CYCLES, SEQUELS, SPIN-OFFS, REMAKES, AND REBOOTS

T0385529

CYCLES, SEQUELS, SPIN-OFFS, REMAKES, AND REBOOTS

Multiplicities in Film and Television

EDITED BY AMANDA ANN KLEIN
AND R. BARTON PALMER

UNIVERSITY OF TEXAS PRESS *Austin*

Requests for permission to reproduce material from this work should be
sent to:
Permissions
University of Texas Press
P.O. Box 7819
Austin, TX 78713-7819
http://utpress.utexas.edu/index.php/rp-form

⊗ The paper used in this book meets the minimum requirements of
ANSI/NISO Z39.48-1992 (R1997) (Permanence of Paper).

LIBRARY OF CONGRESS CATALOGING-IN-PUBLICATION DATA

Cycles, sequels, spin-offs, remakes, and reboots : multiplicities in film
and television / edited by Amanda Ann Klein and R. Barton Palmer. —
First edition.
    pages   cm
Includes bibliographical references and index.
    ISBN 978-1-4773-0900-1 (cloth : alk. paper) — ISBN 978-1-4773-0817-2 (pbk. :
alk. paper) — ISBN 978-1-4773-0818-9 (library e-book) — ISBN 978-1-4773-
0819-6 (nonlibrary e-book)
    1. Film sequels.   2. Film remakes—History and criticism.   3. Film
genres—United States.   4. Television remakes—History and criticism.
I. Klein, Amanda Ann, 1976–, editor.   II. Palmer, R. Barton, 1946–, editor.
    PN1995.9.S29C93   2016
    791.43′6—dc23

                                                                    2015028439

doi:10.7560/309001

CONTENTS

ACKNOWLEDGMENTS

AMANDA ANN KLEIN thanks her faithful writing group at East Carolina University, and the Femidemics (Anna Froula, Marianne Montgomery, Marame Gueye, Andrea Kitta, and Su-Ching Huang), for their helpful revisions and editing suggestions.

R. Barton Palmer is grateful for the continuing support for his research from the Calhoun Lemon family, as well as from Dean Richard Goodstein of the College of AAH at Clemson and chair of English Lee Morrissey.

Both authors owe a huge debt to Jim Burr, Lynne Chapman, and Sarah McGavick at University of Texas Press for ushering this manuscript through its various stages of production, and to Kip Keller for his always on-point copyediting.

Amanda thanks her family—Zach, Jude and Maisy—for their support, and Barton is grateful to Carla Palmer, sons Camden, Colin, and Jeffrey, and daughter Tonya for their tolerance of and interest in his writing.

CYCLES, SEQUELS, SPIN-OFFS, REMAKES, AND REBOOTS

CHAPTER I

INTRODUCTION

AMANDA ANN KLEIN AND R. BARTON PALMER

TEXTUAL TRADITIONS ARE OFTEN UNDERSTOOD as a succession of distinct singularities, that is, as individual texts with a claim to being considered unique. But in practice, individual texts are hardly self-contained in that sense, being joined by various bonds to other texts and often participating in more than one series or grouping. These multiplicities or textual pluralities take a number of distinct but hardly mutually exclusive forms, including adaptations, sequels, remakes, imitations, trilogies, reboots, series, spin-offs, and cycles. The cinema has, from the beginning, depended on such multiplicities, as opposed to promoting the unique value of individual films, and the reason is simple. The reuse, reconfiguration, and extension of existing materials, themes, images, formal conventions or motifs, and even ensembles of performers constitute irresistible adjuncts to continuing textual production, supporting the economies of scale upon which the film, and later the television, industries very quickly began to rely. Furthermore, the connection between texts becomes an important aspect of media consumption as the ties that link texts to one another—what Gérard Genette terms their "transtextuality"—afford the opportunity for complex forms of aesthetic enjoyment. Multiplicities invite viewers to appreciate the new in the context of the familiar and already approved, sanctioning readings that crisscross textual borders. Genette suggests that criticism should focus on *"every* connection *joining* a text B to a text A anterior to it"* (our emphasis), and this is particularly true of cinema and television, textual forms in which reuse and recontextualization are, for institutional reasons, especially prominent (Genette 1982, 11).

This dependence on the transtextual makes all forms of media—including cinema, television, and the Internet—thoroughly traditional, their rich multiplicities having often been anticipated in earlier periods of intertwined production strategies. In the Middle Ages, for example, the ever-expanding and eventually vast corpora of connected texts were recognized as constituting "matters" defined by their general subject. The so-called matter of Britain focused on King Arthur, his Round Table, and the tragic history of his kingdom, affording generations of poets and prose writers unending opportunities for linked intervention and extension, remaking, recontextualization, serializing, and cycling. Medieval Arthurian matter, in fact, can be considered an immense cycle of tales that intersect, repeat, revise, and reformulate in inexhaustibly inventive fashions that remained productive for several centuries. Criticism of this textual tradition, then, searches for "some principle by which individual texts form a meaningful whole, some unity that might be discerned from a multiplicity of parts" (Sturm-Maddox and Maddox 1996, 1). We might say much the same about visual media. In replicating the compositional flexibility of the novel, however, commercial filmmaking and television productions have always been open to the adoption, in every sense of the word, of new material. To date, media studies has not produced a general term to describe the trans-singular results of these joining processes, for which we propose to adopt the term "multiplicities."

Of course, the fact that multiplicities have become a central feature of these media's dedication to continuing forms of textual creation and renewal has hardly escaped critical notice. For example, in "Reification and Utopia in Mass Culture," a seminal essay that, though published in 1979, continues to establish a useful framework for understanding the textual "flow" of mass culture, including the commercial cinema, Fredric Jameson echoes the antipathy of Frankfurt school thinkers toward forms of art produced by industries motivated strictly by the profit motive. Popular films, he avers, are "texts" only in the special sense that they cater to a public eager and willing "to see the same thing over and over again." Such "repetition effectively volatilizes the original object," with the result that those who study mass culture can locate no "primary object of study" (Jameson [1979] 1992, 19–20). Through strenuous efforts to establish originality and uniqueness, so-called high art, by contrast, strives to avoid repetition (Berger 1992, 46). Jameson argues convincingly that modernism, with its aesthetic of textual self-containment, can be seen in part as a reaction to such volatilization, and that it strives, sometimes through extreme measures, to ensure "the survival of the primary text," for such texts can offer "a stable reality" to which the reader "can return over and over again" ([1979] 1992, 20). This is a form of repetition (ironically dependent on a dubious understanding of hermeneutic stability) that Jameson valorizes without further comment. In his view, the opposition of singularity to multiplicity in cultural production is affirmed by the difference between high art, on the one hand, and industrially produced entertainment on the other, in which repetition and other forms of reuse entail a lack of stability even as they allow the cinema to exploit a paradoxical desire for a sameness that is always different.

Jameson emerges as a defender of the customary highbrow understanding of this opposition, but only in general. He parts company with Theodor Adorno, Max Horkheimer, and the other Frankfurtians in declaring that mass culture is no "empty distraction," no purveyor of false consciousness. Like modernism, popular forms such as the cinema entertain, although in different ways, "relations of repression with the fundamental social anxieties and concerns" forming the raw materials to be transformed by both forms of artistic practice (Jameson [1979] 1992, 25). But textual multiplicity poses a problem for the media studies scholar. Volatilization disperses critical attention across textual borders that are readily displaced or replaced by the continuing flow of texts, yielding no "stable reality" that can serve as the object of hermeneutic inquiry. Instead, the critic of multiplicities must attend to the fact of dispersal.

Grounded in an analysis of the cinema's mode of production (which is motivated by the desire to repeat and thus extend pleasure), the concept of volatilization usefully underlines the significance of the textual multiplicities that constitute the continuing manufacture, distribution, and exhibition of commercial media, particularly film and television. Artistic modernism may be characterized by the persistence of the "original object" in cultural circumstances that threaten its autonomy and impermeability, whereas commercial cinema and television have been essentially defined by the genres, series, remakes, adaptations, cycles, remakes, reboots, and spin-offs that enable the continuing provision of a sameness marked indelibly by difference. These processes are obviously not generated by some simple desire on the part of viewers to consume the same object over and over again. The "same thing" that the viewer sees time and time again is always different from the "same things" that precede and follow it. Commercial media production does not support an absolute distinction between modernism's fetishization of individuality, on the one hand, and the devotion of the culture industries in general to assembly-line sameness on the other. Dismissing popular films as essentially "the same" is a cultural judgment akin to Horkheimer and Adorno's of the cinematic medium's purported valuelessness, which fails to take into account the necessarily relentless devotion of the media industry to discover and promote a "new" that is always in some sense the "old." Dispersal of this kind generates different forms of individuated multiplicities more often than singularities *tout court;* that is, it is a process that works with but also against the technologizing of modern industry, which plays an important, even if finally limited, role in film and television production.

The dialectic between "new" and "old" in film and media production answers the industry's need for both regularity (the auditorium seats that must be filled and refilled in order for a studio to stay afloat, the ad dollars or subscription fees that must roll in for a television series to continue to run) and originality (viewers always desire the yet unseen, tire quickly of the "new," are ever susceptible to the exciting promise of "coming attractions"). This paradoxical need can be negotiated and then satisfied to some degree by the assignment of productive capacity to genres. It is self-evident, perhaps, that every genre either lacks (or has somehow lost sight of) an "original object," and that what is repeated through innovation is a pattern whose precise ontology is unclear. That is because a genre exists only culturally, as a transindividual concept, similar to the forms of language, and is capable, like them, of generating an infinite number of "never yet spoken" statements. By contrast, the process of volatilization can be glimpsed more clearly in multiplicities such as the adaptation, the authorial oeuvre, the sequel, the cycle, or the reboot, in which a "new" text (a designation that any given entry can be assigned only provisionally, since it too can be "followed") replaces and yet does not (in fact cannot) replace what has come before. These forms of multiplicity volatilize the original by underlining its insufficiency, by announcing that there is a "more" that the urtext does not contain and likely does not anticipate, in the process revealing that there is a desire for continuation or repetition that the original cannot satisfy. At the same time, the existence of an original text undermines the claim to self-sufficiency of what follows; later texts are revealed to be volatilizations in the sense that, textually speaking, they can be properly understood and valued only when their connection to what came before is acknowledged.

In *Convergence Culture* (2008), Henry Jenkins studies the interdependence of media industries in an era of horizontal integration. No longer regarded as self-contained texts, big-budget blockbusters and high-profile television programs stretch across an extensive landscape of supplementary markets, including sound tracks, video games, toys, comics, and conventions. Jenkins coined the term "transmedia" to describe "a process where integral elements of a fiction get dispersed systematically across multiple delivery channels for the purpose of creating a unified and coordinated entertainment experience" (Jenkins 2007). The essential nature of such multiplicities in film and television is thus a paradoxical transtextual, transmedia textuality dependent on the insufficient sufficiency of the artistic object. A more recent text is characterized as an emergent singularity and a part of what has gone before, as an entity for but not entirely in itself, as a textualization that is sufficiently insufficient, never hermetic, but instead always open to extension. For this reason, multiplicities such as the sequel seem to be a perfect reflection of the mediascape's dialectic of textual provision, which is dependent on the simultaneous valuation of what is present and of what is yet to arrive.

Nowhere is this more obvious than in the cinematic program itself, which has for many decades included an insistent, self-promoting invocation of some awaited form of newness that is always said to up the ante on pleasure, extending the range of the already consumed and enjoyed. At the time of announcement, that pleasure can be glimpsed only in fleeting, fragmented moments stitched teasingly together in a rapid montage that substitutes for, even as it anticipates, the deferred moment of encounter. Jenkins, however, notes an extra dimension of transmedia texts: "We are drawn to master what can be known about a world which always expands beyond our grasp. This is a very different pleasure than we associate with the closure found in most classically constructed narratives, where we expect to leave the theatre knowing everything that is required to make sense of a particular story" (2007). The volatilization of the original object emerges as an essential element of film's and television's modes of production and exhibition, and of their self-understanding. Entertainment now includes the promise that pleasure does not have to end after the lights go up or the series finale airs, that limits can always be exceeded by what the immediate future will bring if only the viewer will return. The moment of enjoyment is thus ritualistically preceded (and its possible satisfaction, in effect, undermined) by an enticing prospection. The essence of the institution, and not just the text, is thus this carefully calculated instability. In the forms of multiplicity in which repetitiveness both defines and eliminates textual boundaries, film and television offer a mass-cultural countermeasure to the "hermetic" text of modernism, characterized by that retreat from context (and thus also from any succession of texts) that Joseph Frank usefully terms "spatial form."

MULTIPLICITIES IN PRACTICE

In 2010, Hollywood industry papers reported that production on a new blockbuster, *Battleship* (2012, Peter Berg), starring A-list talent such as Liam Neeson and Alexander Skarsgård, had begun. The punch line, of course, was that the film was "loosely based" on the popular Hasbro board game of the same name. With this news, the blogosphere exploded with incredulity over commercial cinema's seeming inability to come up with original ideas for motion pictures. For example, Eric Eisenberg (2012) lamented: "More than just being about the quality of *Battleship*, a big part of the reason people were turned off of the movie was because the idea of a film based on a board game is ridiculous. I understand that Hasbro loved all of the money they made from the Transformers movies, but seriously, we don't need a Hungry, Hungry Hippos adaptation."

Although *Battleship* went on to receive a fairly positive critical reception (many reviewers expressed surprise over how "not bad" the film was),[1] the film did poorly at the box office, making only $300 million on its $200 million investment (Guadiosi 2012). Then, in 2012, it was announced that several other board games would receive the big screen treatment, including Monopoly, Action Man, and yes, even Hungry Hungry Hippos (Child 2013). Critics like Eisenberg find it "ridiculous" that Hollywood could found a major blockbuster franchise on a board game adaptation, though it is not strictly accurate to call these films "adaptations" of board games. Hungry Hungry Hippos and Battleship are brands, names, and images, but they are not narratives or characters. And this seems to be precisely Eisenberg's point: the problem with contemporary commercial cinema (epitomized by Hollywood) is that it is more concerned with making money than it is with telling a quality story or creating an indelible character.

As demonstrated by the strong negative reaction to *Battleship*, commercial cinema's attachment to the linked processes of repetition, replication, sequelization, and rebooting—to films that appear in multiplicities—is generally understood in a negative light in the popular press. With the announcement of every new sequel or reboot appears a new think piece decrying the loss of creative innovation and the steady decay of the cinema. Indeed, in a think piece in *Vulture*, Claude Brodesser-Akner (2012) describes the critical reaction to Universal's multimillion-dollar deal with Hasbro toys this way: "The reaction from many in the creative community was scorn, followed by resignation: Had it come to this? A latex rubber doll filled with gelled corn syrup was now what passed for intellectual property?" Brodesser-Akner concludes his piece with a sigh of relief, "With *Candy Land* finally out of its system, here's hoping Universal will recover from its insulin shock soon and get back to making the meat-and-potatoes entertainment that made it great all those years ago." There is a generalized sense that commercial cinema is losing its ability to come up with new ideas and, in its drive for profits, is finally scraping the bottom of the story property barrel.

But most of these think pieces confuse the need to make action-heavy, dialogue-light tent-pole films that do well internationally with the drive to make films out of known story properties, something now called "preawareness" (Epstein 2013). These are two different production strategies that just happen to work well together. For example, Hollywood's dysfunctional love affair with blockbusters—movies that can potentially make or break a studio—is a relatively modern phenomenon. Throughout the 1960s, the major US studios lost money at the box office for several interrelated reasons, including the rising popularity and widespread availability of television, "white flight" to the suburbs, and the slow dissolution of the studio system form of production. To recoup losses, studios began investing their production money in fewer, very expensive "event" pictures. This new mode of production proved problematic when these pictures failed to recover their production costs at the box office. Famous flops like *Cleopatra* (1963, Joseph L. Mankiewicz), *Star!* (1968, Robert Wise), and *Hello Dolly!* (1969, Gene Kelly) put major studios such as Twentieth Century–Fox, Warner Bros., and United Artists on the brink of financial ruin. After a brief flirtation with making films for urban African American audiences, leading to the creation of the blaxploitation cycle of the 1970s, studios discovered that fans would go to see movies like *Jaws* (1975, Steven Spielberg) and *Star*

Wars (1977, George Lucas) over and over, thus ushering in the era of the modern blockbuster.

Ironically, it was the directors of these first blockbusters, Steven Spielberg and George Lucas, who recently made headlines when they predicted the "implosion" of the film industry: "There's going to be an implosion where three or four or maybe even a half-dozen mega-budget movies are going to go crashing into the ground, and that's going to change the paradigm" (quoted in Child 2013). In these formulations, multiplicities (or at least big-budget tent-pole films, which are almost always part of a multiplicity) threaten not simply American cinema's ability to be seen as art—but also its ability to exist. And so, as is often the case, history winds up repeating itself.

Although the US blockbuster did not emerge until the 1970s, the practices of basing films on pop-cultural ephemera like popular board games and duplicating familiar story properties and characters has been common in filmmaking since its origins. For example, in 1905 Thomas Edison released *The Whole Dam Family and the Dam Dog* (Edwin S. Porter), a film based on a popular souvenir postcard image. The film's appeal was based on its ability to create a moving, breathing version of the popular postcard art featuring this humorously named family. According to Charles Musser, Edison put his mark on the film by adding a dinner scene in which the "Dam dog" attempts to steal the father's seat: "On the eve of the nickelodeon era, this combination of novelty and familiarity was the formula for commercial success" (1991, 319). It is not a big leap from a successful film based on a souvenir postcard to a successful film based on a board game. The drive to exploit audience interests in comic strips, magic lantern shows, vaudeville, popular songs, and other films and then to replicate those successful formulas over and over until they ceased to make money is foundational to the origins and success of filmmaking worldwide. Indeed, in his study of cinema produced in the years 1902–1903, Tom Gunning found exactly that: "A large number of films in these two years are based on characters, stories, or situations that audiences would find familiar from other forms of popular entertainment, and often from several such sources in combination . . . Early films offered versions of images that circulated through popular culture, endowed with the novelty of motion and projection" (2009, 120).

In other words, the cinema has always been rooted in the idea of multiplicities—that is, in texts that consciously repeat and exploit

FIGURE 1.1. The Dam Dog was a character in the popular souvenir postcard "The Whole Dam Family and the Dam Dog," which was made into a short Edison film in 1905.

images, narratives, or characters found in previous texts. Carolyn Jess-Cooke explains: "The culture of copying in early cinema was rooted in a collective endeavor both to capitalize on popular trends, themes and productions, and to articulate the ever-changing modern experience" (2009, 22). Self-cannibalizing cycles and sequels, and even the practice of making films out of toys and board games, are filmmaking strategies dating back to the industry's first decade, not a symptom of contemporary culture's inability to create anything new.

It isn't just the cinema that relies on multiplicities to generate sure profits. As this anthology demonstrates, the television industry also relies on the replication and repetition of successful formulas as a central part of its production strategies. And although this process of creative stealing is central to capitalism itself, it is, as in the case of cinema, a generally denigrated process, as if the entry of capitalism somehow contradicts the possibility of art. Unoriginal art, in critical parlance, is an oxymoron. Indeed, a think piece on the blog *Grantland*, that, ironically, can be seen as a copy (or, at the very least, a spin-off) of the numerous similar essays by TV critics lamenting the end of the so-called golden age of television, tellingly attributes the perceived contemporary creative decline of US television to an apparent uptick in multiplicities. Andy Greenwald laments: "Rather than innovating or acknowledging risk, ratings-obsessed programmers at even the most respected channels have fallen back into a disheartening pattern of pandering, copying, and outright cannibalism" (2013). Greenwald offers a quick history of the legitimization of television, a process that, he argues, mirrors the "creative awakening" of US cinema in the 1970s.

Since television is a younger medium than film, the field of television studies is currently grappling with the same conversations that film studies scholars were having in the 1970s, and only recently has television itself reached the stage where it is able to "legitimatize" itself and make claims for its status as art. But critics like Greenwald feel that the current golden age of television (which many critics date to the premiere of HBO's *The Sopranos* in 1999), like the "golden age" of cinema in the 1970s, is in a state of decline due to its insistence on repetition.[2] Greenwald calls the current state of television the "Zombie Age," in reference to the seemingly mindless repetition found in contemporary television: "Yet the Zombie Age is marked by a persistent, undeniable decay. Corpses are picked over. Ideas, once devoured, are regurgitated and feasted on again" (2013). The use of this zombie metaphor, with its concomitant imagery of carrion and scavengers, is unequivocally negative. Of course, as Todd VanDerWerff notes, "The dirty little secret here is that essentially every decade except the 1960s has been proclaimed the 'golden age of TV' at one time or another" (2013). In other words, critics and historians of television, much like their counterparts in cinema studies, are constantly searching for that ideal moment when the art form they love was considered to be at its purest, to be reaching its richest potential. But what tarnishes each of these supposed golden ages? The presence of multiplicities.

In the 1950s, during the early days of television ownership, most American set owners were upscale and urban. They were what we now call "first adopters," and they had the money to invest in a new and untried form of home entertainment. The industry was based in New York, and for a variety of reasons, including sponsors' ownership of time blocks, live televised theater was one of its dominant forms. These teleplays featured adaptations of works by the nation's most notable authors (Tennessee Williams, Ernest Hemingway, F. Scott Fitzgerald, et al.). Television playwrights, especially Rod Serling and Paddy Chayefsky, were national figures. This early tele-

FIGURE 1.2. The HBO slogan from the 1990s illustrates how the channel distances itself from the medium in order to gain cultural capital.

vision programming was modernist in its insistence on the unique, isolated text, and hence was distinct from the forms of multiplicity—especially the situation comedy and the continuing dramatic series—that soon came to dominate programming.[3] The world of television changed as new forms of financing evolved and more Americans acquired sets. Television subsequently became understood as a "lowbrow," commercial mass medium that could be experienced by anyone who owned a television.

In *Legitimating Television: Media Convergence and Cultural Studies* (2012), Michael Newman and Elana Levine argue that beginning in the 1970s and 1980s, when the concept of "quality television" increased the possibilities of targeting programming to desirable (that is, affluent) audiences, television began to once again aspire to become a "highbrow" medium. Other technological changes, such as the practice of putting entire seasons of television on DVD, as well as the amount of serious writing (that is, other than reviews and recaps) that critics began to devote to their favorite shows, like *The Sopranos*, created the sense that US television was finally being appreciated as an art form, but only because television was being compared to already established art forms, particularly the novel and the film (Newman and Levine 2012, 6–10). According to Levine and Newman, "Legitimation always works by selection and exclusion; TV becomes respectable through the elevation of one concept of the medium at the expense of the other" (13). Indeed, HBO's famous ad campaign from the 1990s, "It's not TV. It's HBO," is a good example of how television can be legitimated as art only if it is distanced from the medium of television itself.

As Brenda Weber argues in relation to the current demonization of reality television, we are inherently suspicious of the popular: "Popularity speeds the decline of one's claim to artistry, simultaneously heightening the venom of critique" (2014, 15). Furthermore, those gatekeepers of the world of media appreciation, who are paid to dispense their good taste—film and television critics, but also media scholars—reify and limit the sphere of what constitutes good taste. Therefore, it makes sense that most of the texts that fit under the broad umbrella of multiplicities, such as film sequels and cycles, television remakes and spin-offs, are most frequently discussed as "guilty pleasures," when they are not dismissed outright as harbingers of the end times of cultural production. Newman adds: "Serial forms have historically been associated with children (e.g., comic books) and women (e.g., soaps). In other words, there is cultural distinction, a system of social hierarchy, at play" (qtd. in Bordwell and Thompson 2012, 17). Texts that appear in multiples are most frequently associated with simplistic tastes, and as a result, academia is slow to respond to and analyze these texts, despite their obvious critical value.

Texts that appear in multiplicities are understood to be worth "less than" those texts that stand alone, a model of art appreciation borrowed, to film studies' and television studies' detriment, from the world of fine art and the valorization of "aura." Critical disdain for texts appearing in multiplicities is rooted in the neoromantic belief that art should somehow *not* be concerned with making money, that a television series that unabashedly courts the audience's desires is somehow less artful, less complex, or less worthwhile than one that exists to thwart, complicate, or comment on those desires.[4] Likewise, multiplicities are often viewed with suspicion because they refuse to end, denying the kind of closure necessary in, or at least desirable for, literary forms in which the material object of the book shapes forms of storytelling. Multiplicities insist that no texts have firm limits— they can be constantly told, retold, reconfigured, and spread across platforms, no matter how many times the monster is defeated or the world is saved. But this distrust of texts without end, these multiplicities, belies the fact that narratives themselves are never closed: "There is nothing intrinsically unimaginative about continuing a story from one text to another. Because narratives draw their basic materials from life, they can always go on, just as the world goes on. Endings are always, to an extent, arbitrary. Sequels exploit the affordance of narrative to continue" (qtd. in Bordwell and Thompson 2012, 13). Thus, the study of multiplicities highlights how, as viewers and critics, we simultaneously embrace and disavow what is most central to popular media production: repetition, continuation, and profit.

Film studies scholars have recently begun the necessary work of understanding how multiplicities work. Examples of significant work on multiplicities include Andrew Horton and Stuart Y. McDougal's *Play It Again, Sam: Retakes on Remakes* (1998), Jennifer Forrest and Leonard R. Koos's *Dead Ringers: The Remake in Theory and Practice* (2002), Constantine Verevis's *Film Remakes* (2006), Carolyn Jess-Cooke's *Film Sequels: Theory and Practice from Hollywood to Bollywood* (2009), Claire Perkins and Constantine Verevis's *Film Trilogies: New Critical Approaches* (2011), Amanda Ann Klein's *American Film Cycles: Reframing Genres, Screening Social Problems, and Defining Subcultures* (2011), and Thomas Leitch's *Film Adaptation and Its Discontents: From "Gone with the Wind" to "The Passion of the Christ"* (2007). These monographs and anthologies carve out spaces in film scholarship for serious considerations of sequels, remakes, trilogies, adaptations, and film cycles, categories that are often "absorbed into broader discussions of sequelization, repetition, and recycling" (Perkins and Verevis 2011, 1). While we agree with Verevis and Perkins that sequels, remakes, and trilogies, as well as reboots and cycles, are rich enough to warrant their own book-length studies, this collection seeks to bring these categories together under a single umbrella: multiplicities. We do this not to undo the work of these scholars, but rather because we see value in studying these kinds of texts together in order to make a case for the significance, ubiquity, and critical potential of cinema's long history of investing in and creating multiplicities through reboots, remakes, and cycles.

The study of multiplicities has made its way into television studies, too. Jonathan Gray's *Show Sold Separately: Promos, Spoilers, and Other Media Paratexts* (2010) examines the role that media paratexts play in the way we understand film and television. Jonathan Kraszewski's *The New Entrepreneurs: An Institutional History of Television Anthology Writers* (2010) historicizes adaptations of TV anthology dramas into books, plays, films, and television series. Heather Urbanski's *The Science Fiction Reboot: Canon, Innovation, and Fandom in Refashioned Franchises* (2013) looks at television reboots from the perspective of fandom. Carlen Lavigne's new anthology *Remake Television: Reboot, Re-use, Recycle* (2014) offers a variety of perspectives on remake themes in popular television series. Like these studies, *Multiplicities* offers analyses of series based not on their perceived "quality," but on the way these series rely upon the repetition of familiar characters, plots, and entire series; ultimately, we argue that multiplicities allow the critic to put a particular television series in conversation with a larger body of narratives. Our section on television addresses the value of studying these television series as multiplicities rather than as discrete television genres, modes, or formats.

CONTENT OVERVIEW

The appearance of sequels, remakes, reboots, spin-offs, and adaptations of lowbrow story properties (comics, television shows, toys, theme park rides) most commonly spark debates about the demise of film or television. Despite all the perceived (and real) faults of multiplicities, audiences love them. It is precisely this love, this fan devotion that prompts film and television studios to churn out copy after copy of the next "big thing," and that justifies a critical study of the production, reception, and analysis of film and television not as separate disciplines, but together. *Multiplicities* analyzes popular media texts that appear in multiples: sequels, trilogies, adaptations, and cycles of films; television series that beget other television series (aka, spin-offs); reboots and remakes. We are interested in media texts that are recycled, duplicated, and repeated. We examine how such multiplicities come to exist and why they exist. And most importantly, we feel that the concept of multiplicities is a productive way to highlight the links among all forms of visual media. In light of the increasingly transmedial nature of contemporary screen cultures, it is time to find cohesive ways of discussing transgeneric groupings, and *Multiplicities* stands as an intervention into these discussions.

This collection investigates the relationship between audience, industry, and culture in relation to multiplicities, and reflects on the presence, meaning, and function of multiplicities in US and international cinema, television, and popular culture. The collection places a large emphasis on Hollywood and US television production, since the United States is the source of some of the most pervasive and commercially oriented examples of multiplicities; but the collection covers media production in global markets such as Italy, Japan, and Nigeria as well. It is our intention to promote the use of the umbrella term "multiplicities" in order to emphasize the fundamental relatedness of plural textual forms. Although the studies in this collection center on examples of media multiplicity, the term "multiplicities" is not yet in general use and, therefore, does not make an appearance in every chapter.

The book moves chronologically, beginning with Amanda Ann

Klein's consideration of the cultural and production history of one of the earliest examples of a cinematic cycle, the "kissing cycle" (1896–1906), in order to understand how it evolved from a voyeuristic spectacle of sexual intimacy to a negotiation of the new rules of heterosexual mixing in public. In addition to demonstrating how the kissing cycle managed several intertwined desires and anxieties—the desire to see sex acts filmed in close-up, the changing nature of public heterosocial socializing, the high stakes of objectification, and the (symbolic) policing of white male sexuality—it illustrates how film cycles have been present in US and international cinema from their origins. Next is Robert Rushing's detailed historical analysis of the popular peplum genre—sword-and-scandal epics that have appeared in cycles in Italy, the United States, and beyond—over the last hundred years in both film and television. Rushing acknowledges that the genre as a whole can be analyzed as dealing with a group of concerns: about masculinity, about the concomitant virility of the nation, and about the "West and the rest." But his contribution focuses on how each successive peplum cycle has maintained the continuity of the genre while innovating at the level of the cycle. His analysis reveals how each cycle conveys increasing anxiety about a stable meaning for the heterosexual male body in a world of bodies that are increasingly "other"—belonging to different races, different sexual orientations, different sexes.

R. Barton Palmer's chapter considers Hollywood's postwar semi-documentary cycle, including several true-story-style productions about Nazi espionage (*The House on 92nd Street*), urban criminality (*He Walked by Night*), and counterfeiting (*Southside 1-1000*). Palmer argues that when studied as a cycle concerned above all with stealth assaults on a barely aware US society, the films reveal how the rhetoric employed to persuade isolationist-minded Americans that increased military preparedness was called for was then deployed to rationalize and defend the power of the state. Steven Doles continues Palmer's discussion of postwar cycles in the United States with his analysis of the reception of race-problem films from the 1940s, focusing specifically on *Lost Boundaries* (1949, Alfred L. Werker). He highlights a particular way of writing about these films that expresses an awareness of their membership within the cycle, or what he terms "cycle-consciousness." Doles argues that this cycle-consciousness allowed writers in the black press to draw distinctions between the cycle and earlier representations of African Americans in *The Birth of a*

Nation (1915, D. W. Griffith) and *Gone with the Wind* (1939, David O. Selznick), and to call attention to repeated narrative patterns.

Constantine Verevis's chapter on "revenge of nature" films from the 1970s works as both a micro study of individual multiplicities and as a macro look at the way different forms of multiplicities come together and are understood by the industry, the press, and contemporary audiences. He considers the relationship among terms like "remake," "sequel," "series," "cycle," and "genre," explaining how each category can be contested (or is contested) in or through this description. Verevis's structural study is followed by Chelsey Crawford's work on the cross-cultural nature of multiplicities, specifically, American remakes of Japanese horror films and the way that knowledge of a text works across nations and audiences. The popularity of these films, often even when the originals are available, demonstrates not Hollywood's domination of the global market, but rather a capitalizing on cultural difference and otherness that nonetheless allows for cultural uniqueness.

Elizabeth Birmingham likewise bases her study in Japan, tracing the growth of one anime cycle that developed as a subset of the much-investigated "magical girl" genre. These conservative television shows were about convincing Japanese viewers that girls should be controlled and contained, for if the future is dangerous, it is dangerous not *for* young women, but *because* of them. These series foreground how popular-cultural products situate cultural unease in the *shōjo* body, the bodies of girls occupying that space between childhood's innocence and the feared power of adult female sexuality. Vincent Gaine examines cultural dis-ease, too, with his chapter on US conspiracy films from the 2000s. Gaine argues that films such as *State of Play* (2009, Kevin Macdonald), *Rendition* (2007, Gavin Hood), and *Green Zone* (2010, Paul Greengrass), when treated as a cycle, present a critical view of post-9/11 foreign and domestic policy, expressing concerns over the role of US governmental and corporate entities in the contemporary era of globalization. Gaine highlights how Hollywood films and their viewers participate in the circulation and recirculation of cultural discourses, particularly in the Internet age, when discourses disseminate faster and more widely than ever before.

Next, Murray Pomerance considers the case of the recasting of Michael Gambon as Dumbledore in the *Harry Potter* transmedia franchise, following Richard Harris's unexpected death during production, tracing the practice to other franchises with a rotating cast of leads. Thus, Pomerance shows how this particular multiplatform multiplicity required audiences to both "already love and know" and "awkwardly refuse" the inhabitation of a continuing (and central) character. Noah Tsika continues Pomerance's discussion of casting in multiplicities via his study of the direct-to-DVD releases produced in Nollywood, southern Nigeria's flourishing and idiosyncratic video film industry. The chapter examines three interrelated phenomena: the relationship between Nollywood's rapid, profit-minded pace of production and its self-conscious generation of discrete cycles; the emergence of a particular cycle, the anti-biopic; and the complex and contradictory definitions of race and class that Nollywood's anti-biopic cycle has generated.

Studies of multiplicities ground televisual analysis in pragmatics, that is, in how television is used by audiences, critics, and the industry. Drawing on rhetorical, media, and feminist theories, Sarah Kornfield's chapter differentiates between television subgenres and television cycles. She situates four American prime-time broadcast programs—*Bones* (2005), *Fringe* (2008–2013), *The Mentalist* (2008–), and *Castle* (2009–)—in relation to both previous crime drama programming and contemporary cable and international programming, and analyzes the gendered representations in these popularly celebrated "gender reversed roles." Analyzing these series as a cycle of crime dramas reveals how such programming works to silence feminist voices that call for gender equity by representing US culture as so progressive that it is "gender reversed," and yet simultaneously asserting patriarchal gender norms by systematically favoring the male detectives. While Kornfield looks at how heterosexual TV detective partnerships are circulated across several broadcast networks, Claire Perkins examines how multiplicities function within a single premium cable brand: Showtime's so-called bad mommy cycle of *The Big C* (2010–), *Weeds* (2005–2012), *United States of Tara* (2009–2011), and *Nurse Jackie* (2009–). Perkins argues that by linking the series in its advertising campaigns and other public discourses, Showtime foregrounds its network brand as a venue for scripted shows with subversive content. She considers the internal consistencies of this cycle by examining the series' transposition of the sensibilities of cinematic "indie" culture, specifically the concerns of another cycle: the "smart" cycle of films visible from the late 1990s to the mid-2000s.

Kathleen Williams brings the collection's discussion of multiplicities from text to paratext as she analyzes fan-made recut trailers of popular films (uploaded to YouTube) and how these paratexts often serve as their own form of multiplicity. Williams outlines the numerous ways that recut trailers play with the temporality of a feature film's promotion, as well as the ways that they may shift our understanding of what constitutes filmic multiplicities. Recut trailers allow users and audiences to revisit, rework, and augment their memory of a feature film, identifying latent story lines, shifting the genre of a film, or allowing a character from a film to exist in a newly imagined film. Her work is followed by Faye Woods's examination of the defining drama of the late-2000s blossoming of British youth television, E4's *Skins* (2007–2013), and MTV's efforts to bring the brand to US television. The *Skins* brand thus functions as its own kind of multiplicity by offering a framework of form, aesthetics, and ideology within which each new cast cycle and its accompanying set of stories are constructed. While the US cycle of *Skins* imported key elements of the *Skins* brand of excess and "authenticity," including key motifs, storytelling structures, and the use of youth voices in its creative process, the cancellation of *Skins US* after a single season can be viewed as the result of the incompatibility of the "gritty glamour" of the *Skins* brand and the US teen-television model it was originally created to oppose.

The next chapter in this section examines how multiplicities form not just around a single popular text but also around an entire cultural era, in this case, the 1980s. Kathleen Loock argues that contemporary remakes of beloved and iconic feature films and television series of the 1980s, such as *The Karate Kid* (1984/2010) and *The A-Team* (1983–1987/2010) are openly nostalgic for a decade that directly preceded the radical societal and technological transformations of the 1990s and 2000s. Unlike the majority of remakes, the films in this 1980s retro cycle rely on their source texts' cult status and presence in the collective memory as their primary marketing hook.

Amy Borden focuses her chapter on another contemporary American film cycle, mumblecore, which, she contends, is marked by its engagement with masculinity in its relationship with bisexuality, femininity, and queer femininity; examples include *Hump Day* (2009, Lynn Shelton), *Hannah Takes the Stairs* (2007, Joe Swanberg), and *Alexander the Last* (2009, Joe Swanberg). Though they share certain aesthetic traits, Borden believes that films of the mumblecore cycle have been discussed as such in the context of their protagonists' projects of masculine self-construction, which come in response to the cycle's representations of female sexuality.

The final chapter examines the 2013 premieres of *Bates Motel* and *Hannibal*, two television series that fittingly demonstrate how multiplicities can link up film, television, and popular literature franchises. Andrew Scahill examines how these series function as both prequels and reboots, considering them to be an altogether different mode—an origin remake, or what he calls a "preboot." *Bates Motel* engages in inverted repetition, in which familiar events are replayed with roles reversed as a way to rewrite or deconstruct assumptions about the original text. *Hannibal* engages in incomplete repetition, in which character types or events mimic familiar moments, but in a way that lacks the "trueness" of the original. He concludes that continued study of the preboot offers an opportunity to examine how narrative extension and reiteration may make new and dynamic demands upon audiences' memory, recognition, and identification.

When read together as a collection, the studies in this book offer a broad picture of how cinema and television have used multiplicities to streamline the production process and capitalize on and exploit viewer interest in previously successful or sensational story properties. The authors discuss seriously forms of multiplicity that are rarely analyzed in those terms, including direct-to-DVD films made in Nigeria, cross-cultural Japanese horror remakes, fan-generated trailer mashups on YouTube, and 1970s animal revenge films. By studying these texts as multiplicities, that is, by the way they make meaning when read *together*, this anthology offers important perspectives not available when the texts are considered as singularities. A multiplicity approach allows the critic to create a snapshot of a text's historical moment, because any text that becomes part of a multiplicity, that is, any text that is popular or resonant enough to engender a multiplicity, is a text that is doing important cultural work. By considering the particular bonds that tie texts to one another, the critic can understand more about the audiences for these texts and why they seek out versions of the same story (or character or subject) over and over again. Likewise, a critical turn to multiplicities in film and television (and the way those multiplicities function across time, nation, genre, and media) offers not simply a useful critical lens, but also a method of expanding our definition of which texts justify scholarly attention. The fact that multiplicities have remained a media studies bugaboo—a cause for populist celebration and elitist scorn—makes their study, heretofore neglected, all the more important. As Brenda Weber argues, when we deny certain popular texts the "engaged critical analysis that would better expose their ideological mandates . . . this contempt also plays into centuries-long debates about what constitutes legitimate art, and thus what justifies scholarly attention" (2014, 16). *Multiplicities* therefore functions as an intervention into this historically and critically marginalized aspect of media studies.

NOTES

1. See, for example, Stevens (2012) and Schwarzbaum (2012).
2. See also VanDerWerff (2013), Paskin (2013), and Hinckley (2013).
3. For more on this period of television history, see Kraszewski (2010).
4. Of course, it can be argued that a film like Jean-Luc Godard's French New Wave film *Breathless* (1960), which is purposely obscure, fulfills audience desires by giving viewers the challenging art film they were looking for.

WORKS CITED

Berger, Arthur Asa. 1992. *Popular Culture Genres: Theories and Texts*, vol. 2. Newbury Park, Calif.: Sage.

Bordwell, David, and Kristin Thompson. 2011. *Minding Movies: Observations on the Art, Craft, and Business of Filmmaking.* Chicago: University of Chicago Press.

Brodesser-Akner, Claude. 2012. "What Hollywood Can Learn from the End of Universal's Ill-Fated Hasbro Deal." *Vulture*, 6 February.

Child, Ben. 2013. "Steven Spielberg and George Lucas Predict Film Industry 'Implosion.'" *Guardian*, 13 June.

Eisenberg, Eric. 2012. "Hungry, Hungry Hippos to Become a Movie." CinemaBlend.com, 4 October.

Epstein, Jay. 2013. "Why Hollywood's Business Model Is Bad News for Creativity." *Wrap*, 12 August.

Forrest, Jennifer, and Leonard R. Koos. 2002. *Dead Ringers: The Remake in Theory and Practice.* Albany: SUNY Press.

Frank, Joseph. 1991. *The Idea of Spatial Form.* New Brunswick, NJ: Rutgers University Press.

Genette, Gérard. 1982. *Palimpsestes: La littérature au second degree.* Paris: Seuil.

Gray, Jonathan. 2010. *Show Sold Separately: Promos, Spoilers, and Other Media Paratexts.* New York: New York University Press.

Greenwald, Andy. 2013. "TV Eats Itself." *Grantland* (blog), 6 November.

Guadiosi, John. 2012. "$220 Million Battleship Flop Sinks Not Only Universal Pictures, But Activision Game." *Forbes*, 20 May.

Gunning, Tom. 2009. "1902–1903: Movies, Stories, and Attractions." In *American Cinema, 1890–1909: Themes and Variations*, edited by Andre Gaudreault, 112–132. Piscataway, NJ: Rutgers University Press.

Hinckley, David. 2013. "With the Conclusion of 'Breaking Bad,' TV May Be Nearing the End of the Age of Ultradark Shows." *New York Daily News*, 24 November.

Horton, Andrew, and Stuart Y. McDougal, eds. 1998. *Play It Again, Sam: Retakes on Remakes*. Berkeley: University of California Press.

Jameson, Fredric. (1979) 1992. "Reification and Utopia in Mass Culture." In *Signatures of the Visible*, 9–34. New York: Routledge.

Jenkins, Henry. 2007. "Transmedia Storytelling 101." *Confessions of an Aca-Fan* (blog). 22 March.

———. 2008. *Convergence Culture: Where Old and New Media Collide*. New York: NYU Press.

Jess-Cooke, Carolyn. 2009. *Film Sequels: Theory and Practice from Hollywood to Bollywood*. Edinburgh: Edinburgh University Press.

Klein, Amanda Ann. 2011. *American Film Cycles: Reframing Genres, Screening Social Problems, and Defining Subcultures*. Austin: University of Texas Press.

Kraszewski, Jonathan. 2010. *The New Entrepreneurs: An Institutional History of Television Anthology Writers*. Middletown, Conn.: Wesleyan University Press.

Lavigne, Carlen, ed. 2014. *Remake Television: Reboot, Re-use, Recycle*. Plymouth, UK: Lexington.

Leitch, Thomas. 2007. *Film Adaptation and Its Discontents: From "Gone with the Wind" to "The Passion of the Christ."* Baltimore: Johns Hopkins University Press.

Musser, Charles. 1991. *Before the Nickelodeon: Edwin S. Porter and the Edison Manufacturing Company*. Berkeley: University of California Press.

Newman, Michael, and Elana Levine. 2012. *Legitimating Television: Media Convergence and Cultural Studies*. New York: Routledge.

Paskin, Willa. 2013. "Is the Golden Age of TV Over?" *Ogden (UT) Standard-Examiner*, 29 December.

Perkins, Claire, and Constantine Verevis, eds. 2011. *Film Trilogies: New Critical Approaches*. Houndmills, UK: Palgrave Macmillan.

Schwarzbaum, Lisa. 2012. "Review of *Battleship*." *Entertainment Weekly*, 23 May.

Stevens, James Snyder. 2012. "Battleship: More Fun than a Board Game Blockbuster Has Any Right to Be." *Time*, 17 May.

Sturm-Maddox, Sarah, and Donald Maddox, eds. 1996. *Transtextualities: Of Cycles and Cyclicity in Medieval French Literature*. Binghamton, NY: Center for Medieval and Early Renaissance Studies, SUNY at Binghamton.

Urbanski, Heather. 2013. *The Science Fiction Reboot: Canon, Innovation, and Fandom in Refashioned Franchises*. Jefferson, NC: McFarland.

VanDerWerff, Todd. 2013. "The Golden Age of TV Is Dead; Long Live the Golden Age of TV." *AV Club*, 20 September.

Verevis, Constantine. 2006. *Film Remakes*. Edinburgh: Edinburgh University Press.

Weber, Brenda. 2014. "Trash Talk: Gender as an Analytic on Reality Television." In *Reality Gendervision: Sexuality and Gender on Transatlantic Reality Television*, ed. Brenda R. Weber, 1–36. Durham, NC: Duke University Press.

CHAPTER 2

THE KISSING CYCLE, MASHERS, AND (WHITE) WOMEN IN THE AMERICAN CITY

AMANDA ANN KLEIN

IN THE 1880S, US NEWSPAPERS in the bustling East Coast cities of New York and Washington, DC, reported, with a mixture of concern and amusement, on the burgeoning phenomenon of "mashing." Mashing, or what is now known as street harassment, "occurs when one or more strange men accost one or more women whom they perceive as heterosexual in a public place which is not the woman's/women's worksite." Mashing is an aggressive act: "Through looks, words, or gestures the man asserts his right to intrude on the woman's attention, defining her as a sexual object, and forcing her to interact with him" (di Leonardo 1981, 51–52). Mashing is not the same thing as flirting between strangers in public, an activity that is enjoyed by both parties. Instead, it is perceived as threatening or, at the very least, unwelcome. Mashing was so common in turn-of-the-century US cities that mashers were a familiar trope in early cinema, specifically in the "kissing cycle" (1896–1906). I argue that these short films, which have primarily been understood as providing viewers with an opportunity to witness the act of kissing in close-up, can be collectively understood as a cycle that worked to negotiate the new power dynamics generated by heterosexual mixing in US cities circa 1900.[1]

The kissing cycle is firmly rooted in the first decade of commercial cinema; it begins in 1896, with the release of *The John C. Rice–May Irwin Kiss* (William Heise), and ends in roughly 1906, with the rise and eventual dominance of narrative film. Early film audiences, raised on optical toys like the thaumatrope, stereoscope, and zoetrope, and familiar with elaborate magic lantern shows with colored slides and moving projectors, would have viewed the cinema not as a new mode of entertainment, but rather as an extension of this sort of "magic theater" (Gunning 1997, 129). This emphasis on display over narrative led Tom Gunning to describe this period in filmmaking as the "aesthetic of attractions." Gunning (1997) argues that film audiences before 1906 did not attend the cinema in order to follow a narrative or to identify with characters and their struggles—they attended to be delighted and amazed.

Thus, early entries in the kissing cycle have primarily been understood in the context of the aesthetic of attractions: as examples of the "facial expression genre" or as spectacles of hitherto unseen sexual intimacy. But since film cycles are defined more by their pragmatics (how they are used) than their semantics (Klein 2011, 5), my analysis correspondingly focuses on how the kissing cycle addressed the changing stakes for women navigating public spaces of heterosocial leisure in the late 1880s and early 1900s. These social spaces forced unaccompanied women to negotiate new rules of "acceptable gestures, thresholds for physical contact, [and] permissible conversation topics" with the men they encountered (Cohen 1992, 111). When viewed through the lens of the kissing cycle, these films can be read as interrogations of the role of women in public, and as chronicles of the inception and evolution of mashing in America. In addition, these films highlight how the transgressions of white upper-class men were framed as inappropriate but ultimately harmless, thus leaving undisturbed the dominant fears of African American men as the primary threat to the chastity of white women, and leaving unquestioned the dominant patriarchal establishment.

THE MODERN CITY, COMMERCIAL TRAVEL, AND MASHERS

In nineteenth-century America, bourgeois gender roles were assigned to specific spheres: men held dominion over the public sphere of business, politics, and government, and women were responsible for the private sphere of the home and social events. These roles emerged, in part, from the social and economic changes of the late 1700s: men worked in the city, and women had to remain in the home and tend to the family. In addition, assigning each gender a defined sphere kept white bourgeois men and women from mingling without the supervision of family members (Weiner 1998, 54). Until the end of the 1700s, a journey of more than a few miles was a difficult endeavor, even for men of means. But the rapid development of stagecoach lines, canal boats, steamships, and railroads throughout the nineteenth century made commercial travel a reality, creating new networks of communication and interaction between East Coast cities (Cohen 1992, 112).

By 1900, US cities were spaces in flux: a combination of rapid industrial growth and the movement of people from the country to the city in search of better job prospects changed the landscape of the East Coast. Women, specifically those known as the "New Women" increasingly went out by themselves (or with other women their own age) to window shop or travel in train cars. Temporarily beyond the reach of patriarchal supervision, these women wished to participate in the consumer-oriented, heterosocial culture of the US city. The New Woman discarded the binding Victorian corsets and petticoats of her mother's generation, preferring to wear loose blouses and long skirts that provided mobility when riding a bike or a horse, or while playing a game of tennis. In other words, the New Woman was defined by her freedom of mobility—both in and through city spaces, and socially (Bordin 1993, 2). Men were unaccustomed to seeing women traveling or walking alone or without a male escort. Likewise, women were unsure about how to react when men approached them, leading to what Patricia Cohen has called "cultural improvisations" (1992, 110). One such "improvisation" is the figure of the masher, a (white heterosexual upper-class) man who loitered in public, heterosocial spaces, such as train cars, movie theaters, and parks, and made unwelcome sexual advances to the single women who also frequented these spaces.[2]

Of course, mashers did need not go so far as to steal a kiss. A man could be labeled a masher simply for speaking in a familiar manner to an unaccompanied woman in public. As a *Washington Post* article of the time explains: "Any man who smiles at a woman passing him on the public streets, or who makes grimaces of a flirting or insulting nature such as to incur the displeasure of the woman in question is . . . subject to arrest and fine not exceeding $25" (1905c).[3] An editorial in the same newspaper, entitled "Our Naughty Men," recounts one woman's experience with a DC masher, whom the author describes as an "ogler" and an "insultor of women": "If she took but a twilight stroll a masculine figure would start from out of the shadows and be strolling by her side in a moment, asking 'Can I make a date with you?' or perhaps passing the time of day" (*Washington Post* 1908b). And a later article, titled "Warring on Mashers," recounts how a mother and daughter "of some prominence" were insulted by a

FIGURE 2.1. Accounts of women fighting back against urban mashers appeared in articles, editorials, and letters to the editor throughout the nineteenth century.

man who approached the daughter and said: "Hello kid: want to take a walk?" (*Washington Post* 1911). Here we can see how mashing was a symptom of and reaction to America's shifting notions of class and propriety in the early 1900s: the man mentioned in the last article was a masher because he approached a woman "of some prominence" as if she were *not* a woman of some prominence. This distinction is key: mashers were not characterized as rapists or legitimate threats to white womanhood. Their behaviors were considered disrespectful, crude, and "naughty," but not dangerous.

As the nineteenth century drew to a close, the sometimes despicable but mostly comic figure of the masher was the subject of newspaper articles, editorials, and letters to the editor: "At first newspapers urged respectable men to play a stronger role in protecting women from ogling and catcalls. Gradually though, women began taking matters into their own hands" (Kearl 2011). Indeed, newspapers frequently published exciting accounts of women fighting back against their harassers. One riveting article from 1906 describes how Miss Ellen Pierson, "a modest girl and highly respected," beat two men with her umbrella (sending one to the hospital) as they harassed her on her way home from work: "Each time the umbrella cut deep, and the man yelled like a child. He begged for mercy, but the girl had none for such as he" (*Washington Post* 1906). These stories were such a familiar convention, in fact, that three female "night workers" (a physician, a reporter, and a night school teacher) were interviewed for an editorial called "Women Who Find Streets Safe," which questioned whether the masher scare was an exaggeration (*Washington Post* 1905b). The three women described their encounters with "mashers" as social misunderstandings rather than impertinent violations of a tacit social contract between the genders. Likewise, some men found the prohibitions against mashing or flirting confusing, as one masher, who spent two days in the workhouse for his crimes, explained in 1905: "A 'copper' never bothers you for flirting with women in New York. There is hardly anything but flirting and 'mashing' on Broadway" (*Washington Post* 1905c).

The modern US city, with its ever-evolving technology and constantly moving crowds, altered the way that men and women interacted. And the cinema, like the city, "circumvented [and] quickly undermined many . . . long-established [cultural and social] prohibitions" (Musser 2005, 96). Indeed, the kissing cycle—which showcased images of men and women kissing in public (sometimes consensually and sometimes after being taken by force) undermined prohibitions against the public display of sexual intimacy while catering to the audience's desire to view it. More broadly, the cycle managed fears about what the city unleashed in its white men, who were responsible for the city's thriving economy as well as its looming dangers. Fears about white men and their inability to control their sexual impulses in what was essentially the social-sexual equivalent of the wild, wild West were managed through the figure of the masher. Although the masher was understood differently by different classes of women and even among different classes of women, in accounts of mashers in newspapers[4] and on film, their class, nationality, and racial identity remained constant: middle or upper middle class, American, and white.[5] Thus, "the masher scare minimized the sexual threat of white men while leaving intact dominant fears of black men as violent rapists" (Kearl 2011). White mashers' punishments were largely symbolic: scolding the masher, whether in the pages of newspapers or on movie screens, acted as a safety valve for venting the outrage of bourgeois women who found the improprieties offensive, and of skittish shopgirls who just wanted to ride the train to work in peace—a surface-level checks-and-balances system that did little to change the nature of patriarchal oppression.

By contrast, African American men accused of sexual impropriety were not comical rogues who were fined or sent to jail for a few days; they were often labeled rapists, and the penalty for this suspected sexual impropriety was death, usually by lynching.[6] The film image of what Donald Bogle has termed the "brutal black buck," the African American sexual predator who presents the ultimate threat to white womanhood, reached its apotheosis in D. W. Griffith's *The Birth of a Nation* (1915) and the character of Gus.[7] But in the kissing cycle, which preceded Griffith's film, the figure of the white masher implied what remains unstated, namely, white men were ultimately not a threat to white women: "In southern culture, lynching, imprisonment, and intimidation were all deemed necessary to keep the black man in his place. Within American motion pictures, violence towards African Americans was depicted as humorous and justifiable" (Butters 2002, 28). Thus, the kissing cycle managed several intertwined desires and anxieties: the desire to see sex acts filmed in close-up, the changing nature of public, heterosocial socializing, the high stakes of objectification, and the (symbolic) policing of white male sexuality.

THE FIRST KISS

The first entry in the kissing cycle, *The John C. Rice–May Irwin Kiss*, later known as *The May Irwin Kiss* or *The Kiss*, is believed to be the first kiss captured by the cinema (Musser 2005, 96). John C. Rice and May Irwin were the middle-aged stars of the popular stage play *The Widow Jones* (1895, John J. McNally), and the kiss, filmed in medium close-up, is taken from the final act of the play. Accustomed to performing before large audiences, the two seasoned stage actors know how to build a scene. They press their cheeks together and utter lines of dialogue we cannot hear. Then John Rice smooths down his mustache (a gentlemanly gesture), seizes May Irwin's face, and kisses her on her lips.

J. A. Sokalski argues that the film and its focus on "performed affection" can be traced back to the same tradition on the nineteenth century stage (2004, 299). She argues that performed affection played an important role in turn-of-the-century America: "Where [else] might one watch and learn the methods of intimate kissing without being intrusive? . . . Outside of commercial visual media, it is an event less frequent than one would think" (301). Sokalski explains that an important distinction between the screen kiss and the stage kiss is that the absence of physical bodies allows us to examine the act closely, without the need for the "civil inattention" such an act provokes when performed by present bodies (311). Linda Williams adds that "the excitement around new technologies of vision went hand-in-hand with the excitement around newly mediated revelations of sex" (2006, 291). Indeed, the new cinematic technology displayed by *The May Irwin Kiss* provided voyeurs with a socially acceptable venue for examining the previously intimate, hidden act of kissing, and from a viewing position (a medium close-up) that would be unconscionable in real life.

The success of *The May Irwin Kiss* spawned a series of imitators in the United States and the United Kingdom, each offering a unique variation on the subject, including *The Soldier's Courtship* (1896, Alfred Moul), *Tommy Atkins in the Park* (1898, Robert W. Paul; a "remake" of *The Soldier's Courtship*), *Hanging Out the Clothes* (1897, G. A. Smith), *The Amorous Guardsman* (1898, British Mutascope and Biograph Company), *What the Vicar Saw* (1899, Robert W. Paul), *On the Benches in the Park* (1901, American Mutascope and Biograph), *The Kiss* (1900, Edwin S. Porter), *Photographing a Country Couple* (1901, Edwin S. Porter), *Love in a Railroad Train* (1902, Sigmund Lubin), *A Frontier Flirtation* (1903, G. W. Bitzer), *What Happened in the Tunnel* (1903, Edwin S. Porter), *The Story the Biograph Told* (1904, American Mutascope and Biograph), *A Race for a Kiss* (1904, Lewin Fitzhamon), *Kiss Me* (1904, American Mutascope and Biograph), *Nervy Nat Kisses the Bride* (1904, Edwin S. Porter), *The Misdirected Kiss* (1904, American Mutascope and Biograph), *Kiss Me* (1904, American Mutascope and Biograph), and *A Ballroom Tragedy* (1905, American Mutascope and Biograph), among others. But these films following in the wake of the originary entry in the kissing cycle, *The May Irwin Kiss*, did not replicate Irwin's sense of sexual agency or control.[8]

Sokalski notes that Irwin, being an actress with a formidable stage presence, had a "measure of control" over her performance in *The John C. Rice–May Irwin Kiss*, and therefore she was not, at the time of the film's release, viewed as the passive recipient of John Rice's osculations: "May Irwin's ability to make jests at the expense of men seems to prove that in kissing on stage, May Irwin performed sexuality that enacted female control over the activity" (Sokalski 2004, 316).[9] But the kissing films that followed May Irwin's performance depict women as the recipients of kisses; they are *kissed*, not *kissing*. And thus began the long-standing cinematic practice of depicting women as the passive objects of male heterosexual desire. This scenario is illustrated in *Photographing a Country Couple,* in which a photographer invites a "country couple" (that is, a naïve couple) to sit on a bench and pose for a photograph. But the rube, a stock figure familiar from films like *Uncle Josh at the Moving Picture Show* (1902, Edwin S. Porter) but also common in vaudeville and comic strips, is more interested in looking through the camera himself than in posing with his girl (Hansen 1991, 27–29). The photographer takes advantage of this distraction to steal a kiss, repeatedly grabbing at the woman, who pulls away from him and squirms. When he finally succeeds in kissing her, we see the woman's legs kick out in front of her in a final act of resistance. The rube, meanwhile, has been tied to the photographer's camera tripod by a sneaky boy, and is unable to rescue his girl from this sexual violation. Likewise, in the British film *The Amorous Guardsman,* a member of the royal guardsmen, famous for being impervious to distraction while at their posts, grabs a passing woman and kisses her. When he sees his senior officer approaching, he stashes his conquest inside the guardhouse. But the senior officer sees the girl and gestures for her to come out of hiding. When she does, he kisses her as well, despite the protestations of the first guardsman.

Both the rube's girlfriend in *Photographing a Country Couple* and the woman in *The Amorous Guardsman* are the victims of a public sexual violation perpetrated by white males. Yet these films, like all the kissing films dating back to *The May Irwin Kiss,* were intended to be humorous. At no point during these films is the audience supposed to feel concerned for these women's safety or virtue; we are supposed to laugh at its brazen violation. Sokalski argues that this was a kind of defense mechanism for early film audiences, which were not yet comfortable with witnessing a sexual act in close-up with a group of spectators (2004, 314). When read in the context of the kissing cycle, however, this comedic tone can be understood as an attempt to obscure the fact that the cycle provided an ongoing narrative about what happens to women when they engage with modernity, either through their travels in the city or their exposure to photographic technology.

Indeed, the problematic nature of women who challenge established models of femininity and gender is highlighted in another entry in the kissing cycle, *A Ballroom Tragedy*. The film opens with a sofa, decorated with small pillows, in the midground of the shot, and a party (partially obscured by a heavy curtain) in the background. We see one couple, male and female, dressed in formal wear (a tuxedo and a grey dress), chatting to the right side of the frame. Another couple (wearing a tuxedo and a white dress) approaches and heads toward the sofa. When the woman in white turns her back to the camera, we can see that her gown is low cut, revealing her shoulders and all of her upper back. Not surprisingly, the man escorting the woman in the demure grey dress soon dismisses her in favor of the woman in white's bold, sexualized self-display. This detail is significant because upper-class women were trained to believe that certain costuming choices could provoke male desire: "Men who saw women alone exhibiting freedom of manners, sociability and splendid dress marked them as disreputable and treated them accordingly" (Cohen 1992, 121). In the context of the kissing cycle, which highlighted the irresistibility of white women, the woman in white's "splendid" dress signals that she is consciously provoking the male look, and that she may suffer penalties as a result. Soon, the man and the woman in white are engaged in a passionate kiss on the couch; she wraps her arms around his neck, and we see his hand slip under the folds of her wrap. The woman in grey, who has been lurking in the shadows, then pops out from behind the curtain and stabs the woman in white in the back. The victim pulls out of the kiss, extends her arms out in a gesture of surprise, briefly covers her eyes in despair, and then collapses to the floor. Her assailant dashes off into the background of the party while the distraught suitor holds the limp body of the woman in white.

Although the central spectacle of *A Ballroom Tragedy* is this act of violence, not the kiss, I place it in the kissing cycle because it is the act of kissing that generated the violence. Indeed, the woman in white is not a passive subject here, as was the female figure in *The Amorous Guardsman*. She wears a revealing dress and flirts with her suitor, and when he leans in to kiss her, she moves to meet his lips. The dominant ideology of the time led women to believe that they would be perfectly safe riding on a train, walking down the street, or attending a party without a male escort as long as they were "truly virtuous" and "behaved appropriately" (Cohen 1992, 122). But those who weren't would suffer the consequences. Indeed, the final seconds of *A Ballroom Tragedy* focus on the woman in white, not the woman in grey; that is, we focus on the consequences of the victim's social transgressions, not the assailant's violence. An early form of "victim shaming," *A Ballroom Tragedy* implies that women who don't follow the rules, such as the provocatively dressed woman in white, will suffer for their transgressions. Self-policing, in the form of modest clothing and behavior, is the only way to ensure safe passage in the modern city.

THE KISSER KISSED

Rather than straightforward spectacles of "performed affection," later entries in the kissing cycle provide a commentary on kissing films themselves—specifically, on the figure of the masher. Indeed, later films in the cycle seem to challenge the idea that women who navigate urban spaces automatically become the defenseless victims of mashers. For example, *A Frontier Flirtation* opens with a young woman seated alone on a bench, a familiar staging from kissing films such as *A Soldier's Courtship* and *Tommy Atkins in the Park*. She is framed in a long shot and wears a heavy black veil over her face. A masher, dressed in what appears to be a cowboy's outfit (hence the film's title), approaches the woman and gives the camera a devilish smile. J. A. Sokalski writes that the use of direct address by the male in films like *The New Kiss* marks his control of both the frame and the kiss, since it "trains" the viewer to identify with his point of view (2004, 315). A similar effect is created here: having established his control of the scene, the cowboy leans in and makes a series of advances. The woman pushes his hand away four times until, at last, he lifts up her veil under the pretense (we can only assume, based on other films of this cycle) of stealing a kiss. But what is revealed under the veil is not the face of a lovely young maiden, but a monkey! The cowboy looks again at the camera, this time in horror, and flees the frame to the left. A second later, a man dressed in gentleman's attire enters the frame from the right. He sits down next to the woman and removes her mask, revealing that she is laughing heartily. He puts his arm around her, and she leans against him as he joins her in laughter. In the final seconds of the film, he turns and kisses her on the cheek, which seems to please her. Then the scene fades to black.

The plot of *A Frontier Flirtation* was likely a reflection of, or a reaction to, the many accounts of women who, fed up with the unwanted attentions of mashers, finally began fighting back. For example, an 1895 article titled "Thrashing a Masher" tells of two actresses, Vera Irving and Vivian Pattoe, who were repeatedly harassed by a drunken fan as they took the train home from an evening's performance:

"Quick as a flash Miss Irving's shapely gloved fist shot out straight from the shoulder, landing on the masher's nose with such force that, with a yell of surprise and pain, he staggered back" (*National Police Gazette* 1895). The gleeful tone of this account highlights that the masher was understood to be morally corrupt: the author revels in his comeuppance. The article notes that bystanders witnessing this encounter cheered as an "athletic" man "started in Corbett-like manner to give the masher the most thorough beating he ever had in his life." ("Gentleman" Jim Corbett was a famous boxer of the time.)

Yet the prevalence of these accounts in newspapers and their depiction on the screen highlights that the spectacle of the masher's transgression was too entertaining to ignore: it was something to condemn, but only after it had first been watched and enjoyed. Thus, the films in the kissing cycle, like the exciting accounts of plucky women rejecting lascivious male advances in order to protect their honor, offered audiences an opportunity to negotiate the possibilities of modern heterosocial interactions. The woman featured in *A Frontier Flirtation* was not simply playing defense; that she already had the monkey mask on when the cowboy began harassing her is a sign that she was expecting such an encounter, perhaps even "asking for it." And the final seconds of the film, which display the woman's enjoyment of her own clever trick, further highlight her control of this potentially threatening leisure space.

There is a similar commentary on the male gaze in *Kiss Me*. Like *A Frontier Flirtation*, *Kiss Me* is set in a public space, a boardwalk or a main street, and features four life-size posters advertising contemporary burlesque shows: *The Majestics*, Rose Sydell and the London Belles, Paul Sheridan's New City Sports, and the Rentz-Santley Company. Two well-dressed women enter the frame from the right, walk past the posters, and then shake their heads at the camera, highlighting the vulgarity of the advertised shows. Unlike the two women, who wear long skirts, jackets, scarves, and hats, the women featured in the posters are bare-armed and, in one poster, wear short skirts (the uniform of the showgirl). As the prim women exit, another female couple, perhaps a mother and her adult daughter, dressed in equally conservative outfits, enters the frame from the left. When the daughter pauses to examine the "poster" of Rose Sydell (which is not a poster, but rather a person standing within the ripped frame of what was once a poster), her mother chastises her and then drags her, by her ear, out of the frame. Throughout this exchange, "Rose Sydell"

FIGURE 2.2. In *Kiss Me*, the masher becomes the object of the female gaze.

remains impassive. It is only when an older gentleman, marked by his white beard and unsteady gait, enters the frame and examines the poster that Rose breaks the illusion by turning her head slightly and making eye contact. Obviously startled by this turn of events, the man moves in for a closer look. Rose puckers her lips for a kiss, and the man stumbles backward, rubs his eyes, and then fishes around in his pocket for his spectacles. He circles the poster, stepping ever closer, intrigued, but also clearly shaken by the notion that the body he has been objectifying has suddenly taken on subjectivity. He gets over that quickly, though. Just as he is readying his pucker to kiss Rose, the older woman featured earlier in the film reenters the frame from the right, grabs him by the ear, just as she did with her daughter, and drags him away.

Only when *A Frontier Flirtation* and *Kiss Me* are read in the context of the kissing cycle—and its attempts to grapple with the cultural improvisations necessitated by modernity—can we see how these films are less about the act of kissing and more about the way women tried to make sense of major social shifts. *Kiss Me* is especially interesting in how it plays with the male gaze. The female bodies depicted in the posters were created for male consumption; this is made clear when the mother chastises her daughter for looking at them. But Rose turns the tables on this arrangement by looking back. It is only when a male approaches that Rose shifts from object to subject. She transfers her "to-be-looked-at-ness" from her body to that of the old man, and in that moment our identification shifts to the woman, the former object, as she marshals control of the gaze. As the old man reveals, the effect is unnerving.

Kiss Me offers an interesting counterpoint not just to the kiss-

ing films discussed earlier, but also to the popular cycle of burlesque films produced at the same time, such as *Trapeze Disrobing
Act* (1901, Edison Manufacturing Co.) and *From Show Girl to Burlesque Queen* (1903, A. E. Weed). In burlesque films such as *Pity the
Blind No. 2* (1904, American Mutascope and Biograph), for example,
women are ogled, often unknowingly, by men they encounter in public spaces. In *Kiss Me*, however, the male looker becomes the object
of the female gaze. She becomes the masher, taking advantage of the
disguise provided by the poster to draw in unsuspecting men. Reading these kissing films together as a coherent cycle—one initially
created to satisfy the desires of the gaze (to see the technology of the
cinema on display, to see a sexual act up close) but later appearing to
question the boundaries and penalties of such objectification—highlights these previously hidden connections.

KISSING ON TRAINS

The depiction of objectified women who turn the tables on their male
aggressors was given an even more elaborate treatment in *What Happened in the Tunnel*, an amalgam of two previously successful cycles: kissing films and "phantom rides." Phantom rides were created
by placing portable cameras on moving trains, thus putting the spectator in the position of a passenger on the train. Given the success of
kissing and phantom train rides as subjects in early cinema, it is not
surprising that in 1899 the British filmmaker G. A. Smith decided
to unite these two very popular, though seemingly unrelated, short
film subjects in *The Kiss in the Tunnel*. The first shot is from the
point of view of the train conductor as the train enters a dark tunnel.
The middle shot places the viewer inside a train car, where a young
man and a young woman are seated against a painted backdrop. The
man, taking advantage of the darkness of the tunnel, stands up and
kisses the woman. The final shot returns the viewer to the point of
view of the conductor as the train exits the tunnel. *The Kiss in the
Tunnel* proved to be a viable new formula in early cinema, and soon
imitators such as *The Kiss in the Tunnel* (1899, James Banforth) and
Love in a Railroad Train (1902, S. Lubin) appeared. Since exhibitors
were always looking for products that had proven appeal and yet were
novel,[10] it was only a matter of time before the figure of the masher
entered this new iteration of the kissing cycle, as he did in films such
as *What Happened in the Tunnel* and *Nervy Nat Kisses the Bride*.

What Happened in the Tunnel opens with a medium shot of three passengers—an upper-class white woman, her African American maid, and a masher—seated inside a train car. A window on the left side of the frame offers, via rear projection, the illusion of scenery rushing past the window. As the masher flirts with the woman seated in front of him—picking up her dropped handkerchief and clasping her gloved hand—she smiles and laughs. Her traveling companion, dressed in a maid's uniform and hat, watches the exchange, also amused. Then the image fades to black for approximately six seconds. Unlike *The Kiss in the Tunnel* and its imitators, *What Happened in the Tunnel* never offers the viewer an exterior shot of the train entering or exiting a tunnel, because the director, Edwin S. Porter, was able to assume the audience's familiarity with the context; fans of previous "kiss in a tunnel" films would have been a target market for his variation on the subject. Thus, as soon as the screen goes black, the audience assumes that the masher has achieved his goal of securing a kiss from the young woman. When the black screen fades into a view of the train's interior, the audience discovers that the two women have switched seats. Instead of kissing the upper-class white woman, the masher finds he has kissed her working-class African American maid. Once the man discovers his mistake, he quickly scans the car to make sure no one else witnessed the event and curses the women vehemently. Unfazed by his anger, the two women look at each other and laugh uproariously. The visibly shaken masher, aware that he has been "punished," sits back down and pretends to read his newspaper.

With *What Happened in the Tunnel*, Porter took a well-worn cinematic convention—a man and a woman who use the darkness of a tunnel as an opportunity to steal a kiss—and added several updates that refreshed its appeal. First, it incorporated the women's trick—which hinges on both their cleverness and the visual gag of the switched bodies. Earlier variations on this entry in the kissing cycle, like *Love in a Railroad Train*, likewise relied on the gag of using the darkness of the tunnel to fool a masher (in this film, he is fooled into kissing a baby's bottom). *What Happened in the Tunnel* was therefore extremely timely: it exploited fears about the dangers awaiting young women who traveled without a male escort in the city, yet simultaneously assuages those fears with a comedic comeuppance. Mashers may harass women traveling alone on trains, but ultimately, it is all in good fun.

Of course, what is most interesting about this kissing film is the

FIGURE 2.3. *What Happened in the Tunnel* reinjects the subject of race into the popular kissing cycle.

way it reinjects the subject of race into the kissing cycle, which, up until that point, had been primarily concerned with consensual (or nonconsensual) kissing between heterosexual white men and women.[11] In all of the aforementioned films, the consequences for stealing a kiss are minor: white (upper-class) men who harass or even attempt to rape white (upper-class) women are never arrested or physically harmed for their transgressions. Their unbridled sexual drive, stimulated by the excitements of the modern city and the presence of unattended women, is, for the most part, treated as farcical entertainment. By contrast, Linda Williams points out that while viewers of *The Kiss* were drawn in by the "anatomization" of an on-screen kiss, viewers of *Tunnel* were interested in "the social embarrassment of the man punished for taking liberties with a white woman by the presumed unpleasure of kissing a black one" (2008, 31).

What Happened in the Tunnel thus ups the stakes of the kissing cycle by making an unbidden kiss interracial: "The first interracial kiss is thus staged as a kind of spectacular secret exposed, an 'attraction' advertised by the title that dare not name it but sets us up to want to see and know it" (Courtney 2005, 6).[12] The film portrays this kiss as an embarrassing penalty for attempting to kiss an upper-class white woman, but glosses over the reality of the relationships between upper-class white men and working-class African American women. Jane Gaines analyzes it thus: "It is there in the tryst on the train that would seem to be a remarkable rearrangement of a historical paradigm: the white lady looks on *approvingly* as the white gentleman kisses her black maid, a historical turnabout that would seem to stand in front of the familiar paradigm in which the white lady strenuously *disapproves* of such a relation" (2001, 89). This film defuses the masher's threat with a comic scene and a rousing quasi-feminist vision of a cross-class, cross-racial bond between two women, but behind closed doors this masher could take advantage of the socially powerless maid without fear of reprisals. He could do much more than kiss her, and without any repercussions. Once again, the masher contains and manages the white male's sexual transgressions, distracting audiences from the reality of the rape of African American women by white slave owners for centuries.

EARLIER I DISCUSSED *A Ballroom Tragedy*, in which a woman who dresses provocatively (for 1905) is stabbed to death in public, the victim of another woman's jealousy. The message of the film was that (white) women must be ever vigilant about the impact their sexuality might have on the (white) men around them. While the changing urban landscape and the rise of commercial travel at the turn of the twentieth century necessitated a series of cultural improvisations between American men and women, it was women who ultimately were forced to police their clothing, mannerisms, and travel routines. Women who got kissed were women who had not taken the proper precautions for preventing such behavior—they dressed too provocatively, traveled at an unseemly time of day, or simply failed to arm themselves appropriately (whether with an umbrella or a monkey mask). Thus, as the management of street harassment increasingly became the responsibility of women—not the harassers—women saw the potential freedom of the city become increasingly circumscribed. The promise of access to the public sphere of men, business, and politics was once again foreclosed. As Patricia Cline Cohen explains, "part of the price of respectability was a denial of female competence in negotiating public space" (1992, 122). Likewise, as demonstrated in *What Happened in the Tunnel*, while white women were saddled with the responsibility of managing white male behavior, African

American women were left to absorb this redirected sexual energy as their "sexual surrogates" (Gaines 2001, 89). Meanwhile, African American men continued to be demonized (and murdered) for sexual transgressions that did not take place. These patterns were featured in the pages of the nation's newspapers and on its movie screens. By examining these kissing films as forming a cycle of their own (as opposed to belonging to separate cycles of phantom rides, burlesque films, kissing in tunnels, and racial mistake films, among others), the usually invisible, complex social codes of decorum and resistance circulating around these films are made legible.

NOTES

1. See, for example, Williams (2006), Sokalski (2004), Smith (2012), and Musser (2005).

2. The *New Oxford American Dictionary* dates the word "masher" from the "late 19th century," calling it primarily a "U.S. phenomenon." The earliest mentions of mashers in US newspapers appear in the 1880s.

3. In addition to verbal affronts, some mashers stalked, followed, harassed, and even assaulted or raped the women they encountered in public. Most newspaper accounts of mashing, however, describe some kind of verbal insult.

4. In addition to the many articles cited in this chapter, see Black (1906) and other representative pieces in the *Washington Post* (1905a, 1908a).

5. An article in the *Los Angeles Times* (1903) attempts to distance American gentlemen from the masher scourge: "The curs who insult women are not by any means confined to any one locality. They are to be found in nearly all our larger cities—although (much to our credit as a nation,) they are not, as a rule, American born."

6. Lisa Dorr offers some bleak statistics from just one state: "Between 1880 and 1930, Georgia lynched 460 people, 441 (96 percent) of whom were black" (2004, 17).

7. See the study by Bogle (1993).

8. An originary film is the entry that launches a film cycle, usually because of the timeliness of its subject matter and its easily reproducible semantics (Klein 2011, 11–12).

9. In Jacob Smith's essay on the relationship between performed affection on the screen and performed affection on the phonograph, he discusses how "the potentially egalitarian quality of the kiss can blossom in the context of a sound-only media form like the phonograph" (2012, 126).

10. Gaudreault argues that in addition to preexisting story properties, by 1904 film producers were increasingly reliant on sequels, remakes, and even "duped prints that they bought on the market for that purpose, shamelessly selling them as their own" (2009, 146).

11. *The Misdirected Kiss* offers a similar scenario: a nearsighted man mistakes the African American maid for his white mistress and begins kissing her

hand. And *Negro Kiss* (1903) features an African American man and woman engaged in a consensual kiss, though such intraracial depictions of kisses were then rare.

12. Jane Gaines argues that *What Happened in the Tunnel* is also part of a larger cycle of "racial mistake" films in which "the black female character is accidentally kissed" (2001, 54–55).

WORKS CITED

Benjamin, Walter. 1968. "On Some Motifs in Baudelaire." In *Illuminations: Essays and Reflections*, ed. Hannah Arendt. New York: Schocken.

Black, Winifred. 1906. "How to Avoid Mashers: Women Have the Remedy in Their Own Hands." *Washington Post*, 28 January.

Bogle, Donald. 1993. *Toms, Coons, Mulattoes, Mammies, and Bucks: An Interpretative History of Blacks in American Films*. New York: Continuum.

Bordin, Ruth Birgitta Anderson. 1993. *Alice Freeman Palmer: The Evolution of a New Woman*. Ann Arbor: University of Michigan Press.

Brooke, Michael. "Tommy Atkins in the Park (1898)." *BFI Screen Online*. http://www.screenonline.org.uk/film/id/727290.

Butters, Gerald. 2002. *Black Manhood on the Silent Screen*. Lawrence: University Press of Kansas.

Cohen, Patricia Cline. 1992. "Safety and Danger: Women on American Public Transport, 1750–1850." In *Gendered Domains: Rethinking Public and Private in Women's History*, ed. Dorothy O. Helly and Susan M. Reverby, 109–122. Ithaca, NY: Cornell University Press.

Courtney, Susan. 2005. *Hollywood Fantasies of Miscegenation: Spectacular Narratives of Gender and Race, 1903–1967*. Princeton, NJ: Princeton University Press.

di Leonardo, Micaela. 1981. "Political Economy of Street Harassment." *Aegis: Magazine on Ending Violence against Women* (Summer): 51–57.

Dorr, Lisa Lindquist. 2004. *White Women, Rape, and the Power of Race in Virginia, 1900–1960*. Chapel Hill: University of North Carolina Press.

Gaines, Jane. 2001. *Fire and Desire: Mixed-Race Movies in the Silent Era*. Chicago: University of Chicago Press.

Gaudreault, Andre. 2009. "Movies and Chasing the Missing Link(s)." In *American Cinema, 1890–1909: Themes and Variations*, ed. Andre Gaudreault, 133–157. Piscataway, N.J.: Rutgers University Press.

Gunning, Tom. 1997. "As Aesthetic of Astonishment: Early Film and the (In)Credulous Spectator." In *Viewing Positions: Ways of Seeing Film*, ed. Linda Williams, 114–133. New Brunswick, NJ: Rutgers University Press.

Hansen, Miriam. 1991. *Babel and Babylon: Spectatorship in American Silent Film*. Cambridge, MA: Harvard University Press.

Kearl, Holly. 2011. "A History of 'Aggressive Male Street Flirts, or "Mashers,"' in the U.S." StopStreetHarassment.org. 20 April.

Klein, Amanda Ann. 2011. *American Film Cycles: Reframing Genres, Screening Social Problems, and Defining Subcultures*. Austin: University of Texas Press.

Los Angeles Times. 1903. "Mashing the Mashers." 21 September.

Musser, Charles. 2005. "The May Irwin Kiss: Performance and the Beginnings of Cinema." In *Visual Delights Two: Exhibition and Reception*, ed. Vanessa Toulmin and Simon Popple, 96–115. Eastleigh, UK: Libbey.

National Police Gazette. 1895. "Thrashing a Masher." 11 May.

Smith, Jacob. 2012. "Kissing as Telling: Some Thoughts on the Cultural History of Media Performance." *Cinema Journal* 51, no. 3: 123–129.

Sokalski, J. A. 2004. "Performed Affection: The Spectacle of Kissing on Stage and Screen." In *Allegories of Communication: Intermedial Concerns from Cinema to the Digital*, ed. John Fullerton and Jan Olsson, 299–320. Rome: Libbey.

Urbanora. 2011. "The Soldier's Courtship." *The Bioscope* (blog), 25 July.

Washington Post. 1905a. "Police at Capitol: Special Force Which Guards Building and Grounds." 7 August.

———. 1905b. "Women Who Find Streets Safe: Experience of Three Night Workers Who Have Not Been Molested, Though Unprotected." 5 November.

———. 1905c. "Flirting Is a Crime: District Code Designates It So on the Streets." 30 December.

———. 1906. "Girl Fells Two Mashers: Swings Her Umbrella So Forcibly that One Goes to Hospital." 15 September.

———. 1908a. "Paradise for Masher: Avenue More Lawless than Bowery Says Fair Critic." 23 March.

———. 1908b. "Our Naughty Men." 24 March.

———. 1911. "Warring on Mashers: Women Must Be Guarded, Says Maj. Sylvester." 25 May.

Weiner, Marli. 1998. *Mistresses and Slaves: Plantation Women in South Carolina, 1830–1880*. Urbana: University of Illinois Press.

Williams, Linda. 2006. "Of Kisses and Ellipses: The Long Adolescence of American Movies." *Critical Inquiry* 32, no. 2: 288–340.

———. 2008. *Screening Sex*. Durham, NC: Duke University Press.

CHAPTER 3

DESCENDED FROM HERCULES:
MASCULINE ANXIETY IN THE PEPLUM

ROBERT RUSHING

WORLD CINEMA INCLUDES A CURIOUS GENRE, largely but not exclusively Italian, that has repeatedly appeared and disappeared over
the last hundred years in both film and television.[1] In English, these
films were called "sword and sandals" films, or sometimes were
lumped together with other films set in the classical world as "gladiator movies" (although gladiators are relatively scarce in them).
I should be clear at the outset that the peplum genre does not simply include any film set in the classical world (indeed, in many ways
films of this type are opposed to big-budget Hollywood epics set in
the classical world), but has a distinct set of stylistic and ideological
traits as well as its own history. While serious English-language criticism about these films and television series exists (Günsberg 2005;
Dyer 1997), it has been rare. In Europe, French critics named the
genre after an article of female clothing in Greek antiquity and called
them "peplum" films (Aziza 1998), the term employed here. French
critics took peplums seriously: an issue of the prestigious *Cahiers
du cinéma* in 1962 featured more than one article on the peplum,
including "L'âge du péplum" ("The Age of the Peplum"), in which
Jacques Siclier wondered which peplum director might count as an
auteur, thus rescuing intellectuals who wanted to enjoy these low-
budget, popular, and often right-wing movies without feeling guilty
(1962, 34). Even in Italy, where almost all peplums were made until the 1980s, criticism tends to be limited to simple synopses and
catalogues of the films (for example, Cammarota 1987; Casadio 2007;
Giordano 1998).[2] Because of their low production values and campy
style, particularly their apparently unintentional homoeroticism,
peplum films have remained a curiosity, even within cult cinema, despite the longevity of the genre.

In its most stereotypical form, the peplum depicts muscle-bound heroes (professional bodybuilders, athletes, wrestlers, or brawny actors) in mythological antiquity, fighting fantastic monsters and saving scantily clad beauties. Rather than lavish epics set in the classical world, they are low-budget films that focus on the hero's extraordinary body. Peplums have flourished and declined in popularity for a century, appearing in four discrete cycles: about two dozen Maciste films of 1914–1926 (all starring the same actor, Bartolomeo Pagano, playing the same character, Maciste), made predominantly in Italy; several hundred classic peplums from 1957–1965, starring professional bodybuilders such as Steve Reeves, also made almost entirely in Italy, often as coproductions with other countries; a short burst of films in the 1980s after the success of *Conan the Barbarian* (1982, John Milius), including numerous Italian films such as *The Throne of Fire* (*Il trono di fuoco*, 1983, Franco Prosperi), *Ator the Invincible* (*Ator 2: L'invincibile Orion*, 1984, Joe D'Amato), and *Conquest* (1983, Lucio Fulci), but also several American and US-Argentina productions; and the current cycle of peplum films—*300* (2007, Zack Snyder), *Clash of the Titans* (2010, Louis Leterrier), *Immortals* (2011, Tarsem Singh)—and television series—*Spartacus: Blood and Sand* (2010, but continued under different titles until 2013)—which arrived after the success of Ridley Scott's *Gladiator* (2000).[3] The current surge of peplum films does not appear to have exhausted itself yet: a third installment in the *Clash of the Titans* franchise is planned, as is another Conan film starring Arnold Schwarzenegger. Releases in 2014 alone included a prequel to *300* (*300: Rise of an Empire*, Noam Murro), the volcanic gladiator spectacle *Pompeii* (Paul W. S. Anderson), and Kellan Lutz (of *Twilight* fame) squared off against Dwayne "The Rock" Johnson in dueling versions of Hercules (*The Legend of Hercules* [Renny Harlin] and *Hercules* [Brett Ratner]).

It is tempting to offer a single explanation for the changing fortunes of the peplum. It appears to be particularly well suited to addressing concerns about masculinity, the concomitant virility of the nation, and anxieties about the "West and the rest," and it has arguably appeared during some of the West's more conservative moments. While such arguments offer some of the most productive ways for thinking about the peplum, they also rely on sweeping generalizations and don't account for practical factors that contribute to the rise and fall of a genre, including changing audience tastes and the exhaustion of genres (particularly of a relatively simple genre like the peplum). Although one cannot help speculating on how a genre embodies the spirit of its times, this chapter will focus on how each successive cycle maintained the continuity of the genre while simultaneously renewing it.

Although the peplum genre spans almost a century, it exhibits a remarkable degree of coherence and similarity. This is true regarding plot devices (for example, a hero chained to a stone wheel that he must endlessly turn—in 1914, 1961, and 1982), images (the spectacular collapse of monuments, buildings, or mountains, from 1914's *Cabiria* (Giovanni Pastrone) to 2011's *Immortals*), distinctive camerawork (conditioned by the need to linger over the protagonist's superbly muscled body, and therefore particularly tied to slow-motion photography), and ideology (almost always associated with right-wing politics and colonialism, although in complicated ways).

At the same time, the peplum has also changed significantly: it has gone from being a predominantly Italian phenomenon in its first two cycles to a globalized Anglophone one beginning in the 1980s, and its dominant affect has changed from a sunny confidence in the power of manly muscles to a Nietzschean ressentiment in the face of an overwhelmingly decadent and morally corrupt enemy. Today's peplum hero is not simply resentful, however—since *Conan* and *Gladiator*, his affect had been dominated by loss, melancholy, and a sense that he is "too late" or otherwise out of time. Even in the remote past, the time of heroes is always already over, leaving the peplum hero with one last heroic muscular mission to perform, one that, in productions as diverse as *300*, *Spartacus: Blood and Sand*, and *Immortals*, leads to his death. If there is a narrative arc to the changes that have taken place in the peplum, it would be one of increasing anxiety about a stable meaning for the heterosexual male body in a world of bodies that are increasingly "other"—belonging to different races, different sexual orientations, different sexes.

FROM MACISTE THROUGH THE MIDCENTURY PEPLUM

The Italian film industry in the first decades of the twentieth century was one of the most powerful and influential in the world, with particular advantages in the manufacturing of epics set in the classical world, including temperate weather, abundant light, varied landscapes, and actual classical buildings and ruins. In the 1912 blockbuster *Quo vadis?* (directed by Enrico Guazzoni, based on Henryk

Sienkiewicz's novel), Bruno Castellani appeared as Ursus, the giant slave who fights a bull bare-handed in the arena to save his mistress. Castellani's Ursus was not so much muscled as he was simply huge, but two years later the same type appeared in the even more successful *Cabiria*, this time in the character of Maciste, played by Bartolomeo Pagano. Maciste's body was equally massive, but extremely muscular (for the time—we have a very different, and much more extreme, notion of muscular definition today), and Pastrone made certain that Maciste's body was visible at all times. In the first shot in which he appears, he stands as still as a statue (Dalle Vacche 1992, 27–28), his muscles flexed, before suddenly shifting and adopting a new muscular pose. As the racially ambiguous slave of a wealthy Roman, Maciste wore little besides a leopard-print loincloth and spent his screen time performing typical variety-show strongman feats that could showcase his physique and straining muscles: lifting his comparatively tiny opponents into the air and hurling them over a wall, bending iron bars to escape a jail cell, and turning a millstone for ten years. Maciste was the film's most popular character, and Pagano went on to star, from 1915 to 1926, in approximately two dozen spin-offs that took his formidable body around the globe. Everyone understood that *Cabiria* was a nationalist allegory (it recounted Rome's victory over Carthage just as modern Italy was engaging in its own colonialist adventures in North Africa; see Schenk 2006), but the Maciste cycle suggested, in the years leading up to Mussolini's accession to power, that the virile Italian body could dominate everywhere (Ricci 2008, 84–88): in the Austrian alps (*Maciste alpino* (1917, Giovanni Pastrone), America (*Maciste e il nipote d'America* (1924, Eleuterio Rodolfi), the Middle East (*Maciste contro lo sceicco* (1926, Mario Camerini), entirely imaginary countries (*Maciste imperatore* (1924, Guidi Brignone), and even hell itself (*Maciste all'inferno* (1925, Guido Brignone). The studio ditched Maciste's ancient (and dark-skinned) identity for these later films—in all of the spin-offs, Maciste appears as an equally strong but modern Italian, suggesting that his dominant physicality and overwhelming health and energy transcend both time and space.

As Jackie Reich (2011) has noted, the modernizing and civilizing of Maciste also necessitated covering his body in clothing and rendering it less visible. But there is always a way to expose even the modern male body for the spectator's enjoyment: in both *Il viaggio di Maciste* (1920, Carlo Campogalliani) and *Maciste imperatore*, Pa-

FIGURE 3.1. Maciste as a statue.

gano appears in his original Maciste costume, since, in the fictional world of Maciste films, Maciste sometimes works as an actor who plays Maciste. In numerous films, Maciste has an occupation that leaves his arms bare (a sailor in *Maciste contro lo sceicco*) or his chest entirely exposed (he pays for passage on a ship in *La trilogia di Maciste* [1920, Carlo Campogalliani] by stoking the ship's engines). In other films, a brawling opponent might "accidentally" tear his shirt off—and in *Maciste innamorato* (1919, Luigi Borgnetto) there is a shower scene for no other purpose than to showcase Pagano's body (from the waist up only, of course). In *Maciste nella gabbia dei leoni* (1926, Guido Brignone), Maciste works for a circus as a strongman, and in one particularly impressive demonstration, he lifts his slender female costar, Seida (played by Mimi Dovia) into the air with one hand. She stands in ballet shoes *en pointe* on his palm, and then gracefully begins to dance along his biceps. This sequence emblematizes in many ways the strangely static character of the strongman in peplum films—his strength is best perceived in a frozen and posed body, while the female body is at its most perceptible in the elegant movements of dance, a gendering that has characterized the movements of actors and cameras in the genre from its origins to today. As Wyke has noted, the "living statue" has characterized bodybuilding since Eugene Sandow essentially invented the practice of bodybuilding in the late 1800s (1997, 53, 69), and it continues today to represent the ideal of the peplum masculine body; it goes hand in hand with photographic practices that best present the body frozen in moments of muscular exertion: slow pans and close-ups in the time of the Maciste films and midcentury peplums, slow motion and the artful use of ramping in the contemporary peplum.

The predominant affect in the Maciste films is one of cheerful, ready willingness—Maciste leaps into action at every opportunity, often grinning with delight as he fights, lifts, smashes, and heaves. There are, however, certain kinds of action that he curiously avoids. Maciste, setting a pattern that continued through the midcentury peplums, almost never falls in love (*Maciste innamorato* is perhaps the only exception), but instead facilitates a romance between the female protagonist and another man. Sometimes this match is what we might expect from an ideologically conservative genre (as in *Maciste contro lo sceicco*, in which Maciste brings together two members of the aristocracy), but just as often, Maciste facilitates a match across some sort of barrier. In *Maciste all'inferno*, it is that of a working-class girl to the local aristocrat who has gotten her pregnant, while in *La trilogia di Maciste*, it is the love between a newspaperman and an aristocratic girl. In *Maciste nella gabbia dei leoni*, the strongman brings together Giorgio, the wealthy (white) son of a circus owner, and Seida, a racially ambiguous gamine he rescues while on safari in Africa (her blackface gradually diminishes over the course of the film); in one of the few German-made Maciste films, *Maciste und die Javanerin* (1922, Uwe Jens Krafft), it is a Javanese woman and the Dutch governor of the Indonesian colony, who was her lover and father of her child.

Maciste almost always remains excluded from the romantic plot; in *La trilogia*, he simply rolls his eyes when a besotted girl declares her love for him, preferring the company of his pipe. In *Il viaggio di Maciste*, this attachment to objects rather than girls becomes a running gag when the audience is unexpectedly told that Maciste has a wife, but a wife with the curious name of Diattolina. In a comic revelation, this Diattolina turns out to be a car made by the Diatto firm (which later gave rise to Maserati). "She's cute," Maciste remarks about an American girl, Miss Edith, who pursues him, "but she's not built like my Diattolina!" (Indeed, Maciste's custom-built Diattolina only has one seat because of Maciste's huge body, so romance is structurally excluded.) When it comes to romance, Maciste often appears like nothing so much as a giant, muscled schoolboy—he is uninterested and doesn't really "get" adult sexuality. Ricci nicely calls him "distinctively desexualized" (2008, 81).

The connections between the first cycle and the second cycle of the peplum (again, made almost entirely in Italy, but released around the world) are so numerous and so well established that it almost goes without saying that the midcentury peplum is derived from the Maciste cycle—indeed, the most frequent character in the mid-century peplum is still called "Maciste" (often changed to Hercules in US versions), and several of the midcentury titles are simply taken verbatim from earlier Maciste films, such as *Maciste contro lo sceicco* and *Maciste all'inferno*. These similarities conceal certain important differences—the explicitly procolonialist nationalism of the Maciste cycle (*Cabiria, Maciste alpino, Maciste nella gabbia dei leoni*) is in some ways toned down in the midcentury peplum, not least by using American bodybuilders (or Italian bodybuilders under assumed American names) as the stars. At the same time, midcentury peplums are often racist in ways familiar to contemporary audiences—in the peplums directed by Antonio Leonviola, for instance, African blacks like "Bangor" and "Ubaratutu" immediately assume the "proper" relationship of slave to master once they meet the white hero (Dyer 1997, 179). In *Samson and the Seven Miracles* (*Maciste alla corte del Gran Khan*, 1961, Ricardo Freda), six-foot-two-inch Gordon Scott, waxed and oiled and wearing nothing but a bright red diaper, wanders through a crowd of medieval Chinese peasants without anyone noticing him—a sequence frequently repeated in peplum films set outside continental Europe; see the midcentury version of *Maciste all'inferno* (1962, Ricardo Freda), for instance, or *Goliath and the Vampires* (*Maciste contro il vampiro*, 1961, Sergio Corbucci and Giacomo Gentilomo), once Goliath arrives in the Middle East. The white man is invisible in his universality.

The midcentury peplum begins with the enormously successful 1958 Steve Reeves vehicle *Hercules* (*Le fatiche di Ercole*, 1958, Pietro Francisci) and follows many of the basic structures outlined in the Maciste films, particularly the ensemble of "feats of strength" that structures the wandering narratives of peplum films: the hero once again wrestles an animal, lifts an opponent and hurls him into his other enemies, pries open the iron bars of a prison with his bare hands, and so on. The affect is largely the same as well: the strongman is a big exuberant fellow whose essential attitude is ebullient and happy. The Italians called these figures *"giganti buoni,"* or "good giants" (Giordano 1998), and that is precisely what they are. And the sexuality expressed in the two cycles is also the same: women are definitely attracted to the strongman, but he is generally presented as a big boy who barely understands what is being offered to him. For instance, in *Hercules, Samson, and Ulysses* (*Ercole sfida Sansone*, 1963, Pietro Francisci), when the biblical Delilah attempts to seduce Hercules, she goes skinny-dipping in a pool and coyly invites Hercules to join her for a private bath. He does not accept or reject the invitation, which he clearly doesn't understand; instead, he holds up a dead bird: "I just caught this chicken!" he exclaims proudly, grinning and oblivious. Like the original Maciste, he prefers to arrange matches for others—although, in a change from earlier films, these matches rarely cross racial or class boundaries. In several films, a morose or lethargic sidekick emphasizes the strongman's active optimism: Ilius in *Goliath and the Dragon* (*La vendetta di Ercole*, 1960, Vittorio Cottafavi), or Theseus in *Hercules in the Haunted World* (*Ercole al centro della terra*, 1961, Mario Bava). This does not stop the films from offering heavily eroticized depictions of the female body—the "exotic dance" sequence hinted at by the ballet performance in *Maciste nella gabbia dei leoni* became a fixture in the midcentury cycle of the genre, for example, belly dancing with flimsy silken veils.

But the visual focus throughout is on the male protagonist's body. His muscles take priority—or rather, their presence and power are revealed through tension (for example, the arms straining as they pull on chains). This emphasis often leads to a peculiar kind of antinarrative spirit in the peplum. Focused intently on showcasing a posed body in stasis, it delays or eschews narrative or character development. Most narrative events occur primarily to give the hero another opportunity to lift something heavy or break something hard, and they often crop up without any apparent cause or motivation. *Maciste contro il vampiro* opens with the bodybuilder plowing a field. When his plow runs afoul of a tree stump, he tears the stump from the ground with his powerful body (long, lingering shots of his back and shoulders); as he pulls it free, he hears a cry for help—a boy in the nearby water is being attacked by a sea monster! After defeating the monster, Maciste sees smoke from his village nearby—it is being attacked by marauders! And so on. There is, strictly speaking, not much narrative at all, in the sense of a series of unfolding and concatenated events, each a consequence of what went before. Instead, there is a series of feats of strength connected metonymically in space and time, an anachronistic holdover of the "cinema of attractions" (Gunning 1986). These episodes are held together by the same basic story outline in virtually every midcentury peplum: the rightful power of the state has been usurped by a foreigner or an illegitimate ruler. The strongman's labors restore the proper order so that civilization can go on.[4]

As was the case with Maciste, time and place are surprisingly plastic in the midcentury peplum. The strongman might get swept away from Greece in a storm and washed ashore in pre-Colombian South America, as he does in *Hercules against the Sons of the Sun* (*Ercole contro i figli del sole*, 1964, Osvaldo Civirani), or go to medieval China (*Samson and the Seven Miracles*) or Africa (*Maciste in King Solomon's Mines* [*Maciste nelle miniere di re Salomone*, 1964, Piero Regnoli]) or Atlantis (*Hercules and the Captive Women* [*Ercole alla conquista di Atlantide*, 1961, Vittorio Cottafavi]), or Puritan America (*The Witch's Curse* [*Maciste all'inferno*, 1962, Riccardo Freda]), where Maciste sports an impressive Elvis bouffant. The overall effect is to suggest that heroic white, Western masculinity was universal, dehistoricized, omnipresent (and omnipotent). This was not in any way different from the same temporal and geographic elasticity on display in the Maciste films—Maciste, as the bearer of Western heroic masculinity, was also everywhere, at all times.

The midcentury peplum itself, on the other hand, was not quite so eternal. Audience interest dramatically collapsed in 1964, and the last peplums appeared in 1965. The influence of the films was lasting, however, and appeared in a variety of media—an animated series of peplum shorts for children, *The Mighty Hercules* (1963–1966), ran on American television; Hercules became a character—explicitly modeled on Steve Reeves—in the Marvel Comics universe starting in 1965 (even today, the character retains Reeves's distinctive beard); and the midcentury films continued running for years on American television under the rubric "The Sons of Hercules." In the 1980s, when the pro wrestler Ray Fernandez took the nickname "Hercules," he grew a beard and began carrying huge chains, both references to Reeves's 1958 Hercules. On the big screen, however, the peplum went on an extended hiatus as the midcentury cycle came to an end. The genre (already fairly simplistic) seemed to have exhausted its possibilities, and degenerated into either ultra-low-budget knockoffs of previous films (often by simply reusing footage from those prior films) or simple parody. The apparent requirement to have a bodybuilder in the main role significantly reduced the possibilities for psychological nuance or character-driven narratives, and by 1964 audiences had apparently seen enough bulging muscles heaving (fake) boulders.

THE "BARBARIAN" PEPLUMS OF THE 1980S

The most significant shifts in the peplum's evolution occurred in the next cycle. From 1965 to 1982, hardly anything that might be called a peplum was made in the West, although Schwarzenegger's first film role, in *Hercules in New York* (1970, Arthur Seidelman), was a parody of the midcentury peplum. *Conan the Barbarian* (1982) reimagined the peplum strongman, however, as a typical Reagan-era action star like Rambo or Mad Max—resentful and nostalgic about a past happiness forever lost to him. The preferred setting for these films was still in an ancient mythological past, but one that had all the traits of a postapocalyptic landscape; Western civilization was in disrepair, incapable of protecting anyone, even the strongman and his family. Some 1980s peplum films took this idea—that the distant past might have resembled the near future after a nuclear apocalypse—to its logical conclusion. In both *She* (1982, Avi Nesher) and *Yor, the Hunter from the Future* (*Il mondo di Yor*, 1983, Antonio Margheriti), both Italian productions, the archaic peplum past of swords and sandals is revealed to be precisely a post-nuclear-apocalypse world, a "barbarian" world in our future.

In twenty-odd films made between 1982 and the end of the decade, some in Italy, some in the US and Italy, some in the US and Argentina, the term "barbarian" appears repeatedly in English titles—*Conan the Barbarian*, *The Invincible Barbarian* (*Gunan il guerriero*, 1982, Franco Prosperi), *Barbarian Queen* (1985, Héctor Olivera), *Barbarian Queen II: The Empress Strikes Back* (1990, Joe Finley), *The Barbarians* (1987, Ruggero Deodato), *The Sword of the Barbarians* (*Sangraal, la spada di fuoco*, 1982, Michele Tarantini), also known as *Barbarian Master*—and virtually all of them position their imaginary universe outside the domain of the civilized, generally in a world of anarchy and chaos where a lone hero must struggle simply for survival. The overall effect is to suggest that the time of heroic masculinity is over, lost forever, and can be recuperated only after a rupture in time. The hero is often the last of his tribe, giving the sense of the end of an era that is already far removed from the contemporary viewer of the film.

These films follow a "crisis of masculinity" narrative: critics such as Neale (1993), Savran (1998), and others argued that as social and economic forces gradually eroded traditional gender norms and male privilege, some mainstream films responded by depicting exaggerated and hyperbolic visions of masculinity, male privilege, and violence. The *Rambo* films serve as a convenient touchstone for films in which masculinity is threatened and then reaffirmed in an exaggerated, even hysterical fashion. Similarly, 1980s barbarian peplums intimated what peplum films since 2005 have been suggesting with much greater force—the era of heroic white masculinity is over.

Not all 1980s peplums were as dark in tone as *Conan the Barbarian* or Lucio Fulci's *Conquest* (1983), whose principal character doesn't even live to participate in the final confrontation with the evil queen. Some, like *The Barbarians*, were essentially throwbacks to the cheerful muscularity of the midcentury peplums, and many others simply reveled in the cinematic freedom available in the 1980s: sex and gore. Indeed, the Italian directors of 1980s peplums had previously directed gore and splatter films (Lucio Fulci), pornographic films (Joe D'Amato), and exploitation films such as *Cannibal Apocalypse* (*Apocalypse domani*, 1980, Antonio Margheriti). While many present their principal characters as nominal or ostensible good guys, a few—especially the US-Argentina coproductions—depict completely amoral universes, as in the particularly repulsive *Deathstalker* movies, in which rape is regularly committed by the "heroes," let alone the villains. Although women do appear in the 1980s peplums at times as female warriors, virtually all of them are also victims of rape and torture (*Red Sonja* [1985, Richard Fleischer] and *Barbarian Queen* come particularly to mind), and none has the strongman's physique or impressive strength.

The "barbarian" world, in short, is at least as much a postapocalyptic male fantasy as a fear about the imminent collapse of civilization—yet another example of how "crisis of masculinity" films reaffirm traditional male privileges in an exaggerated or hyperbolic fashion. This point is particularly important for the contemporary peplum, which in some instances—*300* is the most salient case—has relied on a neoconservative "clash of civilizations" model, depicting a protagonist who not only affirms his masculinity and strength in the face of the modern world, but must also defend himself as a Westerner against a decadent and luxurious East. This paranoid narrative, however, is also a wish fulfillment that depicts a world in which tra-

FIGURE 3.2. Conan as a boy, having just lost his mother.

ditional gender roles and hierarchies are reestablished and male violence is no longer restrained.

It is not hard to find most of the stereotyped features of the midcentury peplum in the barbarian peplum—there are fights with wild
animals, the hero is tied to a rack (we watch his muscular struggle
to free himself), and there are eroticized female dance routines. In
Conan the Barbarian, Conan is forced to turn a stone wheel for ten
years, just as Maciste does in *Cabiria*, a film from sixty-eight years
earlier. The films still depend on a series of Orientalized figures—
many of them feature a marauding "horde" that is more or less explicit Mongolian—and exotic locales, costuming designed to maximize exposure of the protagonist's body, and a final sequence that
involves the spectacular collapse of an oppressive building, following
the precedent set in the 1958 *Hercules*.

Even so, the suite of feats of strength disappears, and despite his
muscles, the protagonist no longer has the impossible or superhuman
strength typical of the midcentury peplums. In compensation, he ac-
quires psychological depth, especially Conan (Arnold Schwarzenegger), the only character of the 1980s peplums that was enduring and
influential. Conan's life is marked by double traumas, both of which
are the loss of women. There is his mother, who is decapitated by
Thulsa Doom as she holds little Conan's hand, and later, his lover
and comrade Valeria, killed by Doom's magic arrow. Together, these
lost women form the central absence that organizes a new masculine subjectivity: melancholy, nostalgic, resentful. "For us, there is
no spring," Conan muses regretfully late in the film after fondly re-

calling his childhood.[5] He may become a powerful king, destined to live on forever in legend, but his character and his film are already essentially melodramatic—it is already "too late" (Williams 1991, 10–11; see also Fradley 2004) for Conan, as it will be for the heroes of the contemporary peplum. For the most part, the psychological depth of Conan—such as it was—was not widely imitated by other 1980s peplums, which were largely exhausted by the end of the decade. The vast majority were simply ultra-low-budget exploitation films, devoid of innovation or originality; the bulk appeared in 1982 and 1983, and by 1987 the resurgent genre seemed tapped out again—at least on the big screen.

THE CONTEMPORARY PEPLUM

The contemporary peplum has definitively adopted the psychological depth and haunting internal sadness of Schwarzenegger's Conan, and in so doing, it may have found greater longevity than previous cycles. In the early 2000s, there were occasional peplum films, such as *The Scorpion King* (2002, Chuck Russell), but the genre experienced a major resurgence after *Gladiator* and more particularly after the blockbuster success in 2007 of Zack Snyder's *300*, both of which definitively established the introspective, melancholy, and lonely hero as a staple of the current cycle. The film version of *300* adapted Frank Miller's graphic novel of the same name, which was in turn loosely based on a midcentury classical epic, *The 300 Spartans* (1962, Rudolph Maté). The film notes its own genealogy when the narrator Dilios (David Wenham) proclaims, "We Spartans are descended from Hercules himself," acknowledging not only the mythological strongman, but also the 1958 *Hercules* that initiated the modern peplum cycles. It depicts a rational, civilized West menaced by overwhelming, degenerate hordes from the East: the Persians are tattooed, pierced, scarred, and deformed; they participate in orgies with hermaphrodites and amputees, and so forth. Although many found the film's content objectionable—homophobic, racist, misogynistic, and unusually antagonistic toward bodily difference and disability (see Chemers 2013)—it also developed a remarkably coherent and beautiful visual aesthetic, combining gorgeous computer-generated landscapes, extensive color modification (especially the selective desaturation of parts of the color palette), rhythmic ramping (the smooth change of film speeds), and the almost omnipresent use of slow mo-

FIGURE 3.3. Muscular, athletic bodies in *300*.

tion, which enabled the viewer's unimpeded admiration for the Spartans' muscular, athletic bodies.

The extensive use of slow motion, coupled with the Spartans' scant costuming (naught but leather codpieces and a red cape), may have allowed for the unimpeded appreciation of the male form, but it also exacerbated an issue that had long been visible in the peplum—its powerfully homoerotic undertones. Even as the Spartans in *300* badmouth the Athenians for being "boy lovers," they exchange homoerotic banter with each other, and the extensive use of slow motion and ramping presents muscular male bodies in action as objects to be looked at and admired. Although mainstream audiences of the time understood midcentury peplums as "straight," later viewers saw them as filled with unintentional camp. As Wyke notes, one of the first public gay film festivals in the United States featured a midcentury peplum film in its lineup (67).[6] In the early 1990s, the film critic Michèle Lagny was perplexed by the apparently unintentional homoeroticism of the genre (1992, 171), which, after a hundred years, was starting to look as though it might not be so unintentional. Although some (Pierce 2011) have argued that *300* and other recent epic films are essentially heteronormative, many contemporary peplums do not try to play down their campy homoerotic heritage—indeed, they often strain to maximize it. The Greek gods in the 2011 film *Immortals* are slender but muscular hunks in gold lamé loincloths with fabulous accessories. Nowhere is this more true, however, than in the televisual counterpart to *300*, the Starz series *Spartacus*.

Spartacus, which concluded its fourth and final season in 2013, borrows heavily from *300* and videogames (see Simmons 2011)—the computer-generated sprays of blood, the rhythmic ramping, extensive use of "painterly" and artificial environments—but ratchets up the violence, gore, profanity, and general excess by several notches. At first glance, this excess, including extensive full frontal nudity by both sexes, graphic violence, and graphic sex, appears to be simply a gratuitous, traditional male fantasy.[7] A sustained reading, however, tends to indicate that the show is instead ironic and self-aware, and its ideology considerably more nuanced and thoughtful than that of *300*. Whereas the Spartans of *300* are terrified of admitting any form of difference (sexual, bodily, racial, and so forth), *Spartacus* unites different races, bodies, and sexual orientations under the banner of the "brotherhood" of gladiators. Several of the characters have same-sex romances, and while tribal differences and hostilities are highlighted (Thracians versus Gauls, for example), racial distinctions are mostly ignored.

What unites the gladiators of Spartacus is in fact less their soldierly solidarity and brotherhood than their shared sense of oppression at the hands of the Roman elite. In particular, the show evinces a populist concern with the lives of what are essentially working-class men, whose muscular bodies are put to use and abuse by the soft, decadent Romans. Their bodies displayed on the training grounds, in the arena, and, on occasion, in the bedrooms of upper-crust Roman women. Indeed, the show fetishizes these sequences of display, since they allow the viewers—like the Romans—to examine the muscled male body at their leisure.

In some ways (but only in some), *Spartacus* is like its more famous cinematic predecessor, at heart a left-wing fable. It trains future generations of largely straight male viewers to be comfortable alongside those who are sexually, corporeally, or racially different—largely by depicting all men, gay and straight, white and black, as participating in a common culture. That common culture is violent, muscular, competitive, trash talking, misogynistic, and antagonistic to any form of a cultural elite, but also open to certain forms of difference. When Spartacus (Andy Whitfield) first arrives at the *ludus*, or training camp for gladiators, he is pushed into the middle of a mass of muscular men (some naked, others mostly so) who run the gamut of skin colors. One is disabled, another—who will turn out to be gay—is African, played by the Maori actor Antonio Te Maioha. "Lick my hole," sneers Crixus the Gaul (Manu Bennett, whose father is Maori-Irish) at Spartacus in the scene's opening dialogue. Crixus is presented with full-frontal nudity, standing inches away from the new trainee and backed by the rest of the gladiators—is this the prelude to sexual gang violence? The rest of the sequence, however, defuses that threat, and as Spartacus learns to deliver similar threats and insults, he takes his first step toward being accepted by the group.

Unlike most historical dramas that deal with sensitive issues, *Spartacus* never positions itself as being "tolerant" or "accepting" of racial or sexual difference by having a character anachronistically "speak out against injustice." Instead, sexual orientation and race are simply never mentioned or referred to at all. White and straight are no longer the invisible universal identity—instead, the universal identity is muscled, male, and working class. No difference within the group is acknowledged, and every difference outside it is accentuated. As Spartacus is trained in this world (the locker room of the gym relocated two thousand years in the past), so is the viewer.[8]

What then unites *300*, *Spartacus*, and a recent peplum film like *Immortals*, with its delicate (but muscled) gods clad in gold lamé? All are dedicated to the idea that heroic male subjectivity finds itself "after"—after the loss of the self, of society, of civilization, of one's sexual life. The beloved woman, identity, and homeland have been left behind, lost forever. The sexual trauma implicit in this heroic identity is not contingent, temporary, or metaphorical—indeed, both *Immortals* and *Spartacus* feature castration in its most literal forms. True virility is to be found in an all-male space, but just as importantly, that space is the end of the road. In most contemporary peplums, it represents the hero's drive toward self-obliteration.[9] (This trope perhaps also serves as a guarantee that the protagonist will not find a renewed erotic life in that all-male world.) Since *Conan* and *300*, this condition seems to be the space in which we imagine mythic masculinity: in the doomed melancholy of a hero whose time is over and whose only option is a final, suicidal mission that will, at best, save the world for the lesser men to come.

NOTES

1. I refer to the peplum as a genre because (as this chapter shows) it has a consistent set of themes (such as the struggle against the sexually depraved foreign oppressor); settings (classical or mythological antiquity); characters (Hercules, Maciste, the Titans); and stylistic conventions (particularly the emphasis on the muscular body of the protagonists). It is differentiated from the more general cat-

egory of epic films set in the classical world by its low budget, populist ideology, and popular appeal—and particularly by its focus on the muscular body of the hero. Even Neale, whose notion of genre is more narrow than that of, say, Altman (1999), includes the peplum as a subcategory of "epics and spectacles" (2000, 91).

2. Indeed, what is probably the most theoretical and critical book by an Italian on the peplum was published in French (dell'Asta 1992).

3. For the purposes of brevity, I do not discuss here a wave of peplum television series that appeared in the 1990s (*Hercules: The Legendary Journeys* [1995–1999], *BeastMaster* [1999–2002], and others], made almost entirely in Commonwealth countries.

4. Yet it is clear that the strongman cannot simply represent the state, since he is almost never authorized by the state and usually comes to the aid of an oppressed foreign people. Dyer understands him as representing a fantasy of the power and rightness of the West in its colonial adventures; Günsberg, as the fantasy that muscular power could still have meaning in an industrialized world; I have argued that he is a way of embodying sexual desire that is not limited by a clear recognition of sexual difference. Clearly, the strongman is polysemic.

5. The "crisis of masculinity" narrative would suggest that this constellation of affects (nostalgia, regret, resentment, melancholy) is a way of expressing anger over the loss of traditional male prerogatives in a world where it isn't really socially acceptable to do so—one is supposed to think that modern gender and racial equality, for example, are good things. If feminism and the entrance of women into the workplace were indeed crucial factors in provoking a crisis in masculinity, it might at first seem curious that so many of these films base the hero's nostalgic melancholy on the loss of a woman. But the deaths of Conan's mother, his lover Valeria, and Maximus's wife in *Gladiator* result in the creation an all-male world where strength and courage are paramount.

6. The term "camp" has been used in a number of ways, but generally refers to portrayals so exaggerated that they become indeterminate or convey the opposite impression of the one originally intended, as when exaggerated portrayals of heterosexual masculinity suggest homoeroticism or when something is "so bad it's good." Sontag (1966) calls camp a "sensibility" rather than a clear concept—something so vague and indeterminate that it resists definition but can nonetheless be identified. Pure camp takes itself seriously and thinks that it is doing a good job of conveying, say, virile masculinity. Historical distance, however, makes us later see it as silly, exaggerated, or even strangely gender bending, and this is very much the case with the peplum.

7. A student once told me that the show was kept running on a continuous loop in his fraternity house, and both *300* and *Spartacus* have achieved a kind of cult status among young men.

8. I should be quite clear that the show is hardly a general utopia of difference: its valued masculinity is always set against effeminacy and women, whose concomitant lack of value in a masculine universe is unquestioned. As the gladiators taunt Spartacus about the supposedly nasty smell of Thracians, Spartacus finally shows that he knows how to fit in. "That explains why you smell like a woman," he retorts, and finally all the men laugh together. Also, as in *300*, disability is generally a sign of degeneracy—the lame Ashur, for example, is without honor.

9. This is, of course, not the only possibility in the contemporary peplum:

while the 2010 remake of *Clash of the Titans* adopted much of the same desperate melancholy and loss of the original, its successor, *Wrath of the Titans*, adopted a rather sunnier outlook. *Troy* (2004) also took on something of the midcentury peplum's campy character. Still, the dark, melodramatic desperation of the contemporary peplum hero is the dominant trend, and certainly reflective of the tendency in much contemporary action cinema.

WORKS CITED

Altman, Rick. 1999. *Film/Genre*. London: British Film Institute.

Aziza, Claude. 1998. "Le mot et la chose." *CinémAction* 89:7–11.

Cammarota, Domenico. 1987. *Il cinema peplum: La prima guida critica ai film di Conan, Ercole, Goliath, Maciste, Sansone, Spartaco, Thaur, Ursus*. Rome: Fanucci.

Casadio, Gianfranco. 2007. *I mitici eroi: Il cinema peplum nel cinema Italiano dall'avvento del sonoro a oggi, 1930–1993*. Ravenna: Longo.

Chemers, Michael M. 2013. "'With Your Shield, or on It': Disability Representation in *300*." *Disability Studies Quarterly* 27, no. 3 (2007). http://dsq-sds.org/article/view/37/37.

Dalle Vacche, Angela. 1992. *The Body in the Mirror: Shapes of History in Italian Cinema*. Princeton, NJ: Princeton University Press.

dell'Asta, Monica. 1992. *Un cinéma musclé: Le surhomme dans le cinéma muet italien, 1913–1926*. Translated by Franco Arnò and Charles Tatum. Crisnée, Belgium: Editions Yellow Now.

Dyer, Richard. 1997. *White*. New York: Routledge.

Fradley, Martin. 2004. "Maximus Melodramaticus: Masculinity, Masochism, and White Male Paranoia in Contemporary Hollywood Cinema." In *Action and Adventure Cinema*, ed. Yvonne Tasker, 235–251. New York: Routledge.

Giordano, Michele. 1998. *Giganti buoni: Da Ercole a Piedone (e oltre); Il mito dell'uomo forte nel cinema italiano*. Rome: Gremese.

Gunning, Tom. 1986. "The Cinema of Attraction: Early Film, Its Spectator, and the Avant-Garde." *Wide Angle* 6, no. 2: 63–70.

Günsberg, Maggie. 2005. *Italian Cinema: Gender and Genre*. New York: Palgrave.

Lagny, Michèle. 1992. "Popular Taste: The Peplum." In *Popular European Cinema*, ed. Richard Dyer and Ginette Vincendeau, 163–180. London: Routledge.

Neale, Steven. 1993. "Masculinity as Spectacle: Reflections on Men and Mainstream Cinema." In *Screening the Male: Exploring Masculinities in Hollywood Cinema*, ed. Steven Cohan and Ina Rae Hark, 87–102. New York: Routledge.

———. 2000. *Genre and Hollywood*. New York: Routledge.

Pierce, Jerry B. 2011. "'To Do or Die Manfully': Performing Heteronormativity in Recent Epic Films." In *Of Muscles and Men: Essays on the Sword and Sandal Film*, ed. Michael G. Cornelius, 40–57. Jefferson, NC: McFarland.

Reich, Jacqueline. 2011. "Slave to Fashion: Masculinity, Suits, and the Maciste Films of Italian Silent Cinema." In *Fashion in Film*, ed. Adrienne Munich, 236–259. Bloomington: Indiana University Press.

Ricci, Steven. 2008. *Cinema and Fascism: Italian Film and Society, 1922–1943*. Berkeley: University of California Press.

Rushing, Robert. 2008. "Gentlemen Prefer Hercules: Desire/Identification /Beefcake." *Camera Obscura* 23, no. 3: 158–191.

Savran, David. 1998. *Taking It like a Man: White Masculinity, Masochism, and Contemporary American Culture.* Princeton, NJ: Princeton University Press.

Schenk, Irmbert. 2006. "The Cinematic Support to National(istic) Mythology: The Italian Peplum, 1910–1930." In *Globalization, Cultural Identities, and Media Representations,* ed. Natascha Gentz and Stefan Kramer, 153–168. Albany: State University of New York Press.

Siclier, Jacques. 1962. "L'âge du péplum." *Cahiers du cinéma* 131:26–38.

Simmons, David. 2011. "'By Jupiter's Cock!': *Spartacus: Blood and Sand,* Video Games, and Camp Excess." In *Of Muscles and Men: Essays on the Sword and Sandal Film,* ed. Michael G. Cornelius, 144–153. Jefferson, NC: McFarland.

Sontag, Susan. 1966. "Notes on Camp." In *Against Interpretation, and Other Essays.* New York: Farrar, Straus & Giroux.

Williams, Linda. 1991. "Film Bodies: Gender, Genre, Excess." *Film Quarterly* 44, no. 4: 2–13.

Wyke, Maria. 1997. "Herculean Muscle! The Classicizing Rhetoric of Bodybuilding." *Arion* 4, no. 3: 51–79.

CHAPTER 4

THE AMERICAN POSTWAR SEMIDOCUMENTARY CYCLE: FACTUAL DRAMATIZATIONS

R. BARTON PALMER

IN FEBRUARY 1946, the World Theater in New York, one of the city's established art cinemas, took a chance on a new film from Italy. In defiance of all reasonable expectations, Roberto Rossellini's *Rome, Open City* (*Roma città aperta*) played to overflow audiences for an amazing twenty-one months, breaking theater records previously established by *The Birth of a Nation* (1915) and *Gone with the Wind* (1939). *Paisà* (*Paisan*, also 1946), the second film in what would become Rossellini's war trilogy, met with a similar reaction, including a rave review from the nation's leading critic. Writing in the *New York Times*, Bosley Crowther (1948) found unfamiliar a film committed to limning a "terrifying picture of the disillusion, the irony, the horribleness of strife," accustomed as he was to the more comforting chauvinism of the Hollywood war movie and of American commercial film production in general. Films like Rossellini's war trilogy—which concluded with *Germany Year Zero* (*Germania anno zero*, 1948)—offered authentic visions of a European culture nearly destroyed by war, with a hard-edged approach to dramatizing collective disaster (of which the twentieth century provided what we might call a richness of material) that had never been taken up before by the commercial cinema.

Perhaps most importantly, these films, soon to be known collectively as neorealist, struck American viewers as authentic in large part because they had been quite obviously shot in the locations where the dramas depicted took place, even as they traced the experiences of characters that seemed to have sprung from those places, inevitably embodying and expressing cultural truths. To be sure, of course, neorealist films, as Crowther's "shock" exemplifies, voided the contract of representation that had previously bound Ameri-

can viewers to their cinema; now, in the general spirit of modernist convention breaking, certain forms of living, political realities,
and cultural themes previously off limits to the medium, were being
explored.

Rossellini's images reflected the complex realities of his postwar
world, and were staged in it for the most part. But these images were,
with some minor exceptions, not found in some newsreel and then
creatively redeployed as part of an ontologically complex montage
melding the typically verisimilar with images that were authentic
in a different sense, reflecting in part a world that existed before the
shaping intentions of the filmmaker. In an essay that interestingly
incorporates the insights and blindness of the neorealist position, Cesare Zavattini (perhaps its most eloquent spokesman) proclaims, as
he reflects on the essential difference between this style of filmmaking and entertainment cinema more generally: "The most important
characteristic of neo-realism, i.e., its essential innovation, is, for me,
the discovery that this need to use a story was just an unconscious
means of masking human defeat in the face of reality" ([1952] 1978,
67). Nonetheless, his films, like Rossellini's, remain firmly rooted in
narrative, which, with its twists and turns, sympathetic characters,
thematic concerns, and dramatic resolutions, provides the structure
upon which the evocation and exploration of real place and the various meanings it holds in the contemporary moment might unfold.
He could imagine a time when this tradition of filmmaking would
dispose of "no scenario written before, and no dialogue to adapt," but
in fact that moment never arrived (75).

Crowther, viewing *Paisà*, found himself intrigued by its flouting
of industrial wisdom. Here was a film that did not deploy, much less
focus on, professional actors; exhibited no commitment to glamor-
ization and eroticization; and did not insist on concluding with what
Fredric Jameson ([1979] 1992, 27) has called "the optical illusion of
social harmony," a happy ending that is self-evidently wish fulfillment. And yet Crowther should have also felt a profound sense of déjà
vu while watching *Paisà*. A US film cycle that manifested remarkable parallels to (but also intriguing differences from) neorealism was
already well launched in 1946. Crowther had even been present at
its birth almost six years before, in September 1940, at the impressive Radio City Music Hall, one of the nation's most famous first-
run theaters. There Crowther saw a Louis de Rochemont production,
The Ramparts We Watch (1940), an essay film, or so we might call

it, since we lack a more appropriate label to cover its combination of instruction and exhortation with a dramatically enacted story. In *Ramparts*, de Rochemont unveiled a striking model of cinematic unconventionalism that was a more radical departure than neorealism from the entertainment film model.

Though the film has been more or less ignored by historians ever since, the production, exhibition, and critical reception of *Ramparts* pointed toward an existing vein of popularity to which neorealism subsequently appealed. *Ramparts* proved successful enough to inspire a quite successful cycle of similar semidocumentary films, whose popularity endured until the end of the 1950s. These were intended for general exhibition, not for alternative theaters like New York's World, and they soon came to constitute an important part of Hollywood's range of entertainment options. In the postwar era, in fact, this kind of filmmaking was a defining presence on American screens, with a good number of films (especially those defined retrospectively as "noir") falling into the semidocumentary category properly speaking, and many others that made no use of documentary techniques but were more broadly realist, especially in their use of real locations as "themselves."[1]

Neorealism as a movement had to contend with the debatable place of story in films that also avowed or embodied quite different intentions. And as it turns out, also debatable was the role that story was to play in this developing tradition of the American semidocumentary. What follows is an analysis of how the complex, though ultimately uncommercial, model offered by *Ramparts* was modified in three later releases as the cycle unfolded and audience interest eventually waned: *The House on 92nd Street* (1945), *He Walked by Night* (1947), and *Southside 1-1000* (1950).

THE RAMPARTS WE WATCH (1940):
"A STIRRING DOCUMENT OF PICTORIAL JOURNALISM"

In contrast to both *Paisà* and *Roma*, de Rochemont's film incorporated substantial "documentary" footage into its story; in fact it is dominated by such footage. More importantly, perhaps, the story was illustrative of, and thus subordinate to, the director's avowed intent to limn a history of such sweeping scale that it could be told only through newsreel vignettes fixed by explanatory voice-over narration. Announced in a lengthy precredit scroll, the film's intention is to depict how in the years leading up to the US declaration of war in 1917, public opinion shifted from unconcern about European developments to a troubled neutrality, and then from a barely suppressed partisanship to an embrace of the Allied cause. The film was, quite simply, a call to arms.

In his enthusiastic review, Crowther (1940) could hardly help concluding that the elaborate pastiche that was *Ramparts* was no "entertainment film, in the easy sense of that word," for it "deals in historical facts as they fall into a grim, dramatic pattern." Though warning viewers that "there has never been a motion picture just like this one," he found himself so startled by this thoroughgoing reworking of feature film conventions that his review offers only a vague idea of how the film is structured, instead enthusing that "a more provocative or challenging motion picture has not been placed before the public in years—or maybe, on second thought, never [*sic*]."

De Rochemont's previous career had been spent working not for the studios, but as an employee of Time, Inc., where he started *The March of Time* (1931–1945), a radio news series, and then became involved in producing documentary shorts for a newsreel series, then quite famous, of the same name, which ran from 1935 to 1951. When he set out to create what Crowther (1940) interestingly calls "pictorial journalism" in *Ramparts*, de Rochemont was a documentarist of many years' experience. *March* differed radically from earlier theatrical documentary shorts. By the late 1930s, its shorts were focusing on a single subject, depicted in striking images, imaginatively edited by de Rochemont, and then analyzed, often at some length, by an offscreen narrator, Westbrook Van Voorhis. De Rochemont occasionally used filmed stagings of events, a technique adapted from the radio version of the program, which deployed dramatic readings.

Planning for *Ramparts* began with de Rochemont's intent to portray what he considered to be the "less tangible, less comprehensible, but much more vulnerable rampart of our national defense, the mass mind of the American public," as he confessed to Crowther (1939). Dramatization through individual yet typical characters would be more effective in depicting the change in public attitudes through the dramatic (strictly speaking, fictional) means of conjuring up a typical American small community. De Rochemont searched for a small city not far from his New York City base whose look had not changed substantially since 1919, settling on New London, Connecticut. More interesting perhaps, given what Rossellini and company were to do a few years later, he involved the townspeople themselves heavily in the project. There are no professionals in the cast, and the film omits the usual credit sequences, in which roles are identified by their performers. A reported 1,400 local residents were used in the production, and 73 had speaking roles. Here is Roberto Rossellini describing how he searched for "players" to appear in *Germany Year Zero*: "For my cast I roamed the streets of Berlin, looking for satisfactory physical types . . . Most of my players had never acted before, but anyone can act provided he is in familiar surroundings and given lines that are natural" (quoted in Gallagher 1998, 240). De Rochemont would have agreed with this approach to casting and film performance.

Ramparts set itself the task of educating the public, but it is also a fictional tale of ordinary Americans living in a typical small town. This part of the film consists of a number of short vignettes in which characters act out events that illustrate and exemplify a shifting national mood. A Hungarian immigrant receives a draft notice and returns to fight for the country of his birth; a German American family feels the pull of divided loyalties and is ostracized by the "better" elements in the town; a young man, inflamed by a desire for adventure, joins the Lafayette Escadrille against the wishes of his parents. These dramatic sketches do not add up to a plot in the traditional sense. *Ramparts* is an artful pastiche, deploying four different kinds of footage: newsreel accounts of important international events; shot-on-location footage of the "typical American small town," where the narrative is in some sense set; reenactments of historical events that do not feature identifiable characters; and dramatic vignettes featuring named characters. Story is strictly subordinated to the film's informational and frankly propagandistic aims.

And yet the concluding section breaks this elaborate pattern, and for journalistic rather than formal reasons, as *Ramparts* turns from recounting history to anatomizing and analyzing a contemporary threat, the frightening military strength of America's potential European enemy, National Socialist Germany. To make this case with disturbing effectiveness, *Ramparts* incorporates substantial footage from a captured print of Hans Bertram's *Feuertaufe* (Baptism of fire, 1940), an extended newsreel feature, rather like a *March of Time* episode, dealing with the Nazis' victory over Poland in the fall of 1939. The film, which had premiered that previous April in Berlin, was intended as the first of a projected series of documentaries designed to strengthen domestic morale in Germany and, when exported abroad,

When we are ready to take the
stride into overseas space,....

FIGURE 4.1. *The Ramparts We Watch* incorporates a number of staged sequences; here, a "German" broadcaster explains the Nazi plans for world conquest.

to convince others of the Third Reich's invincibility. De Rochemont somewhat mysteriously obtained a print that had come into the possession of the Royal Navy and used the film's propagandistic rhetoric to offend a then-neutral America, certainly not what Bertram had in mind.

If *Ramparts* inaugurated a tradition, it remains something of an isolated masterpiece, with its hastily revised menu of materials reflecting the exigencies of a rapidly evolving political atmosphere and the rhetoric, as de Rochemont thought, needed to change minds in response. *Ramparts* is not a feature film with documentary stylings, but in fact just the opposite, and this was not a formula that had a chance of enduring for very long in an industry committed to storytelling and, more broadly, to entertainment more than journalism. And yet the semidocumentary developed along more traditional, commercial lines even as it continued, in varying forms, the pictorial journalism at the heart of de Rochemont's first major release, at least until the public tired of such tendentiousness.

More importantly, de Rochemont's film demonstrated the audience appeal, and profitability, of factual-fictional cinematic realism, the approach to filmmaking that, with the help of Darryl F. Zanuck and others at Fox, he subsequently refined in the project that was to become *The House on 92nd Street* (1945), which was directed by

Henry Hathaway, a frequent collaborator and then an apostle of the de Rochemont–Zanuck approach. *House* was the film that firmly established the box-office potential and critical acceptance of semidocumentary films based on actual events and incorporating elements of crime thrillers, which were then also enjoying considerable popularity. Zanuck took credit for the invention of this formula, hit on during his work with de Rochemont, who turned his hand to feature filmmaking after producing more straightforward documentaries released by Fox during the war. In a memorandum written in 1947 during the production of Hathaway's *Call Northside 777*, a semidocumentary thriller on which the two cooperated, Zanuck noted for his production staff the dissatisfaction he had felt with the first draft of the script for *House*, which he faulted for its lack of audience-engaging drama: "If we do not have a vital personal story and characters whom we understand and appreciate, then our film becomes as impersonal as a 'March of Time.' And it loses the very elements that made the aforementioned films [all de Rochemont productions, including *House*] tremendously popular. . . . It is not enough just to tell an interesting story. Half the battle depends on *how* you tell the story" (quoted in Behlmer 1993, 122–123).

Zanuck at first vetoed the project that would become *House*, but he was impressed that de Rochemont had obtained special access to FBI files and facilities through his assiduously cultivated friendship with Director J. Edgar Hoover. The two producers then determined to combine *March of Time* factual materials with what Zanuck termed factual dramatization. What he meant was that in the manner of socialist realism, the film should deploy a narrative featuring illustratively typical characters and situations. And yet, conforming more closely to proven Hollywood formulas, the main characters should be both intriguing and sympathetic, or "dramatic," as Zanuck might have put it (Behlmer 1993, 123). We can probably credit the studio executive with the idea that the dramatic sections should be done in the then increasingly popular style of the crime melodrama, what we have since been taught to call film noir.

Zanuck shifted the formula toward the fictional, making story rather than information the film's emphasis. Still, the film's journalistic bona fides impressed Crowther (1945), who praised *House* for its "headline flavor." With Zanuck monitoring planning and execution, standard Hollywood filmmaking structures could be deployed: a focus on star players; a carefully contrived plot; and suspenseful action sequences built on multiple dramatic conflicts. These staples of fiction filmmaking did not displace the use of either "real" footage or documentary formal techniques, including "voice of God" narration, elaborately explanatory opening credits that glorify national institutions, a pledge that filmmakers are telling a true story, and their solemn commitment to using, when possible, real locations and those inhabiting them.

Ramparts invented the semidocumentary form; *House* provided its apotheosis.[2] Zanuck bragged that he had "personally originated the so-called de Rochemont touch" (quoted in Behlmer 1993, 121). Although the facts speak otherwise, Zanuck deserves a great deal of credit for refining the formula. As a predictably intense wartime interest in politics both international and national lessened with the coming of prosperity and peace, the strident engagement of de Rochemont's informational approach seemed less attractive to filmgoers. The workings of industry cycling soon created and furthered the tradition, which was to last quite a bit longer than Zanuck had predicted. In 1950, looking closely at the disappointing box office of such semidocumentaries as Elia Kazan's *Panic in the Streets* (1950), he opined that films in this category had started to prove a "shocking disappointment," especially those "'downbeat' in nature or deal[ing] with sordid backgrounds, unsympathetic characters, and over-emphasized 'suffering'" (quoted in Behlmer 1993, 193).

Although the semidocumentary series, with its "downbeat" nature, was doomed by a change in audience tastes, postwar realism as a movement had longer legs, extending a popularity established by the earlier cycle. Zanuck sponsored the production of a number of films dealing with the "real events" of World War II, including *The Desert Fox* (1951, Henry Hathaway) and *Five Fingers* (1952, Joseph L. Mankiewicz), whose protagonists, somewhat controversially, were a German general and a German spy. For the offscreen disembodied voice of authority, these films substituted a more dramatic device, in keeping with Zanuck's views: Jamesian narrators, minor characters called upon to record, evaluate, and explain the actions of the not altogether conventional main characters. Only a minimum of newsreel footage was deployed in these films, and there was no location shooting in *Fox*. By the end of the decade, Zanuck was working on a project that usefully joined this kind of historically based narrative with the star-studded extravaganza (in the tradition of the very successful United Artists release *Around the World in 80 Days* [1956, Michael Anderson]). In addition to merging two of the previous decade's most successful production trends, Zanuck's *The Longest Day* (1962) proved to be one of the era's most profitable pictures, an exercise in the re-creation of recent history through the technique of factual dramatization. Key events in the planning and execution of the D-Day landings, involving military and political leaders and occasionally those of the lower ranks, are reenacted, and these tableaux are supplemented by "typical" scenes featuring fictional characters whose purpose is to illustrate various experiences of D-Day, a device drawn directly from *Ramparts*.

The House on 92nd Street was directed by one of de Rochemont's most enthusiastic and talented collaborators, Henry Hathaway. Released in September 1945, a little more than a month after final victory in the Pacific, it is a wartime thriller, and fictional only in two senses. The film expands its spare story, based on a true case whose details came from FBI files to which de Rochemont was given privileged access, with some imagined scenes and confected dialogue constituting sequences that are "true" only in a minimal sense. More problematically, in response to a perceived exhibition imperative, the script rewrites history. To provide a contemporary hook for its release—the dropping of atomic bombs on Hiroshima and then Nagasaki that August—the plot connects the roundup of a German spy ring (which actually took place early in the war, before scientific research on this new weapon was much advanced) with the protection of Manhattan Project secrets.

In the film's often self-consciously noir segments, an expressionist stylization dominates, providing an intriguing contrast with the blank realism of the other segments, many of which are either stock footage of FBI operations (provided to the filmmakers by Hoover) or sequences shot on location, including an interesting panning shot that, with the aid of some processing trickery, suggests an impossible proximity of the FBI building to the White House (both, of course, are on Pennsylvania Avenue). Much of film's footage is either of the actual events that the film treats (the so-called Duquesne spy case) or is straightforwardly documentary in its apparently unstaged recording of police activities and its low-key, though still distinctly celebratory description of law enforcement procedure. Nonprofessional actors were used in minor parts (with some of the roles being played by actual police personnel). Sequences shot silent are explained by a self-assured and omniscient narrator (Reed Hadley, in a role that he would repeat many times in other semidocumentaries).

And yet *The House on 92nd Street* is more than a re-creation of a "true case," since the two tendencies in the cycle's formula (facts and their dramatization) tend to diverge. The film's narrative focus is uneasily split between the Nazi agents, those fascinating perpetrators of an unfathomable and perverse evil, and their pursuers, whose unalloyed and rather flat virtue proves much less appealing, even though it naturally emerges victorious in a finale that celebrates the invincibility of US institutions. The sequences detailing the machinations of the reptilian villains strain to evoke a different atmosphere. These sequences are overly theatrical, barely contained by Hathaway's otherwise subdued and objective approach to his material. That one of the main characters is a double agent, present as either an informant or a "conspirator" in most of the dramatic scenes, bridges the gap between the film's contrasting representational regimes, but only somewhat.

Subsequent entrants in the semidocumentary cycle manifest the same unstable melding of two opposed story worlds: the well-organized modern state, knowable as well as knowing, its irregularities surveilled and corrected by governmental agencies of enormous power that are always put in service of the public good; and the more recognizable realm of everyday experience as understood by Hollywood, a place where personal relationships, difficulties, and triumphs displace from focus the larger picture of US society. This split is particularly pronounced in the semidocumentaries that are noir inflected, but produces a palpable unease even in those that are not, such as Fred Zinnemann's *The Men* (1950), which tells the story of the care and rehabilitation of paraplegic war veterans even as it concerns itself with the difficulties experienced by one veteran (played by Marlon Brando with fierce Method-acting understatement) who decides, against his better judgment, to get married.

HE WALKED BY NIGHT: MORE OR LESS A TRUE STORY

Like *House*, *He Walked by Night* can legitimately be termed a "true story," being based on an actual case: the killing of two policemen by a fellow member of their own Pasadena, California, department, who worked in the fingerprint records division. In the hands of the screenwriters John C. Higgins and Crane Wilbur, this rather mundane criminal, however, becomes a self-taught and sociopathic genius who is not only adept at designing innovative electronic equipment, but is not above stealing what others have invented and selling it as his own. Roy Martin (Richard Basehart), unlike the pathetically inept German agents in *The House on 92nd Street*, is a cunning adversary. After he somewhat rashly kills a policeman who spots him about to burglarize an electronics shop, Martin eludes capture because he proves amazingly knowledgeable about police technique.

He Walked by Night was directed by Alfred L. Werker, with a great deal of help from Anthony Mann, who would later distinguish himself with a number of noir films, some of which belong to the semidocumentary series, most notably, perhaps, *T-Men* (1947). An old Hollywood hand, Werker would later do distinguished work directing two other de Rochemont–produced semidocumentaries, *Lost Boundaries* (1949) and *Walk East on Beacon* (1952). *He Walked by Night* offers much of the same documentary stylization found in *The House on 92nd Street*, even though the "case" in this film is no more than superficially based on actual events. A written title only somewhat misleadingly proclaims: "This is a true story. It is known to the Police Department of one of our largest cities as the most difficult homicide case in its experience, principally because of the diabolical cleverness, intelligence and cunning of a completely unknown killer. . . . The record is set down here factually—as it happened. Only the names are changed, to protect the innocent." These words are echoed by those of the narrator, who, as shots of Los Angeles and its police department play on the screen, provides an overview of the nation's second-largest urban area, whose cosmopolitanism and mixed, transient population, so he avers, provide a challenge for law enforcement. Somewhat wryly, he concludes, "The work of the police like that of woman is never done. The facts are told here as they happened."

Many of the sequences in the film that detail police work meet that standard of authenticity, having been filmed inside the Los Angeles Police Department headquarters (an imposing building shot from a low angle to emphasize its embodiment of well-organized power) and furnished with an appropriate voice-over commentary. The staged sequences are carefully stylized to match the reality footage. The producers Robert Kane and Bryan Foy were so eager for authenticity that they asked the LAPD for a technical adviser. Sergeant Marty Wynn, who wanted the film to avoid the distorting clichés that had dominated Hollywood treatment of crime detection, provided much valuable information about police procedure; under Wynn's tutelage, the screenwriters and performers learned the jargon of the trade, includ-

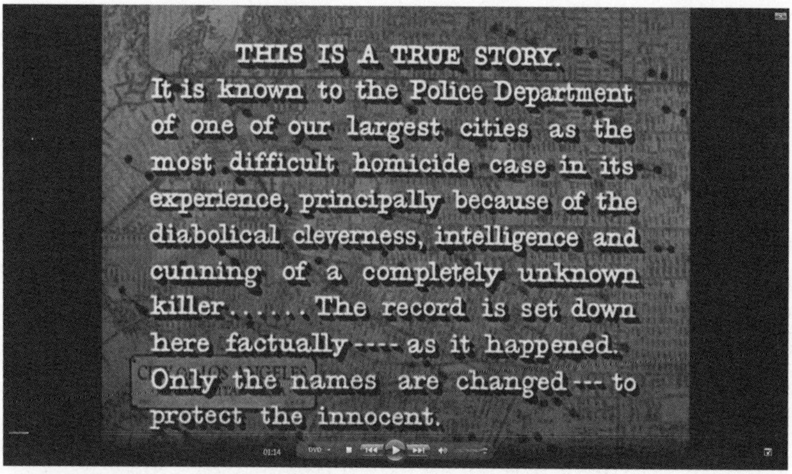

FIGURE 4.2. Like many semidocumentaries, *He Walked by Night* opens with a title card that rather deceptively informs viewers that what they are about to see is a "true story."

ing the abbreviated language of police radio calls and the specialized vocabulary of evidence gathering and testing. The result was, as A. W. (1949) wrote in his *New York Times* review, "more than a modicum of striking realism and authority."

Yet it is important to note that the film, in detailing what it confesses is, for the LAPD, "the most difficult homicide case in its experience," commits itself to focusing on the extraordinary rather than on the everyday aspects of police work. Influenced by film noir's preoccupation with the bizarre and the perverse, Werker and the screenwriters not surprisingly developed Roy Martin, the "diabolical" genius, as a kind of monster who, in fact, cannot be identified and collared by ordinary police procedure. Instead, in a movement of the plot that intriguingly anticipates the spectacular finale of a more celebrated contemporary thriller, Carol Reed's *The Third Man* (1949), Martin must be hunted down and exterminated in his filthy underground lair. Werker and the cinematographer John Alton, famous for his expressionistic setups and visual stylization in such noir classics as *The Big Combo* (1955), *Mystery Street* (1950), and *The Hollow Triumph* (1948), put Martin in control of a shadowy alternative world, a place of darkness, anomie, and reckless self-assertion that the police enter only at their peril. Detective sergeant Marty Brennan (Scott

Brady) is foiled repeatedly by Martin, who seems to know police procedure better than the policemen themselves.

As does the noir–inflected semidocumentary more generally, *He Walked by Night* juxtaposes a city of light (populated by citizens going about their business and surveilled by the benevolent police) and a city of darkness (a criminal underworld that, metaphorized by the night that seems to enfold it, does not easily admit the knowing, official gaze). Like the film's narrative and visual structure, the sound track is schizophrenic, split between the heavy, grim romantic theme that plays over Martin's lurking in the shadows and the upbeat, almost military air that accompanies the work of the police, the grinding routine according to the book that eventually identifies the criminal. The city is the focus of productive communal life (as the opening montage of shots depicting everyday life emphasizes), but its anonymous spaces shield those who, in their exceptionality, would live in defiance of officially imposed law and order. The two worlds found in the contemporary US metropolis seem utterly opposed, but they are actually strangely connected because Martin, as it turns out, is a former employee of a local police department. Like the double agent in *House*, he seems comfortable in both versions of the city.

Appropriately, Martin is hardly, at least at the outset, a career criminal, nor is his lawbreaking to be explained sociologically. The underworld he inhabits is never figured in either economic or class terms. It seems, instead, to be the underside of bourgeois normality. Martin's thefts of electronic equipment are meant to further a career of invention and self-promotion for which his extraordinary mental abilities would certainly qualify him. Because he is never interrogated by the police, Martin's abandonment of a career in law enforcement following military service remains a mystery. This much is clear. Eager to make a mark for himself in a postwar world driven by technological advance, inured to violence, and deploying technical knowledge and skill gained from government service, Martin is yet another version of the returning soldier who cannot fit easily into a changed world despite his exceptional talents and energies.

The damaged veteran is a stock character of film noir, an essential element of its nightmare vision of American life. *He Walked by Night*, as its title suggests, is finally more interested in exploring, even if not explaining, this enigmatic figure. Thus Martin's moral nature is evoked but little through dialogue and mostly, in the expressionist manner, by visual style and mise-en-scène. Despite its opening avowal of truth telling and the narrator's commitment to setting out the facts "as they happened," the film is much more than a straightforward chronicle of the infallible methods, the irresistible institutional power, and the quietly heroic dedication of the police in identifying and capturing criminals.

Boris Ingster's *Southside 1-1000* (1950), which details the exploits of Treasury Department agents in apprehending a gang of counterfeiters, is not the first film in the cycle to focus on this governmental institution, but interestingly exemplifies the representational and stylistic changes that the turn toward documentarism involved.[3] By 1950, the Zanuck formula, with its emphasis on factual dramatization and downbeat subject matter, was wearing thin on Hollywood's customers, as the producer himself, who was a keen observer of the film-going scene, quickly recognized. In particular, the documentary stylizations of the cycle were now so routine as to be invisible. The *Times* reviewer praised *Southside* as a "well-mannered melodrama," ignoring the film's carefully managed documentarism (T. M. P. 1950). This appraisal ignores the subtlety and talent with which Ingster and his creative team managed the formula, which here still clearly betrays its origins in *Ramparts*.

In this film and others of the cycle, the state and its forms of power emerge as forces capable of, indeed irresistibly successful in, surveilling, controlling, and usually eliminating any serious, organized threats to the common good, whether foreign or domestic. By a direct address to the viewer, and the clear ability to collect and assemble a series of persuasive, informative images, the documentary portions of films in this cycle manifest the very power they strive to represent. Criminality in the semidocumentary is thus rarely a matter of inexplicable turpitude or social disadvantage, only seldom reflecting the psychopathological anomie that dominates in wartime noirs like *Double Indemnity* and *Murder, My Sweet* (both 1944). Criminality instead usually figures as a powerful and well-structured opposition to the common good, a rational and calculated force dedicated to the extensive subversion of the public order or even, in those semidocumentaries with Cold War themes, to the overthrow of society. This kind of criminality cannot be countered and defeated by that most prevalent of noir stock characters, the private detective; it requires instead the information-gathering, evidence-sifting, hypothesis-building procedures of a modern intelligence service backed, as necessary, by the fully armed power of the state.

In *Southside*, federal institutions prove invincible, incorruptible, and all-protecting of what the viewer is told is the most important weapon against the forces of darkness, a stable currency. What makes life possible—the money that fuels all social relations—is provided by the state, which is alone capable of marshaling the resources necessary for the protection of its value and utility. Treasury Department operatives provide the final truth that the human experience here considered yields as they first discover the crime and then track down the criminals responsible for it, eventually bringing them all to justice and eliminating the threat they pose to the body politic. In the tradition of *Ramparts*, the semidocumentary often presents a United States bearing up under continual assault from within and without by large-scale efficiently organized institutions whose essential quality is their unflagging devotion to discovering, cataloguing, and interpreting facts. If one purpose of documentary film is informational, that is, making available a knowledge of the world that ordinary people do not possess, then this aesthetic finds its perfect correlative in official institutions whose fact-gathering and hypothesis-building functioning is detailed in this tradition, always with a jingoism suited to exercises in propaganda.

The drive of those willing, in a dangerous world, to destroy collective security for personal gain, set against the dedication of federal forces to providing protection for a key government institution—US currency—generates the tensions exploited in the narrative as two opposed worlds compete, however unequally, for dominance. As the film's narrator proclaims, those who are in command of the facts will always triumph over those who lack the all-encompassing knowledge that only large-scale institutions can provide. This power to know and reveal, and thus to control, finds its material reflex in semidocumentary form itself: in the film's assertion that the stories it tells are true; in its flaunted ability, through the editing process, to yoke together and fix the meaning of disparate kinds of images; and in its carefully calculated deployment of a firm, persuasive, and self-confessedly omniscient extradiegetic narrative voice that recuperates and corrects the contingent truths that emerge within the world of the story.

All the semidocumentaries deploy voice-over narration to solve the problem of melding the documentary and story portions of the text. How this may be artfully accomplished is best demonstrated in *Southside*. The film's introductory section is in effect a cinematic essay that argues for the centrality of a stable currency to the survival of the democratic West. A hand spins a globe and lands on the Korean peninsula as the narrator suggests that the struggle between totalitarianism and democracy, begun in 1914, may be entering its final phase with the outbreak of this proxy war between communism and the free world. A montage of battle scenes from World War II (generic images of huge naval task forces, aerial dogfights, and nighttime artillery fire) offers a catalogue of weapons that the narrator avers are not as powerful as a strong currency in maintaining a free society against threats from within and without.

The United States that emerges from these images is productive and prosperous, seemingly safe from any threat, internal or external. But that appearance of unchallenged social order fostered and protected by impressive institutions is deceptive, even if only in the limited sense that the film will go on to explore. In the manner of a classic documentary, the "point" of individual shots in this essay is not readable without the narrator's explanation. The introductory essay ends with a direct borrowing from *The House on 92nd Street*: a panning shot that links the Washington Monument with the Treasury Department building, affirming by this visual demonstration of the proximity of the two structures and the easy passage between them the centrality to US life of the printing of money. Like the society it supports, the American dollar finds itself vulnerable to threats from within and without that would destroy its ability to function as necessary social glue, a truth that, once enunciated, leads naturally to the exemplification of how Treasury agents prevent such a potentially disastrous debasement.

In *Southside*'s documentary prologue, as in that of *Ramparts*, images serve as metonymic images of the larger points made by the narrator; they illustrate and exemplify what he has to say and have no readable importance in themselves. They are established as pictures of things in general, not of things in particular. The rhetorical space occupied by the narrator is not extradiegetic as such, since at this point there is no diegesis beyond a string of otherwise disconnected illustrations. The point of knowledge from which he addresses us is the only place where meaning and truth can be made available.

The main narrative of *Southside*, interestingly enough, manifests a similar kind of movement away from telling to showing. The primacy of the narrator's well-constructed diatribe yields focus to a story world that by its nature reveals its own meanings. The cinematic essay proper ends, and the exemplum begins, even as a hardly surprising rhetorical shift occurs. The viewer, first lectured effectively on a central truth of modern social life, is positioned to be entertained by a story illustrating important aspects of that truth. But this transition masks, rather transparently, another move as the film assumes a conventional identity as a Hollywood product designed to deliver the pleasure of compelling narrative. In recognition of this delayed but inevitable move away from documentary rhetoric, the film could turn completely from telling to showing. Having discovered effective visual and dramatic ways to present exposition, the classic Hollywood story of this era had no need for voice-over commentary. Voice-over is available to filmmakers only as a stylistic option to be used rarely and then usually as character focalized and associated with subjective flashbacks, often but hardly exclusively in film noir. But the complete abandonment of voice-over at this point would undermine the way in which the film has hitherto carefully constructed a connection between the narrating presence of the cinematic essayist and the powerful state institutions whose nature and purpose he explicates and aurally represents. He constitutes himself, in fact, as their enthusiastic and omniscient spokesman. Should it simply become an unreflective source of entertainment, the story, of course, would lose its value as an exemplum. But the split nature of the noir semidocumentary depends on the maintenance of an admittedly uneasy accommodation of contrasting rhetorics as a somewhat self-contained story world is created, even as it remains subordinate to the ideas and values that call it into being and constitute its intellectual frame.

Only the impossible emergence of a character bearing the full burden of institutional power could compensate completely for the narrator's withdrawal, and this move, as Ingster must have recognized, would have been aesthetically disruptive, allowing the film to collapse into two not coherently related sections. In the story world that *Southside* creates, the narrative voice is carefully calculated and never more than an occasional presence, its function no longer to be the sole source of determining information, but to remind viewers of the presence of an extradiegetic space of meaning making and surveilling power.

At times, the narrator intrudes to summarize the meaning of a scene or to effect a transition to the next stage of the action, functions that could be, and often are, just as readily performed by the narrative itself. The narrator assumes something like his previous role as the assembler of images when a complex montage shows how counterfeit money, once it has been produced in large quantities, is laundered within the economy, especially within seedy institutions where close attention is not paid to individual bills (horse racing and casinos). The retention of the narrator, however, depends on an interesting but hardly obvious transformation. The self-sufficient space of truth telling first established as the only source of meaning making for a succession of disparate images becomes an extradiegetic place for comment, forecasting, recapitulation, and summary, turning *Southside* into something very close, structurally speaking, to a nineteenth-century realist novel, which is characteristically dominated by its omniscient, noncharacter narrator, a voice that also effects, as the critical commonplace has it, the attendant subordination of other voices, a valuing enacted formally in this film by the narrator's positioning outside the world of the story.

No more than the government agents who detect and dispose of threatening criminal conspiracies will this figure surrender his control. Transformed into an extradiegetic narrator in the manner of classic realism, this unseen figure continues, until the credits roll, to marshal and interpret data like his diegetic counterparts, never allowing viewers to forget his authoritative presence and transforming such divided texts into effectively unified "authentic" fiction. It is easy enough, in assessing the semidocumentary cycle, to be overly impressed by its preoccupation with realism, broadly considered, including the incorporation within the text of filmic realia drawn from nontheatrical sources. But from *Ramparts* through the end of the cycle, what is most striking about these ostensibly fictional films is their documentary address, a rhetoric employed first to persuade isolationist-minded Americans that increased military preparedness was called for, but then marshaled, in the wake of the huge expansion of governmental force and institutions that occurred during the war, to rationalize and defend the power of the state. It is an interesting comment on popular taste of the period that filmgoers found such representations appealing, in the wake of their country's war against and defeat of regimes indicted, and correctly, for militarism and totalitarianism.

NOTES

Some of the material in this chapter appeared in a slightly different form in "'The Story You Are about to See Is True': *Dragnet*, Film Noir, and Postwar Realism," in Steven Sanders and Aeon J. Skoble, eds., *The Philosophy of TV Noir* (Lexington:

University Press of Kentucky, 2008). I am grateful to the press for permission to reprint.

1. A partial list of films that could be claimed for such a general movement toward cinematic realism, including an emphasis on location shooting, might include the following, in no particular order: *Call Northside 777* (1948), *Unchained* (1955), *The Wild One* (1953), *The Young Lions* (1958), *Judgment at Nuremberg* (1961), *On the Waterfront* (1954), *The Wrong Man* (1956), *Vertigo* (1958), *Niagara* (1953), *Border Incident* (1949), *The Sniper* (1952), *Wild River* (1960), *The Garment Jungle* (1957), *The House on Telegraph Hill* (1951), *Canon City* (1948), *The Phenix City Story* (1955), *The Intruder* (1962), *Teresa* (1951), *The Iron Curtain* (1948), *Black Like Me* (1964), *A Child Is Waiting* (1963), *The Best Years of Our Lives* (1946), *The Woman on Pier 13* (1949), *The Longest Day* (1961), *The Atomic City* (1952), *Nothing but a Man* (1964), *13 Rue Madeleine* (1947), *Slattery's Hurricane* (1949), *House of Bamboo* (1955), *Night and the City* (1950), *Walk a Crooked Mile* (1948), *Panic in the Streets* (1950), *The Tattooed Stranger* (1950), *New Orleans Uncensored* (1955), *Desert Fury* (1947), *A Foreign Affair* (1948), *Diplomatic Courier* (1952), *The Devil Makes Three* (1952), *Foreign Intrigue* (1956), *Little Boy Lost* (1953), *Chicago Deadline* (1949), *Act of Violence* (1948), *Too Late Blues* (1961), *Trapped* (1949), *T-Men* (1947), *Edge of the City* (1957), *The Long, Hot Summer* (1958), *The Street with No Name* (1948), *Appointment with Danger* (1951), *City of Fear* (1959), *The Day of the Jackal* (1973), and *Southside 1-1000* (1950).

2. In addition to providing an eminently commercial version of de Rochemont's documentary approach, *House* is often considered the progenitor of a noir semidocumentary cycle; see, for example, Walker's (1994) introductory essay on noir. Though this is hardly the place for definitional squabbling, I would argue that, properly speaking, the semidocumentaries should be thought of as constituting the relevant production cycle, with the noir-inflected releases constituting a "period" in the history of the cycle, in much the same way that noir constitutes a "period" in other trends, cycles, and genres (Palmer 1994).

3. For cogent discussions of this shift, see, in particular, the studies by Telotte (1989) and Spicer (2002).

WORKS CITED

A. W. 1949. Review of *He Walked by Night. New York Times*, 7 February.

Behlmer, Rudy, ed. 1993. *Memo from Darryl F. Zanuck: The Golden Years at Twentieth Century–Fox*. New York: Grove.

Crowther, Bosley. 1939. "Time Marches on to the Ramparts." *New York Times*, 22 October.

———. 1940. "'The Ramparts We Watch,' a Stirring Document." *New York Times*, 20 September.

———. 1945. "House on Ninety-Second Street." *New York Times*, 27 September.

———. 1948. "Paisan." *New York Times*, 30 March.

Gallagher, Tag. 1998. *Roberto Rossellini*. New York: Da Capo.

Jameson, Fredric. (1979) 1992. "Reification and Utopia in Mass Culture." In *Signatures of the Visible*, 9–34. New York: Routledge.

Palmer, R. Barton. 1994. *Hollywood's Dark Cinema: The American Film Noir*. New York: Simon and Schuster.

Spicer, Andrew. 2002. *Film Noir.* New York: Longmans/Pearson.

Telotte, J. P. 1989. *Voices in the Dark: The Narrative Patterns of Film Noir.* Urbana: University of Illinois Press.

T. M. P. 1950. "T-Men on Screen at the Palace." *New York Times,* 3 November.

Walker, Michael. 1994. "Film Noir: Introduction." In *The Movie Book of Film Noir,* ed. Ian Cameron, 8–38. London: Studio Vista.

Zavattini, Cesare. (1952) 1978. "A Thesis on Neo-Realism." Translated by David Overbey. In *Springtime in Italy: A Reader on Neo-Realism,* ed. David Overbey, 67–78. Hamden, CT: Archon.

CHAPTER 5

CYCLE CONSCIOUSNESS AND THE WHITE
AUDIENCE IN BLACK FILM WRITING:
THE 1949–1950 "RACE PROBLEM" CYCLE
AND THE AFRICAN AMERICAN PRESS

STEVEN DOLES

IN 1949 AND 1950, Hollywood studios and independent production companies released five films that were commonly identified with one another as constituting a "race problem" cycle because of their narratives centering on representations of African Americans facing segregation and discrimination: *Home of the Brave* (1949, Mark Robson), *Lost Boundaries* (1949, Alfred L. Werker), *Pinky* (1949, Elia Kazan), *Intruder in the Dust* (1949, Clarence Brown), and *No Way Out* (1950, Joseph L. Mankiewicz). The race problem cycle was itself part of a larger postwar trend of social problem films dealing with race and racism, following most directly on two films of 1947 about anti-Semitism, *Crossfire* (Edward Dmytryk) and *Gentleman's Agreement* (Elia Kazan). Contemporary reception materials for the race problem cycle typically group the five films together, taking them seriously not primarily as entertainments, but rather as works making arguments about the desirability of change in the social standing of African Americans and the unacceptability of certain expressions of racism.

Examined textually, however, the films of the cycle evince as many differences as similarities. *Home of the Brave* draws extensively on the generic conventions of the war film, and by focusing on the healing of an African American soldier who becomes psychologically disabled when he joins a reconnaissance mission and faces hatred from members of the otherwise all-white unit, it resembles returning-veteran films such as *Pride of the Marines* (1945, Delmer Daves) and *The Best Years of Our Lives* (1946, William Wyler), with their interest in representing the exterior and interior effects of war trauma. *Lost Boundaries* borrows conventions from producer Louis de Rochemont's *March of Time* newsreel series in adapting a nonfiction story of a family that passed racially in a small New England town, finding acceptance in the community even once their "transgression" is revealed. *Pinky*, another passing narrative, moves its nurse protagonist from the North back to her origins in the South, where she can no longer pass. After Pinky leaves her fiancé, who wants her to conceal her background and move with him to a place where her race will be unknown, the film shifts its focus to legal challenges to Pinky's right to inherit property from a white benefactor, the happy resolution of which allows her to open a (segregated) hospital for the African Americans of the town. *Intruder in the Dust* (an adaptation of the William Faulkner novel) and *No Way Out* are crime films in which investigation narratives drive toward the clearing of their central African American characters for the death of a white person, yet the former features a rural southern setting in which the threat of lynching is key to the story line, and *No Way Out* an urban northern setting in which the conflict between black and white characters erupts in a violent riot. Establishing these films as members of the same cycle is thus a selective process that highlights certain features of the films while filtering out others.

Cycles are constituted as much by their pragmatics—how communities make use of and respond to films—as by their semantics—repeated elements such as settings, character types, and props—and their syntax—narrative patterns common across a group of films. Films do not bear signs of their membership in cycles textually, but rather intertextually, through the work of industry professionals who decide what projects to film and how to promote them, based on commercial precedent and their feel for what audiences will pay for, and through the audiences who view the films, noticing connections between them and giving significance to repeated elements. In this chapter I examine the latter, audience-directed process as it occurred in coverage of the race problem cycle in the black press.[1] This coverage included not only reviews but also production notices, announcements and reports of screenings, gossip columns, editorials, columnists' essays, and letters from readers. This diverse material, ranging from brief items to lengthy articles, was sometimes fragmentary or contradictory, and writers in the same periodicals occasionally offered contrasting responses to the same films. I highlight a specific way of writing about these films, one that expresses an awareness of their membership within the cycle, an awareness that I call "cycle consciousness."

Because cycles demonstrate a temporal dimension, in their rapid emergence and eventual dissipation, the first section of the chapter examines how writers in the black press positioned the cycle historically, either as a break from or a continuation of earlier Hollywood representational practices.[2] Since many cycles are highly topical, they generate interest in their address to specific audiences, a fact that the second section of this chapter examines in coverage of how white viewers responded to *Lost Boundaries*. An examination of these reception materials offers a case study of the pragmatics by which film cycles come into existence and gain significance for their audiences. Perhaps most importantly, the present study suggests how widespread a phenomenon cycle consciousness can be, since not only reviews and critical essays but also more ephemeral forms such as production notices and letters to the editor carry with them an engaged and critical dimension.

CYCLES, FILM HISTORY, AND TIMELINESS

Beginning with early production notices, coverage in the black press referred to the films mentioned above as belonging to a cycle and positioned them in contrast to earlier Hollywood representations of African Americans. A full-page article in the *Chicago Defender* (9 July 1949) by Meredith Johns begins with a series of images suggesting gradual but inevitable improvements in Hollywood practices: "Dawn is slowly breaking over Hollywood, which for so many years has dwelt in the darkness of fear-filled ideas concerning problems of racial and religious prejudice. The dawn is not a bright one, but it holds great promise of blossoming into a bright and cloudless day." The film industry, Johns writes, was both "step[ping] forward" and "growing up," and might thereby take on a new social importance. The text of the article is surrounded by publicity photos from *Pinky* and *Lost Boundaries* as well as from the less prominent *Come to the Stable* (1949, Henry Koster). The last film, a sentimental nun picture rather than a social-problem film, is not typically connected to the cycle in other reception materials, but Johns includes it because of Dooley Wilson's role, which "gets away from the traditional dunce role of the Negro handy man." In this article from early in the life of the cycle, the presence of African American actors on screen serves as a criterion for grouping the films together and opposing them to earlier Hollywood fare.

Johns's language describing the industry as "growing up" was echoed over a year later in "Movies Are Growing Up!—Here's Proof," an article in the *New York Amsterdam News* about the revisionist western *Broken Arrow*. The article depicts *Broken Arrow* as the successor to the "pro-Negro successes" of *Home of the Brave*, *Pinky*, and *Lost Boundaries* and also situates the film in relation to the 1947 pair of *Gentleman's Agreement* and *Crossfire*, as well as *The Lost Weekend* (1945, Billy Wilder) and *The Snake Pit* (1948, Anatole Litvak), social problem films about alcoholism and mental illness. Unlike Johns, who groups films together through the diegetic depiction of African Americans, the writer of "Movies Are Growing Up!" connects this group of films through the rhetorical function of the social problem genre. *The Lost Weekend* and *The Snake Pit* make no direct comment on racial oppression, but they, like the other films, are "brave" and "provocative" in dealing with "previously 'forbidden' subject[s]." The most striking feature of the article is a large illustration depicting an airplane formed out of a film projector, with an enormous strip of celluloid running through it to form the wings. From it fall oversize cartoon bombs, each labeled with the name of a film from the cycle. *Broken Arrow*, the largest, is surrounded by other films mentioned in the article: *Gentleman's Agreement*, *Crossfire*, *Home of the Brave*, *Lost Boundaries*, and *Pinky*. The bombs descend on the walls of a ruined cityscape painted with the names of social ills: "Racial Prejudice," "Discrimination" "Distrust," "Misunderstanding," and "Intolerance." The bombs, it seems, will burst in the blink of an eye, clearing away the rubble of past oppression. The destroyed city, moreover, might call to mind photographs of the bombed-out cities of Europe and Asia, images that powerfully connoted an Old World fate that the United States had possibly avoided in the postwar period. Especially with this "explosive" illustration, the article condenses much about cycle consciousness as it functioned in the black press to express a hope that these films would make a permanent change, both to Hollywood's practices and to social attitudes.

Although much of this coverage invokes a past from which the films of the cycle diverge, the writers do not always specify which earlier films they are referring to. Some, however, evince an extensive and explicit knowledge of cinematic history. An editorial appearing in the *Pittsburgh Courier* (8 October 1949) is quite detailed in its historical references and uses them to make a complex argument. The editorial announces at the start, "Hollywood has definitely come of age in its recognition of the color problem in this country," and contrasts the films of the race problem cycle with "the cinematic fare to which we had become accustomed although never reconciled." After this statement, however, the text complicates a clean sense of linear progress: "In its infancy the film industry made its initial racial bow with its 'Brown and White Comedies' in which the two leading characters were an Irish cook and a Negro porter who were sweethearts. Needless to say, and despite supposed increase in tolerance, such a series could not be shown today."³ Certain forms of segregation, particularly the social norms preventing interracial relationships, remained in effect in these films, despite the rhetoric of newness.⁴ Yet the editorial also sees genuine progress in the impossibility of another *Birth of a Nation* being produced by Hollywood.

The editorial next describes a genealogy leading from the silent era to the years shortly before the race problem cycle, listing *Hearts in Dixie* (1929, Paul Sloane), *Hallelujah* (1929, King Vidor), *The Emperor Jones* (1993, Dudley Murphy), *Sanders of the River* (1935, Zoltan Korda), *Tales of Manhattan* (1942, Julien Duvivier), and *Stormy Weather* (1943, Andrew L. Stone). These films are said to mark a certain amount of progress in including African Americans on-screen even though they failed to eliminate stereotypes and thus escape the regressive pull of the past. Curiously, despite the way the editorial begins by asserting that the current race problem cycle is a sign of Hollywood's maturation, later passages group the films of 1949 with the earlier body of stereotype-afflicted films: "But Hollywood directors seem to be mastering a clever technique enabling them to eat the racial cake and have it too. Stereotypes are juggled around, given new make-up and hairdo, sprayed with perfume making them alternately acceptable by Southern whites, Negroes and Northern liberals. Thus all prejudices are soothed and smoothed; hypersensitive souls in all camps are kept calm while a bit of liberalism is injected, the censors with one eye on the Klan are disarmed while the profits roll into the sadly depleted Hollywood treasuries." The editorial suggests that the films of the race problem cycle still remain beholden to the past, despite the "juggling around" of their representational strategies. Negating the supposed break between the films of the current cycle and earlier representations of African Americans could thus be a powerful way to contest a facile, unqualified sense of progress.

Against the hopes expressed in the earliest coverage of the cycle, the race problem cycle did not mark a permanent shift in Hollywood's hiring practices and representations of African Americans, which continued to fluctuate as cycles emerged and dissipated in the following decades, including the blaxploitation cycle of the 1970s, and the "New Black Realism" or "Ghetto Action" cycle of the late 1980s and early 1990s. These cycles provided occasions for articulating an understanding of film history, much as the race problem cycle had done at midcentury. An article by Stanley G. Robertson in the *Los Angeles Sentinel* (27 May 1971), for instance, provides a history that moves from the silent era to the present and includes a paragraph referring to *Home of the Brave* as "a true milestone in the History of American Cinema." But Robertson asks readers not to long for mythic Hollywood "Good Old Days" and instead emphasizes recent work by filmmakers such as Ossie Davis, Gordon Parks, Melvin Van Pebbles, and Wendell Franklin, the directors, respectively, of *Cotton Comes to Harlem* (1970), *Shaft* (1971), *Sweet Sweetback's Baadasssss Song* (1971), and *The Bus Is Coming* (1971). These films (with the exception of the less well-remembered *The Bus Is Coming*) were soon identified as inaugurating the blaxploitation cycle, although Robertson does not use the term. He values each of the directors as important artists in their own way. Davis is "a consummate creative talent in all aspects of the cinema"; Parks is a "pioneer *Life* magazine photographer who laid aside his still camera for one with motion and sound"; Van Peebles is "aggressive and sometimes erratic," words that seem less to criticize the director than to account for the strange vision of *Sweet Sweetback*; Franklin is "the first black man to be accepted into the Director's Guild." For Robertson, the salient feature of these films is not, as it would soon become in typical definitions of blaxploitation, their semantic depiction of a black underworld, but rather the creative labor of African Americans "before and behind the camera."

A similar piece by the scholar Donald Bogle in the *Philadelphia Tribune* (14 February 1992) responds to the black films of the late 1980s and early 1990s, especially those by Spike Lee, and links them with a longer history of black independent filmmaking, particularly Oscar Micheaux's work and the films of the blaxploitation cycle. Following a lengthy section in which he discusses the emergence of independent African American production companies in the early decades of cinematic history, Bogle includes only a brief, two-sentence paragraph on the race problem cycle: "Following World War II and the subsequent rise of the civil rights movement, many [African American] independents found themselves victims of a changing market. Major Hollywood studios released a number of films such as *Home of the Brave* and *No Way Out* which examined America's race problems." Both writers mention the 1949–1950 cycle without directly criticizing it, but the focus in these articles is on black creative labor, especially in the director's chair, which gives the cycle a subordinate position within the genealogies they trace. Cycle consciousness, whether at midcentury, when the race problem cycle was exhibited, or in later decades, when it was remembered, could thus serve as a prompt for articulating a vision of cinematic history connected with the audience's awareness of its own position within the struggles of its historical moment.

THE VISUAL RHETORIC AND WHITE AUDIENCE OF *LOST BOUNDARIES*

Cycles often have a special tie to contemporary concerns because of their topicality, and make use of cinematic techniques not only to entertain but also to communicate ideas and arguments (Klein 2011, 13, 64). Awareness of a film as part of topical cycle—as seen in the coverage discussed in the previous section—might prime viewers to be attentive to *what* ideas and arguments films communicate, and *to whom* they communicate them. Writers in the black press often identified in the race problem cycle a rhetorical strategy by which, despite the central role given to black protagonists, white characters are often the agents of the final resolution of the narrative.

For instance, the actor William Marshall wrote a guest column for the entertainment writer Izzy Rowe in the *Pittsburgh Courier* (7 June 1952), comparing the films of the cycle with the historical film *Lydia Bailey* (1952, Jean Negulesco), in which Marshall plays a Haitian revolutionary. Marshall begins by reflecting on the historical status of the race problem cycle, noting, "The more recent cycle of films dealing with the Negro problem as such has depicted the Negro in a more realistic light which is a great departure from the stereotype with which we had heretofore been confronted." But the actor criticizes both the separation of the cycle's protagonists from a communal black identity and the prominence the films give instead to white representatives of the social order in resolving narrative conflicts: "These vehicles have viewed the Negro's plight through the highly dramatic experiences of an individual Negro whose way of life had little if anything to do with the life pattern of the great majority of the black population. . . . *No Way Out* pictured the altruistic white doctor as the Negro's champion; in *Home of the Brave* the understanding white psychiatrist dissolved the Negro soldier's problems via shock therapy; in *Intruder in the Dust*, the kind white lawyer; in *Pinky*, the unbelievably good white courts." For these reasons, and also to promote his own film, which he contrasts positively with those of the race problem cycle, Marshall prefers a collective image of black revolution to the white-effected gradualism of the cycle. Because it is one of the films of the cycle that most strongly foregrounds a white community in the climax of its narrative, *Lost Boundaries* serves as a good case study for examining how writers in the black press understood and responded to the cycle's address to a white audience.

Lost Boundaries was produced by Louis de Rochemont, former head of *The March of Time* newsreels. Like the string of detective films that de Rochemont produced at Fox, beginning with *The House on 92nd Street* (1945, Henry Hathaway), *Lost Boundaries* is a semi-documentary that strives to establish its veracity through techniques borrowed from the newsreel, particularly the use of location shooting and the presence of a narrator whose voice-over stresses the origin of the story in actual events. The film's credit sequence calls attention to its status as an adaptation of a *Reader's Digest* article about a family, the Carters, who passed racially as white in a small New England town, thereby allowing the father of the family to find work as the town physician.[5] Over the course of the film, the Carters' act of passing is revealed to the white citizens of the town; the townspeople are at first scandalized by the masquerade, but they ultimately come to accept and reincorporate the Carters into the life of the community, after the pastor of the local church gives a sermon extolling tolerance. Calling attention to the use of location shooting, the narrator repeatedly refers to the film as a "drama of real life" and states that the spectator can visit the scene of the film's events in order to confirm that they did in fact take place. Exterior shots of the town's streets and important buildings, as well as interior shots of institutions such as the post office and church, correspond not only to a changing postwar aesthetic that privileged filming away from studio sets, but also ground a rhetoric by which the events of the narrative, since they occurred at a specific time and place, can be taken as carrying with them a general lesson of tolerance that audience members can apply to their own lives.

An important exchange on *Lost Boundaries* took place in the pages of the *Norfolk New Journal and Guide* over the course of two weeks in September 1949. Focusing on white audiences' pleasure in the film, the series of articles began on September 17 with an article introducing an anonymous "Norfolkian who saw the film but whose complexion is light enough to conceal his racial identity." The correspondent reports on whites' responses firsthand: "For about two hours, and for the first time, this person sat among white persons as one of them." After this brief introduction, the remainder of the article is written in the first person as the viewer recalls what it was like to observe the audience's reactions to the film. The writer makes a strong connection between the site of exhibition and the visual rhetoric of the film, picking up on the "real life" quality of the text while claiming, "My presence among the spectators was proof that its message is 'stranger than fiction.'" The writer reports that upon first sitting down, the white audience for the film appeared tense, expecting to be angered or shocked, only to be relieved at discovering that the film "'twas right nice." This attitude is interpreted as a sign that white audience members could be potential allies in opposition to segregation. For example, during a scene in which a nurse shatters a vial of blood donated by a black chauffeur rather than allow it to be mixed with the blood of white townspeople, the writer records a pair of sailors cursing angrily, "G—D— [sic], did you see that wench," and hears in turn "several grunts . . . from all around that I interpreted as distinct disapproval of the nurse's attitude."

The writer is so willing to see the audience's response to the film as indicative of acceptance of integration that he even reproduces expressions of seemingly condescending pity as evidence. Upon seeing the Carters' daughter Shelley (Susan Douglas Rubes) stand contemplatively near a bridge after learning of her "true" identity, the writer reports that one viewer cried out, "She ought to jump for God knows that's more than I could stand." Rather than interpret the statement as evidence that the speaker believes African American lives are not worth living, the writer sees it as evidence of a strong identification between spectator and character and as a sign that the audience "loves" the Carters.

Three related items appeared in the newspaper the following week. Two were exceptionally positive reviews of the film by the paper's society reporter, Mary V. Ransom, who calls the film in one column "the most outstanding picture of all time" (1949b) and states in the other that "there is not one flaw, one unbelievable incident, one glaring oversight anywhere in this humanly told story" (1949a). Ransom reminds readers of the report in the previous week's issue, linking the white audience's reaction to her positive evaluation of the movie. But the third item in the paper, a letter from Beulah V. Harold, draws on the previous week's story in order to contest its interpretation of the audience's reaction: "It appears to me . . . that the picture defeated its own purpose. True, it did create sympathy for the Carter family, but, in creating sympathy it again brought out the age old idea of white supremacy." Harold uses the affective response of the white audience to call attention to the relationship between their enjoyment of the film and the systems of oppression in which they are complicit. Returning to the incident of Shelley at the bridge, Harold interprets the audience member's exclamation that Shelley "ought to jump" much more harshly than did the original writer: "The attitude of 'sympathy' is clearly ruined in the realization that whites are even more glad that 'they're not a nigger.' Moreover, the white ego is inflated when the picture seems to drive home to them the idea of how 'lucky' they are to be white." Harold thus argues that the white audience's pleasure in the film is not sufficient evidence for solidarity with African American political struggle, since the pleasure of identifying with African American characters might be a masochistic act that maintains whiteness at the top of the racial hierarchy.

Several textual features of *Lost Boundaries* likely influenced the interest that writers in the black press took in how white audiences experienced the film's representation of passing African Americans. The narrator frequently offers explanations of the actions and attitudes of the community of Keenham, New Hampshire, employing the pronouns "we" and "our," thus speaking for the (implicitly white) community of Keenham as a collective whole.[6] For instance, when Scott and Marcia Carter (Mel Ferrer, Beatrice Pearson) first move to Keenham, where they believe they will pass only temporarily in order to jump-start Scott's career, the narrator states: "In tradition-bound New England, we are inclined to be cautious toward those who are young and who have little more than book learning. Even though Scott Carter came to Keenham highly recommended, many of his first patients were not sure he had enough experience to take the place of a doctor who had practiced in our community for fifty years."

A few minutes later in viewing time, but years later diegetically,

FIGURE 5.1. The framing of the post office scene naturalizes the townspeople's view of the Carters.

the narrator reveals that the Carters have now been accepted into the community. The narrator speaks, "In small towns like Keenham, leadership and respect can only be earned." The scene that follows shows that Scott Carter has earned the respect of the townspeople as well as a position as a leader among them. In a long shot, Scott enters the town's post office, where he struggles to unlock his mailbox. The men in the post office stand around and stare, forming a tiny, benign conspiracy. Once Scott is suitably frustrated, they reveal that they switched his mailbox so that it would have the same number as their beloved old doctor's. His phone and license plate, they say, have also been switched to the same number, 519. Moved by the gesture, Scott tells the men, "I hope I never let you down." Camera distance and blocking in the scene position Scott Carter as the object of the communal knowledge and action of the townspeople. He has passed their test and should feel proud to be welcomed into their community.

Lost Boundaries thus endorses the communal values of the town of Keenham. Certain sequences in the film, however, call into question the goodness of the townspeople. The scene discussed above, in which the nurse shatters the vial of blood rather than let it be mixed with that of white donors, is one such moment. Another occurs when the Carters' son Howard (Richard Hylton) invites a black college pal to their home over a school holiday so that the pair can continue work on a song they are writing together. When they attend a dance chaperoned by the women of the community, one of the women speaks disparagingly of Marcia Carter: "Well, I must say, she certainly has the strangest ideas socially. I suppose it wasn't her fault, but no one

FIGURE 5.2. *Lost Boundaries* again calls attention to the agency of the citizens of Keenham to accept or reject the Carters as they enter the church.

with any background invites darkies to her home." The woman even refuses to serve the refreshments that have been brought for the occasion rather than "be a waitress for any Negro." The film's representation of the town is thus somewhat contradictory, depicting its citizenry as at once fundamentally decent and virulently racist.

The question of how Keenham will react to the Carters' passing is central to the film's narrative tension and themes. Once the Carters' black ancestry is revealed to the community, there is a montage of gossiping townspeople, all whispering to one another about the Carters. One woman says, "I just don't know what to think about Doc Carter," and another says, "Sure as shootin', they're black as coal inside." In this sequence, it seems possible that the town as a whole might respond to the family as the woman at the party did to the black student, with dismissal and hatred. The final sequence again raises the question of the community's reaction. The family leaves for church, placing them among the townspeople as a community for the first time since their passing was revealed. They run into the woman from the party and her husband, who both stare straight ahead, refusing to even acknowledge the Carters. At the service, however, the reverend sways the hearts of the townspeople to again accept the family, reading a sermon on tolerance before leading them in the singing of hymn number 519, the same number so closely associated with Scott Carter and his position in the community. As in the earlier scene in the post office, this scene is depicted through images that call attention to the intense gaze of the townspeople on the Carters, who are positioned centrally within the frame and isolated from the others, who are seated when the family enters the church. It is again in the white townspeople's power to accept the Carters into the community.

The consideration of white audiences' pleasure in the black press thus responded not only to extratextual forms of oppression, but also identified a rhetorical strategy common throughout the race problem cycle: positioning white characters as agents of tolerance. Alfred L. Werker, the film's director, responded to criticism of his casting white actors as the film's passing protagonists by arguing that it would have been impossible to cast "passable" African American actors because "the majority of Negro actors are of the Uncle Tom, minstrel show, shuffling dancer type of performer." After the interview with Werker was published by the *Los Angeles Daily News*, a white paper, the director's remarks were reported in many black newspapers alongside a strongly worded letter of protest from the Committee for the Negro in the Arts, which the *New York Amsterdam News* published on 6 August 1949. The letter refutes Werker's claim that African Americans were not suitable for any but the most stereotyped roles, pointing to the vibrant history of the black theater and claiming that Werker's casting decisions were motivated by profit, not by the availability of talented actors. Most interesting, however, is a digression that strongly criticizes how the film portrays the white community as knowledgeable about passing African Americans and as wielding political agency over them: "You dared not show that Negroes do pass freely among white Americans AS white Americans—without the white Americans knowing this. And further that it is only when the Negro reveals it that the white really knows. Thus putting an end to the myth that the white American is superior in his 'knowing how to keep the Negro in his place' as he pretends."

The narrative of *Lost Boundaries* drives toward the moment in which the "truth" of the Carters will be unveiled for the townspeople, who then have the opportunity to respond with acceptance or rejection. This letter from the Committee for the Negro in the Arts turns that logic on its head, acknowledging that the film is addressed to white audiences, but claiming that the audience's belief that it will learn something about blackness and passing from the film, and thereby gain a form of agency, is based on false premises.

CLOSE ATTENTION TO THE PRAGMATICS of a film cycle as recorded in an archive (or indexed in some other way, as through audience interviews and ethnographic work) is necessary to tease out how cycles function in their reception. A study like this, however, should not be taken as representative of the responses of the larger body of "everyday" viewers, even in cases of nonprofessional writing like letters to the editor. To reach that kind of broader understanding of a film cycle, it would be necessary to examine the relationship between how the cycle is constructed in sites of public discourse like newspapers and magazines and how viewers conceive of cycles as they choose which films to see and as they find meaning and pleasure in the act of viewing. Another relationship that might be examined productively is that between public discourse and the decisions of industry professionals to develop or promote films as members of cycles. For instance, the language describing Hollywood as "growing up," discussed in the first part of this chapter, was likely influenced by industry and promotional discourses, and this coverage possibly drew on press releases or other promotional materials. At a time of declining ticket sales, Hollywood studios aimed at positioning themselves as purveyors of quality entertainment, and for that reason, the perception of releasing "unprecedented" firsts could be a powerful means of accruing prestige.[7]

Yet the dynamics of film cycles create risks: a studio might scoop the competition with a highly topical feature, and there is the inevitability of diminishing returns as the cycle goes on. The latter concern seems to have been a problem for Fox's Darryl F. Zanuck, who insisted, in promoting *No Way Out*, that "there is no such thing as a 'cycle' where great stories are concerned" (*Atlanta Daily World* 1950). Given a cycle-conscious, engaged audience, however, such a claim seems destined to backfire.

NOTES

1. By "black press," I mean periodicals written and published by African Americans for African American audiences. Examples in this chapter are drawn from the Black Studies Center online database, which contains archives of the *Atlanta Daily World, Baltimore Afro American, Chicago Defender, Los Angeles Sentinel, New York Amsterdam News, Norfolk New Journal and Guide, Philadelphia Tribune,* and *Pittsburgh Courier,* the African American newspapers with the largest circulation at midcentury. The black press also included magazines such as *Ebony* and *Negro Digest,* which often included reviews, actor profiles, and other forms of coverage for the films of the race-problem cycle. Civil rights groups' publications such as the *Crisis* (NAACP) and *Opportunity* (National Urban League) included film coverage, though less routinely than did newspapers

and magazines. See the essays by Robbins (1949) and Squires (2001) for useful accounts of the black press's complex role in organizing and expressing resistance to the white-dominated social order.

2. For more on film cycles, see the study by Klein (2011).

3. I have been unable to identify the specific film mentioned here. It seems possible that the writer was thinking of a series of silent shorts released by the Historical Feature Film Company that starred the African American actors Bert Murphy, Frank Montgomery, and Florence McClain; the company promoted these films in advertisements as "Black and White Comedies," and they were referred to in the industry press as representing the "Black and White brand," in which "all the players are negroes." If so, the reality would seem to contradict the writer's description of an interracial romance narrative in the films, but remains in line with the article's overall interest in examining the history of representations of African Americans on screen; see the examples in *Moving Picture World* (1914) and *Motography* (1914), both accessed through the Media History Digital Library.

4. This was a common criticism of *Pinky* and *Lost Boundaries*, both films in which a romance between a passing African American character and a white character ends when the "fact" of racial crossing is revealed.

5. The representation of passing in the cycle has been discussed by a number of scholars; see Wald (2000) for *Lost Boundaries*, and Courtney (2005) and Petty (2004) for *Pinky*.

6. The name of the town in the film was changed from the actual location of Keene, New Hampshire. The family's surname was changed from Johnston to Carter, and the parents' names from Albert and Thyra to Scott and Marcia.

7. The slogan "Movies Are Better Than Ever" was commonly used in promotional material by Hollywood studios and exhibitors beginning in 1950, and could be attached to a variety of signifiers of quality, including social-problem narratives and other forms of mature content, high production values, color, and the use of widescreen aspect ratios.

WORKS CITED

Atlanta Daily World. 1950. "'No Way Out' Promises Enthralling Race Theme." 23 July.

Bogle, Donald. 1992. "Black Film: Not Just a '90s 'Thang.'" *Philadelphia Tribune,* 14 February.

Courtney, Susan. 2005. *Hollywood Fantasies of Miscegenation: Spectacular Narratives of Gender and Race, 1903–1967.* Princeton, NJ: Princeton University Press.

Harold, Beulah V. 1949. Letter to the editor. *Norfolk New Journal and Guide,* 24 September.

Johns, Meredith. 1949. "A New Dawn Is Slowly Breaking over Hollywood." *Chicago Defender,* 9 July.

Klein, Amanda Ann. 2011. *American Film Cycles: Reframing Genres, Screening Social Problems, and Defining Subcultures.* Austin: University of Texas Press.

Marshall, William. 1952. "Izzy Rowe's Notebook." *Pittsburgh Courier,* 7 June.

Motography. 1914. "Colored Players Featured." 5 December, 768.

Moving Picture World. 1914. Historical Feature Film Company, advertisement. 28 November 1914, 1279.

New York Amsterdam News. 1949. "Attack 'Lost Boundaries' Director for 'Race Slur.'" 6 August.

———. 1950. "Movies Are Growing Up!—Here's Proof." 5 August.

Norfolk New Journal and Guide. 1949. "Extra!! Norfolkian Crosses Race Boundary to See 'Lost Boundaries.'" 17 September.

Petty, Miriam J. 2004. "Passing for Horror: Race, Fear, and Elia Kazan's *Pinky*." *Genders* 40.

Pittsburgh Courier. 1949. "Hollywood Comes of Age" (editorial). 8 October.

Ransom, Mary V. 1949a. "Motion Picture Is Superb." *Norfolk New Journal and Guide*, 24 September.

———. 1949b. "The Feminine Viewpoint." *Norfolk New Journal and Guide*, 24 September.

Robbins, Richard. 1949. "Counter-Assertion in the New York Negro Press." *Phylon* 10, no. 2: 126–136.

Robertson, Stanley G. 1971. "Blacks and the Movie Industry." *Los Angeles Sentinel*, 27 May.

Squires, Catherine. 2001. "The Black Press and the State: Attracting Unwanted (?) Attention." In *Counterpublics and the State*, ed. Robert Asen and Daniel C. Brouwer, 111–136. Albany: State University of New York Press.

Wald, Gayle. 2000. *Crossing the Line: Racial Passing in Twentieth-Century U.S. Literature and Culture*. Durham, NC: Duke University Press.

CHAPTER 6

VICIOUS CYCLE: *JAWS* AND REVENGE-OF-NATURE FILMS OF THE 1970S

CONSTANTINE VEREVIS

IN A WELL-REMEMBERED SCENE from *Jaws* (1975, Steven Spielberg) the fisherman Quint (Robert Shaw) slowly drags his fingernails across a chalkboard to draw the attention of the townsfolk of Amity, who have gathered to discuss their response to the rogue white pointer shark that is menacing their island community. Quint says:

> Y'all know me. Know how I earn a livin'. I'll catch this bird for you,
> but it ain't gonna be easy. Bad fish. Not like going down the pond
> chasin' bluegills and tommycods. This shark, swallow you whole.
> Little shakin', little tenderizin', and down you go. And we gotta do it
> quick, that'll bring back your tourists, put all your businesses on a
> payin' basis. But it's not gonna be pleasant. I value my neck a lot
> more than three thousand bucks, chief. I'll find him for three, but
> I'll catch him, and kill him, for ten. . . . I don't want no volunteers,
> I don't want no mates, there's too many captains on this island.
> $10,000 for me by myself. For that you get the head, the tail,
> the whole damn thing.

This chapter begins with Quint's words not only because it takes an interest in *Jaws*, but also because—as Gilles Deleuze reminds us in *Cinema 1: The Movement-Image*—we should never confuse wholes (*the whole damn fish*) with parts or *sets*. Deleuze writes: "Sets are closed, and everything which is closed is artificially closed. . . . But a whole is not closed, it is open, and it has no parts" (1986, 10). This is to say, more specifically, that the chapter takes an interest in sets, and precisely in how sets come to be closed. It initially employs the term "set" in a nonspecialized way to describe a group of things—in this case, films—that are connected or collected together by virtue of their authorship, appearance, or subject matter. More particularly, the chapter responds to recent work on a specific type of set—the film cycle—and takes as its example the "revenge of nature" film cycle initiated by the massive commercial success of Universal Studios' *Jaws*. It describes *Jaws* and the revenge-of-nature films of the 1970s as a discrete intergeneric set, but also as a nested intrageneric set: that is, as part of a disaster movie cycle that begins with *Airport* (1970, George Seaton) and concludes with the parodic *Airplane!* (1980, Jim Abrahams, David Zucker, Jerry Zucker), a film that directly refers to *Jaws* in its title sequence. In attending to these films—in particular, *Jaws* and its multiples—the chapter considers the relationship among several more-specialized sets—remakes (*Jaws/Creature from the Black Lagoon*), sequels (*Jaws/Jaws 2*), series (*Jaws–Jaws 4*), "cycles" (the revenge-of-nature cycle), and "genres" (here, disaster movies)—knowing that each of these categories is contested in and through this description.

In *American Film Cycles*, Amanda Ann Klein writes that cycles are like film genres in that they are "a series [a set] of films associated with each other through shared images, characters, settings, plots, or themes." But, she adds, "while film genres are primarily defined by the repetition of key images (their semantics) and themes (their syntax), film cycles are primarily defined by how they are used (their pragmatics)" (2011, 3–4). In work foundational to Klein's, Rick Altman describes the role played by film cycles in the process of genre formation. Taking Hollywood-studio-era films as his example, Altman argues that by analyzing and imitating their own most lucrative films, studios seek to establish cycles that are proprietary, exploitable, and exclusive. He writes that when conditions are favorable, single-studio cycles can become sharable, industry-wide patterns and can play a role in exhibition and reception, but this movement toward genre (sharability) works against the economic interests of the studio that initiated the cycle (1990, 59–61). This description of a cycle— a set of films associated with a single studio and containing easily exploitable characteristics—is consistent with Altman's assertion that generic claims have never really constituted a substantial portion of studio publicity campaigns (except those seeking to capitalize on another studio's success), and that this strategy of exclusivity has continued into the postclassical (or post-*Jaws*) period in and through the legally sanctioned use of proprietary characters and brands to initiate series-oriented production, or franchises (115–121).

DISASTER

In Jim Hoberman's account of a "momentous" decade-long period of new Hollywood filmmaking—the years 1975 to 1985—he begins by describing a particular set. He says that June 1975 offered up two "key movies," each of which in its own way was a "brilliant modification of the current disaster cycle that had its real-world equivalents in Vietnam and Watergate" (1985, 35). The first of these—*Nashville* (1975, Robert Altman)—"exploded" the "multi-star, mounting-doom, intersecting-plot format" of disaster films such as *The Poseidon Adventure* (1972, Ronald Neame), *Earthquake* (1974, Mark Robson), and *The Towering Inferno* (1974, John Guillermin) in order to elaborate on and politicize the cycle. By contrast, the second film—Steven Spielberg's *Jaws*—"imploded" the disaster film, paring the narrative and effects of the disaster cycle back to "pure mechanism" and—as the then top-grossing movie of all time—ushering in a new era of high-concept Hollywood blockbusters and franchises.[1]

Disaster films are sometimes said to "constitute a sufficiently numerous, old, and conventionalized group [set] to be considered a genre rather than a popular cycle that comes and goes" (Yacowar 2003, 277).[2] More often, though, disaster films (and disaster movies of the 1970s) are routinely discussed and dismissed as a cycle, one that is formulaic and spectatorial, wasting ingenious special effects on one-dimensional characters (Keane 2006, 1). In these accounts, disaster movies are an exclusive or restricted set, "entirely predicated around disaster," and hence can be distinguished from films and genres (such as war and science fiction) that contain only elements of disaster and of spectacle (Keane 2006, 1). An example of this approach is Nick Roddick's "Only the Stars Survive," an essay that examines disaster movies of the early and mid-1970s in order to locate the disaster film in the context of a long tradition of screen catastrophe and to identify a historical cycle (or set) defined by a number of industrial (commercial, pragmatic) and ideological (social, political) factors. Distinguishing disaster movies from disaster-ridden movies, Roddick describes three textual categories (or subsets) of disaster films: future worlds, in which disaster on a huge scale has already happened, happens in the course of the film, or is narrowly averted; disasters occurring to, or threatening, mass transport; and natural disasters, including the "virus" and "swarm" films of the 1970s—for example, *Phase IV* (1974, Saul Bass) and *Killer Bees* (1974, Curtis Harrington)—

and so-called monster movies of the time, including films such as *Jaws* and *Piranha* (1978, Joe Dante) (1980, 247–249).

Roddick identifies a number of features that characterize disaster films—the disaster is diegetically central, factually possible, largely indiscriminate, unexpected (though not necessarily unpredicted), and so on—but adds that the industrial imperative to repeat a narrative formula does not preclude an assessment of the ideological meanings and motivations of the cycle (1980, 246; see also Keane 2006, 5, 14). This treatment of the disaster movie cycle as a response to a social problem or a political situation is consistent not only with Hoberman's aforementioned assessment, but also with Stephen Heath's contemporaneous "*Jaws*, Ideology, and Film Theory," which claims that "at one level, the ideology of *Jaws* is clear enough. . . . *Jaws* is a Watergate film: Mayor Larry Vaughan of Amity, Long Island serves his electors . . . by hushing up a shark attack" (1976, 25). The same conclusion can be found in more recent evaluations, such as Nigel Andrews's guide to *Jaws*, which claims that "Spielberg's film is . . . a Nixonish drama about a free-preying malign will—the shark's" (1999, 37), and concludes that "the *message* of *Jaws*" is likewise political: after Vietnam, "the strongest bulwarks of civilization are powerless against a guerilla attack that is fast enough, fierce enough, unexpected enough" (5).

EVENT

Jaws can be seen as part of a specific set—disaster movies (genre or cycle, depending on one's position)—in which Vietnam and Watergate were the real-life disasters, but at the same time, it is part of a larger set (or periodization): the films of the 1970s or, as Hoberman would have it, "ten years [of Hollywood filmmaking] that shook the world." As identified in the subtitle of David Cook's *Lost Illusions* (from the History of the American Cinema series), *Jaws* is representative of a cycle of American films made "in the shadow of Watergate and Vietnam": a set of films that is either implicitly or explicitly critical of American society (*Nashville* is probably the limit case), and one that "expresses a fear of powerlessness or loss of control . . . at a time when leadership at every level of society [was] believed to be wanting" (2000, 251). As described by Cook, the disaster film of the 1970s was a commercial form "rich in possibilities," one that remained popular throughout the decade and beyond, and that trans-

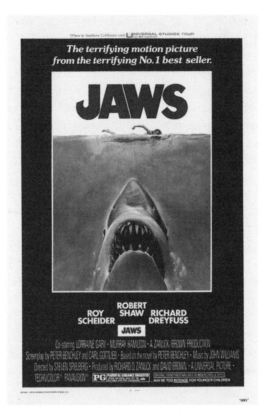

FIGURE 6.1. A new kind of disaster film: *Jaws* (1975).

lated well into international markets; but the cycle "*mutated* in 1975 (like everything else in American cinema) with the appearance of Universal's *Jaws*" (255).

The enormous commercial success of *Jaws* is typically attributed to what Universal Studios (and its boss, Lew Wasserman) described as the establishment of a "*Jaws* consciousness" (Cook 2000, 41–43), one facilitated by a saturation advertising campaign and a wide opening pattern of theatrical release (see also Schatz 1993, 18; Andrews 1999, 114).[3] Although *Jaws* was a multimillion-dollar summer blockbuster based on Peter Benchley's best-selling novel, produced at a negative cost of around $12 million and promoted with a campaign costing more than $2.5 million (Cook 2000, 41), the film was distributed and marketed as if it were an exploitation product: that is, it was "hyped for a quick weekend's profit (*Jaws* grossed $7.061 million in its opening weekend) and sold on the basis of a single sensational image" (43). A film crucial to the blockbuster mentality, *Jaws* is at once a landmark and an aberration in the disaster movie cycle because it combines motifs from several sets in order to create a new kind of disaster film. *Jaws* is an event film, one that associates new types of material with an existing genre: an action-adventure film and a conspiracy thriller, a film that combines elements of monster movies (with a revenge-of-nature subtext), high-gore slasher films, homosocial westerns, and so on (Cook 2000, 256; Schatz 1993, 18).

Jaws was a prototype or blueprint for a new set—the high-concept blockbuster, or event film. The property was later extended through its 1976 theatrical reissue and several official sequels, and has been maintained (decades beyond its initial release) through such events as the thirtieth-anniversary "Jaws Fest" (June 3–5, 2005), during which Martha's Vineyard (the location of the original shoot) once again displayed Amity signage and welcomed back more than twenty-five members of the original cast and crew—including Peter Benchley, Carl Gottlieb (screenwriter), and Joe Alves (production designer)—for a weekend of celebrations (Martha's Vineyard Chamber of Commerce 2005). The most immediate "sequel" to *Jaws* was *The Deep* (1977, Peter Yates), an action-adventure story about a couple, played by Nick Nolte and Jacqueline Bisset, who—with the help of a local waters expert (Robert Shaw, from *Jaws*)—find Spanish treasure when diving near Bermuda. Based on Peter Benchley's first post-*Jaws* novel, *The Deep* was produced by Peter Guber for a rival studio, Columbia Pictures, released to coincide with the paperback publication of the book, and promoted through its merchandizing (which included a translucent blue vinyl album with disco beats by Donna Summer) and a $3 million advertising campaign that featured a vertical poster design (modeled on the one for *Jaws*) depicting a nearly naked female diver rising up through deep blue sea toward a horizontal surface logo (Cook 2000, 45–46; Combs 1977, 257–258).

EXPLOITATION

Jaws is an aberration and a mutant: an A-list action-adventure film that went on to have an enormous impact on films of the later 1970s and beyond (Cook 2000, 256). But generically and genetically, *Jaws* has much in common with B-movie sci-fi, horror, and exploitation films of the 1950s.[4] The family resemblance of *Jaws*, as a Universal

Studios picture, leads most directly back to the *Creature from the Black Lagoon* (1954, Jack Arnold) and before that to its structural analogue in *King Kong* (1933, Merian C. Cooper and Ernest B. Schoedsack) (Verevis 2012). The identification of *Jaws* as part of a creature-feature or revenge-of-nature cycle is consistent with its position in disaster movie subsets—animal attack, ecology of the elements—and is, for instance, further supported by a *New York Times* review headline—"*Jaws* and *Bug*—The Only Difference Is the Hype"—that equates Spielberg's film with producer William Castle's low-budget swarm film *Bug* (1975, Jeannot Szwarc) (Andrews 1999, 117).[5] This type of remark enables some commentators to draw a line from earlier 1970s revenge-of-nature films—titles such as *Frogs* (1972, George McCowan), *Night of the Lepus* (1972, William F. Claxton) and *SSSSnake* (1973, Bernard L. Kowalski)[6]—through *Jaws* and on to later 1970s films such as *Squirm* (1976, Jeff Lieberman), *Empire of the Ants* (1977, Bert I. Gordon), and *Kingdom of the Spiders* (1977, John "Bud" Cardos) (Cook 2000, 255–256; Yacowar 2003, 277–278). Again, this classification is consistent with disaster-cycle subsets, but it ignores *Jaws* coproducer David Brown's comment (itself a part paraphrase of the prologue to *Creature from the Black Lagoon*) that says: "The fear in *Jaws* is [not just] of being eaten. . . . The phobia [of] *Jaws* . . . goes right back to the moment when marine life left the sea and grew legs to stand on land. . . . It is a very primal fear and you don't need to be in a country with a shark-infested coastline to feel yourself involved in *Jaws*" (quoted in Andrews 1999, 63).

The most exploitable feature of *Jaws*—a primal fear of being eaten—was immediately taken up in *Grizzly* (1976, William Girdler), a replica that opens with two young female campers being eaten alive by a mammoth grizzly bear. For viewers of *Jaws*, the scenario is a familiar one: a park ranger (Christopher George) is called in to investigate the girls' disappearance, and when he discovers the teenagers' half-eaten remains, he is joined in his investigation by a naturalist (Richard Jaeckel), who explains that the bear is a survivor of a prehistoric breed. Kelly's endeavor to track and kill the bear is, however, hindered by a park supervisor (Joe Dorsey), whose refusal to close the park to holiday campers leads to further attacks. One of the first in a set of "rogue animal" films to follow *Jaws*, *Grizzly* was immediately recognized as an obvious rip-off—"*Jaws* with Claws"—but its semantics differed substantially enough from those of *Jaws* to avoid incurring the wrath of Universal's legal department. A knockoff from

Atlanta-based Film Ventures International, a production house that specialized in "cheap, ineptly-executed imitations" of blockbusters (Sege 1976), *Grizzly* was directed by William Girdler, who had already made *Abby* (1974), a version of *The Exorcist* (1973, William Friedkin). Girdler later extended the "nature on the offensive" theme through *Day of the Animals* (1978), a film in which a veteran guide (Christopher George, again) leads holiday makers through the High Sierra, where they are attacked by wolves, birds of prey, coyotes, rattlesnakes and—again—grizzlies (Pulleine 1977).

FRANCHISE

The French-language title for *Jaws*—*Dents de la Mer* (Teeth of the sea)—understands the *Jaws* prototype perfectly, as does Andrews when he writes: "Sharks have teeth [as] do aliens, gremlins and werewolves. . . . *Jaws* started it all. The role of teeth as a Vietnam-inspired guerilla war symbolism—deadly weapon concealed behind soft beguiling body part" (1999, 105–107). This comes into sharper focus when *Jaws* is understood as a prototype for a proprietary series: namely, *Jaws 2* (1978, Jeannot Szwarc), *Jaws 3-D* (1983, Joe Alves) and *Jaws: The Revenge*, aka *Jaws 4* (1987, Joseph Sargent).[7] The first of these is often described as a virtual remake of *Jaws*, a film in which the community of Amity Island is again threatened by a giant white pointer. In the film's climatic sea chase, Chief Martin Brody (Roy Scheider) comes to the rescue of his sons and (once again) dispatches the rogue shark, this time by causing it to bite through a high-voltage underwater cable. But as noted by reviewers at the time, the fact that the shark attacks of the first film are acknowledged (sequelized) makes the refusal of Mayor Vaughan (Murray Hamilton) to act on Chief Brody's warning the second time around appear idiotic to a degree that sabotages any real dramatic interest (Pulleine 1982).

As the official sequel to *Jaws*, and (with rentals of $50.4 million) the fifth highest-grossing film of 1978 (Cook 2000, 501), *Jaws 2* demonstrates that the process of continuation (sequelization) is always also one of repetition: of characters and actors, plots and scenarios, themes and styles, and, importantly, title terms (Perkins and Verevis 2012, 2–3). More pointedly, the *Jaws* set (*Jaws–Jaws 4*) constitutes a restricted (blockbuster) cycle: it is "identified with only a single studio" and "retain[s] one or more apparent money-making features from [the] previous success," even if *Jaws 2* and (especially) subsequent sequels

FIGURE 6.2. An unauthorized copy: *Great White* (1981).

immediately fell into so "fully imitable [a] pattern" as to limit the cycle's commercial sustainability (Altman 1990, 59). *Jaws* and its prog-
eny constitute a set, advertised as a proprietary cycle—the famous
tagline for *Jaws 2*: "Just when you thought it was safe to go back in
the water"—and based on characters, plots, and stars of the blueprint.
This set overlaps with a second, unauthorized set, one that, "anxious
to benefit from the success of the proprietary cycle," produced similar films—a generic "rogue animal" set—and sought to advertise or
have the films associated with the success of the *Jaws* prototype and
set (59). The limit case would appear to be *The Last Shark* (*L'Ultimo
Squalo*), aka *Great White* (1981, Enzo G. Castellari), an unacknowl-
edged remake and "carbon copy" of *Jaws* that Universal Studios insisted be withdrawn from theaters for breach of copyright (see Combs
1982, 138). Specifically, the Italian-produced *Last Shark* follows a local shark expert (James Franciscus) and a veteran fisherman (Vic Mor-

row) whose endeavor to capture a white pointer that is menacing a resort town in a lead-up to centennial celebrations is retarded by a local politician (Joshua Sinclair). If Universal's success with *Jaws* exemplifies the strategy of producing a "signature product" (Elsaesser 2011, 283–284) through which to sell a set of films (a cycle) and associated merchandise (a *Jaws* franchise), then Uti/Horizon Productions' *The Last Shark* exemplifies an instance in which it is "more lucrative simply to steal a [blockbuster] property already developed by another studio" (Altman 1990, 121).

CREATURE

The Last Shark is arguably no less a "cod homage" than a film such as *Bacalhau* (*Codfish*, 1975, Adriano Stuart), the Brazilian movie (hastily released to cash in on *Jaws* consciousness) that reimagines Chief Brody as the distinctly unheroic Breda, Matt Hooper as the Portuguese oceanographer Matos, and Quint as the Brazilian fisherman Quico, who attempts to kill the codfish with an archaic bow and arrow (see Vieira and Stam 1985, 31–36). Another was *Tentacles* (*Tentacoli*, 1976, Oliver Hellman), an American International Pictures–Esse Ci Cinematografica coproduction, produced and directed (under the pseudonym Oliver Hellman) by Ovidio G. Assonitis, an exploitation filmmaker who had already made a version of *The Exorcist*—*Beyond the Door* (1974, *Chi Sei?/Who Are You?*)—and would follow *Tentacles* with another "nature on the offensive" production, *Piranha II: The Spawning* (1981, James Cameron). Variously described as a "post-*Jaws* opus" (Pit 1977) and a "devastatingly silly rehash of the *Jaws* formula" (Milne 1977, 129), *Tentacles* follows a reporter named Ned Turner (John Huston) and a marine specialist named Will Gleason (Bo Hopkins) who find themselves drawn into the investigation of several mysterious deaths at a California harborside town. Turner believes the deaths are related to testing for an underwater tunnel, and Gleason gradually realizes they are dealing with a giant prehistoric octopus that has been disturbed by accelerated underwater tunneling authorized by a wealthy industrialist (Henry Fonda). Later—in a scene apparently copied by *Jaws 2*—the octopus attacks a sailing regatta in which Turner's young nephew is a participant. In the final confrontation, Gleason—whose wife (Delia Boccardo), along with her sister, her brother-in-law, and her friend have all been taken by the giant octopus—implores his two trained orcas to help him destroy the monster: "I guess you know now why I brought you here. . . . I've lost a loved one. I need your help more now than ever. . . . I can't ask anybody else, so I'm asking you to help me kill this octopus."

The revenge motif of *Tentacles* is drawn out most evidently in *Jaws* 4—subtitled *The Revenge*—in which Chief Brody's son Sean, the survivor of shark attacks in both *Jaws* and *Jaws* 2—is killed by a white pointer, which convinced Chief Brody's widow, Ellen (Lorraine Gary), that the shark has a grudge against her family, and leads her finally (like her late husband, and with the help of eldest son, Michael) to confront and kill the shark.[8] The revenge theme is in turn inverted in Dino De Laurentiis's epic production (and follow up to his 1976 *King Kong* remake), *Orca: Killer Whale* (1977, Michael Anderson), a film headlined in *Variety* as a "pizza version of *Moby Dick* out of *Jaws*" (Murf 1977). At the start of *Orca*, a Newfoundland boat captain named Nolan (Richard Harris) realizes the commercial value of a killer whale when he witnesses one repel a white pointer shark that threatens the life of a diver. Although a marine biologist (Charlotte Rampling) tries to dissuade him, Nolan undertakes to capture a large male orca for a marine park, but in the process he accidently harpoons its pregnant mate, killing both the female and the unborn calf. The male orca recognizes Nolan as the aggressor and begins to seek vengeance, assailing the local fishing village until it can lure Nolan out to sea and then north, where they duel to the death on the frozen ocean. *Orca* has been described as "another entry in the *Jaws* stakes" (Glaessner 1977), but unlike the low-rent examples of *Grizzly* and *The Last Shark*, *Orca* is a film that "attempts to go one better, at least or bigger," not only by centering its action on a killer whale, but also by investing in international stars (Harris, Rampling), a swelling Ennio Morricone sound track, and—in and through its portentous prologue—themes that are "both epic and ecological" (Glaessner 1977).

MULTIPLES

Perhaps the most enduring recalibration of the *Jaws* formula—maybe also the point at which the cycle exhausted (or reinvented) itself—is the example of Roger Corman's relatively low budget ($676,000) production of *Piranha* (1978), written by John Sayles and directed by Joe Dante (Alexander 2010; Warren 1999). Like *Grizzly*, *Piranha* begins with the investigation of the disappearance of two teenage hikers. A private detective (Heather Waxman) enlists a recently divorced

FIGURE 6.3. An endorsed imitation: *Piranha* (1978).

recluse (Bradford Dillman) as her guide and discovers that the teen-age couple has gone missing at a disused military facility. At the site, they find a scientist (Kevin McCarthy) who explains that he was employed during the Vietnam War to develop a man-eating strain of piranha with which to pollute North Vietnam's waterways. It transpires that the fish have been accidentally released into local waters. In part because of the failure of local officials to heed the warning, the killer fish attack a children's summer camp, which the recluse's daughter is attending. Like other films in the rogue animal cycle, *Piranha* shadows the plotline of *Jaws*, investing in a vicious cycle of marauding seaborne creatures—in this case small and multiple ones—to deliver another knowing entry in the set of exploitation movies from which *Jaws* itself emerged. *Piranha* does this right from the outset: one character refers to the creature from the Black Lagoon, and another plays a video game labeled "Jaws."[9] The film's humor mediates both *Piranha*'s horror and science fiction elements and its social commentary on corporate greed and aggressive militarism to produce a film that—again, like *Jaws*—is "a family film inexplicably floundering with an 'X' certificate" (Forbes 1978).

Additionally, and in the serial pattern that attends all the aforementioned films, *Piranha* was followed by a replica in *Alligator* (1981, Lewis Teague), John Sayles's follow-up as writer, in which irresponsible science unleashes another rogue animal. And (like *Piranha*, it displays a scenario in which the film's "radical message" never overwhelms its schlock-horror premise (Jenkins 1982). *Piranha*—the only *Jaws* imitation endorsed by Spielberg[10]—also led to the Spielberg-produced, Dante-directed *Gremlins* (1984), another work about "bitey" creatures (small and multiple) that thrive in water. Finally, *Piranha* did well enough commercially—especially in Europe and South America—to initiate a new proprietary cycle: *Piranha II: The Spawning*, aka *Flying Killers* (1981); an authorized, made-for-TV remake (1995, Scott P. Levy); a $24 million, theatrically released remake, *Piranha 3D* (2010, Alexandre Aja); and the sequel to the remake, *Piranha 3DD* (2012, John Gulager) (Osmond 2010; Newman 2012; Pulleine 1983).

DISASTER 2

Twenty-five years after *Jaws*, Renny Harlin's (estimated) $78 million blockbuster *Deep Blue Sea* (1999) looks in on an underwater research center off the coast of Mexico where experiments on three mako sharks have seen them grow to forty feet in length and demonstrate intelligent behavior. A violent storm floods the facility, trapping a team of researchers led by Dr. Susan McAlester (Saffron Burrows) three stories under the surface and unleashing the sharks, which stalk and kill their makers. The fact that the scientists must descend through the compound's submerged levels before ascending to surface safety is a return to the disaster movie realm (set) of *The Poseidon Adventure* (1972),[11] and the genetic engineering and digital effects make *Deep Blue Sea* a post–*Jurassic Park* (1993, Steven Spielberg) rogue animal film. It is curious, then, that one reviewer pointed out the obvious—"It is inevitable that any film featuring giant man-eating sharks will be compared to *Jaws*"—but then, somehow failing to recognize the *Jaws* genealogy, went on to say: "*Deep Blue Sea* is ultimately more of a disaster movie teetering on 'B'-movie legs than a *Jaws* rip-off or bizarre slasher-film hybrid" (Graham 1999, 42).

Like *Piranha* before it—or the contemporaneous *Godzilla* remake (1998, Roland Emmerich), which takes its bite from *Jaws*, *Aliens* (1986, James Cameron), and *Jurassic Park*—*Deep Blue Sea* dips into the *Jaws* gene pool, not only through its prologue, with the twist that the shark doesn't get the bikini-clad girl (Koehler 1999), but also by killing the three mako sharks in the same ways as the sharks in *Jaws*, *Jaws 2*, and *Jaws 3D*: blown up, electrocuted, and incinerated. The example of *Deep Blue Sea* seems to demonstrate once again how Spielberg's prototype functions not just as a cornerstone for a revenge-of-nature or rogue animal set, but also as an "operational manual" (Elsaesser 2011, 287) for all modern blockbusters. Ultimately, *Jaws* is not a closed set of image-sounds to be repeated, but—as seen in recent examples such as the Australia-Singapore coproduction *Bait* (2012, Kimble Rendall) and the made-for-television B movie *Sharknado* (2013, Anthony C. Ferrente)—an open whole, one that is endlessly remade and remodeled.

NOTES

1. See also Hoberman (2004) and Wyatt (1994, 113–117).

2. Yacowar (2003, 277–284) identifies at least eight types (sets) of disaster films: natural attack (for example, *Jaws*), the ship of fools, the city fails, the monster, survival, war, historical, and the comic.

3. As Hall and Neale (2010, 211–212) point out, *Jaws* was not the first film to enlist these strategies, but it was the most successful.

4. For an exhaustive account of *Jaws* and its "remakes," see Hunter's (2009) essay, which attends to "*Jaws*ploitation" films with the aim of pursuing "'*Jaws*ness' across numerous adaptations from copying and plagiarism to parody, homage and glancing allusion" (8).

5. Szwarc would go on to direct *Jaws 2*.

6. *SSSSnake* was produced by *Jaws*' producers, David Brown and Richard D. Zanuck.

7. Reviews of the films are instructive for determining their lineages and sets; see, for example, reviews of the *Jaws* series in the *Monthly Film Bulletin* (Milne 1975; Pulleine 1982; Roddick 1977; Newman 1987). Roddick, for instance, writes: "*Jaws 3-D* is pure, unabashed kitsch, with a plot . . . that cobbles together elements from *The Deep*, *The Poseidon Adventure* . . . and *Revenge of the Creature*" (1977, 330).

8. As a sequel, *Jaws 4* establishes continuity with *Jaws* and *Jaws 2* by including Ellen Brody (Lorraine Gary) and featuring some tinted flashbacks of Martin Brody (Roy Scheider), but at the same time it ignores alternate adult versions of

sons Michael (Dennis Quaid) and Sean Brody (John Putch) from *Jaws 3-D* (see Newman [1987, 307]).

9. The opening of *Piranha*—which has teenagers Barbara and David attacked by killer piranhas during a nighttime dip in the dark waters of the military test pool—is a reprisal not only of the opening of *Jaws* (in which Chrissie is taken by the rogue shark while skinny-dipping at night) but also of the lambent swimming excursion by Kay (Julia Adams), and her first encounter with the creature, in *Creature from the Black Lagoon*. Perhaps the most outrageous variant is the nude underwater swim by Danni and Crystal in *Piranha 3D*.

10. The Swedish poster for *Piranha* quotes Spielberg: "The best film inspired by *Jaws* [*Hajen*]."

11. At the tip of the new millennium, *Deep Blue Sea* anticipated a new set of digitally boosted disaster films, including *The Poseidon Adventure* remake *Poseidon* (2006, Wolfgang Petersen).

WORKS CITED

Alexander, Chris. 2010. "When Roger Corman Cleared the Beach." *Fangoria* 296 (September): 50–56.

Altman, Rick. 1990. *Film/Genre*. London: BFI.

Andrews, Nigel. 1999. *Nigel Andrews on Jaws*. Bloomsbury Movie Guide 5. New York: Bloomsbury.

Benchley, Peter. 1975. *Jaws*. London: Pan.

Combs, Richard. 1977. Review of *The Deep*. *Monthly Film Bulletin* 44:257–258.

———. 1982. Review of *L'Ultimo Squalo (Shark)*. *Monthly Film Bulletin* 49:138.

Cook, David A. 2000. *Lost Illusions: American Cinema in the Shadow of Watergate and Vietnam, 1970–1979*. History of the American Cinema, vol. 9. New York: Scribner's Sons.

Deleuze, Gilles. 1986. *Cinema 1: The Movement-Image*. Translated by Hugh Tomlinson and Barbara Habberjam. Minneapolis: University of Minnesota Press.

Elsaesser, Thomas. 2011. *The Persistence of Hollywood*. London: Routledge.

Forbes, Jill. 1978. Review of *Piranha*. *Monthly Film Bulletin* 45:224.

Glaessner, Verina. 1977. Review of *Orca: Killer Whale*. *Monthly Film Bulletin* 44:171.

Graham, Jamie. 1999. Review of *Deep Blue Sea*. *Sight and Sound*, November, 40, 42.

Hall, Sheldon, and Steve Neale. 2010. *Epics, Spectacles, and Blockbusters*. Detroit: Wayne State University Press.

Heath, Stephen. 1976. "*Jaws*, Ideology, and Film Theory." *Framework* 4:25–27.

Hoberman, J. 1985. "Ten Years That Shook the World." *American Film* 10 (June): 34–59.

———. 2004. "*Nashville* contra *Jaws*, Or 'The Imagination of Disaster' Revisited." In *The Last Great American Picture Show: New Hollywood Cinema in the 1970s*, ed. Thomas Elsaesser, Alexander Horwath, and Noel King, 195–222. Amsterdam: Amsterdam University Press.

Hunter, I. Q. 2009. "Exploitation as Adaptation." In *Cultural Borrowings: Ap-

propriation, Reworking, Transformation, ed. Iain Robert Smith, 8–33. *Scope* e-Book.

Martha's Vineyard Chamber of Commerce. 2005. "Jaws Fest." Accessed 28 May 2005, www.mvy.com/jaws (link no longer active).

Jenkins, Steve. 1982. Review of *Alligator. Monthly Film Bulletin* 49:39.

Keane, Stephen. 2006. *Disaster Movies: The Cinema of Catastrophe.* London: Wallflower.

Klein, Amanda Ann. 2011. *American Film Cycles: Reframing Genres, Screening Social Problems, and Defining Subcultures.* Austin: University of Texas Press.

Koehler, Robert. 1999. Review of *Deep Blue Sea. Variety* 138:18.

Milne, Tom. 1975. Review of *Jaws. Monthly Film Bulletin* 42:263–264.

———. 1977. Review of *Tentacoli (Tentacles). Monthly Film Bulletin* 44:129–130.

Murf. 1977. Review of *Orca. Variety*, 13 July, 18.

Newman, Kim. 1987. Review of *Jaws: The Revenge. Monthly Film Bulletin* 54:306–307.

———. 2012. Review of *Piranha 3DD. Sight and Sound*, July, 72.

Osmond, Andrew. 2010. Review of *Piranha [3D]. Sight and Sound*, November, 70.

Perkins, Claire, and Constantine Verevis. 2012. "Introduction: Three Times." In *Film Trilogies: New Critical Approaches*, ed. Claire Perkins and Constantine Verevis, 1–31. Basingstoke, UK: Palgrave-Macmillan.

Pit. 1977. Review of *Tentacles. Variety*, 15 June, 20.

Pulleine, Tim. 1977. Review of *Day of the Animals. Monthly Film Bulletin* 44:166–167.

———. 1982. Review of *Jaws 2. Monthly Film Bulletin* 49:330.

———. 1983. Review of *Piranha II: Flying Killers. Monthly Film Bulletin* 50:233.

Roddick, Nick. 1977. Review of *Jaws 3-D. Monthly Film Bulletin* 44:129–130.

———. 1980. "Only the Stars Survive: Disaster Movies in the Seventies." In *Performance and Politics in Popular Drama: Aspects of Popular Entertainment in Theater, Film, and Television, 1800–1976*, ed. David Bradby, Louis James, and Bernard Sharratt, 243–269. Cambridge: Cambridge University Press.

Schatz, Thomas. 1993. "The New Hollywood." In *Film Theory Goes to the Movies*, ed. Jim Collins, Ava Preacher Collins, and Hilary Radner, 8–36. London: Routledge.

Sege. 1976. Review of *Grizzly. Variety*, 26 May, 18.

Verevis, Constantine. 2012. "Bizarre Love Triangle: The Creature Trilogy." In *Film Trilogies: New Critical Approaches*, ed. Claire Perkins and Constantine Verevis, 68–87. Basingstoke, UK: Palgrave-Macmillan.

Vieira, João Luiz, and Robert Stam. 1985. "Parody and Marginality: The Case of Brazilian Cinema." *Framework* 28:20–49.

Warren, Bill. 1999. "*Piranha*: A Killer Fish Story." *Fangoria* 187 (October): 14–21, 37.

Wyatt, Justin. 1994. *High Concept: Movies and Marketing in Hollywood.* Austin: University of Texas Press.

Yacowar, Maurice. 2003. "The Bug in the Rug: Notes on the Disaster Genre." In *Film Genre Reader III*, ed. Barry Keith Grant, 277–295. Austin: University of Texas Press.

CHAPTER 7

FAMILIAR OTHERNESS: ON THE CONTEMPORARY CROSS-CULTURAL REMAKE

CHELSEY CRAWFORD

AFTER THE 2002 DREAMWORKS RELEASE of *The Ring* (Gore Verbinski)—a remake of Hideo Nakata's *Ringu* (1998)—grossed nearly $130 million in the United States (all earnings figures are taken from Box Office Mojo), Columbia Pictures quickly followed with *The Grudge* (2004). Helmed by Takashi Shimizu, the director of the Japanese original, *Ju-On*, this remake grossed almost $40 million in the United States. After each film's impressive US gross, remakes of Asian horror revealed both a potential American market for an Asian horror cycle and the increased viability of Asian cinema within the global marketplace. In fact, scholars (Park [2009], Herbert [2009]) have suggested that Hollywood's initial decision to draw material from Asia was motivated less by the particulars of the texts than by the mounting significance of Asian countries within the global economy and the increased consumption of Hollywood products in Asia. These scholars claim that Hollywood was driven mainly by a vision of tremendous profits to expand its dominance in Asia. Following this logic, the specifics of the films themselves were of little consequence. They were not chosen for superior story, style, or other admirable artistic or technological achievements; instead, their origins in nations with increased wealth and industrial importance made them worthy of Hollywood's attention. Such a perspective on cross-cultural remaking furthers the widely held belief that Hollywood's industrial and economic goals—to produce the most profitable commodity—outweigh the desire to encourage artistic expression. Akin to the way in which remaking, in general, is condemned for debasing a medium that otherwise might reach the status of a high or fine art, these cross-cultural remakes are disparaged for commercializing an art form, cannibalizing other cultures through imperialism, and corrupting originality, all in the name of financial reward.

This chapter, however, conceptualizes the Asian remake cycle (with a focus on Japanese horror films, or J-horror) beyond Hollywood's economic or imperialistic agenda. While it is not my primary goal to disprove these criticisms (particularly since any claim that Hollywood is not a commercial enterprise would yield limited results), I suggest that the cycle highlights Hollywood's ability to capitalize on cultural difference and Otherness in a way that fails to achieve a totalizing hegemony, but instead permits cultural uniqueness. In other words, these J-horror remakes celebrate difference, but a difference filtered through the lens of comfort and familiarity rather than difference qua difference. By addressing philosophical questions rather than linguistic, industrial, or historical ones, this chapter suggests that the J-horror remakes highlight a valuable cultural overlapping. I use two models (one from within film studies and the other from philosophy) to illustrate both how these films represent moments of cultural contact and how that contact should be understood beyond an exclusively imperialistic model. In particular, translation and communication are the two essential notions I deploy. Film studies has taken up translation as a model for celebrating how cross-cultural remakes reflect new national contexts while retaining a link to the original (Other) film, and I employ this useful framework, with some limitations. The second model, communication, allows me to deploy philosophical concepts from the work of Jean-Luc Nancy in order to conceptualize the cross-cultural contact enacted by these films. Drawing upon Nancy's notion of communication—which emphasizes both distance and touch—allows me to discuss how these films, perhaps unbeknownst to the producers who maintain control of Hollywood's purchasing and remaking of foreign originals, represent a moment in which two cultures come into contact with each other even as they simultaneously maintain their distance and uniqueness. Or as Nancy might say, these remakes reflect how Japan and the United States maintain their status as separate (through distancing) while also highlighting their inescapable overlapping (or touch).

GLOBALIZATION AND THE FEAR OF IMPERIALISM

Asian remakes represent one of two recent examples of Hollywood packaging cross-cultural remaking as an American film cycle. The first of these two cycles occurred between the late 1980s and early 1990s, when American studios focused largely on remakes of French films, and the second instance (the focus of this chapter) followed in the early 2000s, when studios drew material from Asia, with a particular investment in Japan. Though Hollywood has regularly mined the films and cinematic traditions of foreign nations since its infancy, the time between the release of the original and the remake has significantly shortened because of the increase in global interaction resulting from changes to trade restrictions. As Christina Klein explains, "Hollywood, of course, has operated globally since the 1910s. But its global reach expanded dramatically in the 1980s, as the forces of economic globalization—including the opening up of formerly socialist economies, the worldwide reduction in trade barriers, the diffusion of digital technologies—combined to create a global integrated capitalist economy" (2010, 4). This environment has allowed Hollywood to borrow from other cultures more quickly and efficiently than in prior eras. For example, films composing the French and the Asian remake cycles were based on contemporary (rather than classic or older) films and were released with increasing rapidity. In 1993, *Daily Variety* claimed that "studios [were] negotiating English-lingo remake rights for films that [hadn't] even opened in France" (Williams and Mørk 1993, 5), a situation never before witnessed. Typically, Hollywood studios relied upon the successes of a film within a foreign— often European—market to determine which film rights to purchase. But now, negotiations for remakes need not be halted until after a film's initial run.

Though American film cycles did not necessarily benefit from globalization or the quickened pace with which cultural products moved as a result, the increased mobility allowed both contemporary cross-cultural remake cycles to cohere (as cycles) according to their original country or continent of origin. In keeping with Steve Neale's use of the term "cycle" as typically referring "to groups of films made within a specific and limited time-span, and founded, for the most part, on the characteristics of individual commercial successes" (2000, 7), we can extrapolate that the "characteristics" responsible for commercial success were, in the case of the French and Asian remakes, assumed to be causally linked with nation. In other words, whereas a traditional cycle might depend on the assumed value of a given genre or style as evidenced in a foundational film (for instance, Neale cites how *Texas Chainsaw Massacre* [1974, Tobe Hooper] established the slasher film cycle), these cross-cultural remake cycles explicitly link cultural origin with success and then borrow material accordingly. Thus, these cross-cultural remakes can be explicitly defined as cycles because they occur within a particular, finite time span and they descend from a successful foundational film—*Three Men and a Baby* (1987, Leonard Nimoy) in the case of the French remake cycle, and *The Ring* in the Asian cycle—that convinced the studios of an association between the nation of origin and profitability in the US market.

The French and the Asian cycles differ in significant ways—in genre, number of films in the cycle—and simultaneously raise unique issues concerning nation versus continent, and East versus West. Laura Grinsdstaff notes, drawing conclusions from *Daily Variety* data (1987–1993), "Hollywood remade seventeen contemporary French films, all . . . released in the 1970s, 1980s, and 1990s" (2002, 281). The vastness of this remake cycle is not echoed in the Asian cycle. Though the Asian cycle does not have a fully defined time span or a list of included films, scholars generally agree that there are nine films in the cycle. And unlike the French cycle, the Asian cycle includes films from a variety of nations. Though scholars often focus on Japan as the locus of this cycle, films in the cycle originated in other nations as well. After *The Ring*, US studios released *The Grudge* (originally Japanese), *Dark Water* (2005, Walter Salles, originally Japanese), *Pulse* (2006, Jim Sonzero, originally Japanese), *One Missed Call* (2008, Eric Valette, originally Japanese), *The Eye* (2008, David Moreau and Xavier Palud, originally from Hong Kong), *Shutter* (2008, Masayuki Ochiai, originally Taiwanese), *Mirrors* (2008, Alexandre Aja, originally Korean), and *The Uninvited* (2009, Charles Guard and Thomas Guard, originally South Korean). Though this list might seem to indicate American prejudices that overlook differing national identities and boundaries within Asia, it also provides valuable evidence of the relevance of genre to the remake cycle. All the films in the Asian film cycle are remakes of horror films and therefore seem to be capable of more easily crossing national boundaries (an assertion to which I will return).

Lastly, the French and Asian remake cycles raise questions concerning the distinct identities of the Eastern and Western worlds. Remaking Asian films (and, specifically, Japanese films) may present more potential pitfalls than remaking French ones in large part because of producers' unfamiliarity with the films' cultures of origin. Though France's distinct national identity might have been erased through the supposedly homogenizing practice of remaking (an assertion made by French critics; see Bazin [1952]), France and the United States are bound together as members of the Western world. By contrast, the remaking of Asian films is assumed to be a more sensitive process because, as Nicholas Holm claims, "more so than any other national cinema, Japan was considered to defy any Western historical, linguistic, or cultural understanding" (2011, 186).[1] And throughout US film history, there have been fewer remakes of Japanese and other East Asian films than remakes of European films.[2]

Such cultural distinctions reinvigorate the fears of critics who cite cross-cultural remaking as one of Hollywood's most prevalent means of dominating foreign nations through economic imperialism. Though Hollywood's rhetoric might claim that J-horror remakes produce domestic appreciation of a foreign culture and bring unique material to US audiences, scholars such as Myoungsook Park condemn these films for pursuing other goals; protecting the domestic space from unauthorized cinematic commodities remains the ultimate reason for what, on the surface, appears to be a search for narrative or aesthetic Otherness (Park 2009, 114). With respect to these Japanese remakes, the effect of this imperialism and provincialization is felt in the supposed sanitation of many—perhaps all—of the signifiers of Japanese culture. By removing Japanese codes and conventions, American producers have "universalize[d] the text for global reception" (114) and, therefore, supplanted the original with the US version within the confines of both the United States and most foreign nations. In particular, Park dismisses the "remaking as translation" model to which Grindstaff and I subscribe, since one means of universalization is through language. Because Hollywood uses English, these films follow a literary trajectory in which texts translated into English are distributed worldwide, resulting in the English translation becoming dominant—even over the original text—and the English version, rather than the original, becoming the basis for future translations. When an English translation is firmly upheld as the authority, English remains unmarked and "universal," whereas all other languages become inherently marked as Other (118).

The continued homogenization of these Hollywood remakes depends upon the removal of essentially Japanese features as well as elements central to the traditional Japanese *kaidan* narrative—a uniquely Japanese story in which an avenging female spirit haunts the living in an attempt to correct a long-standing injustice she suffered before death. According to Park, the virus structure (which portrays the spirit as infecting all of Japanese society), the female avenger (who becomes almost humanized as the films reveal her deplorable treatment), and the figure of the schoolgirl (who seems to have a unique attachment to the avenging spirit) are all aspects of the *kaidan* narrative that the original Japanese films rely on, but that American producers either diminish to the point of emptiness or remove entirely.

Even if there may be some truth to the critiques that these cross-cultural remakes are merely shallow economic and imperialistic enterprises, I explore three representative films (*The Ring*, *The Grudge*, and *Dark Water*) to suggest a more complex flow of global influence, one that permits us to see the value in such instances of cultural overlapping. Whether or not Hollywood engages in imperialistic domination via remaking, global culture inherently involves a degree of transnationalism and hybridity. The influences exerted between nations in an environment of globalization illustrate how influence flows in an increasingly multidirectional fashion.

TRANSLATION AND THE TRACES OF JAPAN

Though critiques of cross-cultural remaking adopt an attitude that assumes cultural appreciation and respect to be impossibilities, or goals that Hollywood has no interest in pursuing, Grindstaff acknowledges the possibility of a responsible cross-cultural remake and conceptualizes it as translation. Importantly, Grindstaff asserts a particular definition of translation that clarifies her use of the term: "While remakes are not translations in any conventional sense, U.S. adaptations of foreign films certainly raise many of the same concerns about fidelity, superiority, and appropriation as do literary translations of foreign texts" (2002, 277). Though Park would counter that translation merely provides yet another way for Hollywood to displace and unseat foreign products, Grindstaff employs the term to reflect the interrelation of context and content. Translation refers to the way in which a conscientious remake does not attempt to merely transplant the original to a new culture without adequately reflecting the new cultural context. The remake cannot merely erase its origins, but must simultaneously admit the viability and importance of the original. As Grindstaff explains, the remake and the original should be understood as "mutually constitutive concepts" (275). The remake is therefore capable of bringing a new focus to aspects of the original, and the original is equally capable of situating the remake within a broad historical tradition. Conceptualizing the cross-cultural remake as translation, then, demonstrates the inherent link between original and remake; it allows the remake to reflect the new national context while retaining the presence of the cultural Other. Rather than proving Hollywood's exclusively profit-driven interests, these J-horror remakes demonstrate hybridity based on the simultaneous existence of markers of Japanese and American cultures.

Following the logic of translation, then, we can begin to see how the mere fact of a remake being a product of the Hollywood money-making machine does not necessarily, within a given film, guarantee the primacy of one culture or the complete erasure of another. Instead, the model of translation allows for an appreciation of these films as amalgams, sensitive to shifting national contexts. Though they do not frame them as translations per se, Thy Phu (2010) and Eimi Ozawa (2006) provide examples from *The Ring* that display the simultaneous existence of cultures within J-horror remakes. Phu, for instance, acknowledges that the film is often criticized for wholly erasing Japan (as setting or cultural signifier) and the *kaidan* elements. But she counters by pointing out how the *onryou* (the avenging spirit of the *kaidan* narrative) functions as one major way in which "the figure of Japan structures the experience of horror within *The Ring*" (2010, 51). For instance, the fate of both *Ringu*'s *onryou* (Sadako) and *The Ring*'s (Samara) adheres to the basic narrative in which their ghosts haunt the living in order to avenge an injustice they suffered in life. Murdered by a parent and discarded in a well, both Sadako and Samara seek vengeance through videotapes that kill their viewers. Finally, beyond the similarities in the narrative, Samara is visually and physically rendered unmistakably like Sadako. *Ringu* establishes a character trope carried through many of the J-horror remakes (*The Ring* and *The Grudge*, in particular). *The Ring*'s Samara displays many of Sadako's visual characteristics: long, matted black hair flattened across her face like a mask; a pale face and body; a decomposing white dressing gown; and subhuman, broken bodily movements. Such commonalities in narrative and style highlight that even with the differences in language, setting, and actors, stylistic and narrative similarities persist, creating a relation between original and remake that depends on translation, not erasure.

Along with the *onryou*, Phu highlights two other signifiers evoc-

FIGURE 7.1. Samara, *The Ring*'s *onryou*.

ative of Japanese culture within the American film: "Haunting *The Ring* . . . is the figure of Japan, manifest most obviously through the spectre of Samara, whose name refers to the fruit of the Japanese maple, a blood-red visual emblem within Verbinski's film, as well as in the medium from which she emerges, the videotape" (2010, 51). The videotape might seem too universal an artifact to be specifically linked with one culture, but Phu insists that it evokes Japan because of the part it played in copyright legislation and its status as representative of Japan's technological ingenuity. Though, I would argue, both the videotape and the implications of Samara's name narratively further the visibility of Japan within the remake, the iconography of the Japanese maple embeds Japan as a stylistic recurrence as well. Two integral examples highlight how the image of this tree proves useful to the narrative and evocative of the cultural hybridity of Verbinski's film.

The first of these two virtually back-to-back instances occurs when Rachel (Naomi Watts) and Noah (Martin Henderson) discover a barn loft where Samara was held, kept company by only a smattering of toys and a small television set. Noah notices a crack in the wallpaper that exposes something dark beneath. Through a series of close-ups and medium shots, Verbinski slowly reveals tree limbs burned into the wood beneath the wallpaper. Finally, Verbinski's

FIGURE 7.2. The exposed Japanese maple.

camera, situated behind Rachel and Noah, tilts up to reveal the image of a Japanese maple, which Rachel recognizes, stating, "I've seen this tree before . . . I've been there."

Highlighting an important narrative plot point (the connection between this "room" and the Shelter Mountain Inn, where Rachel's niece Katie [Amber Tamblyn] found and watched the deadly tape), the appearance of this tree also connects Samara's ill-fated life, and death, with a Japanese maple. After prompting Rachel and Noah to return to the inn, the vibrant red tree makes another appearance. Following an establishing shot of cabin 12, Verbinski's camera lingers on a close-up of the leaves of the maple tree while using time-lapse photography to show the sun moving across the leaves, altering the hue. Linking the maple simultaneously to Japan, Samara's suffering (as evidenced by its appearance in the barn), her demise (by its appearance at the Shelter Inn, where Samara is thrown down the well), and Rachel's peril (the scene occurs during day seven, at which point previous viewers of the cursed tape have mysteriously died), the image of this tree, in particular, serves as evidence of the concurrent existence of original Japanese and American influences within *The Ring*. At once, the tree represents Japan, Samara, and Rachel, bridging the gap between the two cultures.

Though translation certainly furthers a conception of these remakes that illustrates their value in the face of apparent cultural parasitism, framing these remakes within the theoretical structure of translation holds other inherent obstacles. Grindstaff acknowledges that translation, as she theorizes it, differs from translation in any "conventional sense," but her choice of metaphor (as well as Park's opposition to that metaphor) figures cross-cultural remaking as a linguistic rather than a cinematic concern. In other words, Grindstaff inadvertently risks conflating cinema and language with her use of the term "translation." Though she seeks to emphasize the movement of cinematic material from one cultural context to another, translation implies changing language or dialect. On the other hand, Park critiques the issue of translation not by removing the linguistic underpinnings, but by transforming the central concern from one of cinema as a language into one of language *within* cinema—her objections to these films includes a condemnation of the statement by Hollywood producers that changing the language spoken by the characters represents a *minor* distinction between original and remake. Whereas the limitations of Grindstaff's argument come from the friction caused by treating cinema as a language, Park's result from dismissing the cinematic in favor of the linguistic expressions within the narrative. Neither of these uses of the concept of translation satisfactorily overcomes the potential linguistic underpinnings of such a framework. Although furthering an association between remakes and language, the model of translation is not able to adequately examine the universality of images, which, I insist, remains an important aspect of how these remakes allow for cultural crossover that undercuts claims of imperialism.

DISTANCE, COMMUNICATION, AND THE ONTOLOGICAL MODEL

Though Grindstaff's model, beyond the terminology, is valuable to a reconsideration of this cycle, I want to turn to Continental philosophy in order to elaborate upon her suggestion that these films allow for multiple cultural influences. In particular, Jean-Luc Nancy's theory of ontology, though not explicitly focused on cinema or globalization, offers a satisfying theoretical framework for considering the cultural complexities of difference and sameness presented in this remake cycle. Nancy's conceptual framework takes up questions raised by foundational philosophers (Nietzsche, Kant, Heidegger) in order to develop a theory of Being that satisfactorily counters singularity.

Resting on the notion that Being cannot be conceived of as a singular experience, Nancy sets out to do away with the primacy of the "I." He articulates a theory of ontology that, instead, furthers the notion of a singular-plurality (first-person plural) as the ontological ground of the world. In other words, Being, for Nancy, does not involve my ability to comprehend myself as a singular "me." Instead, one's Being must be understood as an "I" who is nevertheless inescapably part of a "we," though never so much so that one fails to simultaneously maintain one's status as an "I." Each person is, at once, within the plurality and never wholly subsumed by it. As Nancy asserts, "From now on, we, *we others* are charged with this truth . . . the truth of this paradoxical 'first person plural' which makes sense of the world as the spacing and intertwining of so many worlds (earths, skies, histories) that there is a taking place of meaning, or the crossing through of presence" (2000, 5). The truth that all Being is being-with-one-another—being an "I" but also a "we"—makes meaning apparent. Significantly, this quotation includes two additional Nancian concepts that prove integral not only to his theory of singular-plurality, but also to our ability to employ his work as a means for understanding cross-cultural remakes. Both spacing (or distance) and intertwining (or touch) are crucial to the coexistence of the "I" and the "we."

Distance and touch function simultaneously to allow beings to establish sameness (necessary for maintaining the status of the plurality) and distinction (necessary for the continued presence of the singularity). For our purposes, we might say any given nation is simultaneously a singularity and a plurality (or, perhaps either a singularity or a plurality). A nation might be understood as a singularity in that it is thought to have a particular cultural identity shared by its citizens (all identify with a common nomination like "Japanese" or "American," and we typically speak about a country's government or populace). But we simultaneously comprehend a nation as being composed of individual citizens (independent, seemingly autonomous I's) that come together to form a plural we. Similarly, we must acknowledge that distance between one culture and another is necessary to maintain the nations' identities, while the sameness established by instances of contact (such as cross-cultural remakes) exemplifies the intertwining of all people and all beings. In Nancy's words, "All of being is in touch with all of being, but the law of touching is separation; moreover, it is the heterogeneity of surfaces that touch each

FIGURE 7.3. The looming concrete structure.

other" (2000, 5). The logic of touch depends on division and distance; a distance that is not impassable, but is also not negligible. When Japan and the United States come into contact with each other, this touching is exemplified by cross-cultural remakes. These films allow not only the Being of both countries (as well as the beings within them) to maintain distinctness, but also the nations to be connected through sameness. The space that separates these countries remains present yet surpassable. This allows both cultures to celebrate and acknowledge the simultaneous presence of their uniqueness and their commonality.

J-horror remakes, in particular, highlight Nancy's ontology because of the thematic and stylistic overlap between Japanese and American versions. In particular, both versions of *Dark Water* (2002, Japan; 2005, US) visually emphasize the apartment building occupied by the primary female characters. The directors consistently frame the mother (Yoshimi [Hitomi Kuroki]; Dahlia [Jennifer Connelly]) and daughter (Ikuko [Rio Kanno]; Ceci [Ariel Gade]) alone in medium or medium-long shots—occasionally from an overhead angle—that allow the building to dominate and that highlight their lack of contact with others. One representative scene during which the visual supremacy of the building sets the tone for the internal development of the characters occurs in the remake when Dahlia and Ceci initially tour the structure. After riding the tram from Manhattan to Roosevelt Island, during which Ceci highlights their inevitable isolation when she glances toward Roosevelt Island and states, "Mommy, that's not the city. . . . That's the city over there [pointing toward

FIGURE 7.4. Roosevelt Island's desolation and disrepair.

Manhattan on the left side of the frame], that's not the city [point-
ing toward their destination]", the pair walk through near-desolate
concrete walkways and buildings, ultimately arriving at their desti-
nation. Salles signals that they are drawing near by increasingly employing low-angle shots of massive concrete structures, the last of
which shows their future home. Cutting from the low-angle shot of
the building to an overhead shot of the street, Salles emphasizes the
island, and this building in particular, as a location free of any significant signs of activity.

After meeting the building manager out front, the duo proceeds to
the lobby as the film cuts to a long shot down the main corridor. The
long shot becomes a frequently recurring shot distance (employed
to show mother and daughter entering the lobby, to frame the hall-
way outside their apartment, or even to film the apartment itself),
and it emphasizes the desolate and dreary nature of this building.
It highlights the impression that this place lacks the common con-
notations of home (comfort, warmth, family), and instead represents
alienation, isolation, fear, and (ultimately) sacrifice. The building,
stylistically emphasized in this manner, expresses the lack of community resulting from financial constrictions and an impending divorce. Similarly, the building's deterioration highlights the mounting fear over both the source of the water that constantly seeps into
Dahlia's apartment, as well as the failure of motherhood. Ultimately,
both films wed the mother character to the building (and its ghostly
inhabitant) through an inherently maternal sacrifice. Giving her life
to free her child seems an act both necessary to mothering and capa-

ble of being completed only by a mother. This shared concern, stylistically and thematically, over a gendered relation to children, a sense of alienation, and an absence of community demonstrates a significant means by which Japan and the United States become one, overlapping briefly even as the differences remain.

Similarly, the universality of genre-specific images in the Asian horror remake cycle further enhances Nancy's applicability to these films. Because horror is generally defined by feelings of "dread, anxiety, fear, revulsion, surprise, [and] shock" (Klein 2010, 12) created by the alternation of the seen and the unseen rather than by the specific cultural means that trigger such reactions within the viewer, the feelings themselves are understood as "foundationally human and thus common across cultures" (12). These J-horror films explicitly cultivate feelings of fear that depend on characteristics shared by all humans and, they therefore represent a means of making cultural overlap apparent. Such instances of overlapping occur throughout these J-horror remakes, but *The Grudge* represents a particularly poignant example, since the remake directly quotes the original. One such quotation occurs near the conclusion when Karen (Sarah Michelle Gellar) receives a message from boyfriend Doug (Peter Behr), telling her that he has gone searching for her in the house haunted by the *onryou*. Karen returns to the house, only to experience a vision of Peter (Bill Pullman) discovering his unintentional involvement in the death of Kayako (the *onryou*, played by Takako Fuji). As the scene continues, Karen witnesses Kayako's brutal murder at the hands of her husband when he discovers her romantic feelings for Peter. As Karen flees downstairs toward the door, she hears a sound, turns back, and, to her horror, sees Kayako's animated corpse. In a sequence almost identical to the one in *Ju-On*, the film alternates between medium close-ups of her terrified face and Kayako's body, which, with each reverse shot, creeps—broken and inhuman—further into the frame.

In this example, the cultural tension becomes secondary to a common anxiety, cultural differences subsumed by the sameness of the emotion and the cinematic commonality of the two scenes. Rather than remaining entirely distinct because of differing languages and the racially marked faces of Gellar and Megumi Okina (Rika, Gellar's counterpart, in *Ju-On*), two cultures overlap because of the shared fear resulting from the increasing visibility of the feared force, the universality of cinematic images, and the near-total similarity between the two sequences. But even if we acknowledge the touching of two cultures that this scene represents, we cannot ignore the distinction that persists. Though Japanese and American cultures share a common anxiety and almost identical cinematic material in this moment, the differences remind the viewer that *The Grudge* is still a Hollywood adaptation. The scene brings the countries together, but does not allow them either to fully combine or to completely resist combination. Ultimately, these J-horror remakes demonstrate the value of cinema and its medium specificity for bringing cultures into contact with one another without conflating them or allowing one culture to be subsumed by another.

The function of such cinematic instances of cultural touch, like Nancy's general theory of ontology, depends on the interdependence of communication and Being. Nancy asserts, "'Language' is not an instrument of communication, and communication is not an instrument of Being; communication *is* Being, and Being *is*, as a consequence, nothing but the incorporeal by which bodies express themselves to one another *as such*" (2000, 93). Language, then, does not necessarily function as a means through which beings can begin to comprehend one another, since it is not an instrument of communication. Communication, which is essential to Being and to the way in which beings display their nature to one another, can occur through cinema. In other words, even if cinema itself may not adhere to Nancy's definition of communication (in that communication involves only the intangible), perhaps cinema is a means through which communication becomes possible. The ideas and questions raised by the cinematic image might be understood as incorporeal. That is to say, cinema's concreteness does not diminish its ability to both express and create the abstract, ethereal, or immaterial. In fact, Klein's assertion that horror films generate fear illustrates this point. Though these J-horror films remain material objects—created when light passes through celluloid or even when a digital image appears to radiate from a television screen—the anxiety that they elicit is, nevertheless, immaterial. Therefore, cinema's ability to elucidate Nancy's ontology ought to be foregrounded.

Ultimately, the interplay of difference and sameness at the heart of these J-horror remakes enacts an overlapping whereby cultures can reflect on issues or develop new conceptions of identity and ontology. Or as Nancy explains, "The understanding of Being is nothing other than an understanding of others, which means, in every sense, understanding others through 'me' and understanding 'me' through understanding others, the understanding of one another" (2000, 28). Cross-cultural remakes—and remake cycles—provide a point of interaction between seemingly disparate peoples through which each can develop an understanding of self through other, and of other through self. These moments of touch and contact demonstrate the interconnectedness of cultures and peoples even as those groups (and individuals) necessarily maintain their own unique identities.

UNDERSTANDING, IN EVERY SENSE

Hollywood's motivations for remaking films originating in other national cinemas undoubtedly represent one means of attempting to exert global control and influence while simultaneously protecting its own market from undue impact by imports from other cultural powerhouses. But Hollywood's interest in foreign stories and images also provides useful insight into the complexities of globalization and into the philosophical conceptions of cultural and ontological interaction. Similarly, these remakes reinvigorate cinema with medium-specific possibilities for universal expression and experience, even though some argue that such products, benefiting from Hollywood's dominant position in production and distribution, equate universality with Americanness.

And though critics claim that US remakes of foreign films overshadow the originals to the point that the American version wholly supplants the original, a counterargument can be made, namely, that the act of remaking upholds the significance and general relevance of the original film. For instance, as Thomas Leitch argues—not with respect to cross-cultural remakes, but rather when disputing claims that Brian De Palma's references to the work of Hitchcock are hollow, uninspired copying—many cinematic classics become understood as such only because their successors remake or copy them. For example, Leitch asserts, "By ripping off the shower scene [in films such as *Dressed to Kill* and *The Phantom of the Paradise*], De Palma established that scene as a *locus classicus* of commercial cinema" (2006, 269). In De Palma's case, Leitch argues that such blatant, unapologetic copying of Hitchcock's crucial scene actually played an integral role in establishing that scene as canonical within American film history. One could suggest a similar outcome with respect to the Asian remake cycle in that the original Japanese films, and their particular cultural underpinnings and significance, might not have reached a global audience or inspired discussion by international scholars had it not been for the cross-cultural remakes.

In the end, reconsideration of these remakes—rather than mere dismissal on the grounds that they are shameless commercial acts perpetrated by cultural parasites—highlights the point that even as cultural power and influence are defined as unidirectional and the remade films have supposedly been sanitized of anything smacking of the Other, a valuable cultural exchange nonetheless takes place. A close examination of what has been changed, removed, or retained makes visible the identity of two nations—both their sameness and their distinctiveness. Responsible cross-cultural remakes may represent a valuable cultural and historical practice capable of renegotiating the relation between the national identity of the self and the national identity of another, and between the Other and the self.

NOTES

1. We could extend this claim to include East Asian cinema in general.

2. Hollywood attempted Asian remake cycles in the past, the most obvious example being the Samurai films remade as westerns in the 1950s and 1960s.

WORKS CITED

Bazin, André. 1952. "Remade in USA." *Cahiers du cinema* 2, no. 11 (April): 54–59.

Box Office Mojo. BoxOfficeMojo.com.

Grindstaff, Laura. 2002. "Pretty Woman with a Gun: *La Femme Nikita* and the Textual Politics of 'The Remake.'" In *Dead Ringers: The Remake in Theory and Practice*, ed. Jennifer Forrest and Leonard R. Koos, 273–308. Albany: State University of New York Press.

Herbert, Daniel. 2009. "Trading Spaces: Transnational Dislocations in *Insomnia/Insomnia* and *Ju-On/The Grudge*." In *Fear, Cultural Anxiety, and Transformation: Horror, Science Fiction, and Fantasy Films Remade*, ed. Scott A. Lukas and John Marmysz, 143–164. Lanham, MD: Lexington.

Holm, Nicholas. 2011. "Ex(or)cising the Spirit of Japan: *Ringu*, *The Ring*, and the Persistence of Japan." *Journal of Popular Film and Television* 39, no. 4: 183–192.

Klein, Christina. 2010. "The *American* Horror Film? Global and Transnational U.S.-Asian Genres." In *American Horror Film: The Genre at the Turn of the Millennium*, ed. Steffen Hantke, 3–14. Jackson: University Press of Mississippi.

Leitch, Thomas. 2006. "How to Steal from Hitchcock." In *After Hitchcock: Influence, Imitation, Intertextuality*, ed. David Boyd and R. Barton Palmer, 251–270. Austin: University of Texas Press.

Nancy, Jean-Luc. 2000. *Being Singular Plural*. Translated by Robert D. Richardson and Anne E. O'Byrne. Stanford, CA: Stanford University Press.

Neale, Steve. 2000. *Genre and Hollywood*. London: Routledge.

Ozawa, Eimi. 2006. "Remaking Corporeality and Spatiality: U.S. Adaptations of Japanese Horror Films." *49th Parallel*, 1–7.

Park, Myoungsook. 2009. "Hollywood's Remake Practices under the Copyright Regime: French Films and Japanese Horror Films." In *Fear, Cultural Anxiety, and Transformation: Horror, Science Fiction, and Fantasy Films Remade*, ed. Scott A. Lukas and John Marmysz, 107–128. Lanham, MD: Lexington.

Phu, Thy. 2010. "Horrifying Adaptations: *Ringu*, *The Ring*, and the Cultural Contexts of Copying." *Journal of Adaptation in Film and Performance* 3, no. 1: 43–58.

Williams, Michael, and Christian Mørk. 1993. "Remake Stakes are up." *Daily Variety* 350, no. 12: 5+.

CHAPTER 8

ANIME'S DANGEROUS INNOCENTS:
MILLENNIAL ANXIETIES, GENDER CRISES,
AND THE *SHŌJO* BODY AS A WEAPON

ELIZABETH BIRMINGHAM

THE CRITIC CHARLES SOLOMON'S *New York Times* article "Mean Girls" (17 July 2005) attempts to understand the burgeoning trend of violent girl characters in Japanese animation, noting a new "focus on innocent girls who have undergone deadly transformations." Solomon was among the first critics to note the growing number of these deadly innocents in anime and to connect them as a film cycle "crafted to reflect a facet of the contemporary moment—a popular film, a social problem, a cultural trend" (Klein 2011, 16). Studios respond to such moments with films "based on the desires (and anxieties) of the movie going audience" (4).

Those films that in aggregate become a film cycle are often marked by the economic flexibilities of low budgets and quick development schedules, enabling lightning-fast response to consumer interest and desire (Klein 2011, 20). In some ways, anime production at the beginning of the twenty-first century was created during the perfect circumstances for developing media cycles: technological developments in computer animation, combined with the use of minimal original material and characters already popularized through *manga* (comics) or games (Steinberg 2012), allowed anime to be developed and produced increasingly quickly and cheaply (Condry 2013, 137–142; LaMarre 2009, 64–76). In addition, Japan faced a continuing economic crisis after the crash of the Japanese stock market (the Nikkei) in 1990 (Karan 2005, 317; Leheny 2006, 30–34). The number of companies producing and distributing anime grew because, as a medium, anime proved less expensive to produce than live action. Anime's low production costs helped keep the television industry afloat for nearly a decade after the onset of the economic downturn (Poitras 2000, 25–26). Not only was far more anime produced in this period than before, but that anime produced depicted cultural anxieties about girls and women in curious ways, reflecting and inspiring the changing roles of women in Japan, and expressing cultural fears about those changes (Napier 1998, 91).

This chapter traces the development of one such anime cycle in response to a complex Japanese cultural context that includes at least three important strands: a historical-cultural conflation of the female body with the national body; millennial anxieties brought on by Japan's troubled 1990s, a period of economic collapse, domestic terrorism, and national disaster; and shifting gender expectations and cultural hysteria about young women's behavior. This cultural context created the zeitgeist for a cycle of anime series that depict girls who have been fashioned into dangerous weapons, usually by corporate or shadow-government experimentation gone awry. Through surgical, chemical, biological, or genetic alteration, these girls become powerful weapons that must be controlled, defused, or destroyed.

Although there are many anime series about deadly girls, this paper will discuss six that aired for one season on Japanese prime-time television from 2002 through 2005: *Saikano: The Last Love Song on This Little Planet* (2002, Mitsuko Kase), *Full Metal Panic* (2002, Koichi Chigira), *Scrapped Princess* (2003, Soichi Masui), *Black Cat* (2005, Shin Itagaki), *Elemental Gelade* (2005, Shigeru Ueda), and *Speed Grapher* (2005, Kunihisa Sugishima). These series, though quite different in many ways, share two core features. First, young female characters are surgically or genetically manipulated to make them extremely dangerous. Second, and perhaps most central, is the stance of the programs toward these girls: they are to be disciplined, made less dangerous and more controllable, usually through gender discipline and heterosexual love.

During this same period, live-action television in Japan still regularly focused on the conflict between what Gabriella Lukács (2010, 165) calls "the shōjo (the young girl whose life centers on fun and consumer culture)" and the heroine, usually a traditional woman whose values are demonstrated through her skill at cooking or cleaning, or her willingness to be a stay-at-home mother. At the beginning of the twenty-first century, Japanese television told viewers that girls, whether they were destructive weapons or cute (*kawaii*) shopping fiends, needed to make a turn toward traditional values for both individual happiness and national stability.

Although Solomon suggests that these series "touched a nerve in young viewers who feel helpless in a dangerous world," I suggest an alternative reading. Rather than empowering young girls—who were not the intended audience—these conservative shows are about convincing Japanese viewers that girls *can* be controlled and contained; if the future is dangerous, it is not dangerous *for* young women, but because of them. These series foreground how pop-cultural products situate cultural unease in the bodies of girls occupying that space between childhood's innocence and the feared power of adult female sexuality.

Although the term *"shōjo,"* meaning "the not quite female female" (Prough 2011, 7), developed in the Meiji era (1868–1912), the term carried with it the connotation of sexual innocence. Because of its tense location between burgeoning sexuality and innocence, adolescence was a dangerous time for Japanese girls. With little pause, they moved quickly from childhood to married motherhood, because married motherhood was the state in which their value to society was best realized. In a culture in which the bodies of all subjects became associated with the imperial body, according to Noriko Horiguchi, the bodies of women, always already subject to cultural discipline and regulation, "were meaningful and useful only insofar as they enhanced the wealth and strength of the empire . . . when they were subjected, reproductive and productive bodies" (2011, 20). But in Japan, as in many other parts of the world, modernization and women's formal education led to the lengthening of the time between childhood and marriage (and reproduction), even as society continued to maintain rigid state and family control over the bodies of women (19).

As girls and unmarried women increasingly entered the workforce and purchased consumer goods, the term *"shōjo"* came to mean not only the girl herself, but also the products marketed to a powerful consumer base with expendable income (Toku 2007, 30). As the time between girlhood and married womanhood widened, *shōjo* was no longer synonymous with sexual innocence, either. Sharalyn Orbaugh notes that as the Japanese economy shifted from production in the 1960s to consumption, especially by the economically affluent, in the 1980s, *shōjo* "signified a state of passivity, consumerism, commodification, narcissism, consumption without production, moral and ethical emptiness" (2003, 204). *Shōjo* culture reshaped 1980s Japan through its focus on *kawaii* style and that style's values of childlikeness in looks, dress, behavior, speech, handwriting, and available consumer goods (Kinsella 1995, 224; Winge 2008, 47). This style, driven by girl culture and embraced by young women with newly achieved consumer power, "was a model of the Japanese nation" (Orbaugh 2003, 204), a nation that many cultural critics decried as "feminized and infantilized" through its association with girl culture (Prough 2011, 10). This rhetoric cemented the contemporary conflation of the girl's body with fate of the nation.

This consumption-oriented cultural turn was tolerated in the economic boom of the 1980s despite a vague, widespread unease about the youth whose lifestyles seemed in conflict with, and questioning of, the austerity of the previous generation, which had undertaken the hard work of nation rebuilding after World War II. By the 1990s, however, a range of anxieties, many financial, caused cultural concern to coalesce around the figure of young Japanese women, who would not, even at a time when men were out of work, just grow up and get married. Sharon Kinsella writes of these young women, "They were accused of deliberately vying with men for good jobs while simultaneously denying them marriage partners" (1995, 249), a "choice" culturally framed as self-involved and selfish. According to David Leheny, increased societal concern in the 1990s about the personal choices and public behavior of young women, who were marrying and having children later than ever before, became the "gendered symbol of a selfish generation that refuses its most basic responsibility of reproducing a nation" (2006, 40). Many conservative critics expressed frustration at young women's unwillingness to grow up and fulfill their social roles; the childish *kawaii* craze and "Lolita" style were read as material instantiations of this unwillingness.

Seemingly overlooked by these critics was that the social role of a married young woman was overwhelmingly lonely and "oppressive," since women often lived so far from the city center that they spent little time with their husbands and often found themselves parenting alone (Kinsella 1995, 244). In addition, the lives of educated married women often included low-wage part-time work undertaken to pay for the skyrocketing costs of children's education and long-term care for elderly parents, in-laws, and grandparents (Kelly and White 2006, 67). So although young women were denied high-paying, high-status work during the economic boom, and have not experienced material or social benefits from the ensuing cultural shifts, they nonetheless are repeatedly named as the contaminant whose influence is so powerful that it is reshaping the cultural landscape. The named fear is that the culture itself is becoming *shōjo*: feminized, commodified, and narcissistic. As the critic Naoto Horikiri writes, "The 'shōjo,' that new human species born of modern commodification, has today commodified everything and everyone" (quoted in Treat 1995, 282). Contemporary young women are a new species, capable of polluting an entire culture with their insatiable desires. It is not hard to see why Japanese media began to portray fictionalized young girls as dangerous, not-quite-human beings, genetically altered, different in substance from their parents.

As the new millennium approached, Japan's anxieties grew. Worries escalated about the nation's inability to recover from the economic recession and about the impact the related hardships would have on a society whose fortunes had been built on the tightly mortared imbrications of family, school, and work (Leheny 2006, 23; Prough 2011, 5–7). Japan encountered a set of disasters that shook the public's confidence in nation and society. After the Nikkei exchange hit an all-time high in 1989, it lost half its value over the next year, causing economic recession. By 1993, the real estate market had crashed, and soon afterward a set of bank failures led to instability in the national government; new governments were elected, were seated, and then resigned too quickly to respond effectively to the economic crises (Leheny 2006, 37–38). During this time of government ineffectiveness, two major crises shook the nation to its core. The devastating Hanshin earthquake in 1995 resulted in over 6,000 killed and $100 billion in property damage, its effects made worse by the government's disorganized, slow nonresponse. This horror was followed two months later by Shoko Asahara's Aum Shinrikyo chemical attack on the Japanese subway, which killed thirteen and injured (but could have killed) thousands (Murakami 2000, 224–246). The horror of homegrown terrorism, and the dawning understanding that the nation had no mechanism for responding effectively to or even understanding the hopelessness of the young cult members who attempted to murder thousands of their fellow Japanese, shook the nation as powerfully as the devastating earthquake (Murakami 2000, 3–8; Leheny 2006, 38–42). According to William Kelly and Merry White, these problems of the 1990s undermined confidence in the Japanese "family-nation," a tightly connected set of relationships between a protective state, the successful and enterprising Japanese business world, and a nation built around traditional nuclear families, wherein mothers educated the next generation of workers and mothers (2006, 63–65).

As the new century began, a good deal of national anxiety co-alesced around the figure of the "out-of-line girl" (Miller and Bard-sley 2005, 2), the schoolgirl who looked and acted in inappropri-ate ways. She read BDSM (bondage, discipline, sadism, masochism) *manga* (Allison 2000, 61–68; Jones 2005, 102–104); she bleached her hair and tanned her face like a "witch" (Kinsella 2005, 146–149); she sold her panties and up-skirt school uniform photos to men (Arbogli 2009) or engaged in schoolgirl prostitution, also referred to as "com-pensated dating"(McClellan 2011, 10–12; Leheny 2006, 71–81; Prough 2011, 116–121), so that she could consume ever-more designer goods (Bardsley and Hirakawa 2005, 112). Although these behaviors became linked in the cultural consciousness, the one that caused the great-est consternation was undoubtedly *enjo-kosai* (compensated dating). Jennifer Prough describes the media storm in August 1994 after the reporting of a study suggesting that as many as 27 percent of junior high girls "had experience of" phone-dating services: "Mountains of articles, news stories, PTA and government reports, as well as books, both academic and popular, accumulated quickly, all of them trying to figure out what was happening and how many girls were involved" (2011, 119). Prough points out that the anxiety was not just about pro-miscuous girls (similar stories in the United States focused on pro-miscuity), but about middle-class girls selling themselves to buy things, usually the Western designer goods that had been abundantly provided by parents before the financial crash (120). The scandal was not so much that these girls were taking part in illegal behavior, as that they were selling themselves for things that were not "needed," things that their austere and hardworking mothers had done without.

Although, according to Leheny, there was likely a disparity be-tween the prevalence of compensated dating and the media attention it received, the cultural perception remained that this was a serious and pervasive problem. Perhaps most notable about the preponder-ance of the media coverage is that it portrayed the girls involved as dangerous and predatory in their relationships with adult men. The Japanese media coverage of "girls gone wild" continued for more than five years, with an unwavering emphasis: "The spotlight [was] aimed squarely at the girls—why they would behave like this and what kind of society had produced them. Moral responsibility seemed to lie with these 'little sluts' and not with their adult boyfriends or custom-ers" (Leheny 2006, 17). The public concern was rarely for the girls' safety, but more often for their adult partners or, more interestingly, for the nation itself; "social conservatives worried about what a generation of amateur sex workers meant for the future of Japan" (73), particularly when these girls became wives and mothers.

Women in Japan traditionally had been considered the womb of the nation's imperial body (Horiguchi 2011, 23), entrusted with nurturing the next generation to life and greatness, but perhaps placing that trust in this "new species" of girl was a serious mistake. If appropriate motherhood holds the nation together, then surely a nation without appropriate mothers was doomed. These anxieties for the future nation coalesced in the bodies of its girls and gave rise to a cycle of anime series in which girls, if not properly contained, threatened to contaminate and destroy society.

DANGEROUS INNOCENTS: FROM MAGICAL GIRLS TO WEAPONIZED BIOTECHNOLOGY

The nineties saw anime depictions of magical, psychic, alien, cyborg, and vampire girls and girlfriends (Dinello 2005, 140–141; Drazen 2003, 123–124; LaMarre 2009, 209–251; Napier 2005, 195–197). Often, these were girls who used special powers to unquestioningly serve their boyfriends and fight evil. As the year 2000 neared, television series about "magical girls" grew in number and formed discreet cycles (Napier 1998, 91–109; Sweeney 2008, 170–172). Magical girls, such as the internationally popular Sailor Moon, in *Bishoujo Senshi Sailor Moon* (1992–1997, Junichi Sato), and Sakura, in *Cardcaptor Sakura* (1998–2000, Morio Asaka), inhabit true *shōjo* anime, shows written for preteen girls and featuring both a "female aesthetic" and an "eternal theme . . . love" (Toku 2007, 30). In these anime, girl heroes use newly discovered magical powers not for their own gain, but to fight evil and, of course, to find love.

Whereas the magical girls of the 1990s developed from the hopeful source *manga* of the 1980s economic boom, by the early 2000s, the source material for anime, whether *manga*, video games, or light novels, was darker and more anxious, a reflection of the times. This is not to say there were not dangerous girls in 1990s anime. Kanako Shiokawa's "Cute but Deadly" describes these early dangerous girls, such as Lum, from *Alien Girlfriend*, or Princess Kahm, from *Outlanders*; those girls were dangerous in the cause of good and were bombshells of cute, helping their adolescent, average, nerdy boyfriends (1999, 113–115). The 1990s girl characters shifted from *Sailor Moon*—average, even klutzy, silly girls with glamorous alter egos and hidden powers to change the world (Grigsby 1999, 192–193)—to something else. No longer quite human, they fought and killed not for love, but because, in the absence of parents, they had been designed or programmed for destructive power. These new millennial girls were dangerous because although they looked like real girls, they had been significantly altered. These girls were offered a choice between giving up whatever made them exceptional in order to live as average, normal girls and serve their human boyfriends, or else being hunted and killed.

Although Solomon suggested that the dangerous anime girls of the new millennium were a reflection of girls' anxieties, it may be more accurate to understand these girls as a reflection of broader cultural anxieties, even patriarchal anxieties. None of the series in this cycle were created for or marketed to girls. *The Scrapped Princess*, *Black Cat*, and *Elemental Gelade* are all regularly categorized as *shōnen* (boys') anime because the original *manga* were published in weekly magazines of boys' comics. Series such as *Saikano* and *Elfen Lied* (2004, Mamoru Kanbe), the latter of which Solomon reviewed in his article, were *seinen* anime—anime designed and marketed to men, usually in the eighteen-to-thirty-year-old demographic, and scheduled in a late-evening, adult time slot on television. In addition, *Full Metal Panic*, *Speed Grapher*, and the chronologically later *Code Geass* (2006–2007, Gorō Taniguchi) are also usually categorized as *seinen*. The anime in the cycle under discussion here were created for and marketed to teenage boys and men, and the dangerous girls they depict fall into three related categories: weaponized girls, contaminating girls, and genetically modified girls. In each case, the girls are a "new species" of human, usually a "man"-made species purposefully designed to fulfill a deadly purpose. Despite an earlier critical desire to frame the anime girls of the Sailor Moon variety as exemplars of girl power (Sweeney 2008; Napier 1998), the girls in this film cycle, although destructive, are not powerful. They themselves are not in control, but are weapons or tools for powerful men—corporations, religious cults, or shadow governments—to use as they wish. Many of these girls have adult male handlers whose work it is to control and contain their considerable power.

A weaponized girl is a cyborg or a hybrid, neither quite human nor wholly machine. In her essay "A Cyborg Manifesto," Donna Haraway envisions cyborgs as offering women the opportunity to "have less at stake in male autonomy" because they are "not of woman born"

FIGURE 8.1. *Saikano*'s Chise represents the *shōjo* as a dangerous weapon: a uniformed schoolgirl with weapons grafted to her body.

(1991, 177), because they are Other to humans. While Haraway's notion of the cyborg contains a hopeful notion of a posthuman synthesis, there is no such hope for the weaponized girls in this cycle, who exist mainly to extend male autonomy as weapon extensions of a man or of national interests. The weaponized girls in this film cycle, *Saikano*'s Chise or *Elemental Gelade*'s Ren, represent the two most common forms of weaponization depicted: the literal cyborg, a girl who has had weapons grafted to her, and the magical cyborg, who transforms into a weapon as the result of some magical or alien force. Both kinds of girl-weapons exist under the control of human men, and they know and feel their difference from humanity.

In *Saikano*, viewers meet Chise only in her boyfriend Shuji's memory, already an absence, existing only in flashback for the viewer, and through her "exchange" diary, a document she wrote with Shuji as they traded back and forth a notebook in which they described their daily lives to each other. Although viewers meet Chise as Shuji first

remembers her—a cute, clumsy, and exceptionally ordinary girl—
Shuji quickly discovers Chise's secret in a daylight wartime attack on
his town's mall. He follows a small bright weapon to a bombed-out
building and finds a dazed and injured Chise, with metal wings split-
ting her skin.

The story is "about" Chise's dying humanity. At one point, Shuji
notes how cold she is; at another, it is clear that her heart no longer
beats. Though depicted in scene after scene as a heartless killing machine, Chise continues to maintain that she loves Shuji, and he both
fears her power and seems to love her, convincing her that she must
be human, for only a human soul can love. She and Shuji try to escape together to live "as a married couple": Chise wants to have a
baby, but cannot. The weaponization of her body has made her sterile. The thirteen-episode series concludes with Chise destroying the
sterile body in which she is trapped, and the "light" of her soul—the
assurance of her humanity—appears to be contained and consumed
by Shuji's body as he ingests her. "I can only exist inside you now,"
her soul tells him. But she has already made the visible world a sterile wasteland where Shuji is the lone survivor.

The story is perhaps best read as one of containment of the girl's
power: Chise is initially infantilized. She is half Shuji's size and
looks to be eleven or twelve, though as she is surgically weaponized,
boys at school begin to notice her body changing, and remark upon
it. As a result, she begins to show an interest in her power—as both
a woman and a weapon. In the end, this woman-weapon is so powerfully dangerous—she has annihilated whole cities with nuclear
weapons—that she must destroy herself to save her human soul. The
Japanese concept of *gyokusai*, which translates as "shattering jade,"
refers to destroying a thing of great value before giving up honor. The
term has come to mean honorable suicide. For example, after the Battle of Saipan in 1944, as many as 1,000 women and children died by
throwing themselves off a cliff into the sea before they would allow
themselves to be taken prisoner by US forces. The women's deaths
came to represent (in that wartime moment) the noblest act a Japanese woman could make; through her death, she became "the nation's body" (Cook 2008, 349). Chise, through her suicide and the destruction of her sterile body, is redeemed and becomes whole by being
contained by and united with Shuji.

Similarly, *Elemental Gelade* is a boy's story about a girl; the narrator tells the viewer so in the first episode: "This is the story of Coud,

a young sky pirate, and the adventures he experiences in his pursuit of love and freedom." After stealing a coffin-like box in his work as a pirate, he discovers in it a sleeping girl, Ren, who wakes, sees him, and says, "I hate you. You smell just like a human. Therefore I hate you." Although others repeatedly claim that Ren is not human, but an Edel Raid, a creature whose purpose it is to "react" with a human "pleasure" as that human's weapon, Coud, alone among the series' characters, believes in Ren's humanity. After Ren is attacked, she "reacts" with Coud, becoming his weapon. The twenty-six-episode series ends with Coud and Ren journeying to an Eden-like garden designed to contain the Edel Raid girls. Ren questions the containment, which has been framed as being for her own protection: "We did not ask for protection. You isolated us because you thought we are dangerous." Although Ren is offered the chance to be an "infinitely powerful" goddess, and she is freed from her bond with Coud, she reacts with Coud to "give birth to something greater," and with a kiss she chooses life as a "normal" girl with a fifteen-year-old pirate for a boyfriend.

The Edel Raids, mainly depicted as childlike girls, are in slave-like relationships with their "pleasures," some of whom are wicked, and most of whom are controlling adult men who "react" (sometimes by force) with the Raids to fight in despicable ways and to keep them in relationships of servitude. Perhaps these not-quite-consensual relationships with dangerous and controlling adult men are meant to reflect unflatteringly on compensated dating. But perhaps more obviously, they depict what Rosalind Coward calls a kind of immature, "reactive" sexuality, one that reads "young girls as expressing a sexual need, even if the girl herself does not know it." This view of nascent sexual awakening "feeds off the idea of a fresh, spontaneous, but essentially *responsive* sexuality" (quoted in Clammer 1995, 212), in contrast to a more demanding adult sexuality. The "reaction" between a pleasure and his Raid is depicted as mirroring a sexual relationship, and not simply in the language of "pleasures" and "reactions." When Ren chooses Coud (to save his life), she sacrifices her opportunity for freedom and power; she is willing to settle into a productive union not as a powerful weapon, but as a helpmate, "giving birth to something greater." This selfless act echoes the call of conservative cultural critics for women to leave the workforce and marry, for the sake of their male partners and their nation.

I know of no US television series featuring teenage girls with weapons systems grafted to their bodies, as Chise does in Saikano, but there were a number of such series on Japanese television at this time. For example, the orphans of *Gunslinger Girl* (2003, Morio Asaka) have bodies fitted with cybernetic implants and are brainwashed to become assassins for the "Agency," a shadow organization of the Italian government; *Solty Rei* (2005–2006, Yoshimasa Hiraike) and other "resembles" have cybernetic bodies that often include weapons systems; and the protagonists in *Sky Girls* (2006, Yoshiaki Iwasaki) and *Strike Witches* (2007, Kunihisa Sugishima) employ strap-on devices to become weapons of war. Moreover there are numerous additional examples of girls who, like Ren in *Elemental Gelade*, magically fuse with or become weapons: Saber, in *Fate Stay Night* (2006, Yuji Yamaguchi) tells Shiro, the teen protagonist, that she is his "servant and weapon"; Tokiko, in *Buso Renkin* (2006–2007, Takao Kato), fuses with an "alchemic jewel" to become a living weapon.

Like these weaponized girls, contaminating girls occupy both real and imagined space. The teenagers who engaged in compensated dating became such a symbol of this pollution that a picture of schoolgirls in uniforms with short skirts and "loose socks" became "emblems of a larger anxiety in 1990s Japan over the collapse of public order" (Leheny 2006, 81). In the media, these girls represented not just a danger to their paying "boyfriends," but also to the structure of Japanese society as a whole. In many ways, these girls became like the "poison" women of the Meiji era (1868–1912), figures prominent in the literature and legal texts of early twentieth-century Japan, texts that "implicitly argued the need to control all women, whose behavior could not be anticipated, because of their physiological volatility" (Marran 2007, 173). Just as the previous century's millennial anxieties had become inscribed on the bodies of sexually transgressive women, or *dokufu* ("poison women"), and entered into the imaginary of literature as a type, transgressive schoolgirls entered the Japanese cultural imaginary as contaminating girls in anime. Similarly, the stories were not of individual transgressions and punishment, but implicitly about the need to control and contain all young women.

When *The Scrapped Princess*'s title character, Pacifica Casull, is born a twin in the royal family of Leinwan, a religious prophecy declares her "the poison that will destroy the world" if she is allowed to survive to her sixteenth birthday. She is promptly dropped off a cliff, but survives. The story focuses on her travels with her adoptive siblings, who use their considerable powers to protect her from the many religious zealots who would kill her to save the world from her contamination. In the end, it becomes clear that the prophecy is true: Pacifica, despite her appearance as a normal girl, is the "Providence Breaker" and her DNA encodes the power to destroy their world, a Matrix-like artifice of false religion and alien technology with the power to control all humans except Pacifica.

On her sixteenth birthday, she will begin passing that genetic ability to others; it will spread like a virus. Her biological twin stabs her in the back ten hours before her birthday, and she is given a choice: to live as the "god" of this artificial world, or to bring freedom (free will), with its attendant uncertainties, to humankind. Pacifica chooses freedom, not only for humans, but also for herself. "Having to live in a world where you just can't make your own decisions, that seems wrong to me," Pacifica says to her world's god, and her choice unseals their world. She returns with her adoptive siblings to their farm, and in the final scene is shown undertaking physical labor (aiding in the birth of a new foal), as a farm girl, and when she is asked whether she is happy, she says, "Maybe that's what really matters in the end, being able to look back over your life when you're on your deathbed and say to yourself, it wasn't half bad." She has given up what made her special, and accepted a simple but hard life of rural domesticity. Her domesticity is the antidote to the poison.

Similarly, in *Speed Grapher* another fifteen-year-old, Kagura, is the "goddess" at a fetish club, where her bodily fluids contain or combine with a virus that gives club members powers related to their fetishes. These adults pay huge amounts of money to share bodily fluids with the girl. Kagura looks much younger than fifteen, and it becomes clear that her handlers are giving her hormone-suppressing drugs in an effort to hold off menses, since she would become a less valuable commodity as a woman. There is much to unpack regarding the cultural anxieties evident in this plotline: passive schoolgirls in fetish clubs for adult men, the consistent use of the word "goddess" to describe these girls, and the opportunity to be worshipped but not to have real power. Both the suppression of Kagura's womanhood and the "virus" passed through the exchange of bodily fluids seem to question the *kawaii* desire of young women to appear and remain childlike. Christine Marran argues that the "poison women" in the Japanese cultural imagination were, like Kagura, "sexually desirous women created as 'unnatural' subjects—made unnatural through bizarre claims about their physiology and psyche" (2007, 175). Kagura

FIGURE 8.2. In *Speed Grapher*, the child Kagura carries a viral contaminant that Saiga has already ingested through a kiss.

saves the life of a much older journalist who sneaks into the club to photograph its activities, and is discovered. The series ends with the journalist (Saiga) saving Kagura, the world collapsing into financial ruin, and Saiga blinded and separated from Kagura. Five years later, she reunites with him, apparently to live with him and care for him, choosing, like her dangerous-girl sisters, domesticity over power.

A third kind of dangerous girl in this film cycle is the girl whose genetic code has been manipulated. In *Full Metal Panic*, Kaname Chidori, another fifteen-year-old, is a "Whispered," one of a group of girls who have had encoded in their DNA the ability to understand a much sought-after "black technology." Interestingly, while this is the central motivation of the series—many organizations fight to control Kaname—viewers never know much about her powers. She does use them to seemingly hack into the male lead's mecha (a gigantic fighting robot controlled from within by a human) at one point and save his life. Like the other dangerous girls, she is ruthlessly pursued by groups that want to use her power, and she is offered the opportunity to assume a high rank in one (the covert international mercenary force called Mithril). Like the other girls, she refuses, although unlike the other girls' powers, her own is not defused or contained as a result—she simply claims she does not wish to use it. The final, idyllic scene shows her fishing with the male lead and saying, "When

FIGURE 8.3. Eve in a moment of innocence with Sven in *Black Cat*.

I am with you, I feel that I can do anything." She claims she feels powerful despite having just refused real power in an international antiterror organization; she has gained contentment by stepping into a traditional role—as a girlfriend (to a teenage mercenary) in a pastoral environment.

In *Black Cat*, Eve appears to be quite young, eleven or twelve. She is a genetically engineered weapon by nature and nurture, designed to be a powerful soldier and raised not as a child, but as an emotionless killer. She meets Sven, a bounty hunter called a "sweeper," who treats her like a human child, buying her ice cream and reading to her, "saving" her from the many men and organizations that wish to own her. (Her original handler is a weapons dealer who clearly owns her and values her as a weapon.) She attempts to show her thanks to Sven by becoming his weapon, but their relationship is strangely complicated. Eve seems to express feelings for Sven when asked, at the end of the series, why she became a sweeper. She responds, "Because someone cherishes me." And though she doesn't answer when asked by a girl her age whether the very adult Sven is her boyfriend, she blushes. By the end of the anime, Eve wears a school uniform and looks like an ordinary schoolgirl; she is clearly no longer a weapon. In her last line, she states, "Being free is the most wonderful thing."

But she has chosen to give up her powers, those qualities that made her exceptional, in order to be a schoolgirl, whose body is among the most disciplined and regulated in her culture.

These series make it clear that these cute young girls are dangerous and not quite human, and need to be contained; even, perhaps especially, the heroes, who are also their love interests, work to contain them. In fact, the genetically modified girls are categorized as something nonhuman: Kaname is a "Whispered," and Eve refers to herself as a demon; her initial handler calls her "database of stolen secrets." These girls' classification as something not human means that they are available to be owned, traded, and handled. In each show, the central plot surrounds the organization able to own or control the girl, and in each series, it is only in renouncing their special abilities that the girls experience freedom. Once their power is contained, these girls have the "freedom" to be with a male partner, sometimes an inappropriately older one, in a traditional relationship.

Girls' bodies are highly regulated commodities in both traditional and modern cultures. In Japan, where the woman's body has historically been conflated with the "nation's womb," anxieties about girls' bodies and behaviors became a national media crisis in the 1990s. Unsurprisingly, this crisis affected prime-time television for men as girls were repeatedly depicted as a darling but dangerous species, one that needed to be domesticated and diffused, by men, for the good of the future nation.

WORKS CITED

Allison, Anne. 2000. *Permitted and Prohibited Desires: Mothers, Comics, and Censorship in Japan*. Berkeley: University of California Press.

Arbogli. 2009. "Where the Japanese Schoolgirl's Panties Come From." YouTube. June 29. http://www.youtube.com/watch?v=w4KsV4rVINE&NR=1&feature=endscreen.

Bardsley, Jan, and Hiroko Hirakawa. 2005. "Branded: Bad Girls Go Shopping." In Miller and Bardsley (2005), 110–125.

Clammer, John. 1995. "Consuming Bodies: Constructing and Representing the Female Body in Contemporary Japanese Print Media." In Skov and Moeran (1995), 197–219.

Condry, Ian. 2013. *The Soul of Anime: Collaborative Creativity and Japan's Media Success Story*. Durham, NC: Duke University Press.

Cook, Haruko Taya. 2008. "Women's Deaths as Weapons of War in Japan's 'Final Battle.'" In *Gendering Modern Japanese History*, ed. Barbara Molony and Kathleen Uno, 326–349. Cambridge, MA: Harvard University Press.

Dinello, Daniel. 2005. *Technophobia! Science Fiction Visions of Posthuman Technology*. Austin: University of Texas Press.

Drazen, Patrick. 2003. *Anime Explosion: The What, Why, and Wow of Japanese Animation*. Berkeley, CA: Stonebridge.

Grigsby, Mary. 1999. "The Social Production of Gender as Reflected in Two Japanese Culture Industry Products: *Sailormoon* and *Crayon Shin-chan*." In *Themes and Issues in Asian Cartooning: Cute, Cheap, Mad, and Sexy*, ed. John Lent, 183–210. Bowling Green, OH: Popular Press.

Haraway, Donna. 1991. "A Cyborg Manifesto: Science, Technology, and Socialist-Feminism in the Late Twentieth Century." In *Simians, Cyborgs, and Women: The Reinvention of Nature*, 149–181. New York: Routledge.

Horiguchi, Noriko J. 2011. *Women Adrift: The Literature of Japan's Imperial Body*. Minneapolis: University of Minnesota Press.

Jones, Gretchen I. 2005. "Bad Girls Like to Watch: Writing and Reading Ladies' Comics." In Miller and Bardsley (2005), 96–109.

Karan, Pradyumna. 2005. *Japan in the 21st Century: Environment, Economy, and Society*. Lexington: University Press of Kentucky.

Kelly, William, and Merry White. 2006. "Students, Slackers, Seniors, Singles, and Strangers: Transforming the Family Nation." In *Beyond Japan: The Dynamics of East Asian Regionalism*, ed. Peter Katzenstein and Takashi Shiraishi, 63–84. Ithaca, NY: Cornell University Press.

Kinsella, Sharon. 1995. "Cuties in Japan." In Skov and Moeran (1995), 220–254.

———. 2005. "Blackfaces, Witches, and Racism against Girls." In Miller and Bardsley (2005), 142–157.

Klein, Amanda Ann. 2011. *American Film Cycles: Reframing Genres, Screening Social Problems, and Defining Subcultures*. Austin: University of Texas Press.

LaMarre, Thomas. 2009. *The Anime Machine: A Media Theory of Animation*. Minneapolis: University of Minnesota Press.

Leheny, David. 2006. *Think Global, Fear Local: Sex, Violence, and Anxiety in Contemporary Japan*. Ithaca, NY: Cornell University Press.

Lukács, Gabriella. 2010. *Scripted Affects, Branded Selves: Television, Subjectivity, and Capitalism in 1990s Japan*. Durham, NC: Duke University Press.

Marran, Christine L. 2007. *Poison Woman: Figuring Female Transgression in Modern Japanese Culture*. Minneapolis: University of Minnesota Press.

McClellan, Gerry. 2011. "Schoolgirl Prostitution in Japan." PhD diss., University of Sheffield.

Miller, Laura, and Jan Bardsley, eds. 2005. *Bad Girls of Japan*. New York: Palgrave.

Murakami, Haruki. 2000. *Underground: The Tokyo Gas Attack and the Japanese Psyche*. Translated by Alfred Birnbaum and Philip Gabriel. New York: Vintage.

Napier, Susan. 1998. "Vampires, Psychic Girls, Flying Women, and Sailor Scouts: Four Faces of the Young Female in Japanese Popular Culture." In *The Worlds of Japanese Popular Culture*, ed. D. P. Martinez, 91–109. Cambridge: Cambridge University Press.

———. 2005. *Anime from "Akira" to "Howl's Moving Castle."* New York: Palgrave.

Orbaugh, Sharalyn. 2003. "Busty Battlin' Babes: The Evolution of the *Shōjo* in

1990s Visual Culture." In *Gender and Power in the Japanese Visual Field*, ed. Joshua S. Mostow, Norman Bryson, and Maribeth Graybill, 201–228. Honolulu: University of Hawai'i Press.

Poitras, Gilles. 2000. *Anime Essentials: Everything a Fan Needs to Know.* Berkeley, CA: Stonebridge.

Prough, Jennifer. 2011. *Straight from the Heart: Gender, Intimacy, and the Culture of Production in Shōjo Manga.* Honolulu: University of Hawai'i Press.

Shiokawa, Kanako. 1999. "Cute but Deadly: Women and Violence in Japanese Comics." In *Themes and Issues in Asian Cartooning: Cute, Cheap, Mad, and Sexy,* ed. John Lent, 93–125. Bowling Green, OH: Popular Press.

Skov, Lise, and Brian Moeran, eds. 1995. *Women, Media, and Consumption in Japan.* Honolulu: University of Hawai'i Press.

Solomon, Charles. 2005. "Mean Girls." *New York Times,* July 17.

Steinberg, Marc. 2012. *Anime's Media Mix: Franchising Toys and Characters in Japan.* Minneapolis: University of Minnesota Press.

Sweeney, Kathleen. 2008. "Supernatural Girls, Witches, Warriors, and Animé." In *Maiden USA: Girl Icons Come of Age,* 155–174. New York: Peter Lang.

Toku, Masami. 2007. "Shōjo Manga! Girls' Comics! A Mirror of Girls' Dreams." *Mechademia* 2:19–32.

Treat, John. 1995. "Yoshimoto Banana's *Kitchen,* or the Cultural Logic of Japanese Consumerism." In Skov and Moeran (1995), 274–298.

Winge, Theresa. 2008. "Undressing and Dressing the Loli: A Search for the Identity of the Japanese Lolita." *Mechademia* 3:47–63.

CHAPTER 9

IT'S ONLY A FILM, ISN'T IT?

POLICY PARANOIA THRILLERS

OF THE WAR ON TERROR

VINCENT M. GAINE

THE CONSPIRACY OR PARANOID THRILLER has been a Hollywood staple for decades. Since the attacks on the World Trade Center of September 11, 2001, there has emerged a specific cycle of paranoid thrillers that critique policies of the War on Terror.[1] This cycle of policy paranoia thrillers ran from 2004 to 2010, consisting of the following seven films: *The Manchurian Candidate* (2004, Jonathan Demme), *Syriana* (2005, Stephen Gaghan), *Rendition* (2007, Gavin Hood), *Shooter* (2007, Antoine Fuqua), *State of Play* (2009, Kevin Macdonald), *Green Zone* (2010, Paul Greengrass), and *Fair Game* (2010, Doug Liman), all of which offer distinct responses to the politics and policies of counterterrorism.[2] The policy paranoia thrillers share thematic, stylistic, and narrative tropes, including fragmentary and unreliable narratives, disrupted and unsettled styles, and plausible settings that encourage viewers to see the fictional diegetic world as relatable to their own. The cumulative effect of these tropes is to express both explicit and oblique criticisms of foreign and domestic US policy, and for viewers to see themselves as culpable and responsible for the paranoia of the War on Terror.

Ray Pratt's insightful study *Projecting Paranoia: Conspiratorial Visions in American Film* covers paranoid cinema from 1940s film noir to the millennial "demise of citizenship" films (2001, 250). Pratt's book was published before the 9/11 attacks; this study will take up discussions of paranoid films released during the War on Terror. Amanda Ann Klein explains the phenomenon of production cycles, linking them with particular historical contexts (2011, 57), which may be social problems, industrial development, or cultural trends and interests. The contemporary resonance of films is limited by changing social interests and concerns, and cycles are initiated by a film that is either critically or commercially successful, reflects current social interests, and contains elements that can be replicated (61). Such is the case with the policy paranoia thrillers, a term I use to indicate that these thrillers depict a mood of paranoia related to governmental policies enacted and followed during the War on Terror. Some of these films are directly associated with counterterrorism methods (*Rendition* and *State of Play*) or the invasion of Iraq (*Green Zone* and *Fair Game*). The association may also be indirect—the policies that provoke paranoia in *The Manchurian Candidate* (election campaign support), *Shooter* (human rights violations), and *Syriana* (oil) are not explicitly counterterrorist (although the War on Terror is mentioned), but the films nonetheless depict a mood of paranoia related to governmental policy enacted and followed during the War on Terror. "Policy" in this case does not necessarily mean codified legal statutes; indeed, the policies may be blatantly illegal, as seen in *Shooter* and *State of Play*. Instead "policy" refers to US governmental actions such as rendition, the privatization of national security, military action overseas, interference in foreign governments, and the manipulation of domestic election campaigns. The paranoia created by these policies is shared across the films and conveyed through narrative and stylistic devices.

Across paranoid thrillers from all periods, paranoia is created as the individual is oppressed by powerful and mysterious entities—examples include *The Manchurian Candidate* (1962, John Frankenheimer), *The Parallax View* (1974, Alan J. Pakula), *JFK* (1990, Oliver Stone), and *Enemy of the State* (1998, Tony Scott). Pratt defines this element as "visionary paranoia" (2001, 8), visual culture expressing powerlessness and loss of autonomy. Cycles of paranoid thrillers have appeared at particular historical moments, reflecting specific historical anxieties.[3] As the name suggests, the policy paranoia thrillers express specific anxieties over US policy in response to the threat of terrorism.

These films' skeptical treatment of overarching narratives makes them highly postmodern. The scholar of postmodernism Jean-Francois Lyotard argues: "Knowledge . . . is always indirect . . . composed of reported statements that are incorporated into the metanarrative of a subject that guarantees their legitimacy" (1984, 35). A metanarrative is a story into which other stories fit: a subject—such as the threat of terrorist attacks—and the statements about this subject, which are both legitimized by the existence of the metanarrative and serve to reinforce and perpetuate its discursive power. The greatest power of such a narrative is its claim to veracity and truth—a metanarrative has a "totalizing" effect (Booker 2007, xiv), allowing those who accept it the reassurance of knowledge. In the absence of such an overarching narrative, we are left with uncertainty and doubt. This chapter is an exercise in creating an overarching narrative: I argue that a group of films from different directors and studios are all related in an important way. My evidence is my own analyses of the films and their engagement with what I identify as social concerns from the time of their production and release, and I assemble this evidence for the legitimacy of appearing in this book so that I can dissceminate my argument to interested readers.

As Lyotard argues, however, what we think of as "knowledge" is really a composite of views, and the composition does not happen on its own. News media receive a plethora of stories, but only some are disseminated, and those in highly edited form. Government-issued official statements are based on reports and meetings, but the statements are distillations of these processes and are always issued to serve particular agendas. Statements and arguments that contradict the metanarrative supporting the media's or the government's goals may never be known, or can prompt severe repercussions.

The War on Terror is itself a metanarrative. First used by President George W. Bush in an address to Congress on 20 September 2001, the War on Terror unites the foreign and domestic counterterrorist operations of the United States and its allies (George W. Bush 2001). Reports about the likelihood of a terrorist attack, military strikes against training camps in the Middle East, the hunt for Osama bin Laden, and US opposition to Saddam Hussein's alleged programs for weapons of mass destruction (WMDs) were all grouped together under the heading "War on Terror." This political expediency led to many controversial policies, such as increased airline security, extensive background checks of civilians, and the invasions of Afghanistan and Iraq. David Sterritt argues that following 9/11, the popular media emphasized "aspects of the case that [were] readily turned into narrative [and] a fitfully fought, nebulously defined 'war against terrorism'" (2004, 63–64). This metanarrative was a major rhetorical tool of the Bush administration.

There have been attempts to frame the War on Terror historically. President Barack Obama announced on 23 May 2013 that the threat of terrorism had changed, and that America's future counterterrorism strategy would change as well (Bergen 2013). This statement has been interpreted as a declaration that the War on Terror is over (Shinkman 2013; Shapiro 2013), but for the purposes of my analysis, the significance of Obama's speech rests in a shift in political rhetoric away from Bush's totalizing metanarrative—the War on Terror is longer a guiding principle of policy. Obama has distanced himself from the metanarrative of a "war," a concerted, unifying campaign that every American is a part of. This view is not limited to government speeches; a poll found that a majority of respondents regarded the term "War on Terror" as a figure of speech rather than an actual military campaign (Blanton 2013). Possible reasons for this view are the withdrawal of troops from Iraq and the assassination of Osama bin Laden in 2011. Bin Laden's death in particular suggests that a campaign of retaliation for 9/11 is complete, since the mastermind behind the attacks was brought to a form of justice. While counterterrorism is ongoing, the rhetorical War on Terror can be viewed historically as US policy moves away from this metanarrative (Bergen 2013).

As a cycle, the policy paranoia thrillers constitute a critical voice against the War on Terror metanarrative, displaying postmodern "radical suspicion" (Booker 2007, xiv). This suspicion is expressed through narrative content, including oblique and overt critiques of antiterrorism policies, and style, since many of the films deny a totalizing metanarrative (Markert 2011, xviii). Stylistic tendencies such as rapid editing and unsteady cinematography, combined with complex and fragmented narratives, challenge a sense of unity and coherence in these films, indicating suspicion of governmental policy and disillusionment over American moral superiority (xx). Furthermore, the films invite viewers to see parallels between real-world events and what is presented on-screen, indicating that the diegetic world is not simply fictional but reflective, suggesting culpability and responsibility on the part of the viewers. This combination of content and style, which denies unity within a metanarrative and invites a sense of responsibility, is the visionary paranoia of these thrillers.

A key element in identifying the films of this cycle is setting, and they all share contemporary settings of the early twenty-first century. Science fiction films, therefore, including those with superheroes, are not part of the cycle;[4] nor are spy films, because much of their paranoia is common to that genre in all contexts.[5] The CIA does appear in five of the policy paranoia thrillers I cited, but none are solely concerned with espionage. In *Syriana*, a CIA agent (George

Clooney) undertakes missions in the Middle East that serve America's oil interests, encountering an energy analyst (Matt Damon) and a Washington lawyer (Christopher Plummer) who work with the oil industry as well. In *Rendition*, the CIA analyst Douglas Freeman (Jake Gyllenhaal) is no more central than Anwar (Omar Metwally) and Isabella Fields El-Ibrahimi (Reese Witherspoon), Senator Hawkins (Alan Arkin) and Alan Smith (Peter Sarsgaard), and Fatima (Zineb Oukach) and Khalid (Moa Khouas). *Green Zone* and *Fair Game*, which, I argue, close the cycle, also feature the CIA, and demonstrate acute paranoia, since even the very agencies of government are victims of policy.

Shooter and *State of Play* both involve protagonists that uncover conspiracies, as does the film that initiates this cycle, *The Manchurian Candidate*, in which Major Ben Marco (Denzel Washington) discovers that vice presidential candidate Congressman Raymond Shaw (Liev Schrieber) is the puppet of the investment group Manchurian Global, which, in collaboration with Shaw's mother, Senator Eleanor Shaw (Meryl Streep), created a story to make Raymond their candidate, described by Marco as a "sleeper in the White House." Marco's investigation exposes this conspiracy metanarrative, and the plot is thwarted. The film illustrates that paranoid films "simultaneously distance viewers from the reality of events, and increase uneasiness through parallels with real-life events" (Pratt 2001, 91). This simultaneous distancing and discomfiture is apparent in *The Manchurian Candidate*.

Released in the summer of 2004, as the United States headed toward a presidential election between President George W. Bush and Senator John Kerry, *The Manchurian Candidate* can be read as a protest against the Bush administration, in contrast with John Frankenheimer's original film, which expressed Cold War fears of Soviet infiltration. In the remake, the threat is domestic rather than foreign, indicative of concerns in the mid-2000s. George W. Bush had obtained a dubious election victory in 2000,[6] and to imagine Bush or Dick Cheney as the puppets of a multinational corporation was hardly a stretch, a point the film makes clear with reference to Manchurian Global being awarded a no-bid defense contract, much like the ones awarded to Cheney's former employer Halliburton (Teather 2004). Furthermore, the film was released at a time when discontent over the War on Terror was becoming more apparent (Markert 2011, xxiii). Alongside Demme's film, 2004 saw the release of several documentaries critical of the War on Terror, such as *Fahrenheit*

9/11 (2004, Michael Moore) and *WMD: Weapons of Mass Deception* (2004, Danny Schechter).[7] The commercial success of these non-fiction films (according to Box Office Mojo, *Fahrenheit 9/11* is the highest-grossing documentary of all time) and *The Manchurian Candidate* indicates that cinema audiences were willing to see critiques of contemporary US policy.

In Marco's exposure of the Manchurian conspiracy, which debunks the story of Shaw the war hero, the film implicitly criticizes the rhetoric of the War on Terror. Parallels to real-world ideological oppositions are established by the film's fictional presidential campaigns. Shaw espouses a romantic and militaristic position: "I believe democracy is not negotiable. I believe that freedom from fear in the world at large and here at home is not negotiable. I know how much Americans have to fear today. But I can tell you that I've been there. I've faced the enemy firsthand on the battlefront. I know what it is to be afraid. But I am living proof that we can win. We can prevail. We must secure tomorrow today."

Shaw's promise to "secure tomorrow today" (similar to ones made in a contemporary brochure; see Bush-Cheney Campaign 2004) is a vague statement that contrasts with the specificity of presidential candidate Senator Thomas Jordan (Jon Voight), who criticizes the War on Terror much as John Kerry did (Associated Press 2004). Jordan insists: "We need to look inward. We need to attend to our own house." He describes the War on Terror as entering "another year without an end in sight," and blames US foreign policy for the growth of terrorism. The War on Terror is very much part of the diegetic context, a milieu of fear that Manchurian Global seek to exploit. Allegorically, the film suggests extreme paranoia, a political climate in which multinational corporations have the ability to control governments. Through the contrast between Jordan and Shaw, *The Manchurian Candidate* presents the viewer with an ideological choice between critical responsibility and romanticized militarism. The film supports Jordan's position; Marco goes to the senator with his evidence, demonstrating that America must indeed attend to its own house in the face of such conspiracies. The threat to Shaw's election chances leads to Jordan and his daughter Jocelyne (Vera Farmiga) being murdered. Shaw drowns both Jordans, and Jocelyn's death includes a point-of-view (POV) shot from underwater, looking up at Shaw as he holds her under (fig. 9.1). This is the visionary paranoia of the film, oppression by powerful forces that will not tolerate disagreement

FIGURE 9.1. Jocelyn Jordan's distorted view of her murderer, Raymond Shaw.
Copyright 2004, Paramount.

with their metanarrative. Scarily, these are the forces determining
whom to vote for.

The debunking of a metanarrative is also key to *Green Zone* and
Fair Game, while *Rendition, Shooter,* and *State of Play* display skepticism toward film narrative itself. In *State of Play*, the reporters Cal
McAffrey (Russell Crowe) and Della Frye (Rachel McAdams) investigate a series of murders they believe to be linked to a private security
firm, Pointcorp. The visionary paranoia of *State of Play* is different
from that of *The Manchurian Candidate*. Kevin Macdonald uses an
unsteady visual style, as when, in the opening scene, handheld shots
capture a man bursting through a crowd and running desperately before Robert Bingham (Michael Berresse) shoots him and a passing cy-
clist. Sonia Baker (Maria Thayer) is filmed similarly as she walks to a
subway. She then appears in a POV shot before the screen goes black;
we subsequently learn she was murdered (also by Bingham). This unsteady aesthetic is used throughout the film, and the instability it creates is at odds with the assembly of a stable, totalizing metanarrative.
Indeed, the film denies an all-encompassing story. Cal and Della discover that Pointcorp is reaping enormous profits from the US government's privatization of homeland security, but that the murderer,
Bingham, is a mentally unstable former soldier in the employ of Cal's
friend Congressman Stephen Collins (Ben Affleck). The film suggests
a totalizing metanarrative in the form of a grand conspiracy, but then
debunks that possibility by uncovering several stories only coinci-
dentally linked with one another. The unsteady cinematography sug-

gests Bingham's warped perspective. *State of Play* is critical of US policy—the privatization of domestic defense is framed as illegal and responsible for turning self-sacrificing soldiers into mercenaries and madmen—but it is also critical of totalizing metanarratives through its denial of a unifying conspiracy.

Shooter is more cynical than *State of Play.* Staff Sergeant Bob Lee Swagger (Mark Wahlberg) is framed for an attempt on the life of the US president, and in seeking to clear his name, he uncovers a conspiracy. The problem, however, is not a few greedy individuals, including Senator Charles F. Meachum (Ned Beatty) and Colonel Isaac Johnson (Danny Glover)—the entire system of government is implicated in the corruption. Swagger learns that the government is always aware of events such as the torture at Abu Ghraib and the massacre of villagers. Attorney General Russert (Brian Markinson) accepts Swagger's evidence and exonerates him of the assassination charge, demonstrating that the truth can set you free. But the film debunks the metanarrative of the rule of law: Johnson cannot be prosecuted under US law for his actions committed overseas. Russert tells Swagger: "This is the world we live in. Justice does not always prevail. It's not the Wild West where you can clean up the streets with a gun, even though sometimes that's exactly what's needed."

But Swagger does clean up, killing Johnson and Meachum, who protests: "I am a United States senator!" to which Swagger responds, "Exactly," before shooting him. Following these executions, Swagger is captured in full shot, striding in slow motion away from Meachum's exploding house. This is a duplication of an earlier shot in which Swagger strides away in slow motion with the American flag flying behind him. The echo of the earlier scene suggests that reverence for government and the symbols of patriotism have been replaced by destruction and anarchy. The film's paranoia is so strong that everything must be destroyed, making *Shooter* the most nihilistic of the policy paranoia thrillers.

Like *State of Play*, *Syriana* displays cynicism toward metanarrative through its engagement with narrative, because its multistranded story defies easy comprehension. *Syriana* features a merger between the oil companies Connex and Killen, and the interconnections between this merger and the CIA, Washington law firms, the US Justice Department, Middle Eastern governments, and terrorist organizations. So confusing is *Syriana* that it is as though a documentary about the oil industry attempted but failed to construct a comprehen-

sible narrative because of the levels of complexity (Tait 2007, 126).
Green Zone and *Fair Game* are simpler and more defiant, focusing on
the exposure of Iraq's lack of WMDs. *Green Zone*'s protagonist, War-
rant Officer Roy Miller (Matt Damon), investigates the truth behind
WMDs, while in *Fair Game,* Valerie Plame (Naomi Watts) and Joe
Wilson (Sean Penn) are persecuted because they speak out against the
White House's metanarrative about Iraq's nuclear capability. While
Syriana and *Shooter* despair over the possibility of meaningful narra-
tive, *Green Zone, State of Play, The Manchurian Candidate,* and *Fair
Game,* whose characters seek to expose the corruption and injustice
that they discover, suggest that skepticism and pursuit of the truth
are worthwhile.

Rendition likewise involves an exposure of injustice, but also
points to the unreliability of metanarratives. Its plot revolves around
a terror suspect, Anwar El-Ibrahimi, who is abducted by the CIA and
brought to an unnamed African city, where he is tortured for information after a terrorist bomb explodes in the city square. The film
crosscuts between four plotlines, including the interrogation conducted by Abasi Fawal (Igal Naor), observed by the CIA analyst Douglas Freeman. Meanwhile, Anwar's wife, Isabelle, investigates his disappearance, seeking help from Alan Smith, aide to Senator Hawkins
in Washington. At the same time (apparently), young lovers Khalid and Fatima conduct a relationship in secret because Fatima's father, Fawal, would not approve of Khalid. As it turns out, the plotline involving Khalid and Fatima occurs before the other events, and
Khalid was the bomber whose attack prompts the investigation and
Anwar's abduction. The film's presentation of events suggests simultaneous action: no cues prompt the viewer to suspect that the events
are not occurring simultaneously until the final act. Fawal's investigation into the bombing reveals Khalid and Fatima's association,
and his race through the streets to Khalid's home is intercut with
Fatima learning that Khalid is a terrorist who has targeted her father. These scenes are also intercut with Freeman releasing Anwar,
having decided he is not associated with terrorists. The crosscutting
between Freeman and Fatima shows them both racing against time,
one to release Anwar, the other to stop a bombing. As Anwar is released, Fatima reaches the town square, creating the expectation of a
last-minute save. But as Fatima enters the square, the shot becomes
brighter, and footage from the beginning of the film is played again,
only this time we see that Khalid was the bomber, and that he killed
Fatima as well as himself.

This narrative twist demonstrates that totalizing metanarratives, like that of the War on Terror itself, are not to be trusted. The viewer's faith in the narrative is betrayed, and the twist "suggests that events are caught in an almost unstoppable loop, sustained from afar by the cynical interventions of America's spymasters" (Barker 2011, 107). Learning about the events that led to the bombing, such as Khalid's radicalization following his brother's torture by Fawal's security forces, makes no difference; the attack has already happened, and further torture does nothing but continue the loop as we see the attack happen again. The twist therefore supports Freeman's criticism: "If you torture one person you create ten, a hundred, a thousand new enemies." While *Rendition* concludes with Anwar returning to his family, the cycle of violence appears unstoppable, and there is no indication that rendition, let alone terrorism, has been stopped. There is a suggestion that Freeman might initiate a change by leaking the story to the press, but the film does not offer a solution; it would render the film simplistic if this one case suddenly brought about a major shift in US policy. Instead, it presents the uselessness of torture and the responsibility of good people to take action, the open ending suggesting that such action is for the film's viewers to take.

Rendition's style aids its critique, since it presents hideous events with stable, nondisrupted shots and editing. In an early scene, Freeman and his associate Dixon (David Fabrizio) are driven through the busy town square while on the other side Fawal takes tea at a café. Despite the chaos of the square, the camera remains stable rather than shaking, as it does in similar scenes in *Syriana* and *State of Play*, even when a waiter is shot and a bomb explodes without warning. A long take after the explosion captures the scene of devastation, the inflection of muted sound giving the viewer an approximation of the experience. Anwar's torture is presented in stable long and medium shots, the camera maintaining a distance and portraying a gross violation of human rights in the same way that it presents Isabelle playing football with her son. Rather than presenting the torture scenes from Anwar's perspective, which would manipulate the viewer into sharing his experience, the detached presentation of the torture scenes place the viewer in the position of Freeman so that, like him, we can judge the legitimacy of Anwar's treatment.

Other moments in the film create links between the torture of Anwar and the US administration. When Alan explains rendition to Isabelle, the Lincoln and Jefferson Memorials are visible in the background. Later, a scene transition consists of an upward tilt from the roof of Anwar's cell to Alan's desk, creating a link between governmental policy in Washington and the suffering it causes. Visual motifs that indicate criticism of US policy are abundant in *Shooter* too. The mise-en-scène of Swagger's home includes a copy of the *9/11 Commission Report* beside a laptop that displays the left-wing website ZMag.org. Later, Swagger consults a ballistics expert, Mr. Rate (Levon Helm), in Athens, Tennessee, the location of the 1946 Battle of Athens, in which armed citizens removed the corrupt local government and restored free elections (Seiber 1985). The presence of this locale in the film foreshadows Swagger's one-man crusade against corruption. When Swagger is apprehended and brought before the attorney general, his orange jumpsuit is reminiscent of those worn by terror suspects at Guantanamo. *The Manchurian Candidate* likewise features stylistic flourishes that express paranoia, besides the drowning POV shot mentioned above. When Marco talks to Rosie (Kimberly Elise), we see her from his point of view, which becomes hallucinatory as a bullet wound appears on her forehead (fig. 9.2). The strangeness of this shot is continued by a subsequent objective shot that features no injury, indicating that Marco's memories are literally bleeding into his vision. When Shaw is "activated" and becomes an obedient automaton, the shot becomes brighter to indicate his blissful acceptance of his handlers' instructions (fig. 9.3). These flourishes unsettle the viewer, expressing the films' paranoid and untrustworthy worlds.

The untrustworthy worlds of *The Manchurian Candidate*, *Rendition*, and *Shooter* are presented with a classical Hollywood aesthetic: continuity editing and a visual composition of (mostly) stable shots that clearly capture the events before the camera and present them at a distance, giving the viewer a sense of totality and an understanding that the action presented is to be taken at face value. As demonstrated by *Rendition*, this sense can be misleading, and the other policy paranoia films employ a more disconcerting style, as already discussed in relation to *State of Play*. This aesthetic, also used in *Syriana*, *Green Zone*, and *Fair Game*, suggests only a partial vision of events, consisting largely of handheld cinematography, rapid editing, jump cuts, and an uncomfortable proximity to the action. This approach gives the impression of authenticity and intimacy, as though viewers were filming the events themselves, and is similar to the YouTube aesthetic found in Iraq War films.[8] The intimate style provokes paranoia because it denies a sense of control and order. The opening scene of

FIGURE 9.2. Ben Marco's paranoia "bleeds" into his view of Rosie. Copyright 2004, Paramount.

FIGURE 9.3. Raymond Shaw's blissful acceptance of his handler's instructions. Copyright 2004, Paramount.

Syriana features men obscured by fog who jostle to get onto a bus, their struggle presented in discontinuous shots as though the camera could not gather all the footage. A lack of diegetic sound adds to the confusion, and shots of the men's faces staring at the camera heighten a sense of immediacy, as if the viewer were a participant in the unspecified event. The men's faces are noncomprehending, suggesting that they are no wiser than the viewer about what is going on.

This intimate style, used throughout *Syriana*, continually places the viewer uncomfortably close to the characters. The common thread of the film is oil, upon which Western capitalism depends. *Syriana* brings the viewer disconcertingly near the corrupt and murderous machinations that result from our need for oil, and just as our need is (literally) everyday, the interconnections and corruptions that facilitate the oil supply are presented as mundane: *Syriana* depicts Islamic radicalization and CIA assassinations with the same emphasis given to boardroom meetings and a family breakfast. A scene toward the end of the film demonstrates the film's visionary paranoia as the style draws the viewer close to both victims and perpetrators. Prince Nasir (Alexander Siddig) attempts a coup against his brother, who supports US oil interests, so the CIA kills the prince and his family with a guided missile. Bob Barnes (Clooney), disillusioned with the agency's operations, tries to warn Nasir, but is killed in the explosion. When Barnes drives across the desert to intercept Nasir, shots from inside his car place the viewer alongside him, sharing his desperate ride. When the missile strikes Nasir's car, we see it from Bryan Woodman's (Damon) position inside another car, the sudden explosion filling the frame without warning. These shots express the shock and anguish of the strike victims, but the viewer has a similar intimacy with the CIA command center, presented in close-ups that create the same sort of proximity. We share Barnes's desperation and Woodman's shock, but also the CIA's position of power and influence. We see congratulations being offered in the command center over a successful mission, and the scene is intercut with the presentation of an "Oil Man of the Year Award" in the United States. The editing here creates links between the sudden murder of a family (including children) and the success of the oil industry—the sound of applause from the award ceremony continues over images of the smoking crater of the missile strike. The intimate style and intercutting keep viewers uncomfortably close to the events, not allowing them the luxury of distance.

A similarly intimate style is present in *Fair Game* and, especially, *Green Zone*, which has the most mobile aesthetic of all the policy paranoia thrillers, its scenes captured with handheld cameras and the editing's rapid cuts creating a chaotic sense of disorientation and threat. This chaos expresses the doubt that comes from rejecting metanarratives, the uncertainty that results from not accepting the official version of Iraq's WMDs. *Green Zone*'s mise-en-scène includes news footage of President Bush declaring the war in Iraq over, emphasizing the metanarrative of the War on Terror. The policy paranoia thrillers offer an alternative, which is explicated in *Fair Game*, the only "true story" within this cycle.[9] A recurring feature across these films is news images, and *Fair Game*, to a greater extent than *Green*

Zone, features news footage of George W. Bush, Condoleezza Rice, and Donald Rumsfeld speaking about the evidence for Iraq's WMDs. This contradicts CIA meetings in which materials such as aluminum tubes are deemed to be unsuitable for uranium enrichment. As Valerie Plame's colleague Bill (Noah Emmerich) says: "Someone is cherry-picking raw data and serving it up to the press as fact." In both *Fair Game* and *Green Zone*, an Iraqi insider confirms that WMD programs were abandoned after the First Gulf War, giving the viewer an alternative to the totalizing metanarrative.

To speak of the alternative in *Fair Game* is dangerous, even for high-level government employees. The film depicts the CIA's dismissal of Valerie after her husband, Joe Wilson, publishes an article that refutes the government's claims regarding WMDs. The family is subsequently persecuted, not by the government, but by a manipulated population. Joe is described as a liar and a traitor in the pay of left-wing hate groups, their home receives threatening letters and telephone calls, and reporters harass them outside. Joe and Valerie are victims of the War on Terror because they speak against it. Yet the film suggests that sociopolitical engagement can be a possible solution as well as a source of trouble: Valerie testifies before Congress and tells her version of what took place. Her approach to the Capitol is intercut with Joe delivering a lecture to university students in which he speaks about the importance of political awareness and critical thinking rather than media parroting. The lecture develops the conceit of an earlier scene in which Joe writes his article. An extraordinary shot captures Joe from what is effectively the point of view of his computer monitor before he starts typing. The viewer sees Joe looking back at the screen, the cursor blinking expectantly. Joe tells the truth, much as Valerie does at the film's conclusion. When she does so, the camera is in the position of a news camera, so we see her much as the public would have when the real Plame testified. The inclusion of footage of Plame over the end credits supports the truth of the film's story. Joe types his words, Valerie testifies, but as with *Rendition*, *State of Play*, and *Green Zone*, the public exposure of this information is the end of the film, and viewers are left to make their own response.

Fair Game's message reiterates that of the other policy paranoia thrillers: the responsibility for an honest America, one not run by thugs and free from corruption, lies with the populace. These films valorize the truth, championing those who speak out as responsible members of a democracy that values freedom and self-determination rather than deceit and manipulation by the elite and powerful. The protagonists possess or acquire knowledge that they need to share, and we the viewers are the population, the blank screens, ready to receive this knowledge and respond to it. While the films in this cycle vary in their creation of visionary paranoia through setting, narrative, and style, none of them offer a conclusive *answer* to the grim events they portray. *Syriana* and *Shooter* are nihilistic, suggesting, respectively, no hope for change or an anarchic rebellion. Others indicate that getting the story out is the right thing to do, no matter what, as we see in *Rendition, Green Zone, State of Play,* and *Fair Game,* while a noble sacrifice saves the day in *The Manchurian Candidate.* If there is to be freedom from paranoia, these films suggest, it is the responsibility of the cinema-going public to achieve it. This message is suggested through stylistic techniques that prompt questioning on the part of the viewer, such as the unsteady cinematography of *Green Zone* and the crosscutting of *Syriana.* Viewer responsibility is suggested also through narratives that do not resolve the paranoia but end on ambiguous notes, leaving questions open for the viewer to consider and potentially respond to. The films therefore advocate responsible, engaged democracy: governments exist to serve their electorates, and should that covenant be broken, it is the duty of the electorate to oppose corruption and abuses of power. An important aspect of that duty is to remain wary and critical of totalizing metanarratives.

As noted above, the Obama administration shifted its rhetoric away from the totalizing metanarrative of the War on Terror, attempting to frame this controversial period of US policy as having occurred in the past. *Green Zone* and *Fair Game* perform a similar framing, viewing the War on Terror with hindsight, and in doing so, they close the cycle of policy paranoia thrillers. The assassination of Osama bin Laden arguably provided resolution to the grand metanarrative of the war against those who attacked on 9/11, and it has already been the subject of a major motion picture, *Zero Dark Thirty* (2012, Kathryn Bigelow). This closure does not deprive the policy paranoia cycle of its meaning, since the argument for resistance and active engagement in political culture remains pertinent in a democracy that values responsible government. While paranoia and conspiracy films are likely to continue, I suspect they will take a similarly historical view toward counterterrorism policy. The policy paranoia thrillers therefore constitute a significant historical cycle that engages critically with a body of governmental policy, demonstrating a critical engagement of film with public discourse. Through their narratives and style, the policy paranoia thrillers exhibit mistrust and even outright rejection of totalizing metanarratives present in public discourse and government rhetoric. All these films derive a significant part of their meaning from their parallels (and sometimes explicit references) to real-world events. While documentaries like *Fahrenheit 9/11* and *WMD: Weapons of Mass Deception* take explicitly polemical stances, these fiction films encourage the viewer to question totalizing metanarratives and engage critically with their political reality.

NOTES

1. As a rhetorical device, the War on Terror can be dated from 20 September 2001 to 23 May 2013, related to specific speeches by Presidents George W. Bush and Barack Obama.

2. For broader discussions of films that engage with these issues, see the studies by Barker (2011) and Markert (2011), and the collection edited by Dixon (2004).

3. Nick Redfern (2009a, 2009b) identifies three major cycles of paranoia films: anticommunist films released between 1947 and 1959, such as *The Red Danube* (1949, George Sidney) and *Assignment: Paris* (1952, Robert Parrish and Phil Karlson); state-institution films, which were prominent between 1965 and 1979, such as *The Parallax View* and *All the President's Men* (1976, Alan J. Pakula); and a less specific cycle running from 1990 to 2006 that includes nostalgia or history films like *JFK* and new-millennium films concerned with memory and reality such as *The Matrix* trilogy (1999–2003, the Wachowskis) and *The Bourne Identity* (2002, Doug Liman).

4. *Watchmen* (2009, Zack Snyder), *Children of Men* (2006, Alfonso Cuarón), and especially *V For Vendetta* (2005, James McTeigue) all display paranoia, but without direct reference to 9/11 or US policy.

5. There are certainly elements of paranoia in films such as *The Bourne Ultimatum* (2007, Paul Greengrass) and *Salt* (2010, Phillip Noyce), and *Body of Lies* (2008, Ridley Scott) is explicitly about antiterrorism espionage. The spy thriller warrants in-depth analysis in its own right, with particular attention paid to those set in the post-9/11 world.

6. The margin of victory necessitated a mandatory recount in Florida, and further recounts could have continued had the US Supreme Court not intervened and ruled that Florida's votes be awarded to Bush.

7. See Markert (2011, 57–148) for a discussion of these documentaries.

8. For discussion of this aesthetic, see Barker (2011, 34–44).

9. The film is based upon the books by Plame (2007) and Wilson (2004).

WORKS CITED

Associated Press. 2004. "Kerry Criticises Bush's Handling of War on Terror." 27 July.

Barker, Martin. 2011. *A "Toxic Genre": The Iraq War Films*. London: Pluto.

Bergen, Peter. 2013. "Bush's War on Terror is Over." CNN, 26 May.

Blanton, Dana. 2013. "Fox News Poll: Most Disagree with Obama, Say War on Terrorism Not Over." Fox News, 19 June.

Booker, M. Keith. 2007. *Postmodern Hollywood: What's New in Film and Why It Makes Us Feel So Strange*. Westport, CT: Praeger.

Bush, George W. 2001. Address to Congress, 20 September. Transcript available on the CNN website: http://edition.cnn.com/2001/US/09/20/gen.bush.transcript.

Bush-Cheney Campaign. 2004. *Agenda for America: A Plan for A Safer World and More Hopeful America* (brochure). Available at 4President.org, www.4president.org/brochures/2004/bushcheney2004brochure.htm.

Dixon, Wheeler Winston, ed. 2004. *Film and Television after 9/11*. Carbondale: Southern Illinois University Press.

Klein, Amanda Ann. 2011. *American Film Cycles: Reframing Genres, Screening Social Problems, and Defining Subcultures*. Austin: University of Texas Press.

Lyotard, Jean-Francois. 1984. *The Postmodern Condition: A Report on Knowledge*. Translated by Geoff Bennington and Brian Massumi. Theory and History of Literature 10. Minneapolis: University of Minnesota Press.

Markert, John. 2011. *Post-9/11 Cinema: Through a Lens Darkly*. Plymouth, UK: Scarecrow.

Newman, Maria. 2004. "Kerry Says Iraq War Raises Questions on Bush's Judgment." *New York Times*, 20 September.

Plame, Valerie. 2007. *Fair Game: My Life as a Spy, My Betrayal by the White House*. New York: Simon and Schuster.

Pratt, Ray. 2001. *Projecting Paranoia: Conspiratorial Visions in American Film*. Lawrence: University Press of Kansas.

Redfern, Nick. 2009a. "Emotion, Genre, and the Hollywood Paranoid Film." *Research into Film* (blog), 7 May. http://nickredfern.wordpress.com/category/paranoia.

———. 2009b. "Conspiracy and Disaster in Hollywood." *Research into Film* (blog), 22 October. http://nickredfern.wordpress.com/category/paranoia.

Seiber, Lones. 1985. "The Battle of Athens." *American Heritage Magazine*, February–March.

Shapiro, Ben. 2013. "Obama Declares War on Terror Over." Cybercast News Service, 30 May. http://cnsnews.com/blog/ben-shapiro/obama-declares-war-terror-over.

Shinkman, Paul D. 2013. "Obama: 'Global War on Terror' Is Over." *US News and World Report*, 23 May. www.usnews.com/news/articles/2013/05/23/obama-global-war-on-terror-is-over.

Sterritt, David. 2004. "Representing Atrocity: From the Holocaust to September 11." In *Film and Television after 9/11*, ed. Wheeler Winston Dixon, 63–78. Carbondale: Southern Illinois University Press.

Tait, R. Colin. 2007. "Assassin Nation: Theorizing the Conspiracy Film in the Early 21st Century." MA thesis, University of British Columbia.

Teather, David. 2004. "Halliburton Suspends Bill for Army Meals." *Guardian*, 18 February.

Wilson, Joseph C. 2004. *The Politics of Truth: Inside the Lies that Led to War and Betrayed My Wife's CIA Identity; A Diplomat's Memoir.* New York: Carroll and Graf.

CHAPTER 10

DOING DUMBLEDORE: ACTOR-CHARACTER BONDING AND ACCRETIONARY PERFORMANCE

MURRAY POMERANCE

Be not too tame neither, but let your own discretion be your tutor.
Suit the action to the word, the word to the action, with this special
observance, that you o'erstep not the modesty of nature.
HAMLET III.II.1896–1898

THE "ACTOR-CHARACTER FORMULA," as one might call it, is invoked by Erving Goffman in his landmark book *Frame Analysis* (1974) as a means of engaging some vital structural and dynamic issues in theatrical performance. Goffman's theorization, based to some degree on the mid-twentieth-century work of Walker Gibson (1950), and like many of the implications in Luigi Pirandello's *Shoot!* ([1915] 2005), is of paramount importance for understanding the ceremonial basis of performance. But it does not intend to penetrate all the strange aesthetic subtleties of screen characterization. And more crucially for my concerns here, it does not address itself to the structural nature of what I term the actor-character bond. While it is ultimately revealing to suggest how characters belong to one phenomenological world while the actors who play them belong to another, the degree of tenuousness between actors and the characters they play is worth its own investigation. This tenuousness is sometimes apparent in an actor's being so tightly identified with a role that outside the legal boundaries of the performance the role persists, the character seems to continue life, and the actor perforce disappears inside him: Harrison Ford as Indiana Jones; Sean Connery as James Bond; Daniel Radcliffe as Harry Potter. In a related way, it is also possible that in the public mind, the actor identification is not associated with a particular characterization (in no matter how many films: Ford as Jones gave four, Connery as Bond gave six) but with a role type. Thus, John Wayne as indomitable cowboy—essentially a category; Marilyn Monroe as sex kitten; Mickey Rooney as irrepressible teen; Marlene Dietrich as naughty underdog. And this strength of bonding may be notably visible in the work of character performers as well as stars: Robert Englund as Freddy Krueger; Edward Everett Horton (*Top Hat* [1935]; *Arsenic and Old Lace* [1944]) and Kathleen Freeman (*Singin' in the Rain* [1952]; *The Disorderly Orderly* [1964]) as bumbling sidekicks or dutiful retainers. In all these affiliation types, bonding strength leads viewers into a deeply embedded and continuing pattern of identification through which the actor and the character are rendered indistinguishable.

At the other end of the continuum is the exceptionally weak bond typically seen when an actor has almost no public presence and is virtually swallowed by the character being portrayed: while they may remember the character vividly long after he has disappeared from the stage or screen, viewers do not carry associations between him and the actor beneath, so that the actor disappears, in another kind of way, even as the performance begins.[1] With strong bonding, the actor is presumed to *be* or *be like* the character; but with weak bonding, the actor isn't there at all. In the latter cases, the performer works out of invisibility explicitly understood as such (whereas solidly bonded actors work out of an invisibility that is only implicit for audiences). Giovanni Ribisi, at least so far, has remained such an unbonded performer: Parker Selfridge in *Avatar* (2009), Tim Briggs in *Contraband* (2012), Alvin Karpis in *Public Enemies* (2009), Junior in *Cold Mountain* (2003), John in *Lost in Translation* (2003), are all impressive performances and were all recognizably produced by one actor—who can be identified as Ribisi, but typically is not. The actor is not bonded either to any one of these characters or to all of them as a cohesive category, and that is why he can change like a chameleon and play so many very different sorts of people in so many contradictory ways. Dustin Hoffman claimed to Charlie Rose in January 2013 that before he was persuaded to do *The Graduate* (1967), he had wanted urgently to be one of these chameleons, too; he saw himself as a character actor, not a star, and feared that the success of Mike Nichols's film would "ruin his career." Paul Fix (in *El Dorado*), Gale Sondergaard (in *The Letter*), Paul Ford (in *The Teahouse of the August Moon*), Thelma Ritter (in *Pickup on South Street*), Celia Imrie (in *Bridget Jones's Diary*), and Kevin Dunn (in *Transformers*) are all workers whose characters burgeon onscreen and yet whose personae as actors have not as yet caught on with the public.

While it is easy enough to recognize these fluctuations in actors' processes and successes, the theoretical construct of the actor-character bond permits us to investigate more deeply our own way of responding to actorly performance. Especially when a material repetition of character is called for—as in film sequels, prequels, series, or remakes—to some degree the viewer's characterological engagement, as it develops over time, comes from recognizing traces of earlier performances in later ones. For one interesting example, consider the screen incarnations of Abraham Lincoln. Walter Huston played Lincoln in 1930 for D. W. Griffith, efficiently and impressively, but apparently not definitively. Nine years later, Henry Fonda was able to supplant memories of that performance sufficiently to gain his own recognition, with his work in *Young Mr. Lincoln* for John Ford, and a year after that Raymond Massey re-created the character again, but less memorably, in *Abe Lincoln in Illinois* for John Cromwell. When, in 2012, Daniel Day-Lewis performed the role for Steven Spielberg (bringing to fulfillment a more-than-ten-year casting dream of the filmmaker's),[2] knowledgeable critics called out for comparisons with Fonda: Fonda, not Massey or Huston. "Like Spielberg's film, Ford's rendition of Lincoln uses one incident of considerable struggle to represent, and confirm, existing assumptions about the larger legacy of the man himself," writes Landon Palmer (2012), for instance. That is, John Ford's Lincoln, Fonda, was, by the end of 2012, still bonded to the role. No one drew comparisons with what has turned out to be the weakest bonding of all, that between the character Lincoln and the actor Royal Dano, who played him with uncanny sensitivity—but no staying power—for five episodes of the vastly popular television program *Omnibus* in 1952–1953. In all of these cases except Walter Huston's, we have character re-creations; and in and of themselves, these do not generally raise concern or alarm with audiences, it being a part of the ongoing conventions of theatricality as applied to cinema that new productions involving new casts bring new realizations of character. I want to explore some of the limits of such a formula.

ONE SIMPLE APPROACH WOULD BE to recognize that actor-character bonds require some explicit worker identification; otherwise, audiences are in no position to recognize and value the labor connection. Regarding worker identification in general, we can point, in the earliest James Bond films, to the fact that the Maurice Binder title sequence (which quickly became de rigueur in this franchise) typically involved a silhouette shot of Bond shooting his Walther PPK toward the camera through a pipe or other circular structure, this shot specifically color saturated and thereby wedded to the sparkling animation of the credits. For this title sequence, Bond was played by the virtually invisible Bob Simmons, not the well-publicized Sean Connery; visible only in high-contrast graphic composition, Simmons was not distinctly perceivable as a performer and was never explicitly credited on-screen. Let us argue that between Simmons and Bond there was no explicit actor-character bond: the links were entirely "backstage." The palpable link that eager audiences created between Bond and Connery—the Bond bond—was a paradigmatic example, motivated partly by the actor's attractive charm and looks, partly by the often unforgettably spicy dialogue that he was scripted to utter, and partly by the fact that the films emerged, and Connery-Bond was graphically repeated, with a rhythmic and predictable periodicity, from *Dr. No* in May 1963 ("Pure, escapist bunk, with Bond, an elegant fellow, played by Sean Connery" [Crowther 1963]), to *From Russia with Love* in May 1964 (a "snappy actor" in a "delightfully wild film" [Crowther 1964a]), to *Goldfinger* in December 1964 ("James Bond . . . whom Sean Connery so handsomely portrays" [Crowther 1964b]), to *Thunderball* in December 1965 ("still performed by Sean Connery" [Crowther 1965]), to *You Only Live Twice* in June 1967 ("Through it all, Mr. Connery paces with his elegant nonchalance" [Crowther 1967]), to *Diamonds Are Forever* in December 1971 ("Mr. Connery . . . must reconcile himself to the fact that nothing becomes him as much as the character he wanted to leave" [Canby 1971]).

Aside from the last of these, released at a time when Connery and Bond had become indistinguishable to the public, none of these films came out more than a year and a half after its predecessor—often they came out roughly a year apart, as though Bond were having a birthday. The timing is not sufficient in itself to account for the bonding, because with other performers in this role, a similar release pattern did not produce the same results. But it did contribute bonding strength to the arrangement achieved through Connery's personal style and the consistent scripting: aside from *You Only Live Twice*, Richard Maibaum was the principal writer on all these films. The utility of the actor-character bond for the performer lies in the progressive depletion of the work that must be undertaken to establish a character with consistency. For audiences, the bond is a direct source of pleasure through repetition.

My principal focus here is one particular (but hardly infrequent) phenomenon that requires a perturbation in the chemistry of the actor-character bond. I refer to instances in which repeat audiences (for instance, those watching cycle films) have a distinctly difficult time coming to terms with an actor-character formula because it seems to violate a bond that has been accepted, validated, and maintained as part of some prior (establishing) engagement. The actor-character formula is being invoked plainly enough, but in contradiction of an actor-character bond firmly in place and fully alive. In a typical case, a character that was originated (successfully) by one actor must, for some reason or another, be performed by another; and the audience is forced into a position where expectations of continuity will be unfulfilled. As a result, films or characterizations are often rejected outright by viewers; or else, to prevent this, filmmakers must undertake some process of negotiation whereby the change of personnel can be opened to validation.

The underlying issue is continuity itself and what viewers take it to be, an actor-character bond being merely one among many possible instantiations that could be adduced for scrutiny. What is it that audiences take to continue in performances themselves, and in performance repetitions? What are the limits of continuity? And what tacit understandings of the exterior structure of dramatization do audiences bring to their viewing—expectations about themselves in their viewing positions, and understandings of writers', producers', and creative artists' expectations of those expectations—that allow them to feel entitled to some essentially unchanged (or else carefully explained changes in) character representation? John Woo's *Face/Off* (1997) can be read as an essay on such carefully explained changes: John Travolta's character is suddenly stripped of his performing self and laid onto Nicolas Cage's, and vice versa, all this identity switching rationalized by a somewhat extraordinary narrative machine. In most filmic narratives, once audiences have been introduced to a character by means of an actorly gesture (which may be variably complex, and may or may not involve other aspects of filmmaking work [Pomerance 2013]), they believe that they can expect to see the actor's bond to the character persist unaltered at least for the duration of the work; what makes *Face/Off* successful is that both actors and both characters remain consistently interlinked on-screen, although it is admittedly a decoding nightmare to have to keep telling oneself that the one who looks like Travolta is actually Cage, and so on.

An important case study in bonding continuity within a single film was provided in Francis Ford Coppola's *Apocalypse Now* (1979) by Martin Sheen, whose suffering a heart attack during shooting and subsequent withdrawal from the action for a protracted recovery period posed the problem of whether his Captain Willard in the sequences shot when he returned would match, in energy and physical presentation, Willard in the sequences shot before he left. The problem of determining continuity in a performance is aggravated by the normal requirement for character development—that the beings we meet might grow, change, become: in *Stella Dallas* (1937), Barbara Stanwyck must become less and less coarse, and more and more sweetly sympathetic, as the film wears on, without ever ceasing to be Stella; in *Les Misérables* (1935, 1952, 1958, 1998, 2012), Fredric March, Michael Rennie, Jean Gabin, Liam Neeson, Hugh Jackman as Jean Valjean must lose Jean Valjean's servile debasement and gain an ethereal spiritual grace without ever really breaking away from him. Therefore, viewers do become used to seeing radical changes in characterological styling; it remains a critical performative issue whether the actor's continuing presence will in some way be made manifest. This riddle lies at the heart of Fredric March's work in *Dr. Jekyll and Mr. Hyde* (1931) and Spencer Tracy's in the remake ten years later; in Jerry Lewis's version of *The Nutty Professor* (1963), the actor openly plays upon this problem.

Considerably more difficult for audiences, and thus demanding of a much more elaborate directorial address, is the situation in which an actor-character bond is degraded entirely and swiftly in the middle of a production. Once a certain amount of film is in the can, it becomes ruinous to think of abandoning a project altogether. In significant part, this problem constitutes the plot of François Truffaut's *La nuit américaine* (1973). The situation befell Terry Gilliam when Heath Ledger died suddenly during production of *The Imaginarium of Dr. Parnassus* (2009), a film Gilliam was able to finish only by establishing a trio of additional actorly connections for the same character by using (as rumors had it at the time) Ledger's friends, one with Johnny Depp, a second with Jude Law, and a third with Colin Farrell; then by recutting the picture to conjoin these performances with Ledger's in order to make a newly coherent story in what the *New York Times* called a "weird and not entirely successful experiment" (Dargis 2009). As a piece of emergency reconstruction, this film is paradigmatic; but also, none of the actors was in a position to establish a bond with that single morphing character.

Actor-character bonds, which are manifestations of the audience's attachment to particular performances, styles, and stories, and which, as such, flow from audience readings at least as much as from actors' adjustments, register expectations of continuity and perceptions of actor-character fit. The bond is a method of addressing the audience's sense of entitlement when watching characterization and thus, finally, of gauging audience shock and disappointment, even disapproval, when the bond is dissipated or broken. *On Her Majesty's Secret Service*, also written by Richard Maibaum, was released in December 1969, that is, within the eighteen-month window after *You Only Live Twice*, but with the fledgling George Lazenby in the title role after Connery had declined it. The film was critically panned, especially by English critics, who found Lazenby a pale imitation of Connery. And the Americans, who had enthusiastically adopted Connery, wouldn't undo the bond either. "Mr. Lazenby, if not a spurious Bond, is merely a casual, pleasant, satisfactory replacement," wrote the *New York Times* (Weiler 1969). Thus, Connery's character bond was inviolable at the time. And producers did not undertake the kind of advance publicity campaign for Lazenby that would have been required to shift audience expectations in advance of so substantive a change. Lazenby managed to play James Bond without achieving, borrowing, or stealing a character bond: he was a bondless Bond.

THE PROBLEM OF ADDRESSING, mollifying, reorienting, and in general controlling audience expectations is central to the organization of the actor-character bond in industrial cinema, and thereby presents itself as an ongoing problem to casting agents, directors, costumers, publicity agents, marketers, and so on. When an actor becomes unavailable for continuing work in a part, as can happen for numerous reasons—Sean Connery declined a one-million-dollar offer to appear in *On Her Majesty's Secret Service*, and Robert Walker died during production of *My Son John* (1952)—reparative work becomes a dominating issue. The recasting of a popular role, that is, a role for which an actor-character bond has been assimilated by a vast ticket-buying audience, becomes a challenge of both aesthetic and economic proportions. The more widely recognized an actor is, the more likely that he will be overtly detectable in performance and tightly bonded to his character, and thus the more fraught with risk are the circumstances that ensue if he drops out. Further, wide recognition of an actor may flow from his on-screen personality or from popular appeal of the films in which he has appeared. The audience both expects and desires to see him again, and so the alteration visible when another actor takes his place must be accounted for. So it is that we find producers and marketers employing a variety of tactics to make clear to paying customers why, in effect, they are not getting the product they believe they have paid for; or else, why they might reasonably be willing to pay afresh for a product that advance publicity warns them has changed. Such publicity will likely address particular questions—what sort of change is in the works, why it is happening, and how reassuring a claim can be made that no substantial detraction will mar the overall narrative scheme—in some way, not only in the screen credits but also through press reports, industrially circulated gossip, or overt manipulations of screen action. Unless, of course, actor substitutions can be hidden.

On January 12, 1977, for example, twenty-five-year-old Mark Hamill was scheduled to film some work for George Lucas's *Star Wars*, involving some pickup shots with him as Luke Skywalker in his landspeeder. But Hamill was undergoing emergency facial surgery, having suffered a broken nose and cheek in a Malibu automobile accident the previous day. The double who was engaged in his place was indistinguishable from the original, and so he fully inherited Hamill's actor-character bond for those shots, in a sense becoming "Hamill playing Skywalker." Hamill's face henceforward had visible scars and a slightly warped mouth, all this sufficiently detectable to the lens that Lucas felt the need to produce a cover account for *The Empire Strikes Back* (1980), the actor's next appearance as Luke. On the planet Hoth, he is attacked and ravaged by a wampa, suffering "wounds to his face." Now, and at least for the Lucas films, what audiences would have seen on Mark's face was transplanted to Luke's.

In every operative moment of an actor-character alignment, the balance of the audience's attention is thrown to one or the other pole, in this case toward Skywalker or toward Hamill. Directors and producers hope that the gaze fixes on the character and perceives character stability. Yet viewers, no matter their ages, quickly learn that characters themselves do not work in movies, and that when sequels are made, the reprise of an adored performance can happen only if an actor agrees to go along. In Hamill's case, if there had been no account explaining the facial alteration of Luke Skywalker, audiences would have found themselves looking through Luke to the transmogrified Mark, whose face would have irrepressibly emerged from beneath the characterological mask. Once the account was provided, however, it could be only Skywalker whose face had changed, the Skywalker who inhabits the fictional world of *Star Wars*, where he had been, and now presumably remains, embedded. To concentrate on Mark instead of Luke is to withdraw to the production frame—to see editing, scoring, budgeting, contracting, and the exchange of money, rather than to experience the thrill of attacking the Empire. While viewers "see money" when they read about films in the newspapers or on Facebook, they prefer not to see money, unless it is diegetic money, when they are watching an actual film. In his rather discourteous *New York Times* review, Vincent Canby (1980) responded to the "new" Luke by literally erasing the actor beneath him: "Hamill may one day become a real movie star, an identifiable personality, but right now it's difficult to remember what he looks like."

An interesting, purely visual accounting technique was used by Tim Burton in managing the Harvey Dent character between his original appearance in *Batman* (1989) and his succeeding one in *Batman Forever* (1995).[3] Billy Dee Williams, who had established an actor-character bond as Dent in the first film, knew that in the ensuing script Dent would suffer facial alteration and emerge as Two-Face. He accepted the role, indeed, only on the proviso that in *Batman Forever* it would be his privilege to do schizoid Harvey. Warner Bros. made the decision, however, to use Tommy Lee Jones, who came across as a "walking make-up marvel" (Maslin 1995). The transformation of the actor-character bond in this case was optically dramatic, since Williams is African American and Jones is Caucasian. The scarred portion of Jones's Two-Face face was designed by Rick Baker and his team as a very dark purple field, congruent with scarring and circulatory problems but at the same time intermediate as a color between normal Caucasian and normal African American skin tones. The new Two-Face was a kind of hybrid of Jones and Williams in the most superficial way, enough so to make it possible for viewers to see continuity where in fact there was none.

Continuity accounting must often be unpremeditated. Having established a healthy career by playing the athletically gifted Superman again and again between 1978 and 1987, Christopher Reeve more or less retired to television for seven years and reemerged as the wheelchair-bound Dempsey Cain in *Above Suspicion* (1995). On May 27, 1995, only six days after this film opened, he was thrown from a horse in Virginia, received injuries to his spinal cord, and became a quadriplegic. Three years later, after considerable medical treatment, he appeared in a made-for-TV renovation of Hitchcock's *Rear Window*, now paralytically trapped in his wheelchair as both actor and character ("Reeve's 1995 horseback-riding accident has left him with a limited acting vocabulary" [Tucker 1998]). By this point, given that publicity about Reeve's accident had been worldwide and persistent, viewers knew they were watching a wheelchair-bound character being played by a wheelchair-bound actor (played, indeed, triumphantly); when they watched *Above Suspicion*, like audiences watching the original *Rear Window* (1954), they knew they were watching a wheelchair-bound character being played by a fully capacitated actor.

The Reeve *Rear Window* project represents a double transformation, then, since the Hitchcock *Rear Window* is as well known as the tale of Reeve's medical history. The actor-character bond of James Stewart–Jeff Jefferies modulates to that of Christopher Reeve–Jason Kemp, and at the same time the bond of Reeve–Dempsey Cain from *Above Suspicion* morphs into Reeve-Kemp. In the first, the heroism of the debilitated Reeve mounting the television performance obliterated audience concern with the story being retold afresh, since all eyes were riveted on Reeve's inconceivably deft moves and accomplished actorly work. In the second, *Above Suspicion* served fortuitously and handily to erase much of the memory of Reeve as Superman, which would otherwise have contaminated his performance in *Rear Window*; he was already established in a wheelchair, even though now, of course, it was for real. While this kind of reality can contaminate a performance, it can also be enriching: we see in actuality the kind of threat that can be presented to a man who cannot move on his legs, but the actuality is dramatically configured and scripted, although not dramatically bounded.

One particularly fascinating application of actor-character bonding applies to the line of progression from an actor's presence in character at the beginning of a film through his presence in the middle and then at the end. Unless a film embodies some relatively spectacular actor-character arrangement that involves a "logical" internal diegetic transformation—such as, for example, Todd Haynes's *I'm Not There* (2007), in which Bob Dylan is incarnated by Cate Blanchett, Ben Whishaw, Christian Bale, and others; *Casino Royale* (1967), in which Peter Sellers, Ursula Andress, David Niven, Daliah Lavi, and Woody Allen are all, seriatim, James Bond; or *Atonement*

(2007), in which Briony Tallis is played by Saorirse Ronan, Romola Garai, and Vanessa Redgrave—and that has been accounted for in advance publicity to address exactly this feature for its own sake, viewers' normative expectation is that an actor-character bond persists unchanged through a diegesis. Characters develop and go through an arc, but they inherently remain the same recognizable beings (and while watching, we do not expect to see evidence that the actor has gone through a transformational arc in doing the work of causing the character to go through a transformational arc). When the diegesis is extended outside the temporal limits of a single film into a series or sequelization, the same convention applies, unless a disclaiming account announces and explains the changes in some way. The character grows, perhaps even reflects back on the past (as we have observed it in earlier films of the series), and encounters progressively more interesting challenges, but is always our identifiable doll. In this sense, the actor-character bond, perduring and enlivening, is also the viewer's bond to both the screen role and the screen worker bringing it to life. Given that this expectation of work extension on the part of performers, essentially conservative, is a major source of revenue in episodic cinema, producers now more and more frequently establish contracts in advance that bind actors to their characters for a considerable period of time and even, as in the case of the *Lord of the Rings* films (2001, 2002, 2003), sequester the production so that more than one film can be shot at the same time.

NO MORE NOTABLE CASE STUDY of progressional troubles will be found than the Harry Potter series, in which all three principal roles were cast and contracted early on for the full run of eight films, and in which a huge number of supporting players (including Alan Rickman, Maggie Smith, Robby Coltrane, Jason Isaacs, David Thewlis, Julie Walters, Ralph Fiennes, and Tom Felton) made repeated appearances that strongly maintained their actor-character bonds. Although technically a supporting role, the character of Albus Dumbledore, headmaster of Hogwarts, is in many ways the pivotal crux of the Potter saga. He must strike viewers positively as a father substitute for the adorable and orphaned Harry; he must appeal as a wizard beyond wizardry, a consummate storehouse of knowledge in the context of necromantic competition and moral uncertainty; he must be morally authentic as the head of a school for hundreds of precocious children,

FIGURE 10.1. Richard Harris (left) and Michael Gambon as Albus Dumbledore.

patiently and wisely leading a staff of eccentric and brilliant weirdos; and finally, he must turn the fatal action that agonizes and then resolves the tale (in a way that, with respect to adoring fans of the series, I will forbear to recount).

The contract for this portrayal went to Richard Harris, seventy-one years old at the time, and a man who had made almost as many films, notably including *This Sporting Life* (1963), *The Red Desert* (1964), *Camelot* (1967), and *A Man Called Horse* (1970). In August 2002, only weeks before the US release of the second film in the series, *Harry Potter and the Chamber of Secrets*, Harris was diagnosed with Hodgkin's lymphoma, and two months later he was dead, a fact acknowledged forthwith in the *New York Times* review (Scott 2002). For the remaining films, the role went to Michael Gambon. Producers thus had to contend with a central and crucial actor-character disbanding, one that involved a fixation of the audiences' attention. Further, the vast popularity of the J. K. Rowling books had led to enormous international anticipation of the films—in which the trio of Daniel Radcliffe, Emma Watson, and Rupert Grint would watchably age toward and through their teen years on-screen. Audience expectations of continuity made it necessary for production to be mounted on long-term investments, and the extensive cost of the films, owing to elaborate effects and the massive salaries negotiated by the principal cast members (Radcliffe and Watson, at least, became enormously wealthy from the films), meant that profitability was possible only if a broad audience, solicited for the first two episodes, could be both maintained and expanded as the series wore on. Gambon had to become Dumbledore without disturbing the placid waters of belief and expectation in which viewers on five continents bathed.

All "continuing" performances, those given by actors reprising their own work in episodic presentations or by actors filling in work commenced by their peers, can be accretions or renovations. In producing accretions, performers assume that the work already done has been received, acknowledged, and established in the orientation of their viewers. They expect that viewers will look for ongoing work to develop out of what came before, to be taken a step further, perhaps to build a character arc but indubitably to extend a position that has been set and defined. As performers work in subsequent manifestations of a role, they layer the performances one upon the other, piling up an accretion of surfaces. In making *Dr. No*, for example, Connery had to work in an original way to establish his character as a charming, manipulative, witty, physically skillful, and knowledgeable man of the world. By the time he made *From Russia with Love*, all these character traits, painstakingly constructed for original audiences, could be taken as read. Bond already "was" all these, so Connery could proceed to show us new and different sides of the character. Accretion typically occurs in a single film as the character proceeds through the narrative; when the film project is a multiplicity of some kind, the style of accretion remains essentially the same, but its magnitude is increased, especially since months or years, not mere scenes, will elapse between points of viewer exposure to the actor in his performance.

In renovative work, by comparison, actors consider themselves at liberty to re-create a character according to their own lights, making only foundational nods to the labor undertaken by a predecessor. Consider Christian Bale as Batman. Under some circumstances, the same actor playing a role over and over in successive films may find the opportunity for renovation, too: Radcliffe as Potter was moving into his teens, after all, and could be understood by the time *Harry Potter and the Prisoner of Azkaban* was released to be a new kind of fellow, subject to hormones in a different kind of way. He could thus renovate the role of Harry, much as, considerably later, in *The Bourne Legacy* (2012), Jeremy Renner renovated the accretionary work that Matt Damon did in three Bourne films before. Renovation makes explicit the transfer of role performance from one actor (or one personality) to another, turns a light on the worker beneath the work. In renovation, the actor tacitly informs his audience that he is aware the role is not originating with his work, and that he knows, too, the difference between the way he is playing a part and the way an acknowledged other (perhaps even himself at a different stage of life) played it before. As Bond, Pierce Brosnan openly "knew"—through his characteristic gracility, derived largely, like much of his 1990s screen work, from his popular work on television in *Remington Steele* (1982–1987)—that he was not Connery, just as Daniel Craig openly "knows" that he is not Brosnan. The *Doctor Who* television series (1963–) makes plain acknowledgment of renovation as not only a recurring but also a dominant architectural feature of the narration, the central character being played by an actor on a limited contract who knows in advance that he is following a long chain of "Doctors" and will be followed by one in his turn. The pretexts of the narrative include "regeneration" or "renewal" proper to Time Lords such as he, which makes all the recasting logical and, thus, "invisible" diegetically.[4]

In *Harry Potter and the Prisoner of Azkaban*, what we see with Gambon in the Dumbledore role originated by Harris is renovative acting hiding beneath a kind of mock accretion. The character traits of Dumbledore are present in the scripting, all derived from Rowling's books, but their articulation belongs to the performer. Gambon pointedly holds back from making shifts in enunciation. Although he admitted that he did not read the books, he clearly did watch at least some of Harris's work in order to gain a sense of the amplitude of speech, the gait, the metricality of posture, the way the eyes were used in the gaze, and so on. As much as possible, he develops straightforward continuities in all these. As well, a number of technical elements work to assist him in accretionary performance. The elaborate makeup, involving a more than substantial white beard, helps mask facial differences. The costume, large, heavy, and ornate, takes some attention away from the eyes and mouth. Further, production personnel and press critics made no further public announcement of Richard Harris's death, nor did they circulate advance publicity in which his absence on-screen was noted. Peter Bradshaw (2004) noticed after the fact, in the *Manchester Guardian*, that "perhaps in honour of the late Richard Harris," Gambon did Dumbledore "with a faint Irish accent."[5] In short, he worked to match not only the quality and timbre of Harris's voice, but also Harris's accent in his vocalization, and all this work was undertaken under the impenetrable aegis of "honour" and in the face of death. Further, there are relatively few scenes with

Gambon in this film, and in them he is generally shot from a distance. *TimeOut London* unshockingly found his Dumbledore "less reassuring" than the one produced through "Richard Harris' paterfamilias" (W. H. n.d.).

But another, overriding feature of *Harry Potter and the Prisoner of Azkaban* worked to take the spotlight away from Gambon and the performance transformation he had to work, thus giving him the space in which to work effectively in renovation. Other intensified aspects of the film gained prominence in viewers' experience, distracting them from concentrating on the renovated Dumbledore. The directorial assignment had passed from the "literal-minded" Chris Columbus (Scott 2004), who made the first two films in the series, to the recently hailed Mexican filmmaker Alfonso Cuarón, the force behind the challenging and very popular *Y Tu Mamá También* (2001). This is the Cuarón hailed for his work in *Azkaban* by A. O. Scott (2004) of the *New York Times*: "Mr. Cuarón's wizard world, shot by the gifted New Zealand–born cinematographer Michael Seresin, is grainier and grimier than Mr. Columbus's. It feels at once more dangerous, more thoroughly enchanted and more real. While the two first episodes took place mostly in the corridors and classrooms of Hogwarts, this one lingers in the shadowy forests and damp meadows outside the school walls, a setting that emphasizes Mr. Cuarón's knack for evoking the haunting, sensual power of the natural world." Dumbledore being a somewhat ancient sort, he stays inside Hogwarts and does not accompany Harry and his friends into more "dangerous" territory "in the shadowy forests and damp meadows outside the school walls"; in short, the narrative handily escapes Dumbledore's limiting precinct. Further, it is encompassed by a vision that is "enchanted" and "real," that is, attention grabbing, and evokes a "haunting, sensual power" that captivates viewers' focus and centers it, much more essentially, upon Harry and crew.

Nor is Harry anything but a magnetic focus. In this outing, it is less his childlike cuteness and British-schoolboy cleanliness that glow in the center of the frame (Woodward 2012) than a "happy-go-lucky decency [that] is darkened by grief, rage and moral confusion" (Scott 2004): not tranquility but an engaging *sturm*. More than that, however, Radcliffe's own adolescence was tormenting his performative work, according to Scott: "Mr. Radcliffe, arriving at puberty, may also have reached the limit of his range as an actor. When called upon to convey deep or complex feelings, he has a tendency to blink and look nervous." Given the carefully crafted centrality of Harry's appearances, the faltering Radcliffe, if that he was, and indeed the exact tones and foibles of his faltering, took viewers' eyes away from Gambon's more polished performance.

And the eyes of younger viewers, at least—those most likely to look up to Dumbledore and be concerned about his metamorphosis— were distracted by a trump, Cuarón's fascination with, and consistent use of, computer-generated imagery, here manifested for the first time in the Potter series. The film not only was about magic, but also had become magical. What match could the old man be, optically and sensually, for a hippogriff in flight? Considerable theorization points to the historical relation between magical performance and spectatorial frenzy (Mannoni 2001; Solomon 2010). The more that the screen seemed itself to come alive, the less overwhelming (the less spectatorial) it could have seemed that Harris had died. Michael Gambon, wrote Scott (2004), "has gracefully stepped into Richard Harris's conical hat and flowing robes," the word "gracefully" standing in for "quietly."

One might suggest that in "becoming" Dumbledore, Gambon reflected nothing less than Shakespeare's "modesty of nature," not only because his work was so respectful, "honorific," and unobtrusive. Since the succession of generations after death, even generations of working performers after their colleagues have left us, is entirely and only natural, just as an actor's accretion of portraitures is a natural evocation of growth and repetitions through time, the renovation was natural in its essence. To say that it was modest is only to add that it worked without drawing attention to its method of working. (Nature does not beckon the scientist, after all, though he purports that it does; he takes advantage of nature.) To mirror life, as Shakespeare, our greatest teacher of performance, tells us acting must do, is always, in principle at least, to be lively by picking up where liveliness has fallen short.

In further films, and with increasing screen attention and ultimately narrative centrality, Gambon's Dumbledore could have been achieved through a more adventurous gamble on the actor's part. He was in a position to renovate his own performance through rich vocal play or in physically revealing close-ups, becoming Dumbledore-Gambon in a pungent, physical, emotive way that hadn't been struck in the relatively philosophical Dumbledore-Harris. But in *Harry Potter and the Prisoner of Azkaban*, with the sudden and inadvertent perturbation of a central narrative node, it was necessary for many reasons that he not work that way, not renovate so boldly. Accretionary acting both presumes and preserves a strong actor-character bond. Mock accretion gives the impression of doing so while not ultimately being confining. Thus, while he is present in *Azkaban*, Michael Gambon does not much appear to be, having come into possession of, with virtual invisibility, the actor-character bond initiated by Richard Harris. He "is" Harris, indeed, until we notice (if we do) that he is not. As an actor, through the magic of his work before the lens, he vanishes, and a deceased colleague, at least for a time in the light, is brought back to life.

NOTES

1. One night in February 1970, at the Vivian Beaumont Theater in New York—to give an interesting, purely theatrical case—the now-forgotten star of Tennessee Williams's *Camino Real* was unable to appear, and the audience instead met his understudy, Al Pacino. This performer was a consummate nobody, but his unflagging and seemingly unearthly energy lit up the space in such a flamboyant and perduring way that Kilroy, the character, was etched forever into memory. Pacino, however, disappeared. When he reappeared, in *The Panic in Needle Park* (1971) and then *The Godfather* (1972), he was, of course, quite another being. Between Pacino and Michael Corleone, a perduring "bond" was formed.

2. As he told Mark Kermode and Simon Mayo of BBC-5 on 1 February 2013.

3. In the intervening *Batman Returns* (1992, Tim Burton), Dent makes no appearance. I am grateful to Dominic Lennard for sharing this example with me.

4. William Hartnell, who originated the role of the Doctor, became ill and difficult to work with, the story goes. By the series' fourth season, a decision had been made to replace him (with Patrick Troughton); the producer Innes Lloyd thought "regular renewal" would make recasting especially smooth. The effect was originally created on-screen through a kind of optical dissolve from one face to the other.

5. Bradshaw's comment is slightly strange in view of the fact that Harris, Irish by birth and a onetime outspoken supporter of the IRA, hardly had a "faint" Irish accent, and that Gambon is also Irish.

WORKS CITED

Bradshaw, Peter. 2004. Review of *Harry Potter and the Prisoner of Azkaban*. *Manchester Guardian*, 28 May.

Canby, Vincent. 1971. "A Benign Bond." *New York Times*, 18 December.

———. 1980. "'The Empire Strikes Back' Strikes a Bland Note." *New York Times*, 15 June.

Crowther, Bosley. 1963. "'Dr. No,' Mystery Spoof." *New York Times*, 30 May.

———. 1964a. "James Bond Travels the Orient Express." *New York Times*, 9 April.

———. 1964b. "Goldfinger." *New York Times*, 22 December.

———. 1965. "007's Underwater Adventures." *New York Times*, 22 December.

———. 1967. "Sayonara, 007." *New York Times*, 14 June.

Dargis, Manohla. 2009. "A Traveling Show Comes to Town, but Its Guests Are the Ones on a Journey." *New York Times*, 25 December.

Gibson, Walker. 1950. "Authors, Speakers, Readers, and Mock Readers." *College English* 11 (February): 263–269.

Goffman, Erving. 1974. *Frame Analysis: An Essay on the Organization of Experience*. Cambridge, MA: Harvard University Press.

Mannoni, Laurent. 2001. *The Great Art of Light and Shadow: Archaeology of the Cinema*. Translated by Richard Crangle. Exeter, UK: University of Exeter Press.

Maslin, Janet. 1995. "New Challenges for the Caped Crusader." *New York Times*, 16 June.

Palmer, Landon. 2012. "Criterion Comparison: Steven Spielberg's *Lincoln* vs. John Ford's *Young Mr. Lincoln*." *Film School Rejects* (blog), http://filmschoolrejects.com/tag/young-mr-lincoln. 21 November.

Pirandello, Luigi. (1915) 2005. *Shoot! The Notebooks of Serafino Gubbio, Cinematograph Operator*. Translated by C. K. Scott Moncrieff. Chicago: University of Chicago Press.

Pomerance, Murray. 2013. *The Eyes Have It: Cinema and the Reality Effect*. New Brunswick NJ: Rutgers University Press.

Scott, A. O. 2002. "An Older, Wiser Wizard, but Still That Crafty Lad." *New York Times*, 15 November.

———. 2004. "An Adolescent Wizard Meets a Grown-Up Moviemaker." *New York Times*, 3 June.

Solomon, Matthew. 2010. *Disappearing Tricks: Silent Film, Houdini, and the New Magic of the Twentieth Century*. Urbana: University of Illinois Press.

Tucker, Ken. 1998. Review of *Rear Window*. *Entertainment Weekly*, 20 November.

Weiler, A. H. 1969. "New James Bond." *New York Times*, 19 December.

W. H. n.d. Review of *Harry Potter and the Prisoner of Azkaban*. *TimeOut London*, www.timeout.com/london/film/harry-potter-and-the-prisoner-of-azkaban.

Woodward, Steven. 2012. "J.K.'s Potion: Harry Potter, Orphans, and the British Boarding School." In *Popping Culture*, 7th ed., ed. Murray Pomerance and John Sakeris, 353–360. Boston: Pearson.

CHAPTER 11

A LAGOSIAN LADY GAGA: CROSS-CULTURAL IDENTIFICATION IN NOLLYWOOD'S ANTI-BIOPIC CYCLE

NOAH TSIKA

CHRISTENED "SHARON STONE" on account of her sheer sex appeal, a young Nigerian woman seduces and destroys a series of rich businessmen, in the process earning comparisons to the duplicitous female protagonists of such films as *Basic Instinct* (1992, Paul Verhoeven), *The Specialist* (1994, Luis Llosa), and *Casino* (1995, Martin Scorsese). Two promising Nigerian performers whose stage names are Beyoncé and Rihanna develop a rivalry that pivots around a superstar named Jay. A Nigerian village girl who dreams of a better life in Lagos believes herself to be Lady Gaga and eventually achieves fame by publicly lip-synching to pirated versions of Gaga's songs.

In all three examples—which come from the Nollywood films *Sharon Stone* (2003, Adim Williams), *Beyoncé & Rihanna* (2008, Afam Okereke), and *Lady Gaga* (2012, Ubong Bassey Nya)—the biographies of Western media stars are brought to bear upon narratives rooted in the sociopolitical realities of contemporary Nigeria. Not quite biopics, the films nevertheless present accurate information about their eponymous stars. Together, they form a striking Nollywood cycle—one whose unique, contrarian take on the biopic mixes respect for some of Hollywood's biggest names with resistance to Western cultural imperialism. While tracing a young, bullied Nigerian woman's empowering and remarkably evocative imitation of an American pop star, *Lady Gaga* uses unlicensed versions of that star's songs, striking a symbolic blow against Gaga's global dominance. *Beyoncé & Rihanna* pirates and redefines a variety of pop hits, and *Sharon Stone* takes considerable inspiration from Halle Berry's performance as "Sharon Stone" in *The Flintstones* (1994, Brian Levant), further suggesting that whiteness is not the exclusive provenance of a Stone-style seductiveness.

Developed partly as a means of making critical sense of Western media, Nollywood's anti-biopic cycle has demonstrated the industry's capacity to satisfy—as well as irritate—its local and global audiences through complex processes of appropriation, deconstruction, and defiance. In cinema history, there are a few plausible precedents for such films as *Sharon Stone, Beyoncé & Rihanna*, and *Lady Gaga*—even a definite pedigree, dating back to the late colonial period, when the director Jean Rouch cast Oumarou Ganda as "Edward G. Robinson" and Petit Touré as "Eddie Constantine" in his influential film *Moi, un noir* (1958), which toys with American and European star images while exploring working conditions in West Africa. A decade later, the Senegalese actress Safi Faye, touted as the "black Brigitte Bardot," appeared in Rouch's *Petit à petit* (1968), after which she began directing her own films, including *La passante* (1972), in which she interrogates the star images of Bardot, who famously promenades her way through *And God Created Woman* (1956, Roger Vadim), and Jeanne Moreau, who strides at the center of a legendary long take in *La Notte* (1961, Michelangelo Antonioni). In *La passante*, Faye explores what happens when a glamorous African woman does the walking, retracing some of the steps that Moreau takes as the adulterous *flâneuse* of Louis Malle's *Elevator to the Gallows* (1957).

Four years later, Rainer Werner Fassbinder made *Satan's Brew* (1976), in which a German writer (played by Kurt Raab) believes himself to be the reincarnation of the poet Stefan George, plagiarizing George's "The Albatross" and generally conducting himself according to George's biography. Functioning in an equally farcical mode, the Danish comedy *Mifune* (1999, Søren Kragh-Jacobsen) features a protagonist who attempts to "become" the Japanese star Toshiro Mifune, and Pablo Larraín's Chilean film *Tony Manero* (2008) explores John Travolta fandom, offering a hero who patterns himself on the protagonist of *Saturday Night Fever* (1977, John Badham). While these films powerfully anticipate Nollywood's anti-biopic cycle, they are separated historically, nationally, and culturally (not to mention formally, narratively, and thematically); they hardly constitute a coherent corpus, much less a shared set of industrial concerns. Only southern Nigeria's flourishing film industry has managed to consolidate such bizarre, semibiographical investigations of media stardom into a bona fide cycle, and it is to that cycle that I turn here.

FILM CYCLES IN NOLLYWOOD'S GLOBAL CIRCULATION

The study of Nollywood's film cycles has been hindered by the widespread popular stereotyping of the industry as a crassly commercial, self-cannibalizing media phenomenon.[1] Matters of cultural condescension aside, however, it is important to note that the film cycle is one of the most significant casualties of this critical marginalization (or simple misunderstanding) of a thriving industry—something that Nollywood has in common with Hollywood. In her book on American film cycles, Amanda Ann Klein notes that long-standing scholarly reluctance to the adequate investigation of film cycles stems from the fact that cycles "are so transparently associated with commercialism and artlessness" (2010, 6)—associations that continue to cling to Nollywood, as evidenced in a recent *Time* magazine piece that describes the industry thus: "The teeming Nigerian cinema grinds out some 2,500 movies a year, mostly direct-to-DVD quickies mixing melodrama, music, and an evangelical Christian spin" (Corliss 2013). Such comments are remarkably reductive—not to mention mired in the kind of colonialist language that situates Africa and Africans in relation to nature ("teeming" suggesting the heedless fecundity associated with wildlife). Far savvier than *Time* is willing to concede, Nollywood producers have deliberately and consistently used cycles in general—and the anti-biopic cycle in particular—for promotional events both locally and throughout the African diaspora.

In the spring of 2007, the Filmmakers Association of Nigeria (FAN), a Nollywood advocacy and antipiracy group based in New York City, arranged with Sanga Entertainment, a licensed, Bronx-based Nollywood DVD retailer, to screen a four-part entry in the so-called *Beyoncé* series at the National Black Theater in Harlem and at the St. Fortunata School in Brooklyn. While these screenings were especially well attended, spectators at both venues represented an infinitesimal fraction of Nollywood's vast diasporic audience, who at the time had to rely, for the most part, on licensed DVD retailers such as Sanga as well as on vendors selling pirated VHS cassettes and DVDs at media markets and beauty shops in New York, Washington, Atlanta, Houston, Chicago, and London. With a household name like "Beyoncé" providing a globally recognizable point of entry, it is no wonder that Nollywood filmmakers have turned to the biopic genre, but it is a testament to their artistry and ingenuity that they have managed to make Nigerian sense of it—to distort it into something

FIGURE 11.1. Rhyme (Omotola Jalade-Ekeinde) "becomes" Rihanna by singing along to a recording of "Unfaithful" in *Beyoncé & Rihanna*.

as unexpected and compelling as the anti-biopic. Frank Rajah Arase's *The Return of Beyoncé* (2007)—the follow-up to his smash 2006 hit *Beyoncé: The President's Daughter*—may not be "about" Beyoncé Knowles per se, but it does participate in Nollywood's important, attention-grabbing project of recontextualizing Western star images.

For all practical purposes, Nollywood's commitment to the anti-biopic began in late 2002 with the production of the first entry in Adim Williams's *Sharon Stone* series, and it shows signs of having ended with Ubong Bassey Nya's poorly received *Lady Gaga*—a film that generated an unprecedentedly high number of negative responses on various websites, especially iROKOtv.com, one of the Internet's licensed sources for streaming Nollywood films. In the *Beyoncé* series, the Ghanaian-born Nollywood star Nadia Buari plays two roles: a rich, spoiled, extremely media-literate young woman named Beyoncé (in *Beyoncé: The President's Daughter* and *The Return of Beyoncé*), and a woman named Bernice who openly fashions herself according to the contours of Beyoncé's star image, seeing herself as the source of such songs as "Irreplaceable" and "Déjà Vu" (in *Beyoncé & Rihanna* and *The Return of Beyoncé & Rihanna*). Like *Lady Gaga*, which uses no fewer than nine of Gaga's songs for its largely unlicensed soundscape, *Beyoncé & Rihanna*, which was produced in late 2008 (shortly after Beyoncé's album *I Am . . . Sasha Fierce* was released in the United States), opens with a bootlegged version of "Irreplaceable," suggesting the complex coexistence of admiration (for a Western superstar) and resistance (to the licit acquisition of that superstar's hegemonic products) that I take to be characteristic of Nollywood's anti-biopic cycle.[2]

Because this cycle is so alert to the globalizing force of Western media while itself enjoying wide regional and diasporic circulation, it is necessary to clarify some of the central aspects of Nollywood's relationship to local and international modes of production. Scholars of Nollywood have long stressed the industry's Nigerian origins. Mahir Saul and Ralph A. Austen note that while the term "Nollywood" "applies most accurately only to films from southern Nigeria," there are "disputes about whether it should be allowed to cover productions in various languages" (2010, 2). These disputes have led many to question the extent to which Nollywood can be considered a national cinema, especially given the remarkable ethnolinguistic diversity of Nigeria. For Moradewun Adejunmobi (2007), Nollywood represents not a national cinema per se, but, instead, "a minor transnational practice," in that it takes inspiration from a range of West African cultures and contexts, creating a mélange of textual methods.

Precipitated by the spectacular success of the star-inspired (and also star-making) *Sharon Stone* series—in which a woman of color (like Halle Berry in *The Flintstones*) bears the name "Sharon Stone," reenacts more than a few moments from Stone's films, but refrains from crediting or even mentioning Stone the white actress—Nollywood's cycle of anti-biopics adopts a range of Western pop stars as sources of narrative and thematic inspiration, yet avoids standard biographical approaches. But for every warmly embraced film in which a black African (such as Nadia Buari) plays a black American (such as Beyoncé), there is at least one anti-biopic that generates an equally profitable controversy, primarily by structuring multiple similarities between a black performer (such as Oge Okoye) and a white American pop star (such as Lady Gaga), but also by participating in a broad process of cross-cultural imitation—what Frantz Fanon ([1961] 2004) famously referred to as a false universalism, the "pretense" that Western experiences are everywhere applicable. For Fanon ([1952] 2008), the colonized mind remains a mimicking one, enmeshed in neurotic feelings of cultural inferiority and eager to conform to white ideals.

In the Nollywood context, even the most bizarre appropriations of Western star images—those that rely upon a resistant, symbolically

FIGURE 11.2. Sharon Stone (Genevieve Nnaji) schemes in *Sharon Stone*.

charged piracy as well as upon a refusal of the traditional biopic's celebratory prescriptions—may also seem offensively, though implicitly,
pro-West. Nollywood's anti-biopic cycle has frequently found itself at
the center of concerns about what it "does" to Nigeria—from within
as well as from without. Occasionally, Nigerian spectators will aim
their complaints at those responsible for the transnational reach of
the most irreverent Nollywood films—the stars, directors, producers,
and bootleggers who ensure that these films are seen outside Nigeria. Some Nollywood fans, confronted with the strangeness of a *Sharon Stone* or a *Lady Gaga*, worry that the industry's global image will
remain associated with sheer corruption, in keeping with the West's
stereotyped rendering of Nigeria itself, which sees the country as a
"natural" source of Internet scams—a fount of fraudulence. Still others worry that anti-biopics reflect a meaningless adoption of Western star personae and that, as a result, they contribute to the notion
that Nollywood represents a preconscious or prerational media phenomenon, one whose participants are unable to provide coherence of
any kind.

I hope to redress some of these reactionary assumptions by seriously examining Nollywood's anti-biopic cycle, confirming that
many of the prerequisites for the emergence of a Hollywood-style
film cycle—and many of the determinants of its survival—are present in African popular cultures, particularly in Nollywood. While it

is not my intention to extrapolate from this observation a misplaced equivalence between Hollywood and Nollywood, I do wish to explore some of the common global conditions for film cycles while clarifying several aspects of Nollywood's specificity. In addition to providing an extended analysis of a definable film cycle, this chapter indicates the importance of a West African regional framework for understanding that cycle's success.

FROM VIDEO BOOTHS TO BROADBAND: DISTRIBUTING A NOLLYWOOD FILM CYCLE

While there has not yet been a corporatized Hollywood equivalent in sub-Saharan Africa, routinely churning out feature films with high production values and earning impressive returns on their theatrical release, the region has a storied, critically successful history of auteur cinema. The celebrated Senegalese director Ousmane Sembène, for instance, made several classic films in West Africa, although, controversially, those films upon completion were more apt to be screened at European festivals than in commercial theaters in Dakar or Thiès. One cultural obstacle that Nollywood has effectively surmounted is the European-influenced, art-conscious predilection for costly celluloid films. A local film industry that emerged without state support of any kind and without European patrons, Nollywood has long focused on informal distribution and private, domestic exhibition, and it is precisely this relaxed, idiomatic framework that has enabled the industry to embrace cycles as expressions of diverse audience tastes. John C. McCall (2012) has stressed Nollywood's relationship to informal economies, which have imposed severe limitations on the industry while, at the same time, producing untold victories. One such victory, McCall makes clear, is Nollywood's capacity to quickly reach a range of regional audiences through idiosyncratic circuits of distribution, which all but guarantees that the industry will remain relevant to local experiences and will thereby satisfy local tastes.

Consider, for instance, the speed with which Nollywood produced and distributed films about Boko Haram's 2014 kidnapping of nearly three hundred schoolgirls in Chibok: at the height of the global "Bring Back Our Girls" campaign, the industry released two films on the subject, usurping and extending some of the functions of newspaper and television reporting. Several months later, amid the most devastating Ebola outbreak in recorded history, it generated several

Ebola-themed dramas, feeding the perceived popular need to engage with current events. Simply put, Nollywood fans needn't wait for the completion of complicated and long-lasting postproduction protocols, or for films to follow circumscribed exhibition schedules at major multiplexes. McCall, like many Nollywood scholars, decries "the economic apartheid that has isolated Nollywood from the world's formal markets," but concedes that informality lends itself to local relevance, precisely because Nollywood's "fundamentally indigenous foundations make it strongly independent of foreign control or monopoly" (2012, 21). It is clear, then, that Nollywood's resolute independence and idiosyncratic informal infrastructure make it—like mid-twentieth-century American B-movie studios and Hollywood's contemporary direct-to-DVD market—especially amenable to what Klein has called the film cycle's profound "ability to connect with audiences" (2011, 97).

Nollywood's speed, economy, and capacity to quickly reach local audiences are all abetted by additional factors, especially Nigeria's popular press. Numerous Nigerian publications routinely report on the industry, occasionally addressing filmmakers directly, as in the print periodical (and associated website) *Nollywood Forever*, which asks stars and directors to respond to the needs and desires of Nollywood "enthusiasts." Building on this approach, the Nigerian blogosphere abounds with up-to-the-minute assessments of Nollywood casting decisions, generating considerable debate among the industry's Nigerian fans, who dominate web pages dedicated to user comments, and also among its producers, who have been known to respond directly to those comments, often via Twitter. Numerous Nigerian-authored blogs—such as *Linda Ikeji's Blog* and Taiye Suleiman's *Nollywood Photoblog*—archive conversations with some of Nollywood's biggest names, providing not merely publicist-approved sound bites but also evidence that generative ideas have been exchanged and that consumers are as vocal and as viable as producers in shaping an entire popular film industry.[3]

In Nollywood's rapid, low-cost production contexts, filmmakers are able to respond directly and quickly to popular tastes, and to shape cycles according to perceived audience demands. Thus, the multiplication of a discrete filmic approach is possible even before commercial success of any kind has been verified. As Klein argues, swiftness—of both production and distribution—is a condition of cyclical success, even in the typically high-cost, high-pressure practices of mainstream Hollywood. Klein's study centers on films that were "released quickly, with small budgets," and that were thus "better able to capitalize on the contemporary moment than films that took months or years to go from conception to theatrical release" (2011, 20). In Nollywood, which relies almost entirely upon nontheatrical exhibition via videocassettes and video compact discs (VCDs), it is often necessary for a producer to promptly multiply a successful film into a series of cycle-comprising sequels and "sister stories," even at the risk of market saturation. While Nollywood's largely nontheatrical trappings, along with the persistence of piracy, make it difficult to monitor a film's commercial success across a variety of video platforms, the mere fact of a cycle's existence indicates the potential popularity of, at the very least, that cycle's root strategy—the narrative "hook" that first ensured a shooting budget. In the case of the anti-biopic, that strategy has been to exploit the signifying power of Hollywood star personae in order to say something meaningful about fame in today's West Africa.

Film cycles have been central to Nollywood's efforts to expand beyond the perceived confines of local video culture, as can be seen in the joint efforts of FAN and Sanga Entertainment to promote the theatrical exhibition of the *Beyoncé* series in the United States. Given the prevalence of illicit avenues for accessing Nollywood films—a prevalence that has forced FAN to attempt to execute multiple antipiracy measures throughout West Africa and the diaspora—it has been difficult to gauge the cycle-stimulating commercial success of individual Nollywood titles.

There is, however, a new and increasingly popular factor in the Nollywood equation: online viewing. Since the establishment in 2010 of a dedicated YouTube channel named *Nollywood Love*, which later morphed into iROKOtv.com, thousands of Nollywood films have been available online, where traffic can be monitored and commenting recorded—where, in other words, popularity can be gauged through both quantitative (views per video) and qualitative (subjective, prose-based) measurements. A source of considerable stress for many Nollywood producers—but an indispensable, though not yet lucrative, agent in their efforts to reach African diasporic communities—online distribution offers a useful lens through which to study the global audience appeal of Nollywood cycles, at least among fans connected to the Internet.

One of the most popular online sources of Nollywood films, the subscription-based iROKOtv has often confirmed the popularity of the anti-biopic cycle among its millions of visitors, measured both by views per video and by responses recorded in the site's comment section. But in the absence of a designation like "anti-biopic," which I have coined for explanatory purposes in this chapter, iROKOtv is forced to rely on several idiosyncratic strategies for uniting *Sharon Stone, Beyoncé & Rihanna, Lady Gaga, Valentino* (2002, Adim Williams), *Nicki Minaj* (Kunle Afod, 2013), and others—films whose titles alone suggest a certain central connection based on the adoption of globally famous names. In February 2013, iROKOtv listed all of the above films as much-recommended popular titles, showing a certain willingness to consolidate them as the constituents of a cycle. In its efforts to create the semblance of an even broader anti-biopic cycle, however, iROKOtv has retitled many of the cycle's constituent films—and not necessarily with the authorization or awareness of the films' producers. In 2012, it not only divided the four-hour *Lady Gaga* into four parts—a common enough strategy in the distribution of Nollywood films, given their typical length and the storage limitations of the industry's main video formats—but also gave each part a new title: the typographically stylized *Lady GagaA* and *Queen GagaA* and the comparably barebones *Gaga 1* and *Gaga 2*.

The website is hardly alone in imposing this strategy on Nollywood films. When the satellite television channel Africa Magic began broadcasting *Sharon Stone* under the title *Sharon Stone in Abuja*, it suggested a way of highlighting the cultural hybridity of Nollywood's anti-biopics, which filter Western star personae through Nigerian experiences. At the same time, Africa Magic likely counted on a title change to convey the sense that the anti-biopic cycle was more expansive than it actually was—that *Sharon Stone in Abuja* was a completely different film from *Sharon Stone*, rather than a merely retitled rendering thereof.

The fracturing of an individual Nollywood film into multiple parts is a phenomenon with technological roots. It is, in fact, traceable to Nollywood's reliance on videocassettes and VCDs: with their low storage capacities, the formats necessitate the separating of a lengthy film into component parts (as anyone who recalls the two-cassette *Titanic* [1997, James Cameron] can attest)—into, that is, a series of cassettes and discs that may be sold separately or together, depending upon the designs of a distributor. Today, with the rise of Internet distribution, the fracturing of a single film is no longer technologically necessary in most cases, but it remains a popular method. With multiple, often conflicting avenues of distribution—Africa Magic, *Nollywood Love*, iROKOtv, iBAKAtv, Dobox, and numerous other websites—the decision to label and promote a lengthy Nollywood film is often in the hands of programmers who may have little or no contact with producers and distributors operating in the markets of Idumota and Onitsha. In watching what iROKOtv identifies as *Queen GagaA*, for instance, one might be surprised to find that the film's opening credits in fact list the title as *Lady Gaga*, as do the VHS and VCD covers licensed for distribution in southern Nigeria. The division of a single film into multiple parts in these formats can be somewhat misleading: separated onto two VCDs, the continuous anti-biopic *Lady Gaga* becomes *Lady Gaga 1* and *Lady Gaga 2*, as if the latter were a bona fide sequel rather than the spillover of content that couldn't be contained on a single disc.

A common complaint about Nollywood is that the industry lacks a coherent, formal system of production, distribution, and official classification. This isn't simply an ethnocentric Western objection, however. Plenty of Nigerians protest that they don't know what to call—and sometimes cannot even find—their favorite film genres. Such a conundrum is perhaps common to all national cinemas. Before the word "bromance" began to appear in the taglines of numerous Hollywood comedies, how many moviegoers knew to ferret out, say, *Old Joy* (2006, Kelly Reichardt) in order to find the pleasurably awkward mix of self-conscious homoeroticism and old-style stoner anomie that "bromance" so succinctly suggests? That Nollywood's anti-biopic cycle lacks an official or popularly stable name does not make it any less definable as a cycle, however. In fact, the cycle's perceived contours have long been controversial enough to render it a bête noire among Nollywood's biggest fans. For years, and with increasing frequency in online venues, such fans have been protesting what they see as an opportunistic, plagiaristic, and possibly defamatory defiling of the biopic, suggesting not simply a fear of Nollywood's capacity to craft a negative advertisement for Nigeria but also an abiding respect for what a true biopic should be.

THE BIOPIC FROM HOLLYWOOD TO NOLLYWOOD

In response to a short video about the making of *Lady Gaga*, a comment recorded on YouTube asks why "nollywood always has to potray [*sic*] the names of American singers" in its titles, and suggests that the anti-biopic cycle indeed has little to do with the traditionally defined biopic (Tebogo G. 2012). To better understand the negative prefix of this cycle—that is, to make sense of the multiple resistant tactics of *Sharon Stone, Beyoncé & Rihanna,* and *Lady Gaga*—it is necessary to consider the biopic's typical features, especially as they intersect with stardom, genrefication, and cycle creation. When a Nollywood film, operating in the absence of official biographical claims, adopts the name of a Hollywood star, it tends to address the local saturation of that star's image. But according to the logic of Nollywood's anti-biopic cycle, such saturation can lead to crises of identity for young Nigerian women who identify with the likes of Beyoncé, Rihanna, Nicki Minaj, Lady Gaga, and Kesha. Even *Sharon Stone* contends that Hollywood's *Basic Instinct* had, by the early years of the twenty-first century, become so prominent in southern Nigeria—such a popular, hyperfamiliar film—that its star's name could easily serve as shorthand for "femme fatale." Later entries in the anti-biopic cycle, such as *Beyoncé & Rihanna* and *Lady Gaga*, argue that such songs as "Irreplaceable," "Umbrella," "Don't Stop the Music," "Telephone," and "Bad Romance" have influenced Nigerian everyday life—for better as well as for worse. In *Lady Gaga*, the protagonist proudly embraces the emotional and sexual abandon of "Bad Romance," but in *Beyoncé & Rihanna*, Omotola Jalade-Ekeinde's character realizes that while she may well be "one of a kind," the global success of "Umbrella"— a song that she often sings—is conspiring to turn her into a much-loathed Rihanna clone.

Such representations vividly attest to the film cycle's complicated and even, at times, contradictory investment in popular figures and current affairs. Indeed, as Klein argues, cycles—unlike genres—are often insistently topical: "A cycle must capitalize on an audience's interest in a subject before it moves on to something else" (2011, 13). This swift, opportunistic engagement with topicality is rarely more pronounced than in Nollywood's anti-biopic cycle, which cannily incorporates contemporary popular debates. These include the brouhaha over the title icon's queer politics in *Lady Gaga*: situated in a culture that the film depicts as strictly heterosexist, gender normative, and patriarchal, Gaga's alleged "lessons" about gender bending can only create conflict. In *Beyoncé & Rihanna*, the alleged rivalry between two prominent women of color provides the film with a link to local debates about negritude and the notion of a harmonious, universal black culture, suggesting a powerful metacommentary on Pan-Africanism. For its part, *Sharon Stone* centralizes the persistent controversy surrounding the female nudity so famously featured in *Basic Instinct*—a nudity that Nigeria's National Film and Video Censors Board has endeavored to expunge from Nollywood films, even as some Nollywood stars have gained fame by wearing cleavage-baring and semitransparent dresses to red-carpet premieres and televised award ceremonies.

The constituent films in Nollywood's anti-biopic cycle all center on the imagined or culturally translated experiences of hyperrelevant Western pop icons, and they all reflect the kind of wise timing that Klein describes. Ubong Bassey Nya began shooting his *Lady Gaga*, with the Nollywood star Oge Okoye, shortly after Gaga released *Born This Way*, her second studio album; Afam Okereke began directing his *Beyoncé & Rihanna* in late 2008, as both artists were enjoying astonishing success, Beyoncé with *Sasha Fierce* and Rihanna with *Good Girl Gone Bad*. Such topicality is a far cry from the retrospection of most biographical American films—even avant-garde anti-biopics like Todd Haynes's 2007 *I'm Not There*, which queerly considers Bob Dylan's legacy through discrepant lenses.[4]

Biopics, of course, tend to be retrospective for legal reasons. When an authorized biopic's subject is still living, the terms and conditions of contracts typically preclude the dramatization of the subject's present experiences, requiring a focus on previous accomplishments—on a glory safely confined to the historical past. This is true even of what one might call "autobiopics"—films in which stars play themselves, not to illuminate the present, but rather to revive the past. The strategy is twofold: to confirm the star's continued existence and to construct a false equivalence between past and present, particularly as situated on the star's allegedly unchanged face. Beginning with classical Hollywood's *Rhapsody in Blue* (1945, Irving Rapper), in which the aged Al Jolson plays his much-younger self, and *Night and Day* (1946, Michael Curtiz), in which the thirty-three-year-old Mary Martin impersonates her erstwhile teen pluck, and proceeding through Sophia Loren's performance in *Sophia Loren: Her Own Story* (1980, Mel Stuart) and Joan Rivers's work in *Tears and Laughter: The Joan and Melissa Rivers Story* (1994, Oz Scott), such films have routinely relied on celebrity self-representation in order to sidestep what Mary Desjardins reads as "inherent representational problems for traditional film biographies of well-known media stars." For Desjardins, conventional biopics "must represent, rather than present, the aura or uniqueness of their star subjects . . . must convince us of the star's worthiness for narrativization, while another star or performer portrays the star subject of the biography." She points out that "biopics have their ways of compensating for this lack, this falling away from 'wholeness'"—methods that most often rely on "a major star with his or her own aura power [to] play the star subject" (2004, 29).

While Nollywood's anti-biopics do not bother with the familiar trappings of conventional biographical ventures—they refuse to narrate birth-to-death trajectories, and they certainly shy away from bombastic allegations of their subjects' historical import—they do rely on stars who exhibit (as Dejardins puts it) "aura power": the glamorous Genevieve Nnaji, Nollywood's fabled beauty, plays Sharon Stone; Nadia Buari, one of Ghana's biggest names, plays multiple versions of Beyoncé (in a strategy not unlike that of Haynes's kaleidoscopic *I'm Not There*); Omotola Jalade-Ekeinde, named to *Time* magazine's 2013 list of the 100 most influential people in the world, offers her own take on Rihanna; and Oge Okoye, a habitually in-demand actress, does a variation on Lady Gaga's sartorial risk taking that reflects her own famously bizarre red-carpet fashions. In each case, an African icon appropriates a Western pop persona, suggesting that even an anti-biopic can still consolidate stardom. Opposing the conservativeness of the conventional biopic does not, in other words, entail eluding glamour.

Some of Nollywood's most prominent detractors, failing to appreciate such glamour, dismiss the sheer queerness of Nollywood's anti-biopic cycle. A plethora of negative user comments about the low-rated *Lady Gaga* appear on YouTube and iROKOtv, suggesting the anti-biopic's potential to stir up controversy. The majority of these responses tend to decry the film's "pirating" of Gaga's pop persona; only a few of them point out that this piracy extends to the film's sound track, which makes illicit use of Gaga's music in a manner that conceivably represents symbolic resistance to the star's global commercial dominance, her position within Western circuits of economic imperialism. One of the most illuminating online responses to Nollywood's anti-biopic cycle, however, came in a user review posted to the IMDb page of *Beyoncé & Rihanna* in 2008. Titled "Art Immitating [sic] Life . . . or is it?," the review begins by linking *Beyoncé & Rihanna* to Nollywood's collection of quasi-biographical films—the anti-biopic cycle: "Hot off starring in Beyoncé [. . .] the president's daughter [*sic*], Nadia Buari steps into yet another role . . . [based on] her idol, the real Beyonce Knowles. She walks like her, tries to talk like her, dresses like her and even wears her hair like Beyonce." Shifting into a second-person address, the reviewer offers some advice to Nollywood's leading Beyoncé interpreter: "Honestly, Ms. Buari, try and give it a rest. I'm sure the real Beyonce is flattered but you need to give your Beyonce-philia a rest" (Sherazade 2008). Interpreting Nollywood's anti-biopic cycle strictly as a function of a star's personal, imitative pretensions, this particular reviewer also assumes that flattery rather than deconstruction is the purpose of films that feature Western star personae. Still other viewers, on IMDb, YouTube, and iROKOtv, complain that Buari is "stealing" Beyoncé's star persona without properly "honoring" it. For instance, a 2012 user comment on iROKOtv notes that Buari, in singing several Beyoncé songs in *Beyoncé & Rihanna*, hasn't "Learn[ed] The Full Lyrics"—as if imitative precision were the principal objective of this particular anti-biopic (Ramyrosy 2012).

Several entries in Nollywood's anti-biopic cycle appear to anticipate such negative spectatorial responses. In *Lady Gaga*, the namesake imitator, being confronted for the umpteenth time by her chief tormentor (played by the Nollywood star Funke Akindele), defends her "Gaga act" against the accusation that it represents a childish mimicry that is "bad for Nigeria." Claiming not only that Lady Gaga's queer-friendly stance speaks to her but also that she has shared it "since birth," Oge Okoye's title character comes to complicate any easy assumptions about cross-cultural imitations, the best ways of resisting Western cultural hegemony, and the "correct" style of feminine self-comportment. Extremely media savvy, she looks to the life of her idol as a means of learning something about herself, and of questioning some rather limiting prescriptions for "being Nigerian." The study of Nollywood's cycles can serve an equally illuminating, stereotype-shattering function, helping combat the Western cultural condescension that so often positions Nollywood as an accidental or otherwise "mindless" media phenomenon—one that evolves according to chance and without the awareness of its participants.

In Nollywood, film cycles tend to thrive on controversy, and it is difficult to imagine an industrial context whose leading producers are less consciously responsive to dynamic public debates—and less willing to address those debates through diverse narrative forms. In recent years, spectatorial concerns about certain Nollywood film cy-

FIGURE 11.3. Stefani (Oge Okoye), publicly performing as Lady Gaga, lip-synchs to Gaga's "Speechless" in *Lady Gaga*.

cles, whether voiced in the traditional public sphere or confined to the Internet, have often centered on the politics of cultural appropriation, citing Nollywood's complicated references to Hollywood star personae. Nollywood itself has responded to these debates with self-reflexive gestures, such as the depiction of two women who quarrel over the sociopolitical value of the cycle of which they are a part, in the process offering dramatically divergent readings of Lady Gaga's life story. While Oge Okoye's character, the Gaga-loving Stefani (who even shares Gaga's real name), claims that Gaga "is everywhere" and that it would be futile to resist imitating her, Funke Akindele's Luisa, a Yoruba cultural nationalist, maintains that mimicry "is a problem"—one that, in Fanonian terms, "makes Nigeria look bad." But to whom, exactly? In addressing that question, Luisa claims that she is as concerned about her homeland's global reputation as she is about the self-esteem of young Nigerian girls—those who might feel pressured to adopt an imported persona, whether that of Gaga or Nicki Minaj.

The film seems to side with Luisa, at least at first. It lets her serve as the source of several chagrined point-of-view shots that take stock of Stefani's absurd Gaga costumes, from gaudy, bejeweled blue shoes to an equally outré hat. (In addition, the director often cuts to Luisa laughing derisively and expressing her principled disapproval of Stefani's "act.") But by the end of the film, Luisa's lover has left her for Stefani, the professional Gaga impersonator. Stefani, for all her mendacity, isn't punished; Luisa, in familiar melodramatic fashion, is. Shortly before the closing credits roll, it is clear that the film is aware of its own complexities, that it is working to evoke contradictory responses. On the one hand, Gaga worship has empowered a bullied, gender-bending village girl, giving her a life that she would not otherwise have had—and a hot boyfriend to boot, one who seems to believe that she actually is the white Western star she claims to be. But at the same time, a certain cynicism creeps in: the one character who defends an "unspoiled" local culture is left cold and lonely.

For all its obvious and seemingly puckish genre play, *Lady Gaga* remains a powerful, important film, one that reflects the impact of the anti-biopic cycle of which it is a part. From *Sharon Stone* (2003) to *Lady Gaga* (2012), the cycle's constituent films adopt yet estrange Western star personae, subverting the biopic's typical terms and conditions. *Lady Gaga* ends with Oge Okoye's character actually becoming her idol: Terpsichore, one of the nine muses of Greek mythology and the ruler of dance and the dramatic arts, descends to earth to enable this transformation. Suddenly, everyone—with the signal exception of Funke Akindele's Luisa, who successfully "sees through bullshit"—accepts the Lagosian Stefani as the "real" Lady Gaga. Her transition thus complete, Stefani proudly announces—in what might seem an amusing variation on *The Wizard of Oz* (1939, Victor Fleming)—that she was "always Gaga, from the very beginning," with "Bad Romance" in her blood.

NOTES

1. For more on the prevailing popular and scholarly approaches to Nollywood, see Haynes (2010).

2. For more on bootlegging, see Krings and Okome (2013).

3. This confirms—and extends—a point that Karin Barber (1987) famously makes about the relationship between producers and consumers of African popular arts.

4. For an account of this film's relationship to the biopic genre, see Bingham (2010, 377–404).

WORKS CITED

Adejunmobi, Moradewun. 2007. "Nigerian Video Film as Minor Transnational Practice." *Postcolonial Text* 3, no. 2: 1–16.

Barber Karin. 1987. "Popular Arts in Africa." *African Studies Review* 30, no. 3 (September): 1–78.

Bingham, Dennis. 2010. *Whose Lives Are They, Anyway? The Biopic as Contemporary Film Genre.* New Brunswick, NJ: Rutgers University Press.

Corliss, Richard. 2013. "Omotola Jalade-Ekeinde." *Time*, 18 April. http://time100 .time.com/2013/04/18/time-100/slide/omotola-jalade-ekeinde.

Desjardins, Mary R. 2004. "The Incredible Shrinking Star: Todd Haynes and the Case History of Karen Carpenter." *Camera Obscura* 19, no. 3: 23–55.

Fanon, Frantz. (1952) 2008. *Black Skin, White Masks.* Translated by Richard Philcox. New York: Grove.

———. (1961) 2004. *The Wretched of the Earth.* Translated by Richard Philcox. New York: Grove.

Haynes, Jonathan. 2010. "What Is to Be Done? Film Studies and Nigerian and Ghanaian Videos." In *Viewing African Cinema in the Twenty-First Century: Art Films and the Nollywood Video Revolution,* ed. Mahir Saul and Ralph A. Austin, 11–25. Athens: Ohio University Press.

Klein, Amanda Ann. 2011. *American Film Cycles: Reframing Genres, Screening Social Problems, and Defining Subcultures.* Austin: University of Texas Press.

Krings, Matthias, and Onookome Okome. 2013. "Nollywood and Its Diaspora: An Introduction." In *Global Nollywood: The Transnational Dimensions of an African Video Industry,* ed. Matthias Krings and Onookome Okome, 1–24. Bloomington: Indiana University Press.

McCall, John C. 2012. "The Capital Gap: Nollywood and the Limits of Informal Trade." *Journal of African Cinemas* 4, no. 1: 9–23.

Ramyrosy. 2012. Comment on *Beyoncé & Rihanna.* iROKOtv. http://irokotv.com /video/211/beyonce-rihanna#comment-733088524.

Saul, Mahir, and Ralph A. Austen. 2010. Introduction to *Viewing African Cinema in the Twenty-First Century: Art Films and the Nollywood Video Revolution,* ed. Mahir Saul and Ralph A. Austin. Athens: Ohio University Press.

Sherazade. 2008. "Art Immitating Life . . . or is it?" User review of *Beyoncé & Rihanna.* Internet Movie Database, 1 August. http://www.imdb.com/title /tt1266629.

Tebogo G. 2012. User comment on "Nollywood Movie Lady Gagaa (Behind the Scene)," YouTube, http://www.youtube.com/watch?v=ZJLPEu6K9WEdjena bou12341, 30 August.

CHAPTER 12

RE-SOLVING CRIMES: A CYCLE OF TV DETECTIVE PARTNERSHIPS

SARAH KORNFIELD

TELEVISION GENRES FLUCTUATE, often following a rhythm of innovation, imitation, and saturation as they adapt to changes in the television industry, evolving technology, and cultural shifts in audience preferences (Gitlin 1979). Recently, the familiar crime drama was reimagined when four prime-time TV programs, *Bones* (2005–), *Fringe* (2008–2013), *The Mentalist* (2008–2015), and *Castle* (2009–), broadcast a new iteration of the detective partnership. As Andrew Marlowe—*Castle*'s creator and executive producer—remarked, these series have taken a familiar genre and "blow[n] it up" (Ng 2011). This "blown-up" genre had an inauspicious beginning: during Fox's premiere of *Bones*, on September 13, 2005, two characters argued extensively until Temperance Brennan (Emily Deschanel), a forensic anthropologist who works at a museum, finally agreed to partner with FBI special agent Seeley Booth (David Boreanaz), but only if he granted her full participation in their cases instead of relegating her to lab work. Booth acquiesced, responding, "What? Do you want me to spit in my hand? We're Scully and Mulder." In this brief dialogue sequence, *Bones* forged a new cycle of TV detective partnerships.

When *Bones* premiered, TV reviews heralded it as an exciting new show (Gilbert 2005), as just another crime procedural (Laurence 2005), and as a remake of Fox's previously successful "will-they-won't-they" romantic partnership on *The X-Files* (1993–2002) (Bianculli 2005). All these reviews were correct: *Bones* was exciting, it fit the classic crime procedural formula, and it established a running romantic thread between the lead detectives—clearly building on *The X-Files*' cachet with the reference to Scully and Mulder. But *Bones* differentiated itself from generic predecessors and contemporary crime programming like *CSI* (2000–) and *NCIS* (2003–) by capitalizing on an unusual dynamic between the detective partners. The series paired an FBI agent and a civilian, heightening the tension by casting the male detective as an intuitive, easygoing character and the female anthropologist as a socially awkward, disconnected person who approaches her work with scientific precision.

The dynamic between these partners is often understood as a gender reversal, as noted by Sean Mitchell in the *New York Times*: "The traditional male-female roles are reversed in *Bones*" (2006). His review elaborated on this gender reversal by describing Brennan as a "scientist" and a "lonely careerist," and Booth as "emotional and caring." Popular TV reviews routinely code the female detectives on *Bones*, *Fringe*, *The Mentalist*, and *Castle* as "masculine" because of their use of science and their emotional detachment, and herald the male detectives as "in touch" with their "feminine nature," since they follow their "guts" and understand emotional responses (Bianco 2005; Cohn 2006; Elfman 2005; Mitchell 2006; Owen 2008; Willow 2005).

In analyzing these detective partnerships, I work to make sense of this new TV crime cycle and its emphasis on "gender reversed" detectives, exploring the form and style of *Bones*, *Fringe*, *The Mentalist*, and *Castle*, and their function within a broader social moment. Specifically, I argue that these crime series—through their unusual detective partnerships— present false but reassuring images of gender equality that can stretch from the office to the bedroom. This reassurance is, in part, a response to the sociopolitical unease regarding women's roles in society. Currently, Western popular culture oscillates between the opinion that women have, in fact, "arrived" and now dominate higher education and other patriarchal strongholds, and the contrasting opinion that sexism remains a debilitating force in women's lives. This new cycle of crime dramas steps into this uneasy question of women's status with ameliorating images of detectives who work on a basis of equality and ultimately wind up living together. Unfortunately, these series actually re-create patriarchal relationships and pass them off as progressive, pro-women equality. They accomplish this sleight of hand through the ways in which they adapt the classic generic elements of crime dramas, specifically through their juxtaposition of the detectives' characteristics.

To establish these claims, I first briefly explore the contours of how *Bones*, *Fringe*, *The Mentalist*, and *Castle* distinguish themselves from other crime dramas. Second, I differentiate the concepts of genres, subgenres, and cycles, developing a better theoretical under-standing of television's repetitive system and grounding these four programs in their cyclical and televisual contexts. Specifically, un-derstanding these programs as a cycle—not as a subgenre—grounds this analysis in the timeliness of these series and their viability within the television industry as they replicate one another's charac-ters, plotlines, settings, and story arcs while competing for the same audiences. Finally, this chapter analyzes the construction of gender reversals in the programs, arguing that this cycle meets the current debate on women's status in our society with claims of pro-women progressivism while effectively reasserting patriarchal gender norms.

JOINING THE LINEUP

Bones, Fringe, The Mentalist, and *Castle* clearly belong to the crime genre (Harriss 2008). They draw their supporting characters from a stock of law enforcement officials, forensic scientists, and lawyers. Their scenes are set against the backdrops of police headquarters, morgues, interrogation rooms, and crime scenes. And they structure each episode by the logic of crime drama formulas in which a mur-dered corpse is discovered, an investigation commences, suspects flee the scene, a chase ensues, witnesses are interrogated, trace evidence is discovered, and, finally, a startling revelation leads to a climactic arrest and admission of guilt (Harriss 2008).

The TV crime genre has a culturally familiar history. For exam-ple, in the 1970s, buddy cops solved crimes on programs such as *Star-sky and Hutch* (1975–1979) and *Chips* (1977–1983). This dynamic gave way to romantic "coed" detective agencies in the 1980s on se-ries such as *Hart to Hart* (1979–1984), *Remington Steele* (1982–1987), *Scarecrow and Mrs. King* (1983–1987), and *Moonlighting* (1985–1989). *The X-Files* joined and extended this trend in the 1990s, adding sci-ence fiction into the mix; in the early 2000s, graphic forensic work became popular on series such as *CSI* and *NCIS.* Familiar with these versions of the crime drama, both producers and audiences approach *Bones, Fringe, The Mentalist,* and *Castle* through their conceptual-izations of earlier crime dramas.

Bones, Fringe, The Mentalist, and *Castle* differentiate themselves from their predecessors by combining five essential qualities. First, each series pairs together male and female detectives as career part-ners. Second, one of the detectives is a law enforcement officer, and the other partner is a civilian consultant. Third, the programs characterize the male detectives as laid-back, fun people who bend the rules and follow their guts, while the female detectives follow the rules and struggle to emotionally connect with others—and these characterizations are portrayed, in part, as gender reversals. Fourth, the series develop a slow-moving romance between the partnered detectives. And finally, the programs are episodic serials (Mittell 2006). Crime series have combined the episodic approach (in which each episode features a discrete story) and the serial approach (in which the narrative spills from one episode into the next) since at least the 1980s, when series such as *Moonlighting* began featuring "serialized relationships and episodic plots" (Mittell 2006). But *Bones*, *Fringe*, *The Mentalist*, and *Castle* move beyond this model, developing narrative complexity by featuring long-running plotlines in addition to serialized relationships and an open-and-shut case in each episode. For example, while developing a romance and solving a murder in each episode, the first three seasons of *Bones* focus also on the mysterious murder of Brennan's mother; *Fringe* is concerned with a "pattern" of super-scientific crimes; *The Mentalist* focuses on catching a serial killer named Red John; and *Castle* comes full circle by reusing *Bones*' plot, featuring a running story line concerning the murder of the female detective's mother.

Unlike the earlier coed detectives on *Remington Steele* and *Scarecrow and Mrs. King*, whose romantic tension was largely rooted in their inequality, these new coed detective series portray their protagonists as equals: the promos feature them side by side, TV reviews focus on their shared power, and the characters themselves regularly lay claim to this equality.[1] For example, in the "Red Alert" episode of *The Mentalist*, Patrick Jane (Simon Baker) explains that he is neither "above nor below" his partner, the California Bureau of Investigation senior special agent Teresa Lisbon (Robin Tunney); rather, he is "to the side." The narrative setting works to reinforce this claim of equality. Since the partners draw paychecks from different sources, they have no common boss to whom they are accountable—and therefore no one to play favorites between them. Additionally, although one partner has "seniority" as the law enforcement official, the other's civilian expertise is needed to solve crimes, which equalizes the power dynamic in relation to job experience. Finally, the female detectives have formal positions of power; they oversee their own scientist teams or police units. To balance the women's authority, these series give the male detectives informal power: they are more popular and generally more financially successful than the men who are in supporting roles and, therefore, become mentor figures for the other men.

By combining these elements, *Bones*, *Fringe*, *The Mentalist*, and *Castle* position the detectives as equals and then build tension between the partners by juxtaposing their incompatible characteristics. Indeed, moving beyond the norm of flirtatious bickering between television couples, these detective partners must merge wholly incompatible investigative techniques, personalities, values, and life experiences. *Bones*, *Fringe*, *The Mentalist*, and *Castle* are familiar as narratives, drawing on prior television series as reference points, and yet they distinguish themselves, constituting a cycle within the TV crime genre.

GENRES AND CYCLES

The familiar elements of *Bones*, *Fringe*, *The Mentalist*, and *Castle*, such as episode formulas and televisual styles, are familiar because these series borrow or repeat prior crime drama motifs. This is not unusual; television—as a medium—is repetitive. Television's repetitive nature is perhaps best demonstrated by the game show genre in which formulaic series, such as *Wheel of Fortune* (1983–), air indistinguishable episodes daily (Moran 2009). But this logic of repetition permeates even new scripted programming. Some series remake previous story lines; for example, the CW's *Nikita* (2010–2013) reinvented the Canadian series *La Femme Nikita* (1997–2001), itself a remake of a French film (1990) of the same title. In other instances, a successful narrative generates spin-offs: for example, CBS's *CSI: Crime Scene Investigation* (2000–) has generated three spin-off series, *CSI: Miami* (2002–2012), *CSI: NY* (2004–2013), and *CSI: Cyber* (2015–) (Caldwell 1995).

Given this seemingly endless recycling of previous entertainment, genres have a clear and important role in understanding TV programming. Indeed, TV scholars such as Edgerton and Nicholas (2005) recognize that networks often use genres to crystallize their brand in logos, taglines, and program recognition. For example, TNT's tagline, "We know drama," asserts that TNT features a selection of dramas as opposed to sitcoms, talk shows, variety shows, soap operas, cooking shows, or cartoons. Moreover, genres can operate as cultural categories for producers, reviewers, and audience members, who use genres, respectively, to think through what type of stories and aesthetic styles to produce, to assess the quality of a program, and to decide what to watch (Mittell 2004).

While genres now seem indigenous to television scholarship, the concept of cycles stems primarily from film studies. At one level, a cycle, defined as a "series of films [or TV series] associated with each other through shared images, characters, settings, plots, or themes," could seem almost undifferentiated from the concept of genre (Klein 2011, 3–4). Using this definition, for example, one could use either "genre" or "cycle" to characterize *Bones*, *Fringe*, *The Mentalist*, and *Castle*. But the theoretical distinctions between a genre and a cycle become clear when placed in the contexts of the entertainment industry and broader public discourse. Genres have a nearly timeless utility for producers, directors, writers, and creative executives: they serve as templates that one might—at any time—draw upon to generate a new narrative. In contrast, a cycle has a discrete lifespan, and its "formation and longevity" depend upon its "financial viability" and the "public discourses circulating" around a set of narratives (4).

Distinguishing cycles from genres, then, provides a theoretical apparatus and the terminology to explain fundamental differences in entertainment. For example, TV spy dramas and parodies such as *The Man from U.N.C.L.E.* (1964–1968), *I Spy* (1965–1968), and *Get Smart* (1965–1970) shared similar content, televisual styles, narrative forms, and cultural meanings. They became popular—for a time—largely in response to the Cold War (Gitlin 1979; Lisanti and Paul 2002). Thus, they are better understood as a cycle than simply as part of the spy genre, which stretches from *Mission: Impossible* (1966–1973) to *Alias* (2001–2006). Granted, these Cold War spy programs could be classified as a subgenre of the larger spy genre. Yet the concept of a subgenre is counterproductive here: by approaching television entertainment through the logic of subgenres, one merely slices TV programming into smaller and smaller slivers, attaching a label to each slice and then typically constructing complex family trees to map the relationships among subgenres. For example, Joe Bellon (1999) placed *The X-Files* into the subgenre of "non-sci-fi ontological detective story," of which it seems to be the first and only example, and then classified it in relation to the genres and subgenres of science fiction, mystery, and detective show. This serves a taxonomic impetus, but fails to make sense of the television series' form, style, and function within a broader social moment.

Distinguishing between genres and cycles provides at least two clear critical and theoretical apparatuses. First, it sidesteps the quagmire of "taxonomic fascination" into which subgenres can lead critics, but still fosters understanding of a group of narratives in relation to a larger body of narratives (Hart 1986). That is, understanding *Bones, Fringe, The Mentalist,* and *Castle* as a cycle groups them as a discrete set while keeping them in conversation with generic reference points (such as the 1980s coed TV detective agencies). Without the taxonomy of subgeneric classification, this cycle can be critically contextualized by its crime genre predecessors, offshoots on cable programming, and international TV hits (such as BBC's *Sherlock* [2010–]). Indeed, recognizing *Bones, Fringe, The Mentalist,* and *Castle* as a cycle underscores how these programs draw upon previous crime drama cycles, appropriating the narrative forms, gender-sensitive portrayals, and televisual styles from series such as *Cagney & Lacey* (1981–1988), *The X-Files, CSI,* and *Prime Suspect* (1991–2006), Britain's female-oriented series of miniseries. Second, distinguishing between genres and cycles emphasizes cultural considerations, since cycles become viable for a time in relation to specific cultural sentiments. Thus, recognizing *Bones, Fringe, The Mentalist,* and *Castle* as a cycle emphasizes their place in US culture. By re-creating patriarchal relationships and portraying them as equality, this cycle mediates the reality of gender inequity—which manifests in unequal pay, unequal opportunities, the control of women's bodies, and violence against women—and the cultural sentiment that feminism is no longer necessary.

REVIEWING THE CASE

At the heart of each series stands an unusual and romantically oriented detective partnership. *Bones* premiered on Fox in 2005, airing for three seasons before *Fringe, The Mentalist,* and *Castle* joined it in prime time; its narrative is therefore more advanced than those of the other series. On *Bones,* Booth and Brennan have married and are raising their first child together. Also airing on Fox, *Fringe* (created by J. J. Abrams) adds a science-fictional component to the crime narrative as FBI agent Olivia Dunham (Anna Torv) leads the Fringe Division, investigating super-scientific murders that fit a "pattern" caused by the existence of a parallel universe. She works with a crazed scientist, Walter Bishop (John Noble), and partners with his son, Peter Bishop (Joshua Jackson), a former con man.[2] In contrast, CBS's *The Mentalist* remains deeply rooted in real-world possibilities, and the story line centers on Patrick Jane, who previously worked as a fake psychic until a serial killer, Red John, murdered his family. Jane now consults for the California Bureau of Investigation, where he partners with Teresa Lisbon; together they track down Red John. Finally, ABC's *Castle* creates its unlikely partnership by featuring a novelist, Richard Castle (Nathan Fillion), who finds new creative inspiration by shadowing NYPD detective Kate Beckett (Stana Katic). They eventually become partners, and together solve the mysterious murder of Beckett's mother.

While these series seem to diversify their partnerships by pairing a law enforcement official with a museum anthropologist, a fake psychic, a con man, or a novelist, they actually create nearly identical partnerships by characterizing all the detectives according to the same six key, dichotomous attributes. First, the detectives can be either law enforcement officials or civilians. Second, the detectives proceed logically and use the scientific method or else follow their intuition and act impulsively. Third, they are either morally upstanding characters or vice-ridden people who work in moral gray areas, believing that the ends justify the means. Fourth, they either follow legal procedures or work outside the law. Fifth, they can connect emotionally with other people and recognize both their own and others' emotions, or they are emotionally stunted. And finally, the detectives are either capable of developing and maintaining meaningful domestic relationships, or else they struggle to develop intimate relationships.

Bones, Fringe, The Mentalist, and *Castle* juxtapose the detective partners' characteristics by pairing one law enforcement official with one civilian and then divvying up the rest of the characteristics between them. But these characteristics are not randomly ascribed, nor are they portioned out by job description (that is, it is not necessarily the case that the law enforcement partner is also the moral one). Instead, *Bones, Fringe, The Mentalist,* and *Castle* divide the characteristics by gender. Despite the fact that Brennan works as a civilian consultant while the other women are law enforcement officials, all four female detectives are logical and scientifically inclined, morally upright, legally constrained, emotionally stunted, and inept at creating or maintaining long-standing, meaningful relationships. Meanwhile, the male detectives are intuitive, morally ambiguous, legally unconstrained, emotionally attuned, and relationally adept, despite the fact that Booth is an FBI agent and the others are civilians.

Through these opposing characterizations, *Bones*, *Fringe*, *The Mentalist*, and *Castle* depict a world in which female characters may have strong personalities and earn as much as or more than men, but ultimately lack agency—the ability to close cases—and are often portrayed as emotionally damaged characters. Indeed, only the male detectives' love can rescue these women from their emotionally traumatized pasts. To demonstrate this, I analyze, first, the contrast in these series between scientific and intuitive investigative methods; second, the detectives' characteristics of morality and legality; and finally, the detectives' emotional and relational skills. This analysis demonstrates how the distribution of these characteristics undermines the premise of equality on *Bones*, *Fringe*, *The Mentalist*, and *Castle*.

Much like Arthur Conan Doyle's Sherlock Holmes, these female detectives depend on the scientific method as they gather evidence and slowly piece together clues. The male detectives, however, prefer to follow their instincts. For example, in the pilot episode of *Bones*, Temperance Brennan and her team at the Jeffersonian Museum use holographic technology to re-create a murder, thereby learning important details about the assailant. Brennan presents this evidence to Booth, recommending that he arrest a US senator based on her findings. Booth, however, rejects her holography as a "crystal ball," choosing to follow his gut instead. As the investigation continues, both detectives follow their own paths toward solving the murder: Brennan through science and Booth through his gut. But the narrative privileges Booth's intuitive methodology. Brennan's scientific approach assesses only tangible evidence, and there are always more clues to find: the analysis of further evidence reveals that, contrary to Brennan's initial findings, the senator did not commit the murder. Her approach works, but slowly. Booth, on the other hand, follows his gut straight to the villain.

Additionally, Booth's intuitive method provides motives. Booth understands the crimes, whereas Brennan simply collects evidence. After finding and apprehending the murderer on *Bones*' pilot episode, Brennan states, "The evidence said he did it but . . . I don't know why.

You know what? It doesn't matter. Motive does not matter." But Brennan remains troubled, despite her dismissal of motive. Motive clearly matters in crime dramas: the denouement unveils how and why the murderer committed the crime. Unlike Brennan, Booth understands human emotions and recognizes that the murderer was motivated by greed: "He did it to save his job . . . It's that simple." While both scientific and intuitive methods contribute to solving cases and apprehending criminals on *Bones*, *Fringe*, *The Mentalist*, and *Castle*, these series privilege the intuitive over the scientific, especially since the male detectives' intuitive methods explain the crime.

Moreover, the intuitive approach is privileged in these narratives only when performed by a man. They have no use for women's intuition. For example, Patrick Jane repeatedly coerces his partner, Teresa Lisbon, into working intuitively in the *Mentalist* episode "Blinking Red Light." While working a case involving a serial killer, Lisbon starts by digging through old case files. Realizing that the investigation will proceed quite slowly, Jane complains until Lisbon finally allows him to teach her his more intuitive methods. Throughout the episode, Jane encourages Lisbon to follow her gut instead of relying on her more scientific approach to police work. Using Jane's intuitive methods, Lisbon apprehends a pervert. But the man she arrests is not the serial killer, she cannot prove that he has broken any laws, and she releases him at the end of the episode. Lisbon succeeds as an intuitive detective—she catches a pervert—but the narrative refuses to reward her. Instead, it punishes her, since her boss reprimands her for failing to close the case. Meanwhile, Jane follows his own intuition, and—based on the "evidence" of a neatly organized medicine cabinet—correctly identifies the serial killer. US culture celebrates *Bones*, *Fringe*, *The Mentalist*, and *Castle* as narratives in which "the traditional male-female roles are reversed" (Mitchell 2006), yet these series reward "feminine" characteristics—such as intuition—only when they are associated with male characters. Lisbon was successfully intuitive, and yet she turns up empty-handed at the end of the episode; Jane, however, catches a serial killer.

Beyond rewarding the male detectives' intuitive approaches, *Bones*, *Fringe*, *The Mentalist*, and *Castle* reward the male detectives' amorality and willingness to work outside the law. These series present the female detectives as good, upstanding citizens who function within moral and legal boundaries. The male detectives, however, have shady, vice-ridden pasts: Booth was a compulsive gambler,

Bishop and Jane were con men, and Castle was a playboy. Taking *The Mentalist*'s "Blinking Red Light" episode as an example again, we see that the female detective's morality and legality ultimately constrain her. In "Blinking Red Light," both Lisbon and Jane identified villainous men, and neither gathered enough evidence to make an arrest. Lisbon released her suspect, but Jane chose a radically different option.

Attempting to console Jane and convince him to move on, Lisbon states, "Our hands are tied"; Jane, however, replies, "Maybe yours are." He then joins the serial killer—who is a journalist—on the evening news, badgering him by comparing his recent killings to Red John's murders. Jane goads the serial killer into denouncing Red John as an amateur murderer, knowing that Red John will kill the journalist–serial killer in retaliation—which is how the episode ends. Here, Jane works outside moral and legal codes, purposely manipulating two serial killers and using one to bring the other to "justice." Unlike the female detectives, Jane and the other male detectives rarely find their hands tied by a sense of morality or the nuances of legal procedure.

The female detectives—especially Dunham, Lisbon, and Beckett, who work for law enforcement agencies—are ultimately constrained by their adherence to moral and legal codes. The crime genre is premised on the formula of finding and apprehending criminals, yet in this cycle the women's moral and legal compasses keep them from closing cases. The male detectives, however, regularly lie, tamper with evidence, refuse to wait for warrants, use underworld contacts, torture suspects, and generally get the job done through morally ambiguous or illegal means.

Furthermore, the female detectives on *Bones, Fringe, The Mentalist,* and *Castle* have difficulty in recognizing their own emotional responses, relating to others' emotions, and forming meaningful relationships—especially domestic ones. For example, in the *Bones* pilot, the female detective's emotional ineptitude frames her as cold and insensitive. After identifying a murder victim, Booth and Brennan break the news to parents that their daughter was found dead. Booth and Brennan sit side by side, directly opposite the parents. Although the detectives and parents are similarly seated, this scene uses camerawork to emphasize Brennan's emotional ineptitude. Although the father is seated farther from the camera than the mother, the parents are filmed in profile with a midrange shot, so both are in focus re-

FIGURE 12.1. In *Bones*, Temperance Brennan becomes blurred in the foreground as the camera shifts focus to her partner, FBI agent Seeley Booth.

gardless of who is speaking. Similarly in profile, Booth and Brennan are filmed with a much closer shot, so only one of them can be in focus at a time. During this scene, Brennan answers two questions, and each time Booth interrupts her; as he does so, the camera shifts focus to blur Brennan and bring Booth into focus. Specifically, when the father asks, "You're positive it's our Cleo?" Brennan clinically responds, "We established twenty-two points of comparison—" and Booth interjects, "Yes. We're certain." His response provides closure for the parents, whose daughter had been missing for two years. Similarly, when the mother asks whether her daughter suffered, Brennan begins, "Given the state of her skull—" and Booth interrupts, "Cleo never saw it coming." Brennan's answer would have deeply unsettled the parents, since the state of Cleo's skull suggested that Cleo died slowly, painfully, and gruesomely. Throughout this scene, the camerawork reinforces the dialogue: this scene visually and aurally privileges Booth's interruptions as the emotionally correct answers and highlights the inappropriateness of Brennan's emotionally detached statements.

As these series develop, the male detectives teach their partners how to understand emotions. On *Bones*, it took Booth seven seasons to teach Brennan how to recognize others' emotions, adequately respond to those emotions, and experience her own emotions. But

FIGURE 12.2. In *Fringe*, Peter Bishop attempts to console Olivia Dunham as she crouches in the corner of a dark room.

even in the seventh season, when she can openly state that she loves Booth, and when they are living together and preparing for their first child, Brennan still struggles to recognize or value emotions. Instead, she approaches decisions through what she claims are rational, objective, and logical processes. For example, in the episode "The Hot Dog in the Competition," Brennan reasons that Booth would not enjoy attending an ultrasound of their pregnancy, since he does not enjoy black-and-white films. Based on this "logical deduction," Brennan does not invite him, has the ultrasound alone, learns the sex of their child, and announces it to a group of friends without first telling him—and then is surprised by his frustration.

These series often link the female detectives' emotional disabilities to the plotlines. On the *Fringe* episode "Jacksonville," for example, Dunham's inability to feel fear jeopardizes New York City in this sci-fi-imbued program. Scientific experiments conducted during Dunham's childhood altered her brain chemistry. This enables her to identify particular technological incongruities, and thereby prevent crimes, but only if her brain is awash with fear. Thus, her fearlessness—which in other crime dramas might be featured as courageousness—is a negative quality here, since it prevents her from recognizing technologically altered substances. Soon after Dunham learns

FIGURE 12.3. In *Castle*, Richard Castle brings flowers to his partner, Kate Beckett, in the hospital.

that her fearlessness prevents her from solving crimes, she retreats to a dark room and dejectedly slumps down into the only lit corner. Her partner, Bishop, follows her into the room and asks, "Are you okay?" to which Dunham responds in a defeated tone, "No. I'm not afraid of anything anymore." This scene verbally codifies fearlessness as a negative attribute—Dunham is "not okay"—while visually alienating Dunham and positioning her as subdued and defeated. Rather than marking Dunham as courageous, her fearlessness is portrayed as emotional ineptitude.

In direct contrast, the male detectives are always emotionally adept. Their emotional acumen is rewarded in three ways throughout these series: they can solve crimes by identifying villains' motives; they can maintain happy domestic spheres and caring relationships with their children, parents, friends, or extended family; and they succeed romantically. Essentially, these series originally promise a romance between the detective partners and then—slowly—navigate the characters into a relationship. For example, on the third-season finale of *Castle* ("Knockout"), when NYPD detective Kate Beckett is shot, Richard Castle confesses his love for her as she loses consciousness. When the fourth season opens (with the episode "Rise"), Castle rushes to her side with flowers as she recovers in the hospital.

But rather than acknowledging Castle's confession of love, Beckett pretends to have amnesia, thereby avoiding any emotional entanglements, and she goes to great lengths to prevent him from reconfessing his love. These stories encourage viewers to expect romance, and then present men who work toward it as the women they love ignore, thwart, or reject it. *Bones, Fringe, The Mentalist,* and *Castle* privilege the male detectives' emotional and relational skills as viewers root for them, hoping in each new episode that the men will finally break through their partners' emotional barriers and make good on the romantic story lines implied in the pilot episodes.

These series portray emotionally damaged women who cannot process emotions and cannot build or maintain domestic relationships: all four women have tragic or abusive backstories, strained relationships with their siblings and parents, and very few friends. The male detectives, by contrast, are deeply connected to the domestic sphere, have strong familial relationships, and enjoy a wide variety of friends. Even Peter Bishop, who is estranged from his scientist father at the beginning of *Fringe,* develops a close relationship with this well-meaning but troublesome parent.

As a cycle of the crime genre, *Bones, Fringe, The Mentalist,* and *Castle* characterize their detectives through a narrow set of six binary characteristics. Yet by dividing these characteristics by gender—not profession—the series refuse to reward the female detectives: they successfully employ scientific methods in series that privilege intuition; they are good moral characters who uphold the law when shady practices and minor illegalities get the job done; and they are emotionally stunted and relationally inept in series that focus on romance as a running plotline. *Bones, Fringe, The Mentalist,* and *Castle* operate as a cycle, in part, by building their story lines on what they claim are equitable partnerships and reversed gender portrayals. Yet the narratives consistently reward the male detectives, privileging them over their female counterparts.

CONTEMPORARY CULTURE OFTEN BEMOANS a so-called masculinity crisis. Blaming feminism for the problem, pop psychology claims that US culture oppresses men, making them inessential for the family, portraying them as "dolts, bullies, brutes, deadbeats, rapists, sexual predators, and wife beaters" in entertainment, undervaluing them in the workplace, and harming young boys who struggle to establish their identities in a "go-girl" society (Parker 2008). US women have made substantial strides toward equality; for example, women make up 47 percent of the workforce and have "outpaced" men in college attendance since the 1980s (Stevens 2012). But despite the popular celebration of women's success (which often rings the death knell for feminism) and the coinciding concern for men's well-being, US women still earn 77 percent as much as men (AAUW 2012), are grossly underrepresented in Congress (Manning and Brudnick 2014), and suffer violence at the hands of men (NOW 2012).

This recent cycle of crime dramas meets this conflict of perception and reality with ameliorating narratives of gender equality and romantic partnerships. But an investigation of whose methods solve the crimes and which characters are privileged by the narrative structures reveals a basic inequality between the male and female detectives in which the men are systematically favored. Despite reproducing patriarchy, these series are acclaimed as progressive narratives that feature gender reversals. This is particularly troubling because it suggests that sexism is passing for equality in US society.

These series are not inconsequential. In 2013, the average adult in the United States watched approximately four and a half hours of television a day (Kleinman 2013). Within this considerable media industry, these series have enjoyed longevity, stability, and sizable audiences: *Bones* viewership has averaged between 8.9 million and 11.57 million viewers (ABC MediaNet 2008; Gorman 2011); *Fringe*—which aired primarily on Friday nights—averaged between 4.22 million and 10 million viewers (ABC MediaNet 2009; Gorman 2012); *The Mentalist* consistently had strong ratings, averaging between 11.82 million and 17.52 million viewers (ABC MediaNet 2009; Bibel 2013); and *Castle* has averaged between 10.19 million and 12.26 million viewers (ABC MediaNet 2009; Bibel 2013). Although *Fringe* aired its final season in 2012–2013 and *The Mentalist* concluded in 2015, this cycle of the crime genre is far from over. Not only are *Bones* and *Castle* still going strong, but the cycle has been extended through programs such as *Warehouse 13* (SyFy, 2009–2014) and *Elementary* (CBS, 2012–).

As the cycle gets older, these new series have begun to tinker with the formula. For example, *Elementary* is a "new" take on the Sherlock Holmes story: Watson is female, played by Lucy Liu. The series was hailed as "TV's newest will-they-or-won't-they couple" (Stanhope 2012). In *Elementary* the emotionally detached character is male, and the emotionally attuned character is female, reasserting traditional gender norms for emotional acumen. But despite being inspired by Doyle's mysteries, the detectives in this series primarily resemble the partnerships on *Bones, Fringe, The Mentalist,* and *Castle.* This new Sherlock (Johnny Lee Miller) gathers evidence less like an armchair detective who eschews guesswork and more like the work-outside-the-law mavericks on *Bones, Fringe, The Mentalist,* and *Castle.* Similarly, while Liu's Watson is emotionally attuned, she has a dark backstory that effectively cuts her off from friends, family, love, prosperity, and happiness: she abandoned her career as a surgeon to become a sober companion, helping addicts—like Sherlock—recover. Moreover, like the female detectives on *Bones, Fringe, The Mentalist,* and *Castle,* this Watson finds herself constantly attempting to rein in her partner. Except Watson is denied the term "partner": in the pilot episode, she allows Sherlock, through the privilege of companion-client confidentiality, to introduce her as he pleases. He promptly abuses this concession, taking great gusto in presenting her as his personal valet. Later, she becomes Sherlock's apprentice after she quits working as a sober companion to become a full-time detective.

Only time will tell whether Lucy Liu's Watson will be sidelined for Holmes's continued preeminence—a status that the women of *Bones, Fringe, The Mentalist,* and *Castle* are systematically denied despite having deductive skills and emotional detachment comparable to those of the original Sherlock Holmes. Liu is hopeful, believing her character is more than a "sidekick" (Abrams 2012). Unfortunately, as *Bones, Fringe, The Mentalist,* and *Castle* have demonstrated, rising from the rank of sidekick to full partner does not ensure gender equity.

Bones, Fringe, The Mentalist, and *Castle* clearly participate in the crime genre. But recognition of their generic elements does little to contextualize their presence, explain their cultural resonance, or help analyze their relationship with one another, prior crime series, or contemporary competitors. By theorizing these series as a cycle within—not a subgenre of—the crime genre, I focus on their lifespan within the television industry and the public discourses circulating around them. Analyzing these series as a cycle of crime dramas reveals their function within US culture. These series, to some extent, silence feminist voices that call for gender equity by representing US culture as so progressive that it is gender reversed while simultaneously asserting patriarchal gender norms by systematically favoring the male detectives.

NOTES

1. On *Remington Steele*, Laura Holt (Stephanie Zimbalist) owns her own detective agency and employs Remington Steele (Pierce Brosnan); on *Scarecrow and Mrs. King*, Agent Scarecrow (Bruce Boxleitner) is a consummate spy, and Mrs. King (Kate Jackson) is a housewife and part-time spy assistant. Their roles on these series are not equal: one of them is officially in charge, and the other officially subservient. These series derive a significant amount of the tension between the otherwise romantically inclined detective partners by having the officially subservient partner routinely disobey, misunderstand, argue with, and generally thwart the authority of the senior partner.

2. The first two seasons of *Fringe* closely follow the crime drama formula, and the science-fictional elements function primarily as extreme versions of technological innovations. But Fox booted the series to Friday night in the third season, and the number of science-fictional elements increased exponentially, so during the later seasons the FBI team must contend with a parallel universe, alternate histories, doppelgangers, and time travelers.

WORKS CITED

AAUW (American Association of University Women). 2012. "The Simple Truth about the Gender Pay Gap." www.aauw.org/research/the-simple-truth-about-the-gender-pay-gap.
ABC MediaNet. 2008. *2008 Ranking Report*. ABC Television Network, 20 May.
———. 2009. *2009 Ranking Report*. ABC Television Network, 2 June.
Abrams, Natalie. 2012. "Despite Changes, CBS' *Elementary* Captures the Spirit of the Original Sherlock Holmes." *TV Guide*, 29 July.
Bellon, Joe. 1999. "The Strange Discourse of *The X-Files*: What It Is, What It Does, and What Is at Stake." *Critical Studies in Mass Communication* 16:136–154.
Bianco, Robert. 2005. "The Stars Flesh Out *Bones*." *USA Today*, 13 September.
Bianculli, David. 2005. "*Bones* Needs More Meat; Fine Cast Tries to Flesh It Out." *New York Daily News*, 13 September.
Bibel, Sara. 2013. "Complete list of 2012–13 Season TV Show Viewership: *Sunday Night Football* tops, followed by *NCIS, The Big Bang Theory* & *NCIS: Los Angeles*." *TV by the Numbers*, 29 May.
Caldwell, John T. 1995. *Televisuality: Style, Crisis and Authority in American Television*. New Brunswick, NJ: Rutgers University Press.
Cohn, Angel. 2006. "'*Bones*' Booth Gets His Sexy On." *TV Guide*, 30 August.
Edgerton, Gary R., and Kyle Nicholas. 2005. "'I Want my Niche TV': Genre as a Networking Strategy in the Digital Era." In *Thinking Outside the Box: A Contemporary Television Genre Reader*, ed. Gary R. Edgerton and Brian Rose, 247–267. Lexington: University Press of Kentucky.

Elfman, Doug. 2005. "*Bones* Star Is One Strange Agent." *Chicago Sun-Times*, 13 September.

Gilbert, Matthew. 2005. "Human Drama Brings Fox's *Bones* to Life." *Boston Globe*, 13 September.

Gitlin, Todd. 1979. "Prime Time Ideology: The Hegemonic Process in Television Entertainment." *Social Problems* 26:251–266.

Gorman, Bill. 2011. "2010–11 Season Broadcast Primetime Show Viewership Averages." *TV by the Numbers*, 1 June.

———. 2012. "Complete List of 2011–12 Season TV Show Viewership: *Sunday Night Football* tops, followed by *American Idol, NCIS & Dancing with the Stars.*" *TV by the Numbers*, 24 May.

Harriss, Chandler. 2008. "Policing Propp: Toward a Textualist Definition of Procedural Drama." *Journal of Film and Video* 60, no. 1: 43–59.

Hart, Roderick P. 1986. "Contemporary Scholarship in Public Address: A Research Editorial." *The Western Journal of Speech Communication* 50 (1986): 283–295.

Klein, Amanda Ann. 2011. *American Film Cycles: Reframing Genres, Screening Social Problems, and Defining Subcultures.* Austin: University of Texas Press.

Kleinman, Alexis. 2013. "Americans will Spend More Time on Digital Devices than Watching TV This Year: Research." *Huffington Post*, 1 August.

Laurence, Robert P. 2005. "Fox Throws *Bones* onto That Heaping Pile of CSI Imitators." *San Diego Union-Tribune*, 13 September.

Lisanti, Tom, and Louis Paul. 2002. *Film Fatales: Women in Espionage Films and Television, 1962–1973.* Jefferson, NC: McFarland.

Manning, Jennifer E., and Ida A. Brudnick. 2014. *Women in the United States Congress, 1917–2014: Biographical and Committee Assignment Information, and Listings by State and Congress.* Congressional Research Service Report 7-5700. Washington, DC: Government Printing Office.

Mitchell, Sean. 2006. "Ex-Vampire Turns into Regular Guy." *New York Times*, 27 December.

Mittell, Jason. 2004. *Genre and Television: From Cop Shows to Cartoons in American Culture.* New York: Routledge.

———. 2006. "Narrative Complexity in Contemporary American Television." *Velvet Light Trap* 58:29–40.

Moran, Albert. 2009. "Global Franchising, Local Customizing: The Cultural Economy of TV Program Formats." *Continuum: Journal of Media and Cultural Studies* 23, no. 2: 115–125.

Ng, Philiana. 2011. "*Castle* Creator Talks Season 4, Future of the Castle-Beckett Relationship and the New Captain (Q&A)." *Hollywood Reporter*, 19 September.

NOW (National Organization for Women). 2012. *Violence against Women in the United States.* http://now.org/resource/violence-against-women-in-the-united-states-statistic.

Owen, Rob. 2008. "TV Preview: Ex-*Guardian* Baker Lightens Up as *The Mentalist.*" *Pittsburgh Post-Gazette*, 23 September.

Parker, Kathleen. 2008. *Save the Males: Why Men Matter, Why Women Should Care.* New York: Random House.

Stanhope, Kate. 2012. "Comic-Con: Can CBS' *Elementary* and BBC's *Sherlock* Co-Exist?" TVGuide.com, 12 July.

Stevens, Heidi. 2012. "Marissa Mayer: Why Is Everybody So Surprised?" *Chicago Tribune*, 1 August.

Willow, Molly. 2005. "Pair Sure to Heat Up Morgue." *Columbus Dispatch*, 13 September.

CHAPTER 13

SMART TV: SHOWTIME'S "BAD MOMMIES" CYCLE

CLAIRE PERKINS

IN AUGUST 2010, THE SHOWTIME NETWORK promoted the premiere of its original program *The Big C* (2010–) in a spot linking the series to its existing hit *Weeds* (2005–2012). In a scene mimicking the scenario of neighbors meeting over their fence, the star of each series—Laura Linney and Mary Louise Parker—approach each other in a long shot divided between a lush suburban garden and a barren desert landscape. Birdsong plays on the sound track. As the scene cuts to a shot reverse shot of each regarding the other warily, a riff rings out on a banjo and—*Deliverance* style—continues to echo the defensive statements that each woman puts to the other:

Parker: I started selling pot to support my family.
Linney: I just found out I've got the big C. Cancer.
Parker: Now I'm married to a crime lord, I've had his baby, and my son has committed murder.
Linney: Well, my husband is a big baby, my son thinks I'm a joke, and the only person I can trust my secret with is my neighbor's dog.
Parker: My brother-in-law told me he loved me . . .

At this point the call-and-response banjo pattern escalates into a combined swirl of music played against the characters venting madly and indistinguishably about their lives. After twenty seconds or so, they pause and look at each other incredulously:

Linney: You get me.
Parker: I do.
They hug across the fence.

By linking the two series in this way, Showtime foregrounds its network brand as a venue for scripted shows with subversive content. Parker as Nancy Botwin and Linney as Cathy Jamison sit neatly alongside other provocative Showtime characters, such as the vigilante serial killer of *Dexter* (2006–2013), the uncompromising playboy of *Californication* (2007–), and the volatile heroes of *Homeland* (2011–). As this promo makes clear, though, *Weeds* and *The Big C* demonstrate a more specific Showtime preoccupation, namely, with the white middle-class wife or mother as an unconventional "dysfunctional" figure.

Together with *United States of Tara* (2009–2011), in which Toni Collette plays a character with dissociative identity disorder and several alter personalities, and *Nurse Jackie* (2009–), in which Edie Falco is a sardonic drug-addicted nurse, these four series make up a contemporary television cycle anchored by an interest in what is broadly seen as "imperfect" womanhood. This commercial orientation has been characterized in various ways. Emily Nussbaum (2009) suggests that "it's as if everyone at [Showtime] was bingeing on the books *The Madwoman in the Attic* and *Gender Trouble*, with study breaks to mosh to Courtney Love," and Nancy Franklin (2010) describes them as "a collection of series centered on women who at first pass for normal but very soon reveal themselves to be in dire, most likely irreversible, trouble." In a more specific evaluation, Mark Harris (2009) defines these series (sans *The Big C*) by their "bad mommies": "The shows—all black comedies about the impossibility of perfect parenting—share a bracing lack of sentimentality about their (anti)heroines." In this chapter I consider the bad mommy as a new feminine-feminist television type that anchors this cycle of Showtime series with a persona that is simultaneously presented as "good" and "bad." I also consider the internal consistencies of the series' transposition of the sensibilities of cinematic indie culture, specifically addressing the concerns of another cycle: the "smart" cycle of films visible from the late 1990s to the mid-2000s.

CYCLES

Assuming that cycles form only because an originary text creates a financial or critical buzz around easily reproducible elements (Klein 2011, 11), *Weeds* can be viewed as the first entry in the "bad mommies" cycle in its presentation of a disruptive female protagonist in a conventional family environment. Further, Showtime played to the burgeoning rhetoric of quality television by couching this definitive element in a dubious ethical scenario and inflecting the writing and characters with a smart, deadpan verbosity.[1] The style and sensibility of *Weeds* played directly to audience desire for what Kim Akass and Janet McCabe have called the "institutionalized" controversy, pioneered by HBO, in which profanity, sex, and violence mark a cable network as having cultural prestige, creative integrity, market influence, and broadcast freedom (2007, 63–64). As Jenji Kohan, the creator of *Weeds*, describes the genesis of the show, "I pitched a one-liner to Showtime: suburban, widowed, pot-dealing mom . . . and they told me to run with it. [Showtime] had a mandate at the time to make noise . . . because they wanted to come out from under the shadow of HBO. I guess this was noisy enough for them" (Eckerling 2007, 72). The high-concept, "noisy" quandary posed by Nancy is refracted across the cycle in the questions that the figure of Tara raises over mental illness, Jackie over drug addiction, and Cathy over cancer. Each character iterates the figure of the bad mommy by mapping previous television types like the "new woman," the "single mom," and the "unruly woman" onto ethical questions and scenarios.

The function and effect of supposed controversy can here be taken up to illustrate significant commonalities between the discourses of quality TV and indie cinema. The latter is taken to mean the post-1990 institutionalized mode of practice that is marked by characteristics such as a broadly realist imperative that elevates character over plot, the mannerist stamp of a (typically male) maverick author, and a mode of stylistic presentation that is often called up as ironic or quirky. In addition, indie film is distinguished by a set of implicit viewing procedures that seek an engagement from audiences that is both emotional and intellectual (Staiger 2013, 23). In recent years, many indie practitioners have mobilized these traits in critically successful television series, praising the creative freedom that cable networks—like specialty major-independent studio divisions Fox Searchlight or Sony Classics—offer for experimentation with both content and form.[2] In the promotion and reception of this work in film and television, the industrial sites of indie production and quality television have been distinguished from the mainstream as smarter, artier, and more liberal realms. Both sites favor a style of dramedy that centers on the emotional dysfunction of the white middle-class, which is understood to open directly onto the excess, failure, and desperation of contemporary American culture.

With the objective of focusing on and examining this broad analogy, this chapter argues that the controversial protagonists and themes of *Weeds, United States of Tara, Nurse Jackie,* and *The Big C* can be likened to similar content in the niche cycle of American smart cinema. Best understood as a sensibility within the broader category of indie film, smart films are distinguished by a detached and disaffected tone that uses irony to position them as too clever for—and thus in opposition to—the mainstream (Sconce 2002; Perkins 2012). Specifically, smart films use irony to destabilize audience responses to moral issues. Narratives often include hot-button topics such as death, pedophilia, abortion, adultery, and incest, which divide audiences into those who get a film, and those who don't. A concentrated example of the logic of distinction that governs indie cinema and culture in general, the smart film in this way flouts its distance from mainstream registers of taste and value. Given that cycles emerge pragmatically but also temporally, with semantics that are crafted to reflect a facet of the contemporary moment, it can be argued that Showtime's bad mommies cycle capitalizes directly on the critical and popular success of smart cinema as a cultural trend as well as on the changing issues and priorities of contemporary feminist perspectives.

Elsewhere, I have discussed how the smart film's interest in small stories about ordinary lives is couched in a narrative style that emphasizes life as a constant and circular process of adapting to the expectations raised by everyday events and other people (Perkins 2012, 58–73). Smart films are, at heart, ethical deliberations on how best to live. They are broadly definable by Stanley Cavell's notion of perfectionism, which suggests that the quest for human fulfillment is a moral imperative that structures film narrative. The central point of narrative intrigue is an implicit line of questioning in which characters reflect on "how they shall live their lives, what kind of persons they aspire to be" (Cavell 2004, 11) as they are caught up in processes of questioning, judgment, confusion, and attempted transformation. In the most caustic films of the cycle—such as Todd Solondz's *Palindromes* (2004), Noah Baumbach's *Margot at the Wedding* (2007), and Jason Reitman's *Young Adult* (2011)—it is implied that genuine change is impossible for the alienated characters. The moralizing and judgmental perspective that is frequently perceived in this work implicitly depicts how *not* to live: presenting a narcissistic "limit situation" that provides a scathing critique of the ethical potential of the white middle class.[3]

TELEVISION FEMINISMS

The broad syntactical link between the smart cycle and the Showtime series under consideration here, then, is that both foreground ethical situations to frame an interest in how people cope with life circumstances. In the absence of tightly plotted scenarios, smart films proceed as a type of observational cinema, weaving together episodes from lives that palpably but invisibly extend before and after the narrative. The punch lines of these films lie in the self-awareness, or lack thereof, that characters attain, and its implication for how they will live in the future. The format of serialized television enables the continuing depiction of such lives, carrying the overarching theme of perfectionism across seasons. In the Showtime cycle, this is taken up in the examination of female experience, which in the smart film frequently appears as a brittle archetype that carries the empty malaise of middle-class life. Television narrative necessitates the serialization of this limited situation, which in these four series can be read as a reaction against the cinematic model: Nancy, Tara, Jackie, and Cathy exist in a temporal structure where the anger and contradictions that are smothered and curtailed in film are mobilized as the very substance of the ongoing narratives, and the possibility of transformation is consistently negotiated.

The actions of these four women are anchored by the Showtime motif of the conflicted protagonist who is neither straightforwardly good nor bad. Each is a mother facing a unique set of challenging life circumstances: Nancy is widowed, and Tara, Jackie, and Cathy are all defined by a diagnosed disease. In each case, the premise functions to metonymically express a larger concern with moral perfectionism: the question of how best to live in order to achieve a fulfilling existence. Initially, the trope of the divided character puts this question in overtly ethical terms by ascribing each character's bad conduct to their effort to do good in overwhelming circumstances: Nancy's criminal lifestyle is referred back to the necessity of providing for her family; Tara's rebellious and destructive alter egos emerge beyond her control; Jackie takes painkillers to better help the desperate patients in her New York City hospital; Cathy starts break-

FIGURE 13.1. Edie Falco as Jackie Peyton in *Nurse Jackie*.

ing the rules of being a good wife when she receives her terminal diagnosis. Each is presented as a strong woman facing her lot with courage and determination and exhibiting behavior that is at once saintly and taboo. This foundational idea is most precisely allegorized in *Nurse Jackie*'s "Holy Shift" promo shot—which poses Edie Falco with a halo of syringes and pills. As each series settles into a serialized state, though, the clear-cut ethical setup gets blurrier. It becomes obvious that Nancy likes being a gangster; Tara's good and bad alters become harder to distinguish; Jackie realizes her pills are more than a "little bump" to get her up and running; and Cathy's behavior becomes less about her cancer and more about how she has lived her life. Actively aware of the conflicts they sustain, the characters oscillate wildly between different desires, attitudes and actions, and the conflicted figure becomes a trope with which to reflect and rework historical discourses of television feminism.

Historically, there is a notable absence of US dramatic television series centered on female leads; the situation comedy is the genre most consistently associated with female heroines and a progressive politics of liberal feminism (Rabinovitz 1999, 145). As a circular format striving always to reestablish a norm, the sitcom employs narrative and generic qualities that simultaneously introduce and restrain subversive content, thereby functioning as a safe site for feminist discourse (Lotz 2001, 111). It is only relatively recently that women have started appearing as leads in series such as *Ally McBeal* (1997–2002), *Desperate Housewives* (2004–2012), and *Grey's Anatomy* (2005–)—"flexi-narratives" that delay resolution in order to construct "open" rather than "closed" story lines (Creeber 2004, 2–7). Drawing on Umberto Eco, Angela Ndalianis has discussed how such television narratives draw audiences in multiple directions in a "neobaroque" form that displays "a loss of entirety, totality, and system in favour of instability, polydimensionality, and change" (2005, 86–87). This narrative structure is compelling, from a feminist perspective, for its potential to maintain the middle section of a narrative in a state of "liminality," in which the possibility of change and movement is celebrated (Mulvey 1987, 15).

Showtime's "bad mommies" cycle is a central part of a new wave of female-centered television that mobilizes this liminal serial format to engage with complex and contradictory issues of contemporary white middle-class female experience. The four series can be understood as postfeminist for the way that they—like *The Good Wife* (2009–), *Enlightened* (2011–2013), *Revenge* (2011–), *Girls* (2012–), *Veep* (2012–), *Top of the Lake* (2013) and *Orange Is the New Black* (2013–)— deliberately and self-consciously engage previous cultural discourses concerning marriage, romance, career, divorce, and motherhood. In the popular press, this engagement is generally read as a positive and progressive trajectory away from the "perfect" women of *Leave It To Beaver* (1957–1963) and *The Donna Reed Show* (1958–1966) toward states of independence, uncertainty, and imperfection. The contemporary moment is characterized as a period when there are more complex representations of female subjectivity than ever before. Here, strength and dramatic appeal is associated explicitly with verisimilitude. The claim is that nothing within the realm of experience is unrepresentable, and that women are no longer confined to being one thing on television.[4]

In the popular reviews that connect the four Showtime series in a cycle, this innovation is routinely linked to three points of reference. In the broad rhetoric of equality, the first is that the complex and flawed nature of these figures signals that female characterization is finally "catching up" to how men have always been represented on television (see, for instance, Young 2009). The second is that the emphasis on middle-aged women in these series has allowed Showtime to tap into a famously ignored talent pool of actresses; the network chairman and executive Matthew Blank has described the casting of these women as "a formula that works for us" (Chozick 2010). The initial success of Parker in *Weeds* gave Showtime a platform for pitching scripts to actresses like Collette, Falco, and Linney. Third, it is frequently noted that these four series were all created by women: Jenji Kohan, *Weeds*; Liz Brixius and Linda Wallem, *Nurse Jackie*; Darlene Hunt, *The Big C*; and Diablo Cody, *United States of Tara*. Together, the three points give a powerful discursive impression that television is a contemporary site for the best, richest roles for women—both in front of and behind the camera.

While many of these shifts are undeniably welcome and positive, the overarching paratextual message of "progression" needs to be carefully contextualized and historicized. Both the industry and the press promote the Showtime cycle according to a strategy of "affirmative access" that has in the past framed the representation of racial, gender, and social difference on television, typically with the objective of attracting particular target audiences. As Lauren Rabinovitz has discussed in relation to feminist and single-mom sitcoms of the 1970s and 1980s, popular media paratexts perpetuate the presumption that female audiences have shared the life experiences and values that are incorporated into television fictions. In this way, they encourage the notion that these shows are the ideological mirror of a democratic women's culture (Rabinovitz 1989, 7). As Rabinovitz's work shows, the value and interest of any television series that marks itself as a feminist discourse rests in an ability to instead "inscribe, blur and diffuse feminist attitudes that are distinct, mutually antagonistic, and necessarily contradictory" (5). As indicated, the cable environment and the liminal serialized format of *Weeds*, *United States of Tara*, *Nurse Jackie*, and *The Big C* are two factors that directly affect the capacity of this cycle to depict such contradictions. The remaining part of this chapter examines how these contradictions are borne out in the way each series iterates the key semantic element of the bad mommy and reaches back to historical television types in doing so.

BRING IT ON

In a poster that supported the double *Weeds* and *Big C* promotional campaign described at the beginning of this chapter, Mary Louise Parker and Laura Linney stand tall like Amazons. Clad in skimpy singlets and shorts, with their long hair blown out, they stare ahead defiantly. The background behind them bears the words "BRING IT ON." The fearless stance and message openly reject historical associations of the "good" woman as self-sacrificing, passive, cowed, and victimized. Instead, the two characters present the independent woman as a hell-raiser and a shit-stirrer. Nancy and Cathy temporally frame the bad mommies cycle by couching this message in uneven narratives of self-actualization. Their circumstances are framed not as a burden that they must suffer through, but as a wake-up call: a catalyst for changing their lives to something more authentic and fulfilling. It is implied that both played passive and self-sacrificing roles before their sudden change in circumstances and that they are now beginning to empower themselves.

In the poster image, this notion of empowerment is presented with the grammar of individualism that is central to a postfeminist sensibility. Illustrating and aligning the choice of both women to independently take control of their lives, the sexualized image presents them as "autonomous agents no longer constrained by any inequalities or power balances whatsoever" (Gill 2007, 155). It frames the cycle in a postfeminist subjectivity founded upon what Rosalind Gill, paraphrasing Nikolas Rose, calls the "choice biography": "the contemporary injunction to render one's life knowable and meaningful through a narrative of free choice and autonomy, however constrained one might actually be" (156). In the series, this positive trajectory of personal choice and self-determination is presented much more ambiguously. Each woman's potential for personal transformation is circumscribed by her role in the family, with all the inequalities and imbalances that it carries. The bad mommy is not an iteration of the new woman, who takes charge against bourgeois family roles (Deming 1992, 203), but is instead a comment on the "superwoman" capable of balancing a successful career and conventional family life (Lotz 2001, 108). In each of the four series, this balancing act is the site of the imperfection that distinguishes the cycle, in which each character's autonomous transformation is constantly weighed against her loss of moral authority as a wife and mother.

At its core, *Weeds* is a glorious fantasy of female power in the mold of Harmony Korine's *Spring Breakers* (2012), in which young women swagger safely through absurdly dangerous situations, fueled only by audacity and hype. Nancy Botwin resembles a teenager with her cut-off jeans and cowboy boots; her ever-present, oversized drinks; her uninflected drawl; and her partly faux naïveté. She gets into and out

FIGURE 13.2. Mary-Louise Parker as Nancy Botwin in *Weeds*.

of criminal scrapes based purely on the force of her personality and sexual bravado, and much of the series' humor arises from the juxtaposition of her dry and emphatically white manner with the modus operandi of African American drug gangs, Mexican crime lords, and ever-escalating regimes of law enforcement. In this, *Weeds* inherits from indie and smart cinema an anthropological interest in the values and absurdities of the North American white middle class—the world of "sarcasm and iced coffee," as Nancy self-reflexively describes it at one point. Against this measure, the audacity of her behavior is coded as her transgression of social space; she goes to places and meets with people that a good woman should not. In varying ways, each of the series in the bad mommies cycle takes up this theme— mobilizing the issue of whiteness as part of its protagonist's recognition and critique of her safe and entitled niche.

Nancy's will to transgress makes her a single mother who can't be contained by the domestic mold. She takes the tentative assertiveness of the sitcom's version of this figure and amplifies her into a fantastic but still identifiable character who breaks out of traditional iconographic patterns in her depiction of the conflicts of female self-actualization. The circular narrative that routinely returns the woman to the home is here replaced by a serialized story whereby she ascends the drug-dealing chain of command. Each time stability is offered—through marriage, a normal job, or a safe domestic environment—it is rejected in favor of a new start that continues the adventure. This passage is summed up in a number of powerful images of Nancy in motion, as when she rides off on a Segway from the suburban home that she has deliberately set on fire, or progresses determinedly, like Alice in Wonderland, through an illegal tunnel to Mexico.

A number of elements in this scenario resonate closely with the smart film: the dysfunctional family, the ethically charged situation, and the understated delivery of wordy and knowing dialogue. In Nancy's relentless passage onward, though, she reacts against the smart film's cynical vision of the woman frozen in a state of snarkiness or ennui. Selling weed is a choice biography that she finds authentic and fulfilling, and that allows for constant transformation across different roles and types. But it is a mode that she must consistently negotiate with her sons Silas (Hunter Parrish) and Shane (Alexander Gould), who during their tween and teen years protest against her insistence that it is their normal. Weeds in this way initiates the bad mommies cycle as a reaction against what Susan Douglas and Meredith Michaels have called "the new momism": a romanticized and demanding view of motherhood carrying the insistence that "to be a remotely decent mother, a woman has to devote her entire physical, psychological, emotional, and intellectual being, 24/7, to her children" (2004, 4). These series reject this standard of constant presence by locating the role of mothering as just one, compartmentalized part of their characters' personalities. Further, though, they put the scenario in explicitly ethical terms by representing the characters' other traits as bad: selfish, rebellious, addicted.

The last two seasons of Weeds make this conflict a key point of narrative intrigue by thematizing the question of how Nancy's sons have been affected by their upbringing. Jumping forward in time three years to a point when both are young adults, Silas struggles with Nancy for control and direction of the family business, and Shane starts training for the police force. Each ambition reflects the pole to which the two boys have consistently gravitated: Shane to normalcy, and Silas (like Nancy) to chaos. The final episode jumps forward several more years to a futuristic world where weed is legal and Nancy owns an empire of marijuana cafés. In this quasi-fantastic scenario, in which she is normal, she has obscured her past from youngest son, Stevie (Mateus Ward)—who claims her history is "very confusing" to him. Each member of the extended Botwin family is living a full life away from Nancy, and the episode implicitly asks whether she is in this way paying for her "sins." Ultimately, though, *Weeds* ends on a note of benediction. Nancy is alone but also free, and when she decides to sell the business (to Starbucks), she is again rejecting a safe and static life in favor of movement toward the unknown—crystallizing her commitment to her life as an autonomous, self-determining being.

In *United States of Tara* and *Nurse Jackie*, a different narrative setup distinguishes the bad mommy. Tara's and Jackie's circumstances do not suddenly befall them, but extend back beyond the beginning of each series. Diablo Cody describes Tara's disorder as a "primal wound" that she has been living with her entire life (Young 2009); while in rehab, Jackie admits that she started taking pills when her teenage daughter Grace (Ruby Jerins) wouldn't stop crying as a baby. The addict that she tells this to points out that it makes Grace her "ground zero," starkly locating Jackie's addiction in motherhood. In *Weeds*, the pull toward chaos that structures the narrative and its moral inquiry is externalized in the capitalist system of criminality in the United States that Nancy locates and taps into at every turn. In *United States of Tara* and *Nurse Jackie*, the pull is internal, personal, and constant, making the arc of each series less about self-actualization than about survival.

These two series are visibly concerned with the concept of female experience as comprising a set of different and incompatible roles. The orientation is built into the premise of each: Jackie's identity as a wife and mother is saved as a revelation for the end of episode 1, which has introduced her firmly by profession and addiction; *United States of Tara* takes the audacious and fantastic step of allegorizing these different states in distinct characters anchored by one performer. The choice biography that *Weeds* and *The Big C* render as a passage toward an uneven goal of fulfillment is here restricted to a smaller compass: Tara and Jackie present the imperative of appearing as a normal, stable woman as a set of "decorative choices" or disguises (Nussbaum 2009). The difficulty of maintaining control over this process is the central point of each show's dramatic intrigue, since the internal chaos of both characters constantly undermines its operation.

In this way, each of the bad mommies of *United States of Tara* and *Nurse Jackie* acts out the predicaments of femininity. Her conflicted status is inscribed bodily: in Collette's physical transformation from the controlling alter of the 1950s housewife, Alice; to the rebellious teenager, T; to the unexpressive Buck; and in Jackie's movement between using and being clean. Their embodiment of different physical states is a point of fascination and spectacle that marks the characters as unruly—they constantly carry the threat of a transgressive eruption or change (Rowe 1995, 3). The most dramatic and emotive potential for this transgression tends to lie in encounters with their children: in, for instance, the unnerving way that Tara bonds with her teenage daughter Kate (Brie Larson) when in the alter of T—smoking, shopping, and spending money—or in Jackie's barely concealed panic when she misplaces her stash of Percocet on a weekend away with her daughters.

The serialized format allows this unruliness to be presented in a syntagmatic manner that builds toward and retreats from explosion. Initially, Jackie performs and conceals her addiction right under the noses of her family and coworkers, a tension that is represented through space and gesture as she furiously imbibes pills in a toilet stall or slides offending items into the front pocket of her scrubs. When she stops using in season 4, her sobriety itself becomes the spectacle as her body literally erupts with emotion that has hitherto been anesthetized. This behavior—crying, *feeling*—is presented as a transgression of the prickly, tough Jackie of seasons 1–3 and is coded as part of her humiliation. Jackie changes across the course of the series as surely as Nancy does in *Weeds*, but her arc is restricted to the stark process of everyday survival, and her fundamentally contradictory status is borne out in a series of intimate events that Liz Brixius describes (in the "Independent Woman" episode of the PBS series *America in Primetime*) as "little earthquakes . . . slowly but surely destabilizing the ground that she walks on, the world that she inhabits."

In *The Big C*, the bad mommies cycle poses most bluntly the question of how one should live. The pull toward a chaotic unknown is put concretely as a terminal diagnosis, which establishes the serial arc and its protagonist's style of living as a version of being toward death. Cathy Jamison is a perfect enactment of the unruly woman erupting against its opposite: the self-sacrificing wife and mother (Rowe 1995, 88). On receiving her diagnosis, Cathy cuts this lifelong persona loose in order to start behaving in a way that, within the tight confines of her suburban life, offends and is offensive. Her anger is ostensibly driven by her cancer, but is immediately readable as

FIGURE 13.3. Laura Linney as Cathy Jamison in *The Big C*.

a response to her life choices. The ambivalence that she feels toward her family and teaching job is the focus of her rebellion in season 1, in which she kicks her husband, Paul (Oliver Platt), out of the house, fakes suicide in order to scare her son, Adam (Gabriel Basso), and has an affair with a hulking painter named Lenny (Idris Elba). As the series continues, this behavior is modified into subtler action and interaction as Cathy, couched once more in her traditional family role, explores possibilities for transformation within it. Like Nancy, she demonstrates how the attachments and inequities of being a wife and mother affect an autonomous, "bring it on" attitude.

Cathy is unruly insofar as she faces her circumstances as a subject of laughter rather than with the doomed suffering of melodrama. A cancer comedy, *The Big C* uses Cathy's laughter to express her contradictory emotions of anger, hope, resistance, joy, and disappointment. Comedy is used in the sense described by Rowe when she argues that genres of laughter most fully employ the motifs of liminality (1995, 10). Cathy's being toward death is a liminal space where her terminal status endows her with a dimension of the grotesque that allows her to challenge the social and symbolic systems that have kept her in her place all her life. There are two throughlines that govern this: the negative trajectory of her illness, and the broadly positive narrative of self-determination by which she sticks staunchly to not doing things as she has in the past. Throughout the series, many of the choices that signal this shift are paradigmatic and somewhat cartoonish: for instance, Cathy buys a sports car, runs the Minneapolis marathon, and gets a *C* tattooed across her surgery scar. Other actions are syntagmatic and, in their larger scale, more poignant: Cathy takes her initially rebellious African American student Andrea (Gabourey Sidibe) into her family, explores and invests in the option of adopting a baby, and constructs an alternative identity, "Alexis"—a pilot whose husband has recently died—in her visits to a nearby pub, where she drinks martinis during the day.

Marking out the distance from her previous persona, these choices make Cathy a target of Paul's incredulity and Adam's embarrassment. As a positive subversion of their expectations, her behavior appears to find an adequate metaphor in the season 3 story line that introduces the "joyologist" Joy Kleinman (Susan Sarandon). Joy starkly embodies the ideology of happiness that powers the choice biography of the neoliberal subject. Life can be different, she insists, but we have to put ourselves first: "Anybody gets in the way of our joy, and we tell them to go fuck themselves." As a cancer survivor herself, Joy makes literal the *Big C*'s subtextual message of empowerment through illness. But she is another perfect woman, and Cathy rejects her style of living—a move that finds vivid expression when Joy is hit and killed by a bus. The event is a turning point in the arc of the series. Cathy learns that her tumors have returned, and her grandiose patterns of rebellion become modulated in line with the way every dying person's world necessarily narrows. Rather than planning to extend her family, she goes back to eating her favorite pie, and quits chemo, claiming she wants to feel "like me" for as long as she can. As the series winds down, Cathy's bad behavior is channeled into the complex question of what constitutes a good death.

THE FOURTH AND FINAL SEASON of *The Big C* took the highly unusual step of altering its format. Cathy's last few months are depicted in four episodes that expand from twenty-five to sixty minutes under the subtitle "Hereafter"—"a limited series event." With new title sequences and music, and a new promotional image of a short-haired Cathy clad in a black turtleneck with a crow perched on her head, the season was framed as a coda that hyped itself as "event TV." The shift also represented a refusal to neatly absorb Cathy's demise into the existing serialized infrastructure. Even when expected, it says, death is never neat. The move was a compelling one for the bad mommies cycle, since it drew attention to the expectations and values surrounding different television formats. Like almost all the series in the "new wave" of female-centered television, these four shows have a running time of around twenty-five minutes an episode, a length traditionally associated with the safe and restraining site of comedy. Edie Falco famously lashed out against this preconception when she won an Emmy for best actress in a comedy for *Nurse Jackie* in 2010, claiming, "This is just the most ridiculous thing that has ever, ever happened in the history of this lovely awards show. Thank you so much. I'm not funny" (McNamara 2010). Her comments sparked speculation around the orientation of the series and, specifically, the question of how many comedic elements it takes to make a comedy. With its longer episode length, season 4 of *The Big C* presented a direct retort to the question of format, proving that the series worked equally well in the "serious" dramatic mold of male-centered shows like *The Sopranos* (1999–2007), *Mad Men* (2007–2015), and *Breaking Bad* (2008–2013).

The point illustrates how the "dramedic" tone of the bad mommy cycle allows each of its series to break out of rigid and traditional categorizations. By concentrating the conflicted Showtime protagonist into a new television type, the bad mommy perforates the frame of comic and serious formats, of good and bad archetypes, and of right and wrong ways of living. These series reflect the smartness of smart cinema in their black humor, their preoccupation with ethically charged situations, and their promotion of controversy as a mark of distinction. In addition, they mobilize the liminal, serialized space of cable television and the technique of "nonfunny" laughter in order to expand the representation of female experience—from the smart film's blank archetype of narcissism, and from historical television types bound by traditional and patriarchal patterns of iconography. Across these strategies, all bear the mark of the self-determining, autonomous agent who seeks empowerment, but they couch this narrative in a style of living in which the choice biography is constantly and necessarily beset by the demands of a family role. They reject the historically perfect woman who showed no flaws and operated in binary terms, and instead explore the grey area of perfectionism—where the question is not how to live right, but simply how to live.

NOTES

1. For comprehensive coverage of the industrial and discursive emergence of this phenomenon, see the essays collected by Akass and McCabe (2007).

2. For instance, Alan Ball created *Six Feet Under* (2001–2005) and *True Blood*

(2008–); Diablo Cody, *United States of Tara*; Todd Haynes, *Mildred Pierce* (2011); and Lena Dunham, *Girls* (2012–). Nicole Holofcener, Allison Anders, Gus van Sant, and Alexander Payne have directed episodes of *Sex and the City* (1998–2004), *Hung* (2009–2011), *Parks and Recreation* (2009–2015), *Boss* (2011–2012), and *Enlightened* (2011–2013). Steven Soderbergh, an important figure in the history of indie film, made *Behind the Candelabra* (2013; HBO), making good the subtext of his 2013 "State of Cinema" speech, which implied a move into television.

3. For an extended discussion of this idea, see Perkins (2014).

4. See, for instance, the "Independent Woman" episode of the PBS series *America in Primetime* (2011).

WORKS CITED

Akass, Kim, and Janet McCabe, eds. 2007. *Quality TV: Contemporary American Television and Beyond*. London: Tauris.

Cavell, Stanley. 2004. *Cities of Words: Pedagogical Letters on a Register of the Moral Life*. Cambridge, MA: Harvard University Press.

Chozick, Amy. 2010. "Television: Showtime's Bad Girls Make Good." *Wall Street Journal*, 19 March.

Creeber, Glen. 2004. *Serial Television: Big Drama on the Small Screen*. London: Palgrave Macmillan.

Deming, Robert. 1992. "Kate and Allie: 'New Woman' and the Audience's Television Archive." In *Private Screenings: Television and the Female Consumer*, ed. Lynn Spigel and Denise Mann, 203–214. Minneapolis: University of Minnesota Press.

Douglas, Susan, and Meredith Michaels. 2004. *The Mommy Myth: The Idealization of Motherhood and How It Has Undermined Women*. New York: Free Press.

Eckerling, Debra L. 2007. "Weeds." *Script Magazine*, July–August, 72–77.

Franklin, Nancy. 2010. "Old Mortality." *New Yorker*, 16 August.

Gill, Rosalind. 2007. "Postfeminist Media Studies: Elements of a Sensibility." *European Journal of Cultural Studies* 10, no. 2: 147–166.

Harris, Mark. 2009. "TV's Great Bad Mommies." *Entertainment Weekly*, 28 August.

Klein, Amanda Ann. 2011. *American Film Cycles: Reframing Genres, Screening Social Problems, and Defining Subcultures*. Austin: University of Texas Press.

Lotz, Amanda. 2001. "Postfeminist Television Criticism: Rehabilitating Critical Terms and Identifying Postfeminist Attributes." *Feminist Media Studies* 1, no. 1: 105–121.

McNamara, Mary. 2010. "A Funny Old Business." *Sydney Morning Herald*, 28 December.

Mulvey, Laura. 1987. "Changes: Thoughts on Myth, Narrative, and Historical Experience." *History Workshop Journal* 23, no. 1: 3–19.

Ndalianis, Angela. 2005. "Television and the Neo-Baroque." In *The Contemporary Television Series*, ed. Michael Hammond and Lucy Mazdon, 83–102. Edinburgh: Edinburgh University Press.

Nussbaum, Emily. 2009. "Women on the Verge." *New Yorker*, 1 February.

Perkins, Claire. 2012. *American Smart Cinema*. Edinburgh: Edinburgh University Press.

——. 2014. "Beyond Indiewood: The Everyday Ethics of Nicole Holofcener." *Camera Obscura* 85.

Rabinovitz, Lauren. 1989. "Sitcoms and Single Moms: Representations of Feminism on American TV." *Cinema Journal* 29, no. 1: 3–19.

——. 1999. "Ms.-Representation: The Politics of Feminist Sitcoms." In *Television, History, and American Culture: Feminist Essays*, ed. Lauren Rabinovitz and Mary Beth Havalovich, 144–168. Durham, NC: Duke University Press.

Rowe, Kathleen. 1995. *The Unruly Woman: Gender and the Genres of Laughter*. Austin: University of Texas Press.

Sconce, Jeffrey. 2002. "Irony, Nihilism, and the New American 'Smart' Film." *Screen* 43, no. 4: 349–369.

Staiger, Janet. 2013. "Independent of What? Sorting Out Differences from Hollywood." In *American Independent Cinema: Indie, Indiewood, and Beyond*, ed. Geoff King, Clare Molloy, and Yannis Tzioumakis, 15–27. New York: Routledge.

Young, Susan. 2009. "Flawed Females in Favor on TV Series." *Variety*, 10 June.

CHAPTER 14

MY GENERATION(S): CYCLES, BRANDING, AND RENEWAL IN E4'S *SKINS*

FAYE WOODS

IN AN ERA OF FRAGMENTING AUDIENCES and ever-expanding viewing platforms, youth television needs to move fast and make a lot of noise in order to capture and maintain the attention of the teenage viewer. The defining drama of the late-2000s blossoming of British youth television, E4's *Skins* (2007–2013), called attention to itself with its high doses of drinking, drugs, chaotic parties, swearing, and casual attitudes toward sex—its title refers to the cigarette rolling papers also used to fashion joints, but could equally apply to the bounty of teenage flesh on display. The show moved quickly, shedding its cast every two seasons as they finished school at eighteen, renewing itself with a fresh cycle of sixteen-year-old characters—three iterations before its cancellation in 2013. This chapter examines how *Skins* sought to maintain cohesion across these cycles (or "generations"), exploring how it maintained connections with its audience while disposing of entire casts.

I suggest that the development of the *Skins* brand was key to the program's success, cemented by its transmedia storytelling (Jenkins 2006), which expanded its story world across a range of media platforms: the TV program itself, books, websites, webisodes, and social media. Branding is particularly important in constructing relationships with an audience that increasingly consumes its television outside of broadcast flow; in particular, branding is essential for a program that renews its cast every two years. The *Skins* brand offered a framework of form, aesthetics, and ideology within which each new cast cycle and its accompanying set of stories were constructed. Thus, *Skins* remained ever youthful; the cast never aged out of their "scandalous" exploits. This program's brand was built on an assertion of authenticity by foregrounding the creative input of youth voices in the discourse surrounding the program. Each cast cycle—commonly termed "Gen 1," "Gen 2," and "Gen 3"—wrestled with a need to maintain continuity and familiarity, alongside a desire for freshness and originality. Yet the inevitable need to top what had gone before brought the danger of a drift away from character-based intimacy and the everyday to high-stakes drama and violence.

Broadcast on the youth-focused British digital channel E4, *Skins* was an ensemble teen melodrama that echoed US teen-TV predecessors such as *Dawson's Creek* (1998–2003) and *One Tree Hill* (2003–2012)—popular imports broadcast on E4—yet loudly asserted its difference. The program's tone swings between comedy (both mundane and surreal) and dark melodrama as it follows a group of sixteen-year-olds through their last two school years in the southwestern UK city of Bristol. But their schooling is relatively decentered; Roundview College forms a location rather than a narrative focus.[1] The ensemble eases the boredom of teenage routine with leisure time spent partying, casually (yet ostentatiously) consuming a range of pharmaceutical substances, and engaging in the ebbs and flows of tempestuous friendships, relationships, and identity formations.

The *Skins* origin story—endlessly repeated in surrounding press discourse—and its ongoing production process, both of which centralized youth voices, were basic to the program's brand identity of authenticity. The story finds the television writer Brian Elsley having his television pitches critiqued by his nineteen-year-old son, Jamie Brittain, who suggested that he write about teenagers. From there the pair developed *Skins* (Pile 2007; Widdicombe 2011). Brittain based "the characters on his friends, and creat[ed] the teenage 'writing room' in order to keep the language and plots authentic" (Wiseman 2010). By season 3, it was reported that the average age of a *Skins* writer was twenty-one (Armstrong 2009).

Each episode focuses on a single character. This structure ostensibly simplified things for the team of young writers, who were inexperienced in juggling serial television's multiple, interweaving story lines (Rochlin 2008), yet also centralized the role of point of view within the program. The focus on point of view and character interiority highlighted the single-minded narcissism of the unformed teenage identity and built close audience relationships through the intense focus on subjectivity. This relationship was maintained across the cycles of cast changes via the dedicated program website and social media.

The *Skins* brand spread beyond E4 and these transmedia spaces to include a US remake by MTV that imported the series wholesale—branding, format, characters, production process, and all; some episodes offered virtual shot-for-shot remakes of the UK originals. Since this US remake was so closely tied to the continuities of the preexisting brand, I frame its single season as an addition to the *Skins* cycle. Yet *Skins US* (as I refer to the series) served to highlight disparities between the two countries' televisual representation of teenage life; in addition, it fell afoul of both fans' and critics' comparisons with the original and suffered from aggressive negative campaigning by the Parents Television Council (Stelter 2011). The UK run of *Skins* came to a close after three cast cycles in the summer of 2013 with a seventh season of three two-part dramas that caught up with popular characters from the first two cycles as they struggled with twenty-something life.

CATALYZING BRITISH YOUTH TELEVISION

As the first original drama commissioned by E4, a free-to-air digital channel and sister to Channel 4 (one of the UK's five major broadcast channels), *Skins* set out markers for the blossoming of British youth television during the commercial expansion of the digital television era at the turn of the millennium. Targeting the sixteen-to-thirty-four-year-old demographic, it placed youth-focused US imports at the heart of its schedule, including *Dawson's Creek*, to *The O.C.* (2003–2007), and *New Girl* (2011–). E4 built its audience through these US imports—as well as with low-budget reality TV—until it could afford and sustain original scripted programming.

Other than Channel 4's long-running early-evening youth soap *Hollyoaks* (1995–), British youth-focused comedy and drama appeared only in fits and starts across the 1990s and early 2000s. The arrival of *Skins* in 2007 represented the tipping point of British youth television. Similar to how the WB's breakout hit *Dawson's Creek* coalesced that channel's identity in 1997 and set US teen TV rolling, *Skins* proved that the audience was there, forming the model for what followed. The resulting late-2000s boom in the broadcast of high-profile original British content on both E4 and BBC Three (the BBC's youth-focused digital channel) solidified the identity of British youth television.

While E4 anchors its schedules with imported US programming, it has sought to position itself as a particularly British youth channel through the tone and voice of its channel branding and its original British programming, such as *Skins, The Inbetweeners* (2008–2010), *Misfits* (2009–2013), and *My Mad Fat Diary* (2012–). British youth television is a national form with a transnational gaze across the Atlantic, one eye fixed firmly on what has gone before as it determines how to assert its own difference. This first wave of British youth television favored comedy-drama and constructed its identity through a particular tone in which a comic flippancy, a pleasure in excess, and a fondness for surreal moments played off a desire for authenticity, whether through forms of speech, a gritty setting, the mundane and everyday, social humiliation, a desire for rebellion, or the intensity of emotion.

SKINS HITS HARD

The publicity and press discourse surrounding the debut of *Skins* hyped the program's anarchistic excess and made an interlinked assertion of its authenticity regarding teenage experience. Throughout the program's run, British critics noted its attempt at balancing the glamour of its indulgence in teen vices with a more delicate emotional nuance. They suggested that there was "no point in denying that the drink, drugs and reckless shagging are a huge draw for its teenage audience" (Nicholson 2010), yet argued that behind the attention-seeking acts, *Skins* was "one of the few shows to depict teenagers working out their sexuality without criticism or judgment" (Tsjeng 2010). The *Skins* creative team viewed its "non-moralistic take on teenage problems and dilemmas [as] a source of pride," yet critics noted that behind its "heightened, even over-the-top" activities were lovable characters, "vulnerable and impulsive, but essentially good and loyal" (Jardine 2008). When the show was transferred to the United States, this lack of moralizing was at the root of the controversy surrounding the program's debut. The critic Mo Ryan suggested that US audiences had been trained by US television's prevalent conservative ideologies to expect consequences for characters' actions (Ryan 2011). Yet it was precisely this potentially contradictory combination of excess and authenticity that formed the central elements of the *Skins* brand, which carried the program through its cast cycles.

This brand identity leaned heavily on excess at the outset and cir-

FIGURE 14.1. Promotional imagery for season 1 of *Skins* centered on a trailer depicting a hedonistic party; the resulting tangle of bodies became the central image of the campaign.

culated via a range of paratexts that aimed to scandalize (Gray 2010); promotional materials including trailers, billboards, and print ads employed imagery of a hedonistic, destructive teen party, depicted through an aesthetic akin to the titillating, soft-core-porn-tinged style of the controversial fashion photographer Terry Richardson. The trailer featured the Gossip's raucous rock track "Standing in the Way of Control" playing over a furious montage of teenage partying as the bright light of the camera sought out teen bodies in a series of darkened rooms. The partyers rage with messy, childlike abandon, playing with foam, water guns, and a giant soft toy. These symbols of childhood foregrounded the sexualized youth of the program's cast in order to titillate and scandalize, intermingling them with images of booze, drugs, and intense make-out sessions amid scenes of destruction. The protagonists are picked out among the crowd, dazed and blank eyed in close-up, ecstatic in dance, partially clothed and tumbling in a mess of limbs onto floors and beds.

Jonathan Gray suggests that paratexts like this trailer "establish frames and filters through which we look at, listen to, and interpret" the program (2010, 3). This promotional imagery helped mythologize the "*Skins* party" even before the series debuted; the term entered the cultural lexicon, and was used in press reports of destructive teen house parties and hedonistic French club nights (Chivers

2008; Tasserit and Burtin 2009). The drugs, sex, debauchery, and near nakedness of the lifestyle on display formed central motifs of the *Skins* brand, creating continuity across the cast cycles and forming the centerpiece of a similar promotional campaign for *Skins US*. The drugged-out, messy, teen hedonism depicted in these paratexts also sought to establish *Skins'* difference from the imported US teen melodramas—with their glossy, aspirational, upper-middle-class lifestyles and perfect teenage bodies—that had previously dominated E4's drama output.

Valerie Wee suggests that the WB—home of *Dawson's Creek*, *One Tree Hill*, and *Smallville* (2001–2011)—offered "morally idealistic" teens and adopted relatively conservative ideologies and representations in order to avoid controversy (2008, 49). Later teen dramas such as *The O.C.* and *Gossip Girl* (which aired on the digital youth channel ITV2 in the UK) marked out their difference from the WB dramas by playing up scenes of teen excess early in their runs; *Gossip Girl*, for instance, showcased titillating imagery in its Parents Television Council–baiting "OMFG" promotional campaign for season 2 (*Variety* 2008). This content, however, was largely framed within an ideology that positioned partying excesses as signals of emotional disconnect and distress, particularly through the alcoholism of *The O.C.*'s doomed damsel in distress Marissa (Mischa Barton) and the self-serving nihilism of *Gossip Girl*'s bad boy Chuck (Ed Westwick).[2] Whereas the language and sexual content of British youth programming such as *Skins* and *The Inbetweeners* meant they could not air before ten p.m. in the United Kingdom, *The O.C.* was able to air with minimal edits in a Sunday-afternoon slot on Channel 4.

Skins cocreator Bryan Elsley supported the promotional paratexts' assertion of the program's difference in press interviews that hyped its authenticity. Elsley repeatedly (and, arguably, unfairly) asserted that before *Skins*, televisual teens were "either dying of a drug overdose because they have been f***ed by their father or they [were] impossibly bland" (Pile 2007), obliquely referring to social-realist-informed British soaps and dramas and the imported WB teen programs. Yet while *Skins* sought to distance itself from what cocreator Jamie Brittain described as "stupid issue-based stories" (Elsley 2008), it still chronicled a litany of teen problems, including eating disorders, teen pregnancies, and struggles with sexuality and mental illness. In interviews, Elsley asserted that *Skins'* authenticity and its difference from its predecessors were the result of the centrality of youth voices in the creation and writing of the programs, from his then-teenage son's role in the creation of the series to the "teen advisors" employed to vet scripts and provide stories (Green 2008; Barshad 2011).

The central imagery of excess depicted in the show's prolific, hedonistic parties formed a key part of the *Skins* brand identity, as did the production discourse highlighting the youth of the show's creative team and the attending authenticity of its voice. These elements remained central to the *Skins* brand, providing continuity as the program cycled through its three generations of cast changes and its journey to America.

CAST CYCLES

In shedding its cast virtually wholesale every two seasons, *Skins* sought to avoid the problems encountered by US teen TV—exemplified by *Beverly Hills 90210* (1990–2000), *Dawson's Creek*, and *Buffy the Vampire Slayer* (1997–2003)—when its ensembles graduate from high school and age beyond their teenage years. Popular opinion is that teen TV's "magic" fizzles when it reaches beyond the universality of high school life (Berman 2012; Hughes 2007).

The *Skins* brand is built on teenage life's collision of boredom and hedonism, of its emerging identities, of struggles to rebel or to fit in. The show wanted to live fast, die young, and leave a good-looking corpse, rather than age awkwardly into adulthood responsibility (or, more accurately, the extended adolescence of one's twenties). Thus, *Skins* shed its cast members once they reached eighteen (Holmwood 2008). The season 2 finale left shambling loser Sid (Mike Bailey) setting out for America to reclaim spacey, anorexic Cassie (Hannah Murray), formerly swaggering Tony (Nicholas Hoult) still recovering from a debilitating brain injury, and wannabe classical musician Jal (Larissa Wilson) dealing with the fallout from her pregnancy and the death of her boyfriend Chris (Joe Dempsie). Their stories ended there (although one of two-part specials in season 7 caught up with a twenty-something Cassie struggling to get by in London).

The silent, mysterious Effy (Kaya Scodelario), Tony's younger sister, had stalked the edges of Gen 1's narratives, and the season 2 finale closed with a shot of her under Tony's iconic naked-bodies duvet cover, her direct gaze at the camera signaling her role at the center of a new *Skins* generation. Season 3 started afresh, introducing Effy and

FIGURE 14.2. At the close of season 2, Tony's sister Effy is signaled as the centerpiece of the next generation of *Skins* cast.

the Gen 2 cast on their first day of term at Roundview College. When this group finished their sixth form stint after two seasons, the slate was cleaned for Gen 3 to arrive at the start of season 5. This cast had no connection with its predecessors except Roundview College and Bristol itself, and viewers were introduced to the new group through the point of view of awkward, androgynous new girl Franky (Dakota Blue Richards). Each cycle offered an unfamiliar cast with new stories, yet stories and characterizations that strongly echoed what had gone before.

The cyclic generations of *Skins* allowed another central selling point of its program brand to be maintained—the youth of its cast. Unlike US teen TV's tendency to favor twenty-something actors to play teenage roles—for production, creative, and aesthetic purposes—*Skins* touted the youth of each cycle's largely unknown cast. Each generation blended professionals (Hoult and Richards had both starred in US films as children) with amateurs sourced from open castings. These "real" teenagers fed *Skins'* claims of authenticity, the open castings serving as a promotional tool akin to the mass *X-Factor* auditions (2004–) (Wiseman 2010; Parker 2011). Yet while these cast cycles were framed as a refreshing of the program, they could potentially result in a loss of viewers who had built close emotional connections with characters, such as the intense fandom (Hunn 2012) surrounding Gen 2's lesbian couple, "Naomily" (Lily Loveless and Kathryn Prescott as Naomi and Emily). The introduction of a new cast every two seasons meant that the *Skins* brand itself formed the central point of connection with audiences.

Skins' casting choices constructed continuities in other ways, however, filling parental roles with a string of cameos by British stand-up comedians (Bill Bailey as Maxie's dad, John Bishop as Emily and Katie's dad), sketch-show performers (Harry Enfield as Tony and Effy's dad), and sitcom actors (Peter Capaldi as Sid's dad). Within a sea of unfamiliar young faces, this parental generation of comic talent provided viewer connections while also serving to assert *Skins'* comedic credentials, offsetting the intensity of its melodrama. Since *Skins* was tied closely to the point of view of its teen protagonists, parents and teachers were, unsurprisingly, depicted as outsize figures of mockery, lacking discipline or control. Tony and Effy ran rings around their oblivious, buffoonish dad, and Cassie's oversexed artist parents doted on their new baby and each other, paying only cursory attention to Cassie's eating disorder. *Skins'* parental generation of comic fools could never really pull itself together, to grow up itself and parent the teen protagonists.

RENEWED OR RECYCLED?

While each cycle offered a group of new faces, they charted familiar narrative trajectories. In each generation, the second season shifted to a darker tone, undermining "happy endings"; emotions unraveled as characters lost control of themselves and their relationships in the rush to the end of college and impending adulthood. This structure proved problematic in *Skins US*. The critic Mo Ryan (2011) noted that even these consequences were too mild for US audiences: "American cultural sensibilities, especially in the TV realm, generally demand that rule-breaking characters, especially younger ones, pay much bigger prices much sooner than the 'Skins' characters do." The dark shifts of each cycle's second season demonstrate *Skins'* hidden moralistic ideology; the effects of hedonistic lifestyles and punishments for bad behavior just take awhile to get there.

In season 1, the charismatic group leader Tony plays power games and trifles with his girlfriend, Michelle (April Pearson), for the hell of it, but the season ends with him bleeding and broken in Effy's arms after a hit and run. Season 2 charts his physical recuperation, alongside the rebuilding of his friendships. Effy's emotional detachment and nihilistic blankness cast her as an inscrutable object of desire; she toys with Cook (Jack O'Connell) and Freddie (Luke Pasqualino) in season 3, yet this detachment loosens into mental illness in season 4 (her emotional vulnerability ultimately causes Freddie's death at the hands of her therapist). The reset of each cast cycle allows an emotional renewal as new beginnings flush out the darkness—character deaths, broken relationships, shakily healed bonds.

The speed at which *Skins* chewed through its cast cycles could be seen as reflecting the fast pace of youth culture, the slang picked up and dropped like a stone, the ever-shifting vagaries of fashion, music, popular culture, and trends in illegal substances.[3] Yet some things remained the same: the parties, drugs, fights, parents, and struggles for selfhood. While this continuity illustrated the universality of teenage experience, it also created a sense of déjà vu for longtime viewers. Story lines were repeated: love triangles wrenching apart friendships—Gen 1's Tony, Sid, and Michelle; Gen 2's Effy, Cook, and Freddie; Gen 3's Frankie, Matty (Sebastian De Souza), and Nick (Sean Teale); mismatched romances producing teen pregnancies—Gen 1's Chris and Jal, Gen 3's Mini (Freya Mavor) and Alo (Will Merrick); parents finding unsuitable new partners—Sid, Michelle, Minnie; innocents dying—Chris, Freddie, Gen 3's Grace (Jessica Sula); teenage girls teetering on the brink of mental illness—both Effy and Gen 1's Cassie spent time at a surreal mental health clinic. Each cycle offered new interpretations of the same song, though at times these came close to being uninventive covers. Here the rewards for the series' long-term viewers were lessened as *Skins* sought to renew its target teenage audience with each cast cycle (Parker 2011). Whereas an audience's knowledge of a program's narrative history brings depth and narrative complexity to soap operas and "quality" serialized narratives alike (Allen 1985; Mittell 2006), with *Skins* the faithful audience's televisual memory exposes repetition. Rather than the pleasurable layering of memory traces found in long-running soaps and serial dramas, there is a sense of déjà vu, a "haven't we been here before" sensation that suggests limitations in creativity.

Skins faced an internal battle familiar to many long-running film franchises—the need to maintain continuity across discrete narratives, to remain familiar yet avoid repetition, and to top what had gone before. These escalations potentially tipped the careful balance between the show's much-vaunted emotional authenticity and its aspirational glamour of absent parents, parties, and ever-ready supplies of booze and drugs. The season 1 premiere climaxes with a comic set piece: the car that the gang has "borrowed" from the rich kids trundles slowly into the river with everyone inside. Everyone gets wet, and Sid loses a bag of marijuana, which puts him in humorous conflict with a tiny, comically mustached local drug dealer. The season 6 premiere repeats this scenario and ratchets it up a few gears: three characters, who are involved in a car chase with a drug dealer in Morocco, drive off a cliff, and the wreckage reveals multiple packs of stolen cocaine. The crash puts Grace in a coma and Matty on the run from the police. Character deaths repeat across cycles: season 2 killed off hard-partying yet emotionally lost Chris with complications from a heart condition, and season 4 topped this when the slacker romantic hero Freddie is beaten to death with a baseball bat by his girlfriend Effy's obsessed therapist.

ASPIRATION AND AUTHENTICITY

While the centerpiece of the *Skins* brand identity is the show's authenticity and emotional resonance—promoted via the emphasis in surrounding discourse on its young creative voices—the increasing excesses of later seasons illustrated the tensions at the heart of the show: the pull between ideologies of realism and aspiration, recognition and wish fulfillment. The program *was* able to portray relationships delicately and recognize the self-destructive tendencies and casual cruelties of youth; it highlighted the permeable boundary between teenage emotional turmoil and mental health struggles and, as noted above, tended not to immediately moralize its characters' flippant indulgence in sex, drinking, and drugs. When Company Pictures sought to sell *Skins* in the United States, Charlie Pattinson, a company executive, presented it "as an antidote to network teen shows . . . *Gossip Girl* and *90210*" (Frost 2011). But in fact, *Skins* drew strongly on the melodrama-infused storytelling and aspirational lifestyles modeled by US teen TV, just smudging on a bit of British "grit" to conceal the glow.

The TV critic Boyd Hilton suggested that *Skins*' audience appeal lay in its depiction of "teenagers in a quite glamorous, visually ap-

FIGURE 14.3. Bodies and mundane domestic spaces show the aftereffects of a debauched house party.

pealing way," combined with the thrill of seeing "teenagers depicted without treading on eggshells" (quoted in Frost 2011). The aspirational representations found in US teen TV—*Dawson's Creek*, *The O.C.*, and *Gossip Girl*, for example—tended toward golden-lit landscapes, perfectly sculpted and slender bodies, a voluble mastery of language, and the safety of white upper-middle-class lifestyles. *Skins* asserted its difference from these US tendencies through the everyday anonymity of its Bristol location, the bodies and faces of its nonprofessional "real" teens (though nearly all the actresses maintained the regulation slenderness of television femininity), and a tendency toward spare dialogue. The "glamour" of *Skins* lay in the parentless partying excess of its Bristol sixth-formers. The US television critic Matt Zoller Seitz described the program as "an escapist fantasy in which teens carried themselves like seen-it-all rock stars" (Seitz 2011). *Skins* louche glamour is displayed in its characters' artfully bedraggled hair and costumes, the pale clusters of teens stumbling home in the weak light of dawn, the wide-eyed high captured in close-up amid a crowd of bodies pressing together at a club as the bass thumps or a guitar wails, the tangle of bodies passed out amid the morning-after destruction.

Throughout *Skins'* run, nuanced writing and characterization sat alongside hedonistic partying, recurring clashes with drug dealers and criminals, and a normalized middle-class lifestyle in which no one needed a job to fund their prolific drug intake (this normalization is compounded by a tendency to maroon "othered" characters— gay Maxxie (Mitch Hewer), African immigrant Thomas (Merveille Lukeba), stalker Sketch (Aimee-Ffion Edwards)—on council estates).[4] All these activities are carried out against a background of largely absent parents (they leave, die, are frequently on convenient holidays, or are too wrapped up in their own emotional troubles or sexual indulgences) and few ties to schooling, offering an aspirational fantasy for a millennial generation brought up in a landscape of helicopter parents, homework, and overscheduled leisure time.

Yet ultimately this hedonism, like the consumption- and status-based lifestyles found in US teen-TV fare such as *The O.C.* and *90210* (2008–2013), is exposed as empty, particularly in the comedown of each cycle's second season, as darkness engulfs characters and the strain shows.

CONTINUITY THROUGH BRANDING

Skins' "gritty" glamour feeds into certain motifs that repeat across each generation, acting as signifiers of the show's brand: the profligate consumption of drugs, the lingering on teenage female bodies undressing or in underwear (despite its female-friendly melodrama, the male gaze remains strong in *Skins*), and the "*Skins* party," cemented in the public imagination via that first trailer. Throughout the cast cycles, continuities in aesthetics and storytelling tied together the generations. The program's structure of single-character episodes formed a key part of its brand identity, and the focus on characters' interiority forced a close identification with each member of the ensemble in turn. This structure was compounded by aesthetic elements that reflected the myopic teenage focus on selfhood, being trapped in one's own head, and the confusion and illegibility of adult life.

A fondness for the surreal—sometimes woozy, sometimes comic, sometimes threateningly unstable—permeates the series: anorexic Cassie finds Post-it notes on bus windows urging her to "Eat," and patients at the local mental health clinic bounce around the grounds in formation on space hoppers; Chris finds a tramp living in his bath after one too many pill-filled house parties; the mysterious scarred army general who Tony meets on the train to his university interview turns out to be the double of the pompous lecturer who later interviews him. This speaks both to the characters' predilection for intoxication and to the worldview of spacey, disconnected characters such as Gen 1's Cassie or the more willfully detached Effy of Gen 2. As *Skins* cycled through casts, and its faces and stories changed, these aesthetics and motifs maintained its program brand.

The *Skins* program brand formed the fixed point throughout the cast fluctuations, maintaining audience relationships across its seven seasons, and was exported nearly wholesale to MTV for the US version. Catherine Johnson suggests that "programmes are now being constructed as brands designed to encourage audience loyalty and engagement with the text beyond the act of television viewing" (2012, 1). In the digital era, with its wealth of competing channels and platforms, program brands like *Skins* are essential in constructing relationships with a youth audience whose media consumption decenters the television set.

Johnson identifies three characteristics central to the success of a program brand: longevity, multiplicity, and transferability (2012, 159). *Skins* achieved significant longevity (seven seasons of up to ten episodes each) within a British television system that tends toward short seasons and limited runs, and its diverse ensembles and distinctive individualized narrative form offered the multiple points of viewer engagement that Johnson suggests are key to a program brand's success (160). The transferability of the *Skins* brand came via its transmedia storytelling (Jenkins 2006), which expanded its story world across a range of platforms, including promotional music tours, books, and the online worlds that its audience inhabited (Armstrong 2009; Wightman 2010). The spaces between episodes (and sporadically, seasons) found characters conversing in real time over Facebook and Twitter, continuing televisual narratives or setting characters on new adventures. The *Skins* website collated these social media threads, which sat alongside character blogs, music playlists, behind-the-scenes videos, and chats with the program's stylists. Short videos added further details to televised narratives; in season 2, one web video chronicled Tony's nightmares as he struggled to recuperate from his brain injury; in season 6, another featured CCTV footage of a tryst in a school corridor, capturing a secret couple. These videos, character blogs, and social-media presences served as training grounds for the program's young writing team and were thus strongly integrated into the "voice" of *Skins* (Lovett 2012; Green 2008).

CREATIVE PROCESS AS BRAND CONTINUITY

Johnson notes that the digital era has made television's paratextuality more visible than before and suggests that we think of television programs as part of a network of paratexts generating meaning within a brand (2012, 146). As noted above, recurring motifs of the *Skins* brand—drugs, bodies, parties—were established in the promotional paratexts at the program's outset. The press discourse surrounding the program contributed to this network of paratexts by circulating details of the *Skins* creative process that contributed to the program brand's markers of authenticity and the prioritizing of youth voices. The show's cocreator Brian Elsley explicitly connected its "brand values" to the writing, which was "about staying close to the audience and selecting the right storylines for them. . . . about letting our audience feel they are not alone" (Armstrong 2009). In press reports accompanying the debut of each new cast cycle, and later the debut of *Skins US* on MTV, continuity amid change was asserted by emphasizing the program's young production team, particularly the collaborative interaction with "real" teens offered by the *Skins* writing process (Wiseman 2010; Frost 2011; Widdicombe 2011).

While most British television is written solo, in duos, or—in the case of longer-running series—by a series of individual writers, Elsley imported the US writers'-room model, in which a team of writers works to shape story arcs and break down the beats of episodes before assigning individual episodes to writers. The *Skins* writing team brought together experienced television writers with young playwrights and comedians, alongside teen and early-twenty-something writers new to television (Green; Barshad). These were supported by a group of teenage consultants who contributed story ideas and vetted scripts. Young writers—including competition winners—progressed through the ranks, via online written and video content, to the writers' room and eventually to their own episodes (Lovett 2012; Hunter 2012).

MTV bought the rights to *Skins* in 2009 in a deal that saw both Company Pictures and Brian Elsley retain their production roles, serving to "preserve the authenticity" of the UK original (Holmwood 2009). The US channel imported not just the program's characters and narratives, but also the production and casting processes that informed the program's brand identity of authenticity. Press reports continued the UK narrative of promoting the program's production process as a signifier of the authentic youth voice of *Skins US* (Bennett 2011; Widdicombe 2011; Barshad 2011). The development of *Skins US* formed part of MTV's attempt to rebrand itself following the cancellation of its hit scripted-reality series *The Hills* (2006–2010). The channel sought to reorient its brand away from the artifice of Hollywood-set *The Hills*, whose romantic narratives, designer clothes, and perfectly composed widescreen images drew from the aesthetics and storytelling of US teen TV. This stated move toward authenticity was built around the new hit reality series *Teen Mom* (2009–) and *Jersey Shore* (2009–)—both markedly less glossy than *The Hills*—alongside MTV's move into original dramatic programming with the *Skins* remake (Stelter 2010).

The UK *Skins* episodes had aired in the United States on BBC America in an edited version, with relatively clean-cut promotional portraits that were markedly less risqué than E4's. While E4's targeted demographic was sixteen-to-thirty-four-year-olds, BBC America's promotion reflected that channel's address to a much wider audience via its mixture of highbrow and genre British imports such as the long-running family sci-fi series *Doctor Who* (1963–) and the 1950s period drama *The Hour* (2011–2012). In contrast, MTV targets the same youth demographic as E4, thus the scandal-seeking debauchery of E4's promotional paratexts were strongly echoed as the channel sought to make "a huge noise" around the debut of *Skins US* (Ng 2011). Promotional imagery featured parties and piles of partially dressed bodies, and a lengthy promo rewound a teenage girl's journey from collapse to setting out for the night, via a smoke- and drink-soaked teen party (though here at a relatively brightly lit, wealthy suburban home). While *Skins US* was rated TV-MA, signaling that some content was inappropriate for viewers younger than seventeen (in comparison, *Gossip Girl* is rated TV-14) and was scheduled at ten p.m., the Parents Television Council, a conservative pressure group, took the bait and labeled *Skins US* "the most dangerous show for children that we have ever seen" (Bennett 2011) and campaigned for corporations to pull their advertisements (Stelter 2011).

Alongside these promotional paratexts, MTV's importing of one of the key signifiers of *Skins'* authenticity—the use of "real teenagers" in its young cast—contributed to a further media storm. The PTC—

incorrectly—claimed that the use of underage actors in scenes with "sexual content" violated federal child pornography statutes, causing consternation at MTV (Stelter 2011). While the PTC has a long history of targeting teen TV—the *Gossip Girl* OMFG campaign appropriated the PTC's criticism of the program as "mind-blowingly inappropriate" (*Variety* 2008)—MTV's replication of the *Skins* program brand, which was designed originally for a more lenient British broadcasting environment and for audiences familiar with risqué black humor, nonetheless was at odds with the expectations of teen-targeted content in the United States.

While the US cycle of *Skins* imported the key elements of the *Skins* brand of excess and authenticity (the inclusion of youth voices in its creative process, the use of key motifs and storytelling structures), the ultimate cancellation of *Skins US* after a single season—MTV stated the show "didn't connect with a US audience as much as we had hoped" (Ng 2011)—can be viewed as the result of the incompatibility of the "gritty glamour" of the *Skins* brand and the US teen-TV model it was originally created to oppose. Yet the experience of producing *Skins US* helped MTV discover how original fiction programming could serve both its channel brand and the US teen-TV context. This resulted in the teen sitcom *Awkward* (2011–), whose relatively casual attitude toward teen sexuality and drinking shows traces of *Skins'* influence, yet frames this within the safer world of romantic comedy in a brightly lit middle-class suburban milieu.

SKINS RETURNED TO E4 in the summer of 2013 for the final cycle, *Skins Redux*, formed of three two-part dramas—*Fire*, *Pure*, and *Rise*—that caught up with some of the most popular characters as they entered their twenties. Catherine Johnson argues that a program brand is not a static, singular object (2012, 157), yet was the *Skins* program brand, built on the excess and authenticity of the teenage lifestyles it depicted, transferable to (emerging) adulthood? *Skins Redux* found Gen 1's Cassie and Gen 2's Effy and Cook each struggling to find their place in the lonely city expanses of London and Manchester, far from the safety of Bristol, their families, and their friends. Teen hedonism gave way to characters scrabbling to succeed in cutthroat work environments or searching to solidify personal identity in the adult world. Drinking, drugs, and sex remained—those central motifs of the *Skins* brand—and the characters slipped a little too easily into the aspirational glamour offered by the worlds of high finance, fashion, and crime, yet each ultimately rejected these temptations.

The key signifiers of the *Skins* brand, asserted throughout the earlier cycles—the authenticity conferred by the fresh casts of teenage unknowns and the young writers' room—were no more. Murphy, Scodelario, and O'Connell were up-and-coming British actors with West End plays, feature films (*Wuthering Heights*, 2011), and BBC and HBO "quality" dramas (*Dive*, 2010; *Game of Thrones*, 2011–) under their belts. The authentic youth voices of the writing room were abandoned; instead, *Skins Redux* was kept in the family as Brian Elsley and his son and daughter, Jamie and Jess Brittain, wrote for, respectively, Cassie, Cook, and Effy. The cycles of *Skins*, with their shedding of ensembles at eighteen and their clamoring noise of teenage voices, were built on raciness, rebellion, and renewal, on never growing old. Yet with *Redux*, *Skins* abandoned its teenage self and stopped running from adulthood; we saw what happened next, and with that, *Skins* finally died.

NOTES

1. In the United Kingdom, compulsory schooling ends at sixteen, when students sit for the GCSE (General Certificate of Secondary Education). They can study for further qualifications—most commonly, A ("Advanced") Levels—for two more years, either at their high schools or at a separate college. These two years are commonly termed the "sixth form." College in Britain is not the same as university, but immediately precedes it.

2. *The O.C.*'s creator, Josh Schwartz (2004), noted that the network initially encouraged them to "push the envelope" in order to mirror the teenage excesses that audiences experience on reality TV. Yet in the more conservative televisual climate that emerged in the wake of Janet Jackson's "wardrobe malfunction" at the 2004 Super Bowl, incidents of sex, drugs, and debauchery noticeably decreased through *The O.C.*'s first season.

3. A *New Yorker* article quotes the teenage advisers of *Skins US* discussing whether a script was using the most up-to-date slang (Widdicombe 2011).

4. In British film and television, sprawling public housing complexes, with their small, poorly insulated flats, are an easy signifier of struggling, working-class lifestyles and of lives lived on the edge of poverty.

WORKS CITED

Allen, Robert Clyde. 1985. *Speaking of Soap Operas.* Chapel Hill: University of North Carolina Press.

Armstrong, Stephen. 2009. "Loyalty Points." *Guardian,* 11 May.

Barshad, Amos. 2011. "Skins Co-creator Bryan Elsley on Adapting His Show for MTV." *Vulture*, 17 January.

Bennett, Jessica. 2011. "The Most Dangerous Show on Television." *Newsweek*, 14 January.

Berman, Judy. 2012. "9 Signs a Teen TV Show Has Exceeded Its Expiration Date." *Flavorwire*, 13 September.

Chivers, Tom. 2008. "'Skins Party' Wreaks Havoc in Suburban Street." *Telegraph*, 5 March.

Elsley, Bryan. 2008. "Introduction to Skins." *Skins Online* (blog), 14 September. http://skinsonline.blogspot.co.uk/2007/09/introduction-to-skins-by-bryan-elsey.html (access to the blog is by invitation only).

Frost, Vicky. 2011. "The Return of Skins." *Guardian*, 25 January.

Gray, Jonathan. 2010. *Show Sold Separately: Promos, Spoilers, and Other Media Paratexts*. New York: New York University Press.

Green, Chris. 2008. "Teen Writers Show Their 'Skins.'" *Independent*, 11 February.

Holmwood, Leigh. 2008. "Skins 3: The Hunt for the New Tony Begins." *Guardian*, 28 March.

———. 2009. "MTV to Remake E4 Hit Teen Drama Skins for the US Audience." *Guardian*, 24 August.

Hughes, Sarah. 2007. "So Long Veronica Mars: Why Can't TV Do College?" *Guardian*, 31 May.

Hunn, Deborah F. 2012. "'The Dark Side of Naomily': Skins, Fan Texts and Contested Genres'." *Continuum* 26, no. 1: 89–100.

Hunter, Laura. 2012. "Skins Writer: 'Teen Shows Should Be Written for Teens, by Teens.'" *Radio Times*, 16 February.

Jardine, Cassandra. 2008. "Skins: The Wild Bunch." *Telegraph*, 31 January.

Jenkins, Henry. 2006. *Convergence Culture: Where Old and New Media Collide*. New York: New York University Press.

Johnson, Catherine. 2012. *Branding Television*. Abingdon, UK: Routledge.

Lovett, Daniel. 2012. "Daniel Lovett: Interview." Interview by Matthew Bell. *BAFTA Guru*, 30 January.

Mittell, Jason. 2006. "Narrative Complexity in Contemporary American Television." *Velvet Light Trap* 58, no. 1: 29–40.

Ng, Philiana. 2011. "MTV Cancels 'Skins.'" *Hollywood Reporter*, 9 June.

Nicholson, Rebecca. 2010. "Skins Comes Out . . . as a Thoughtful, Heavyweight Drama." *Guardian*, 23 January.

Parker, Robin. 2011. "Skins (Series 5): Youth TV With the X-Factor." *Broadcast*, 28 January, 32.

Pile, Stephen. 2007. "The Naked Truth about Being Young." *Telegraph*, 20 January.

Rochlin, Margy. 2008. "A Show Written for the Young by the Young." *New York Times*, 17 August.

Ryan, Mo. 2011. "'Skins' Creator Defends the MTV Show's Morals, but What about the Edgy Drama's Other Problems?" AOL.com, 25 January.

Schwartz, Josh. 2004. "Josh Schwartz of The O.C. Interview." Interview by Daniel Robert Epstein. UGO.com. The original website is no longer active; the interview is archived on the Internet Archive's Wayback Machine: http://web.archive.org/web/20050430053016/http://www.ugo.com/channels/filmtv/features/theoc/default.asp.

Seitz, Matt Zoller. 2011. "'Skins" Salacious Teen Thrills." Salon, 18 January.

Stelter, Brian. 2010. "MTV Reinvents Itself for the Millennial Generation." *New York Times*, 24 October.

———. 2011. "Taco Bell Pulls Ads from MTV's 'Skins.'" *New York Times*, 21 January.

Tasserit, Maxence, and Steven Burtin. 2009. "'Skins' Parties, Even Trashier than Woodstock? Really?" France24.com, 1 October.

Tsjeng, Zing. 2010. "'Skins': It's Not Just about the Sex and Drugs." *Guardian*, 18 March.

Variety. 2008. "'Gossip Girl': Harsh Reviews Make for Good Quote Ads." 31 July.

Wee, Valeria. 2008. "Teen Television and the WB Television Network." In *Teen Television: Essays on Programming and Fandom*, ed. Sharon Marie Ross and Louisa Ellen Stein, 43–60. Jefferson, NC: McFarland.

Widdicombe, Lizzie. 2011. "Expert Witnesses." *New Yorker*, 10 January.

Wightman, Catriona. 2010. "E4 Announces New 'Skins' UK Tour." *Digital Spy*, 16 December.

Wiseman, Eva. 2010. "Teenagers: Under Their Skins." *Guardian*, 19 December.

CHAPTER 15

EXTENDED ATTRACTIONS: RECUT TRAILERS, FILM PROMOTION, AND AUDIENCE DESIRE

KATHLEEN WILLIAMS

THE LENGTH OF A PROMOTIONAL CYCLE for a film generally begins with the emergence of a poster or a film trailer that attempts to both "announce wares" and "win patrons" (Staiger 1990, 3). Traditionally, film trailers and posters have been used to draw audiences to the cinematic space to consume a feature film. But as film promotion has increasingly shifted from the spaces of the cinema and television, and from being tied to the event of film going, objects of film promotion can be consumed and enjoyed for their own sake at any point in a film's promotional life. The presence of trailers on DVDs and on the Internet mean that consumers can watch a trailer well after a film has been released and for purposes other than choosing which upcoming feature to watch.

Recut trailers, which are typically uploaded to the video-sharing site YouTube, involve the recutting or splicing together of footage from one or more sources to create a trailer for a film that does not and will not exist. In some instances, footage is shot specifically for the trailer. Recut trailers alter the typical path of film promotion, which seeks to announce a film, build an audience, and draw viewers to the space of the cinema. Famous examples of recut trailers include *The Shining* (1980, Stanley Kubrick) recut as a family comedy, or footage from *Back to the Future* (1985, Robert Zemeckis) recut to mimic the narrative of *Brokeback Mountain* (2006, Ang Lee). Although they take the form of an advertisement, recuts seek to advertise something that cannot be obtained, since a hybrid film such as *Brokeback to the Future* (Chocolate Cake City 2006) will not eventuate. Recut trailers reflect and embody audience desire to see an existing feature be extended into a sequel, create a cycle of films, or generate multiplicities through a series of links between disparate films.

This chapter outlines the numerous ways that recut trailers play with the temporality of a feature film's promotion, as well as how they may shift our understanding of what may constitute filmic multiplicities. Recut trailers allow users and audiences to revisit, rework, and augment their memory of a feature film, identifying latent story lines, shifting the genre of a film, or allowing a character from a film to exist in a newly imagined film. They consequently disrupt the typical longevity of a film, leaving tangible objects of audience desire that can be revisited to keep a film almost timeless, allowing an older feature film to be reinvigorated through any of the aforementioned strategies.

I discuss the creation of multiplicities through three case studies in this chapter. First, through an analysis of recuts and originally shot trailers created in the wake of *Snakes on a Plane*'s release (2006, David R. Ellis), I position the recut trailer as a form through which audiences can mock and subvert attempts by Hollywood studios to create film cycles and multiplicities. Second, I use *Inception* (2010, Christopher Nolan) to demonstrate how sound can be used to create multiplicities of a singular film, drawing connections where none were thought to exist. Finally, I discuss fake sequels created for the blockbuster historical action film *Titanic* (1997, James Cameron) to establish how recuts can act as material traces of audience desire to extend a singular film into a series, in particular by combining intertextual references to locate the narrative of *Titanic* as one part of the larger narrative of the characters Jack (Leonardo DiCaprio) and Rose (Kate Winslet).

Though recut trailers are typically considered singular objects that bear little relation to one another (for instance, *The Shining Recut* (Neochosen 2006) as a family feel-good film seems to have little connection with *Brokeback to the Future*), I look at recut trailers that do foster connections and encourage multiplicities. The presence of one recut trailer sparks mimicry to see who can create the most absurd connections between films or generate the most unlikely of story lines.

Throughout this chapter, I discuss these case studies in relation to anticipation and memory, that is, how temporality guides the production and consumption of recut trailers. I argue that anticipation is a driving force behind users wanting to extend a feature and intervene in cinematic memory. Film trailers require us to anticipate—to look forward to the release of a film, but also to anticipate its content and to speculate on its possibilities. We anticipate the content of a film based on our knowledge and cinematic literacy: hearing that Samuel L. Jackson is in *Snakes on a Plane* helps guide our expectations for the feature by drawing on our memories of other films he has appeared in. This is also true for the potential pull of directors: *Avatar*'s trailer listed *True Lies* (1994), *Terminator 2* (1991), *Aliens* (1986), and *Titanic* (1997) as among James Cameron's other directorial achievements. The trailer may nod to this knowledge that is implicit in the audience, drawing attention to the director's body of work and guiding the audience to consider the new film in relation to his or her prior successes.

While recut trailers place past footage in the anticipatory mode through the use of techniques commonly used in trailers and by employing anticipatory reading from audiences, they also evoke memories of past films. Throughout the case studies discussed here, I look at how memory is playfully augmented, shifted, and reworked into new narratives, eras, and genres through the production and consumption of recut trailers. While playfully mocking Hollywood studios' attempts to sell films by appealing to all, recut trailers reflect and embody audience desire to extend the length of a film or to see elements of it play out in a series of newly connected films.

THEATRICALLY RELEASED FILM TRAILERS, MARKETING, AND RECUT TRAILERS

Recut trailers have been continually uploaded to YouTube since its launch in 2005. They have become one of the most consistently popular forms of remixed video online (Horwatt 2009, 82). Recut trailers vary in the types of content being adapted and augmented, and in intent. While some creators demonstrate a fanlike adoration for the source footage they are manipulating, such as fan trailers created for the *Twilight* films (Williams 2012), others manipulate content to demonstrate their knowledge of a film and their cinematic literacy. The trailers examined in this chapter reflect how audiences enact desire and anticipation. The recut trailers remain as traces of the event of cinematic anticipation—serving as material objects of the desire to extend the world of a film beyond its theatrical release.

The most common form of recut trailers involves "genre-shifting" (Tryon 2009), or taking a film and switching its intent by editing footage to make it appear as though the film belongs to another genre.

Popular examples of this include *Mary Poppins* (1964, Robert Stevenson) recut as a horror film in *Scary Mary* (Moviemker 2006), or *Jaws* (1975, Steven Spielberg) recut as a love story between a man and a shark in *Must Love Jaws* (Vayabobo 2006). Genre shifting is successful not only because of the absurdity of a story line of love between a man and a shark, but also because enjoying a recut trailer involves an audience drawing upon its memory of a film and looking for latent story lines hiding in the margins. *The Shining* recut as a family comedy suggests that the editing of a feature can unearth a different perspective or an entirely different film altogether. Meaning is not fixed in a feature film; it is up for negotiation and manipulation by viewers through their memories and by creating their own objects such as a recut trailer.

Before analyzing specific examples of recut trailers, it is important to consider the function and history of theatrically released trailers. Throughout this chapter, I refer to those trailers created by a studio as official or theatrically released, and to user-generated trailers as recuts. Film trailers have been screened in a variety of ways throughout cinematic history. Trailers came to prominence by advertising upcoming attractions in the space of the theater or cinema. Trailers were then introduced as one of the earliest types of advertisements on television. Although appearing in a constant stream of other advertisements, television trailers sought to draw audiences to the space of the cinema. Following the evolution of home theaters, trailers were later included on videocassettes to advertise upcoming video releases, and then on DVDs as "special features." On a DVD, rather than acting as an advertisement for something to be obtained, the "special features" trailer was watched as a promotion for a feature already consumed. As bandwidth and video capability increased online, trailers began appearing on the Internet. They can now be watched on sites such as YouTube at any point in a film's promotional life. Yet they occupy a unique temporal position: they are suspended in an anticipatory state, always claiming that the subject of the trailer is "coming soon."

Since trailers can now be seen in a variety of ways at any point in a film's promotional life, it can no longer be assumed that audiences will watch a trailer before consuming the feature it depicts. Trailers can introduce an audience to the look and feel of a feature film, but they—crucially—also act as a way to *reenter* the world of a feature. This can be achieved by watching a trailer that has been included on a DVD as a special feature or by rewatching a trailer online after the feature has been released.

Trailers and other promotional material mean that audiences are generally familiar with a film before watching it (Burgin 2004, 14). Jonathan Gray argues: "We may in time resist the meanings proposed by promotional materials, but they tell us what to expect, direct our excitement and/or apprehension, and begin to tell us what a text is all about, calling for our identification with and interpretation of that text before we have seemingly arrived at it" (2010, 48). Consequently, film promotion not only makes viewers aware of a film before they watch it, but also allows them to make judgments about it. We anticipate its content and share our anticipation of the film (or our lack of excitement) with others. The trailer has always played a crucial role in the marketing of a film, but as Lisa Kernan (2004) and Keith M. Johnston (2009) have argued, the trailer has played a pivotal role in cinema more broadly, since it not only is how we become familiar with a film, but increasingly, also is how we interact with cinema outside the space of the theater. Theatrically released film trailers "refer to the process of production" of feature films; the names of the studio, the director, and other people and groups involved in the making of the film draw the audience into the world of a feature and into the world of filmmaking (Marshall 2002, 69). Promotional materials such as the trailer "deepen the significance of the film for its audience" by working within the "industrial strategy of massaging the filmic text into something larger" (69). Trailers make this explicit by pointing out other films an actor has appeared in or other films created by the director or producer. Over the past century, as Marshall notes, the evolution of cinema has led to "the intensification and elaboration" of what he refers to as "the intertextual matrix" (69). Audience members do not learn about a feature film by showing up at a cinema unprepared and just watching it—they learn about a film through other platforms, most notably through the trailer and other promotional material.

Since the 1970s there has been an enormous increase in the number of objects used as tie-ins for a feature film, including clothes, toys, and games, meaning that the presence of a feature film is delineated from the cinema and then spread across everyday urban life (Burgin 2004, 14). While items such as promotional T-shirts and toys may be more readily seen as commodities, they play a temporal role by extending the spread of a feature film. A studio may intend a trailer or a poster to be the entry point to a feature, but those sorts of texts act as only one part of a network that circulates around a feature. That network extends the experience of the feature film outside the film's running time and outside the cinema, and can be evoked by a toy in the likeness of a character or by a poster hung on a wall years after the commercial release of a feature.

Thomas Elsaesser describes the act of going to see a movie as a type of contract between audiences and the studios:

> When buying a movie ticket, we are effectively taking out a contract, by which in exchange for our money, we are guaranteed (temporary access to) a normative, quality-controlled product. Conversely, our part of the deal is to be prepared to pay: not for the product itself and not even for the commodified experience it represents, but simply for the possibility that such a transubstantiation of experience into commodity might "take place." Neither the term "product" nor "service," neither the idea of "consumption" nor the concept of "leisure" quite capture the nature of this act of faith. (2001, 16)

Film trailers have often acted as an entry point for audiences into this contract, helping guide decisions about which films to see. They reinforce taste and value judgments and frequently make rhetorical appeals based on particular stars, genres, or narratives (Kernan 2004). In addition, they make technological appeals (Johnston 2009) by drawing attention to technology associated with a film—whether it is sound, 3D vision, or CGI (computer-generated imagery).

In recent years there have been examples of patrons demanding a refund or even attempting to sue studios and cinemas over allegedly misleading trailers. In one case, a woman claimed that there was an enormous discrepancy between the trailer for *Drive* (2011, Nicolas Winding Refn) and the actual film, particularly that the violence of the film was not adequately depicted in the trailer, and thus left her unprepared for it (Child 2011). In 2013, a New Zealand man demanded a refund because an explosion seen in the trailer for a film was omitted in the final cut (Chapman 2013). These two examples play out to excess the contract described by Elsaesser, and they attracted derision because audiences increasingly expect a trailer to amplify or omit parts of a film in order to increase the film's appeal.

Recut trailers have emerged from these cultural expectations surrounding the role of the trailer as an entry point into the narrative world of a film, and as a way to guide cinemagoers into the practice of consumption. They adopt the methods used by studios to sell a film, yet ensure that no end product, no feature, can be attained. Recut trailers demonstrate the underlying potential of any film to be augmented or read differently, reflecting on the role of the audience as a producer of knowledge, and playing with the expectation that Hollywood studios manipulate films through trailers in order to appeal to audiences.

SNAKES ON A PLANE, BUS, BOAT, CARAVAN . . .

In 2006, New Line Cinema announced the release of a film titled *Snakes on a Plane*. It was rumored that Samuel L. Jackson became involved in this production merely because of the name alone (IMDb 2006). The high-concept film played with audiences' expectations of what might be the story line of a feature film with that title, how such a film would be marketed, and how the trailer would differ from the eventual feature.

In the lead-up to the release of *Snakes on a Plane*, users made recut trailers and circulated them online (acts encouraged by the studio), bloggers wrote blog posts, news articles were published about the hype surrounding the movie, and even a participation script (a prompt sheet for audience reactions) was written and distributed online before the film's release—and before its author had seen the film. If film advertising seeks to announce its wares and win patrons, as Staiger (1990) argues, *Snakes on a Plane* suggested that the name of a film alone could announce wares and build anticipation. New Line did not ignore the amount of hype and anticipation building online— it famously responded to suggestions from bloggers and preemptive fans by shooting new footage to move the film from its original PG-13 rating to R (Waxman 2006). It was the name and premise of the film that captivated the imagination of audiences and generated online appropriation and subversion of the concept. In short, you didn't need to see the final product in order to understand it, co-opt it, and parody it.

The MTV parody *Snakes in a Boardroom* (DeNigris 2007) plays with the role of Hollywood studios in the creation of content for box-office success. The fictional film studio PairEmUp Productions workshops a new film that will capitalize on the online success of

Snakes on a Plane. One executive claims that the studio needs to reach the "MTV, Internet generation." When another executive tells him of the success of *Snakes on a Plane*, he responds, "We have our formula then! Animals on transportation, vermin on vehicles." This leads to a ridiculous series of potential film titles such as *Rabbits on a Rollercoaster, Salmon on a Speedboat, Rats on a Razor Scooter,* and *Beavers on a Bullet Train*; they finally settle on *Tarantulas in a Town Car*. This parody makes explicit the playfulness of the *Snakes on a Plane* recut trailers—that this concept was brought into being in a boardroom by executives trying to create vehicles for box-office success.

Each of the parody trailers follows the same principle: an animal that should not be on a particular mode of transport wreaks havoc. One of the most-watched trailers, *Goats on a Boat* (3rd Floor Productions 2006), includes footage from *Snakes on a Plane* to make its connection explicit. The story line involves underworld criminals releasing killer goats on board an ocean liner, where they terrorize passengers. The joke works predominantly in two ways: first, by making goats a source of horror (the worst damage they appear to inflict is shredded clothes and chewed cans), and second, by building upon the absurdity of *Snakes on a Plane*, implying that the original film was part of a cycle that would result in numerous films drawing out the original concept to its least logical conclusions. As one You-Tube commenter posits, the following sequels do not seem too far removed from reality: "Duck on a truck, spiders on a glider and llamas on a farmer."[1]

Besides putting animals on unlikely vehicles, the *Snakes on a Plane* recut trailers create multiplicities from the source film by playing with the role that actor Samuel L. Jackson took in the marketing and legacy of the film. Indeed, his infamous line "I have had it with these motherfucking snakes on this motherfucking plane" is replicated throughout the parody trailers, with "snakes" and "planes" replaced by "goats" and "boats," and so on. The line was a suggestion from online fans (Li and Bernoff 2011, 8); New Line took it on, with the intended result of the film losing its PG-13 rating. As Li and Bernoff claim, "New Line had lost control of the movie and its marketing," since "it had to court these hard-core fans to succeed" (8). In a sense, *Snakes on a Plane* was "co-created" by online audiences (Fisher and Smith 2010, 241), leaving the potential for a cycle of re-

FIGURE 15.1. Samuel L. Jackson in *Snakes on a Plane.*

lated films up to the imagination of online fans. Snakes could have been interchanged with cakes, as in the *Cakes on a Plane* trailer (Media Junkyard 2013), if fans had called for it.

The ability of recut trailers to generate multiplicities frames the appearance of footage from older films in a new light. Rather than being seen purely as footage combined for comic effect, recut trailers as multiplicities respond directly to the role of film literacy and knowledge of the industry and its marketing attempts in guiding the reading and enjoying of recut trailers. The *Indiana Jones on a Plane Parody Trailer* (Goldentusk 2006) recuts footage from the *Indiana Jones* franchise (1981, Steven Spielberg) to focus on instances when snakes were mentioned, in order to draw connections between the two disparate films. In this trailer, *Indiana Jones* in a sense acts as a prequel to *Snakes on a Plane*—by unearthing the common thread between the two films (snakes, planes), it allows audiences to retroactively augment their memories of *Indiana Jones*. This confusing and disjointed temporality is not limited to user-generated objects such as recut trailers. Prequels—by definition—are released after the original films, and often after sequels—as can be seen in both the *Star Wars* (1977, George Lucas) cycle and the *Silence of the Lambs* (1991,

Jonathan Demme) cycle. *Snakes on a Plane* in turn spawned an off-shoot film of its own, created by the imitative, "mockbuster" studio The Asylum. *Snakes on a Train* (2006, Peter Mervis) was released straight to DVD in order to beat the release of *Snakes on a Plane* (a tactic often used by The Asylum). While it could be considered a follow-up of sorts to *Snakes on a Plane* in a cycle, it was released before New Line's *Snakes on a Plane*—demonstrating that influence and intertextuality can result in the circulation of a film's title alone. The *Snakes on a Plane* recut trailers play on this temporal inconsistency.

ITERATIONS OF *INCEPTION*

Christopher Nolan's blockbuster action film *Inception* inspired countless recut trailers that take the distinctive dramatic music from the *Inception* trailer and place it alongside footage from completely unrelated—and often inappropriate—films. In addition, these recuts shift the genre of existing films and turn older films into multiplicities of *Inception*.

Genre shifting involves editing footage from an existing film to make it appear as though it belongs to another genre. Tryon's notion points to the importance of genre in attempting to appeal to audiences through a trailer; as Kernan argues, genre, along with stars and narrative, is one of the central methods used to appeal to audiences. In discussing *The Shining Recut* trailer—which recuts the thriller *The Shining* into a feel-good family comedy about a boy and his father trying to bond while his father finishes writing a novel—Tryon notes that "the use of the Peter Gabriel song [upbeat "Solsbury Hill"] and the voiceover seem to suggest that it is the trailer itself that is the object of parody" (2009, 162). The form of the trailer is mocked for its inconsistencies and the expectation that it could mislead audiences. In the above quotation, Tryon demonstrates the centrality of music and sound in establishing filmic genre—and the potential for a subversion or "shifting" of genre to occur simply through inappropriately deploying a song that evokes a particular genre or emotion. The family comedy *Ace Ventura: Pet Detective* (1994, Tom Shadyac) is recut into a tense crime drama in *Ace Ventura Re-Cut Inception Trailer* (Burian 2010)—which, despite Jim Carrey's comedic delivery, is able to build tension and suspense. Likewise, the comedies *Happy Gilmore* (1996, Dennis Dugan), *The Big Lebowski* (1998, Joel and

Ethan Coen), *Ghostbusters* (1984, Ivan Reitman), and *Superbad* (2007, Greg Mottola) have all been subject to genre switching through a reordering of footage and the presence of a new sound track.

Music has played a crucial part in cinema's history; it has been used to mimic narrative, induce particular emotional reactions in audiences, or even drown out the sound of a loud projector (den Hartogh, Hsu, and Groshek 2013). Music can likewise be applied to evoke a film while displacing memories of it. As den Hartogh and his colleagues argue, "Music holds the opportunity to substantially change the spirit of a scene and might even change the expectations a viewer has of the scene development." Music, as in the case of the recut *Inception* trailers, can also create multiplicities and connections—establishing a network between texts where none previously existed.

As mentioned earlier, the presence of a recut trailer can incite and encourage others to create their own. The spike in recuts following the release of the official *Inception* trailer can be explained by elements of YouTube's architecture that allow recuts to infiltrate a user's attempt to watch an official trailer—the recut then becomes a multiplicity of the official trailer as well as of the feature film. The "related video" function in YouTube presents material traces of intertextual connections: the official trailer for *Inception* may populate the page for a recut *Inception* trailer, the pages of other recut trailers, and pages featuring interviews with the cast of *Inception*. YouTube's design encourages these multiplicities and connections, and the sheer quantity of footage available across YouTube seems only to encourage viewers to make bizarre connections between films through the identification of latent story lines or genre shifting. Since recuts often convey their meanings through their titles, the constant stream of related content helps articulate the relationship between one recut and others, and between all of them and the official source material.

WHILE RECUT TRAILERS CAN BE UNDERSTOOD as a form of mockery or play, the target of their mockery may not be the originary feature film (as is the case with *The Big Lebowski* or *Happy Gilmore* in the examples cited above). Instead, they seem to "aim at an easier target, the Hollywood marketing machine that relentlessly promotes the latest films and by doing so emphasizes the formulaic quality of all trailers and the Hollywood marketing machine in general" (Tryon 2009, 162). The *Inception* recuts indicate that small changes can be made to change the genre of a film, and that regardless of how famil-

FIGURE 15.2. Leonardo DiCaprio and Kate Winslet in *Titanic*.

iar viewers are with a feature, their memories of a film can be up-ended and reordered by drawing it into the world of a seemingly un-related feature film. By using genre shifting, recut trailers extend the life of a feature beyond the consumption of the film itself, thereby disrupting the typical promotional life of a film. By using short mon-tages to present a hybrid film that will never screen in theaters, re-cut trailers give us insight into the imagination of their creators, and the extent to which a film's textuality can spread across multiple narratives.

MY HEART WILL GO ON AND ON: MULTIPLICITIES OF *TITANIC*

Titanic was an incredibly critically and financially successful film—it won eleven Academy Awards, and was the first film to reach one billion dollars at the box office in its initial release. Detailing the sinking of the luxury cruise liner through the fictionalized love story of Jack (Leonardo DiCaprio) and Rose (Kate Winslet), *Titanic* seemed to have something for everybody—a disaster, a romance, a tragedy, even a deep-sea exploration led by Bill Paxton. While *Titanic* cannot have a sequel, since the ship cannot sink twice, numerous recut trail-ers uploaded to YouTube explore imaginary sequels to *Titanic*—trac-ing connections based on the presence of actors in unrelated features.

The recut trailer *Titanic: The Sequel* (Mrderekjohnson 2006) depicts Jack Dawson (whom the audience is left to assume died in freezing waters at the end of *Titanic*) being unfrozen by scientists as text implores the audience to reengage with Jack's story: "as one journey ends, another begins." The trailer uses footage from a number of films that include Leonardo DiCaprio and from other, disparate films such as *Austin Powers: International Man of Mystery* (1997, Jay Roach) for the unfreezing sequence. After Jack is found and thawed out, he attempts to navigate an unfamiliar world while searching for Rose—the woman who went to live on as a (fictional) survivor of the *Titanic*. The trailer directly mocks the attempt made by studios to bring a character back to life or to extend a film into a cycle when it seemed logically impossible to do so. This recut plays with notions of intertextuality directly; Jack is seen in the audience of *Titanic: The Musical*,[2] which extends Jack's narrative not only into the future as an individual, but also as someone who must navigate the permutations of their experience and their character. By including references to the reception and new texts that have arisen out of the story of the Titanic (and therefore the film itself), *Titanic: The Sequel* reflects how the textual representations of Titanic have become part of its story.

A number of other trailers for fake sequels to *Titanic* put multiplicities of that film into the narrative world of other features. *Titanic II: If Jack Had Lived* (Ryoungjohn85 2009) contains footage from *Titanic* interspersed with footage from *Revolutionary Road* (2008, Sam Mendes), which also stars Kate Winslet and Leonardo DiCaprio. *Revolutionary Road* follows the evolution of a relationship (marriage, children, breakdown) during the 1940s–1950s. *Titanic II* demonstrates that characters can be interchangeable with the actors who play them; the presence of Winslet and DiCaprio in any film can be read as a progression of the story of Jack and Rose. This recut also cleverly plays into discussions of *Revolutionary Road* as a reunion of the two actors (see, for example, Child 2008).

The recut's creator claims to be promoting an authentic film that will be released in 2012 (three years from the trailer's upload date). This attempt to induce suspension of disbelief would work only for those not familiar with the footage from *Revolutionary Road*. In part, this is an element of the appeal of recut trailers—the resulting hybrid film is so unlikely that it becomes a parody of the types of films released and marketed by studios. Recut trailers such as *Must Love*

FIGURE 15.3. Leonardo DiCaprio and Kate Winslet in *Revolutionary Road*.

Jaws seem to ask of their audience whether it is any more unusual to have a love story between a man and a shark than it is to have a story of friendship between a boy and a whale, as seen in *Free Willy* (1993, Simon Wincer). Indeed, since the story of *Titanic* is finite—the ship sank and one of the two main characters died—the *Titanic* recuts play with the notion that Hollywood studios will do anything to capitalize on the popularity of a film for financial benefit. The resulting multiplicity is one of a series of connections between films made by recut trailers rather than by the creation of a feature-film sequel.

By drawing upon representations of Kate Winslet and Leonardo DiCaprio in other films and reordering them into the narrative world of *Titanic*, recut trailers for Cameron's epic turn *Revolutionary Road* and *The Reader* into multiplicities of *Titanic*. Like *Titanic II*, *Titanic 2: Rose's Secret* (Rianieltube 2010) employs techniques typical of film trailers in order to revisit the narrative world of *Titanic*. Footage of Jack's death is accompanied by text claiming, "This is not the end . . . but just the beginning." Footage from several films starring Leonardo DiCaprio, spanning several decades and film genres, is used. After Rose is saved, Jack resurfaces and is helped by a rescue boat. Rose continues to live in New York—footage that depicts this is taken from *The Reader* (2008, Stephen Daldry)—and Jack eventually makes his way there with the help of scenes from *Gangs of New York* (2002, Martin Scorsese). Though the shots are not connected, the use of fading to black in a montage (a device commonly used in trailers) lets the audience use their imaginations to connect the scenes.

Many users seem to come across the *Titanic* sequel trailers while searching for a sequel to *Titanic,* rather than while searching for re-cut trailers. Many of the comments on *Titanic 2: Rose's Secret* point to the disappointment felt upon realizing that it was not a "real" film—"Dude that's not the real trailer that's the Gangs of New York movie," and "Is this real or fake." Others praise the effort that went into making the recut: "This must have took a while, well done." One commenter confuses the trailer for *Titanic: The Sequel* with the trailer for the feature film, and recalls how Jack survives while point-ing out how unrealistic *Rose's Secret* is: "Jack was preserved in the ice. But by the time that he got unfrozen rose was already dead (in ti-tanic 2)." This points to what Marshall refers to as "the intensifica-tion and elaboration" of the "intertextual matrix," (2002, 69), that is, through the sheer abundance of material available online, what could be considered intertextual is intensified. Rather than *Rose's Secret* merely being connected to *Titanic,* it represents textual connections to *The Reader, Gangs of New York,* and other recut trailers. Thus, just as promotional materials such as T-shirts or lunch boxes form a part of the intertextual matrix surrounding a film, so too do user-made creations such as completely implausible recut trailers, which generate complicated multiplicities.

RECUT TRAILERS OFFER A SITE where audiences and users can proj-ect their cinematic imaginations, revisiting and augmenting their memories of feature films. By co-opting techniques used by studios to market films—such as amplifying or omitting parts of the nar-rative or falsely representing the genre of a film—recuts parody the ways that studios attempt to appeal to audiences and create hype for their features. Recuts take the form of an advertisement, but deny the user the end product of the feature film; the trailer can be consumed and appreciated, but it will not lead to a feature. The popularity of recut trailers signals two things: first, that there is a willingness in audiences to enjoy the form of the trailer, which is no longer forced upon them before a feature screening in a cinema, and second, that audiences enjoy seeing an older film in an anticipatory mode as well as appreciating the creativity of those who made the recut trailer.

Crucially, recut trailers demonstrate the desire in audiences to create connections and links between films—to unearth latent story lines, to shift genres, or to generate multiple incarnations of a film across decades of film history. By playing with cinematic temporality, recuts evoke memories of films that have been consumed, even as they place footage from the past into the anticipatory mode. Recuts allow viewers to project their memories of a feature onto the form of the trailer and allow those memories to be remolded. In the process, recut trailers parody attempts made by studios to create and market multiplicities.

Recut trailers conflate the past with the future, the new with the old. By universally applying a series of techniques familiar to moviegoing audiences, recuts place older films into a suspended state of anticipation, in which a feature cannot be consumed but is always "coming soon." In this juggling of time, memory, and footage, recuts are acutely self-aware as well as attuned to studios' attempts to manipulate audiences. But these attempts are themselves up for negotiation and subversion. The popularity of recuts on YouTube demonstrates that by allowing films to exist in multiple sites in a state of anticipation, recuts act as a site for audience pleasure in revisiting films and creating connections among them.

NOTES

1. This comment (by "InvalidUser") is on the reposting of *Goats on a Boat* by Hidden Track TV (30 July 2007).

2. The musical was first performed on Broadway in 1997.

WORKS CITED

Burgin, Victor. 2004. *The Remembered Film*. London: Reaktion.

Burian, Karl. 2010. *Ace Ventura Re-Cut Inception Trailer*. YouTube, 8 November.

Chapman, Paul. 2013. "Hollywood Pays Out to Film Fan over Missing Explosion." *Telegraph*, 2 April.

Child, Ben. 2008. "Trailer: Winslet and DiCaprio Reunite for Mendes' Revolutionary Road." *Guardian Film Blog*, 30 September.

———. 2011. "Woman Sues to stop Drive Getting Away with a 'Misleading' Trailer." *Guardian*, 10 October.

Chocolate Cake City. 2006. *Brokeback to the Future*. YouTube, 1 February.

den Hartogh, Rudolf, Cheng Heng Hsu, and Jacob Groshek. 2013 "Music in the Eyes: Contextual Framing and Emotional Attributions in User-Generated Content and Culture." *Widescreen* 1 (18 April).

DeNigris, Paul. 2007. *Snakes in a Boardroom (MTV SPOOF)*. YouTube, 29 May.

Elsaesser, Thomas. 2001. "The Blockbuster: Everything Connects, but Not Anything Goes." In *The End of Cinema as We Know It: American Film in the Nineties*, ed. Jon Lewis, 11–22. New York: New York University Press.

Fisher, Dan, and Scott Smith. 2010. "Consumers Bite on the Social Web about the Film *Snakes on a Plane*." *International Journal of Electronic Marketing and Retailing* 3, no. 3: 241–260.

Goldentusk. 2006. *Indiana Jones on a Plane Parody Trailer*. YouTube, July 14.

Gray, Jonathan. 2010. *Show Sold Separately: Promos, Spoilers, and Other Media Paratexts*. New York: New York University Press.

Horwatt, Eli. 2009. "A Taxonomy of Digital Video Remixing: Contemporary Found Footage Practice on the Internet." *Scope* 15:76–91.

IMDb (Internet Movie Database). 2006. *Snakes on a Plane*. Trivia page.

Johnston, Keith M. 2009. *Coming Soon: Film Trailers and the Selling of Hollywood Technology*. Jefferson, N.C.: McFarland.

Kernan, Lisa. 2004. *Coming Attractions: Reading American Movie Trailers*. Austin: University of Texas Press.

Li, Charlene, and Josh Bernoff. 2011. *Groundswell: Winning in a World Transformed by Social Technologies*. Cambridge, Mass.: Harvard Business Press.

Marshall, David. 2002. "The New Intertextual Commodity." In *The New Media Book*, ed Dan Harries, 69–82. London: British Film Institute.

Media Junkyard. 2013. *Cakes on a Plane*. YouTube, 1 April.

Moviemker. 2006. *The Original Scary "Mary Poppins" Recut Trailer*. YouTube, 8 October.

Mrderekjohnson. 2006. *Titanic: The Sequel*. YouTube, 5 April.

Neochosen. 2006. *The Shining Recut*. YouTube, 7 February.

Rianieltube. 2010. *Titanic 2 Rose's Secret—Full Trailer*. YouTube, 16 October.

Ryoungjohn85. 2009. *Titanic II If Jack Had Lived*. YouTube, 3 August.

Staiger, Janet. 1990. "Announcing Wares, Winning Patrons, Voicing Ideals: Thinking about the History and Theory of Film Advertising." *Cinema Journal* 29, no. 3: 3–31.

3rd Floor Productions. 2006. *Goats on a Boat*. YouTube, 24 October.

Tryon, Chuck. 2009. *Reinventing Cinema: Movies in the Age of Media Convergence*. New Brunswick, NJ: Rutgers University Press.

Vayabobo. 2006. *Must Love Jaws*. YouTube, 14 March.

Waxman, Sharon. 2006. "After Hype Online, 'Snakes on a Plane' Is Letdown at Box Office." *New York Times*, 21 August.

Williams, Kathleen. 2012. "Fake and Fan Film Trailers as Incarnations of Audience Anticipation and Desire." *Transformative Works and Cultures* 9.

CHAPTER 16

RETRO-REMAKING: THE 1980S FILM CYCLE IN CONTEMPORARY HOLLYWOOD CINEMA

KATHLEEN LOOCK

IN THE EARLY 2000S, *Miami Vice* (2006, Michael Mann), *Transformers* (2007, Michael Bay), *Fame* (2009, Kevin Tancharoen), and *Friday the 13th* (2009, Marcus Nispel) made their comeback on the big screen and initiated a film cycle that consists of high-concept blockbusters based on feature films and television series of the 1980s. Critics were quick to recognize the trend, and when *Clash of the Titans* (2010, Louis Leterrier), *A Nightmare on Elm Street* (2010, Samuel Bayer), *The Karate Kid* (2010, Harald Zwart), *TRON: Legacy* (2010, Joseph Kosinsky) and *The A-Team* (2010, Joe Carnahan) appeared on Hollywood's annual production slate, they confidently predicted that 2010 would become "the Year of the '80s Remakes" (Allen 2010; *Time* 2010).

In the end, 2010 did not turn out to be exceptional for film studios' revival of the 1980s. The next year followed suit with new cinematic versions of *Footloose* (2011, Craig Brewer), *Conan the Barbarian* (2011, Marcus Nispel), *Arthur* (2011, Jason Winer), *The Thing* (2011, Matthijs van Heijningen Jr.), and *Fright Night* (2011, Craig Gillespie). In 2012, *21 Jump Street* (2012, Phil Lord / Chris Miller) and *Red Dawn* (2012, Dan Bradley) came to the cinemas, and 2013 saw the release of *Evil Dead* (2013, Fede Alvarez), a remake of Sam Raimi's 1981 horror classic. José Padilha's new *RoboCop* premiered in 2014, and more blockbusters are yet to come: George Miller's *Mad Max: Fury Road* was released in 2015, and both Kenny Ortega's take on *Dirty Dancing* and many other films are rumored to be in different stages of development.[1] Altogether, up to thirty feature films and television shows from the 1980s will be remade in the 2010s—a number that has led *Variety*'s Marc Graser (2010) to describe the long-past decade as "a dynamo for contemporary remakes."

While these movies belong to different genres (and therefore do not share images, characters, settings, plots, or themes),[2] they can still be regarded as forming a film cycle because they remake iconic feature films and television series of the 1980s and because they are all being released within a short period of time. Michael Cieply (2012), who writes for the *New York Times*, remarked that we are currently witnessing "an '80s moment" in Hollywood. His observation is especially appropriate, since contemporaneity is a defining feature of the 1980s (and any other) film cycle. In general, film cycles last only about five to ten years before they lose their financial viability (Klein 2011, 4). As a consequence, studios try to capitalize on the current trend by producing more of the same before audience interest wanes.

In keeping with the timeliness factor, Cieply sees Hollywood's revival of the 1980s as "part of a retro mood that has revved up the careers of baby-boom performers while providing comfort food for the audience" (2012). An entire generation of today's filmmakers, actors, and cinema goers grew up with and still remembers television shows and films of the 1980s (including their related lines of merchandise). But this "retro mood"—or "retromania," as Simon Reynolds (2011) calls it—is neither new nor unique to the film industry. As a trend, it currently pervades almost all areas of cultural production, including music, fashion, toys, food, and interior design (Reynolds 2011, xvii–xviii; see also Loock and Verevis 2012b, 1). According to Reynolds, our culture celebrates nostalgia and "obsesse[s] with the cultural artifacts of *its own immediate past*" (xiii).

Along these lines, I want to suggest that the industrial and cultural practices that have given rise to the 1980s film cycle in contemporary Hollywood cinema can best be described as "retro-remaking." This term is not supposed to add to the conflated vocabulary that can be found in trade, mainstream, and academic publications dealing with Hollywood remaking. On the contrary, "retro-remaking" is an attempt to tackle the linguistic and theoretical challenge at hand.

"Remaking," as used in this chapter, does not exclusively refer to the production of a film remake in the more restricted sense of a filmic iteration; rather, it describes a practice that generates different cinematic formats of innovative reproduction, such as the film remake, the sequel, the prequel, or the spin-off.[3] All these formats are driven by commercial imperatives and rely on pretested material that they repeat, modify, and continue in order to ensure box-office success. This broader understanding of cinematic remaking becomes productive when studying films such as the *Karate Kid* remake, the sequel *TRON: Legacy*, and the TV-to-cinema adaptation, update, and prequel *The A-Team* as examples of one and the same 1980s cycle and as films that share industrial, narrative, and cultural conditions as a result of the remaking practice from which they emerged.

The prefix "retro" (in "retro-remaking") stands for the specific modes and strategies that characterize the practice's current relation (or obsession) with the immediate past. It accounts for the fact that the film cycle returns to the 1980s as part of living memory, recalls and replicates elements of iconic pop-cultural artifacts of that decade, and takes an overall playful approach to the past (Reynolds 2011, xxx–xxxi). As I show in this chapter, many films of the cycle tend to celebrate the originals and their 1980s aesthetic: they directly rely on their cult status and presence in cultural memory and explicitly draw attention to the earlier texts. On the one hand, Hollywood's interest in reviving that particular decade is openly criticized in newspapers and trade publications: the *Telegraph*'s Tom Chivers (2010) writes of "that anti-golden age of cinema, the 1980s," and his colleague David Gritten (2010) asks: "Synthetic music, largely mediocre movies, cheesy hairstyles, absurd fashions and unlovable political leaders. Who'd want to be reminded of such an era?" On the other hand, the decade evokes sentimental attachments to its films and television series, and to associated childhood memories, and there is a general apprehension among audiences that cinematic remaking will destroy these personal ties to the past (Adams 2010; Gritten 2010).

This film cycle thus speaks to a troubled relationship with the 1980s, one raising interesting questions about cultural memory and feelings of generational belonging and the ways in which popular culture participates in their ongoing negotiations and reconstructions. This chapter explores these issues against the background of the timeliness of the film cycle and its particular retro-sensibility. Focusing on both the cinematic texts and the critical discourses that surround them, I first address commercial aspects of retro-remaking and analyze the practice as part of the big-budget, low-risk business model Hollywood has embraced, then turn to the textual level of the movies and closely examine codes and iconographies that evoke the 1980s, and finally end with a discussion of nostalgia and the cultural dimension of retro-remaking.

BUSINESS AS USUAL: COMMERCIAL IMPERATIVES
AND THE 1980S FILM CYCLE

The preeminent driving force behind cinematic remaking is the profit principle. From the film industry's point of view, remaking is a profitable business because it minimizes costs and risks by repeating existing stories and by putting presold products back on the release schedule. Critics often regard this conservative, risk-averse practice as a symptom of a "creative vacuum" in contemporary Hollywood (Adams 2010), but they tend to forget that remaking has been a constant feature of American cinema: the dupes (duplicated positive prints) and remakes of the early silent era were followed by film serials (the chief mode of production between 1906 and 1936), which served "first and foremost, [as] commercial vehicles . . . [using] cliffhangers, publicity [and] literary tie-ins . . . with the intent of keeping audiences coming back for more" (Jess-Cooke 2009, 29). The remakes and sequels released during the classical Hollywood era and ever since the 1970s stem from that practice, as do the recent reboots of the Batman, Spider-Man, and James Bond franchises.[4]

The 1980s film cycle is not different or new in that regard. Studios invest in the recycling of individual properties hoping for a box-office hit and the chance to "open up and exploit new markets, or . . . to revive and create cross-media franchises" (Verevis 2006, 38). What Constantine Verevis has pointed out for 1990s remakings of classic television series from the 1960s and 1970s[5] also applies to the films of the 1980s cycle: they "provide recognizable, and relatively inexpensive, self-promotional devices with which to market and *brand* new 'high-concept' feature films and media franchises" (38, emphasis in the original).

The commercial incentive for remaking, then, is not new but it is nonetheless singled out by film critics whenever properties of the 1980s cycle are concerned. During the recent financial crisis and global recession, these critics argue, remaking has become a very attractive business plan for Hollywood. "Studios pin their hopes on the belief that cinemagoers will return to what they know in difficult financial times," writes Nick Allen (2010) in the *Telegraph*; he considers the "revival of classic Eighties films [to be] a well-trodden path toward shoring up bank balances in Hollywood." For Chivers (2010), too, the return to the 1980s "seems to be a symptom of the credit crunch: a sort of security blanket for studio execs in their late

30s with a nervous eye on the bottom line." And the strategy can pay off handsomely: "The recent success of the dreadful Transformers movies, among other things, [has] suggested that there is money to be made from shameless nostalgia-exploitation, no matter how ridiculous."

New ideas are, in fact, riskier than old ones, representing a considerable gamble for the film industry because it is difficult to predict whether audiences will relate to them and buy a movie ticket. This calculation is crucial—enormous sums of money are at stake. Since the immense success of James Cameron's *Titanic* (1997), which spent part of its $200 million budget on innovative special effects and massive promotional campaigns, Hollywood has embraced a big-budget production model that has rapidly increased the studios' overall expenses (Adams 2010). In 2011, producing a film cost an average of $78 million—as opposed to $42 million in 1995 (Hakashima 2011). Under these circumstances, studios depend on the financial success of their investments, which is why they decide to develop fewer and (supposedly) safer properties, namely, presold remaking formats such as the remake, the sequel, and the prequel—films, in short, that they think will resonate with audiences and that come with built-in franchise opportunities.

For example, *Clash of the Titans* grossed $493 million worldwide and had estimated production costs of $163 million; *TRON: Legacy* made $400 million at the box office and cost $170 million to make; and *21 Jump Street* earned $202 million yet cost (only) $42 million (all figures from Box Office Mojo). In the aftermath of these successful endeavors, the *Clash of the Titans* producers quickly released the sequel *Wrath of the Titans* (2012, Jonathan Liebesman) and started work on a third installment while *Wrath* was still in postproduction (Kit 2011); another *TRON* sequel was rumored to be filming in 2014 (Wickman 2012); and *22 Jump Street* landed a prime release date in June 2014. The financial success of 1980s remaking formats can thus pave the way for sequelization and prolong the film cycle. But not all films meet the expectations attached to them: *The Thing, Footloose, Arthur, Fright Night,* and *Conan the Barbarian* were commercial disappointments, some of them not even covering the production costs (Grierson 2011; Zeitchik 2011).[6]

The case of *The A-Team* (budget: $110 million; gross: $177 million) illustrates how poor commercial performances or failures complicate matters and affect the symbiosis between narrative form and the industry's economic logic. In his discussion of media convergence between cinema and television, Thomas Elsaesser states that cinema "has adopted one of television's most defining characteristics: episodic storytelling and open-ended narration in a series format" (1998a, 18). "More and more feature films are given an 'open' ending, presumably in order to have the option of a sequel," he explains (1998b, 143). Joe Carnahan's high-budget, high-concept *A-Team* movie was planned as a reboot of the franchise because it had the kind of open ending and built-in option for sequelization that Elsaesser describes.

The film tells the origin story of the A-Team, consisting of Colonel Hannibal Smith (Liam Neeson), B. A. Baracus (Quinton "Rampage" Jackson), Templeton "Faceman" Peck (Bradley Cooper), and H. M. "Howling Mad" Murdock (Sharlto Copley). Based on the original premise and opening narration of the 1980s television series (1983–1987), the four US Army Rangers who work for a Special Forces unit in Baghdad during the Iraq War (in the updated version, they are no longer Vietnam veterans) are framed, dishonorably discharged, and imprisoned for "a crime they didn't commit." In an action-laden two hours, they escape, try to clear their names, and eventually become the four soldiers of fortune the audience is familiar with from the television show.

The A-Team ends with an offscreen narration announcing: "Still wanted by the government, they survive as soldiers of fortune. If you have a problem, if no one else can help, and if you can find them, maybe you can hire the A-Team." This coda not only echoes the opening narration of the original series but is also a reminder of the A-Team's weekly presence on television. With the reference, the film therefore hints at its own serial potential: it writes an openness for further adventures into its closure, clearly anticipating further installments. Yet because of the poor earnings of the 2010 summer blockbuster, the production of a sequel was quickly cancelled (Plumb 2011). The narrative logic of the remake, which manifests itself in the open ending, fell victim to the same economic logic behind its creation as a reboot of the popular 1980s *A-Team* franchise.[7]

Regardless of its success or failure, *The A-Team* serves as a good example of the commercial strategies typically involved when a 1980s feature film or television show is recycled for the big screen. First, the film is designed as a spectacular, high-concept blockbuster with an emphasis on Hollywood stars, production design, and state-of-the-art

FIGURE 16.1. One of the many explosion-heavy action scenes in the *A-Team* film.

special effects (Verevis 2006, 48). In the case of *The A-Team*, a well-known premise and a simple story line are combined with explosion-heavy action sequences that are, as one critic pointed out, "in accordance with modern big screen box office standards . . . [and] even more exaggerated and outrageous than anything seen on NBC way back when in the 1980s" (*The Movie Report* 2010). There are elaborate helicopter chases in Mexico, a parachuting tank that plummets into a lake in Switzerland (with the A-Team on board still able to maneuver it, of course), shipping containers on a dock in the Los Angeles harbor that topple like dominoes, and many, many explosions.

The other films of the cycle similarly invested in replacing once innovative—but now outdated—visual effects of the 1980s originals with the latest CGI (computer-generated imagery) technology. About *TRON* (1982, Steven Lisberger) and its belated 2010 sequel, for example, the film critic Roger Ebert writes:

> The first "Tron" (1982) felt revolutionary at the time. . . . It was the first movie to create a digital world and embed human actors; always earlier that had been done with special effects, matte shots, optical printers, blue screen and so on. "Tron" found a freedom of movement within its virtual world that was exhilarating. The plot was impenetrable, but so what? "Tron: Legacy," a sequel made 28 years after the original but with the same actor, is true to the first film: It also can't be understood, but looks great. Both films, made so many years apart, can fairly lay claim to being state of the art. 2010)

For *TRON: Legacy*, "state of the art" includes a digitally rejuvenated, completely computer-generated Jeff Bridges combatting the computer program CLU, and the use of 3D—an additional strategy of visually surpassing earlier versions that has also defined the comebacks of *Transformers, Clash of the Titans, Conan the Barbarian*, and *Fright Night*.

Furthermore, the release of a film in the 1980s cycle is accompanied by massive marketing campaigns and cross-media merchandise. To promote *The A-Team*, a comic book series, a line of action figures, and an iPhone application were introduced. In fact, the comic books and toys have extended the remaking practice to cross-platform productions through the revival of merchandise that was successfully sold in the 1980s. The comic books *A-Team: War Stories* and *A-Team: Shotgun Wedding*, both published during the months preceding the film's release in June 2010, served as prequels and tie-ins to the film. They were designed "to build a solidly action-packed foundation for a new generation of A-Team fans," according to the *A-Team* comic editor and cowriter Tom Waltz at IDW Publishing (IDW 2010). The executive vice president of sales at Jazwares, Laura Zebersky, makes similar claims when advertising the new action toys: "The release of *The A-Team* film will introduce a new generation of fans to the heroes of the popular series. . . . *The A-Team* is a part of pop culture history and we look forward to playing a role in its return" (quoted in Densetsu 2009).

As these presentations of recycled product lines reveal, the producers' marketing of *The A-Team* to a new, young target group heavily relies on the iconic status of the 1980s series in American popular culture. Indeed, the marketing strategies shed light on how American popular culture historicizes itself: in the context of retro-remaking, the pop-cultural—and classic—status of 1980s films, series, and characters, as well as the entire decade itself, is re-created, reconfirmed, and reoffered for consumption to a new generation.

Yet these films are not pitched exclusively at cinema's largest target audience (eighteen- to twenty-four-year-olds), but also to the generation that grew up in the 1980s and is familiar with the cultural products of that time. To them, films of the 1980s cycle sell a living memory endowed with new cultural capital and a notion of timeless significance. The branding concept of the *TRON: Legacy* franchise, for example, clearly built on nostalgia for the 1980s. It included a viral campaign, the screening of teaser trailers and footage at special

FIGURE 16.2. A first look at the grid design of ElecTRONica, the months-long dance party at Disneyland Resort that prepared the release of *TRON: Legacy*.

events, a comic book series, theme park attractions, dance parties, video games, fashion, and jewelry.

"Catapult Back to 1982," urged Robin Trowbridge (2010), the entertainment show director at Disneyland Resort, in a blog post about the (then) upcoming, months-long dance party ElecTRONica at the park. Flynn's Video Arcade from the film had been re-created for the event, and Trowbridge invited potential guests to "peg those jeans, crimp that hair, and get ready to take a trip back to 1982. . . . Yes, before you know it, you'll be playing TRON and other classic 80s arcade games all night long!" In the viral campaign preparing for the release of *TRON: Legacy*, "Flynn's Arcade" tokens and flash drives were sent to selected news websites. They contained codes and a countdown leading to the 2009 Comic-Con in San Diego, where a scavenger hunt revealed another reconstruction of Flynn's Video Arcade, this one with retro coin-operated games and actual Space Paranoids machines, as they had been developed by Kevin Flynn (Jeff Bridges) in the original film (Short 2010).

At first sight, then, the 1980s film cycle does not seem to be all that different from other supposedly low-risk, high-concept, high-budget remaking formats and franchises in contemporary Hollywood cinema. Even the heavy marketing machines accompanying these film releases appear to be similar to those used for other blockbusters. As Carolyn Jess-Cooke has pointed out for Disney's *Pirates of the Caribbean* franchise, the marketing and merchandising "creates *generational* communities, perpetuating experiences and memories . . .

from one generation to another, so that the act of engaging in a . . . film . . . becomes heavily invested with emotional ties" (2010, 220, emphasis in the original). The examples of *The A-Team* and *TRON: Legacy* show that "generational memory-making and transference" (220) are also central to 1980s remaking formats. What distinguishes the films of the 1980s cycle from other properties, however, is the fact that they not only keep the memory of the original alive, but also explicitly capitalize on the 1980s past of the originals. And this extends beyond the commercial level of marketing and merchandising to the textual strategies of the movies themselves. For the knowledgeable audience comprising the 1980s generation and the increasingly pop-culture-literate new generation, the film cycle has many textual "bonus[es] of pleasure" (Leitch 2002, 42) in store.

PLEASURE IN RECOGNITION: TEXTUAL STRATEGIES OF THE 1980S FILM CYCLE

When it comes to the originals, almost none of the films in the 1980s remake cycle resorts to what Thomas Leitch has termed the "rhetoric of disavowal." Unlike most film remakes, they do not "simultaneously valorize and deny [earlier texts] through a series of rhetorical maneuvers designed at once to reflect their intimacy with these texts and to distance themselves from their flaws" (Leitch 2002, 53). Instead, they attempt to maintain a recognizable textual relation to their originals in order to both create and confirm the pop-cultural status of the earlier versions and canonize them as 1980s (cult) classics from which the film remakes of the 1980s cycle derive their own pop-cultural value.

Whereas Verevis has suggested that high-concept films based on American prime-time television series from the 1960s and 1970s are "less interested in recreating the detail of their originals than in adapting the (previously market tested) source material to the conventions and expectations of the contemporary genre movie and/or blockbuster" (2006, 49), this indifference no longer seems to be the case for remaking formats of 1980s television shows and feature films. To be sure, the films of the 1980s cycle still follow the cinematic imperatives Verevis mentions, but they also use textual strategies that revive and foreground important details of their 1980s predecessors. In Philip Drake's words, they mobilize "particular codes that have come to connote a past sensibility as it is selectively re-

remembered in the present . . . as a structure of feeling, and these codes function *metonymically*, standing in for the entire decade" (2003, 188, emphasis in the original).

For the 1980s film cycle, these codes include unchanged, immediately recognizable titles that locate the films in the 1980s; the recycling of sound tracks, along with trademark haircuts, accessories, and signature lines; metareferences to the original and the remaking practice as such; and cameo appearances by original cast members. While most of these strategies can be detected in other remaking formats, I would argue that films of the 1980s cycle employ them in order to produce a specific retro-sensibility.

A presold title already contains the basic premise of a high-concept film and promotes it by recalling an earlier version of the story; its familiarity "arouses the audience's pleasurable anticipation" (Leitch 2002, 40). Viewers know what to expect when they encounter titles like *Friday the 13th, A Nightmare on Elm Street, The A-Team, Miami Vice, 21 Jump Street, Fame, Dirty Dancing, Footloose,* or *Conan the Barbarian.*

Accordingly, the 2010 *Karate Kid* retells the story of a boy (Jaden Smith), who is forced to move far away with his divorced mom (Taraji P. Henson), is threatened by neighborhood bullies in the new place, and eventually makes friends with a reclusive janitor (Jackie Chan), who teaches him martial arts and ways to solve his problems. The overall plot remains basically the same as in John G. Avildsen's 1984 version—including an updated version of the memorable "wax on, wax off" routine and a climactic tournament at the end. This time, however, *The Karate Kid* is set in China, and, most importantly, does not feature karate but kung fu. During production, it was therefore rumored that the film would (and should) be marketed as *The Kung Fu Kid.*

Yet rather than pitching the film as something new, Sony Pictures, wanting to profit from its valuable 1980s property, insisted on maintaining the original title in the interest of rebooting the long-dormant franchise, which had once spawned three sequels, an animated television series, a video game, action figures, headbands, posters, and T-shirts (Horn 2010; Sofge 2010). In an article published in the online magazine *Slate,* Erik Sofge (2010) suggested that "a reboot of the franchise seem[ed] better positioned for nostalgia-driven ticket sales." By preserving the well-known title, the new *Karate Kid* thus encouraged recognition of, and invited engagement with, the popular original, which has maintained a high degree of circulation through television reruns, DVD sales, merchandising, and catchphrases (like "wax on, wax off") that have entered the pop-cultural lexicon. The title itself activates memories of the original and the 1980s past to which it belongs.

Retro-remakes also take up songs, musical themes, and details such as trademark haircuts, accessories, and signature lines from their 1980s sources. Thus, *Fame* includes new versions of the popular, Academy Award–winning title song, "Fame," and the ballad "Out Here on my Own," both sung by Irene Cara in the original. Similarly, *Footloose* recycles not only the story but also the sound track of the earlier film. Many critics have commented on the fact that Craig Brewer's remake is strikingly faithful to the original, or as Roger Ebert (2011) puts it: "This 2011 version is so similar—sometimes song for song and line for line—that I was wickedly tempted to reprint my 1984 review, word for word."

Brewer's *Footloose* opens with an updated version of Kenny Loggins's original theme song, and "the first impression is one of reverence," remarks the film critic William Goss (2011). He adds that other rerecordings throughout the film speak "to that earlier sense of admiration for the original." A long sequence shows (once more) how Willard (Miles Teller), Ren's (Kenny Wormald) rhythm-less sidekick, learns dance moves to a new take on Deniece Williams's "Let's Hear it for the Boy"; Brewer also works in "Almost Paradise" and a sloweddown version of "Holding Out for a Hero" before the film ends yet again with the teenagers dancing to the "Footloose" theme.

In these instances, the songs enforce the overall sense of homage that these retro-remakes render to their originals. In Leitch's words, they intend to "pay tribute to an earlier film rather than usurp its place of honor" (2002, 47). What is more, most of the songs mentioned here became number one hits and gained pop-cultural currency in their own right. They function, so to speak, as a recognizable sound track of the 1980s, one that is replayed in the remakes and evokes the memory both of the original films and the decade itself.

The cinematic adaptation of *The A-Team* retains not only the characteristic title theme of the television series, but also the distinctive appearances of its four characters: Hannibal constantly lights up a cigar and remarks, "I love it when a plan comes together"; Faceman remains the well-dressed womanizer and con man; Murdock is seen in his typical ball cap and leather flight jacket; and B. A. wears his (actually, Mr. T's) trademark haircut, expresses his fear of flying in the catchphrase "I ain't gettin' on no plane!" and has the words "pity" and "fool" tattooed on the knuckles of his left and right hand, echoing another of his signature lines. The film even provides the backstory for B. A.'s characteristic features, which were simply taken for granted in the series. Again, the film's fidelity to the depiction of the characters in the television show both pays homage to the original and speaks to audience expectations, since viewers will quickly recognize their 1980s heroes and take pleasure in identifying their iconic traits.

While *The A-Team* more or less faithfully replicates the almost cartoonish portrayal of the characters as well as the 1980s aesthetic of the episode finales (showcasing over-the-top violence, gunfights, and massive explosions), *21 Jump Street* takes a tongue-in-cheek approach to its original series (1987–1991) and toys with audience expectations by acknowledging and playfully analyzing its own status as a cinematic remaking format.

That film adaptations of long-running television shows comment on the practice of remaking series for the big screen is not entirely new.[8] Yet *21 Jump Street* goes further by turning the revival and remaking of its own original into a basic plot element of the comedy spin-off. In the movie, former high school enemies Schmidt (Jonah Hill) and Jenko (Channing Tatum) meet again at the police academy, where they eventually befriend each other and prepare for graduation. After passing the exams, they are assigned to bicycle park patrol but are immediately transferred when they fail to make their first arrest properly. Captain Hardy (Nick Offerman) tells Schmidt and Jenko: "Fortunately for you two, we're reviving a canceled undercover police program from the '80s and revamping it for modern times. You see, the guys in charge of this stuff lack creativity and are completely out of ideas, so all they do now is recycle shit from the past and expect us all not to notice. One of these programs involves the use of young, immature-seeming officers." These lines recall the original series, introduce its familiar premise of fresh-faced police officers who work undercover as high school kids, and comment on the nature of remaking in general and on the 1980s cycle in particular. On the one hand, the "canceled undercover police program from the '80s" is a stand-in for the television show, which is also evoked when the captain wants to send Schmidt and Jenko to the Jump Street Chapel headquarters but cannot remember the correct street number: "[It's] down on Jump Street. 37 Jump Street," he says, pauses, and mutters: "No, that doesn't sound right." This joke draws on the cult status of the television show, which took itself quite seriously and incorporated many social issues of its time. The captain's memory gap implies that the undercover program—which really means the show—has long been forgotten and no longer occupies a place in the American imagination (although it in fact does), thereby announcing the film's own mockingly affectionate relation to its original. "The guys in charge," on the other hand, can be easily replaced with studio executives, who green-light the remaking of successful 1980s properties for want of original ideas.

21 Jump Street thus takes up and reflects on the critical discourse surrounding cinematic remaking and, more specifically, the 1980s cycle. With the verbs "revive," "revamp," and "recycle" in the captain's remarks, it even echoes the typical word choice of the (generally negative) reviews. The comment, then, knowingly exposes the commercial imperatives that have informed the production of *21 Jump Street* and other 1980s remaking formats. It is further directed at a knowledgeable, pop-culture-literate audience that is not really "expect[ed] . . . not to notice" but to find pleasure in the film's metareferences and winks at the 1980s past.

The television series eventually takes center stage in the *21 Jump Street* movie when Johnny Depp and Peter DeLuise from the original cast return as the DEA undercover cops Tom Hanson and Doug Penhall.[9] Cameo appearances of actors from earlier films or television series are a common strategy in cinematic remaking (Leitch 2002, 42; Loock 2012, 138–139; Verevis 2006, 20). They provide "a special reward for knowledgeable viewers" but can also suggest a sense of continuity (Loock 2012, 138). Once more, *21 Jump Street* intends to surpass other films with its playful attitude toward the source material and the now-famous actor that comes with it.

"We had no idea. You're like an amazing actor, man," Schmidt says to Hanson (and Johnny Depp) when he and Penhall reveal themselves to be, in fact, DEA undercover cops in elaborate disguise and not members of the drug ring that Schmidt and Jenko plan to arrest. Just as they realize their common Jump Street history—"Come on, you guys are Jump Street? That's funny, because we were actually Jump Street"—Hanson and Penhall are wounded in the gunfight finale. Hanson's last words, in the subsequent death scene, serve as an ironic comment on his 1980s fashion faux pas on the television show:

FIGURE 16.3. Tom Hanson (Johnny Depp) and Doug Penhall (Peter DeLuise) from the 1980s television series return as DEA undercover cops in the *21 Jump Street* movie.

"All the stuff that I wore, like the bracelets, the rings, the tight pants was just so that people would think I'm cool." The cameos provide a retrospective backstory for the two officers because they tell the audience what happened to them after the Jump Street program, and they satisfy the desire for final closure through the death scene.

The entire premise of "reviving" both the undercover police program and the successful *21 Jump Street* property "for modern times" draws attention to the difficult negotiation of timeliness and timelessness that concerns all films of the 1980s remaking cycle. In her study *American Film Cycles*, Amanda Ann Klein explains: "The film cycle is a commodity to be assembled, packaged, and sold as quickly as possible, not a timeless piece of art" (2011, 8). In contrast with film genres that "gained cultural capital once they were associated with timelessness—or what audiences are interested in watching for decades to come[,] film cycles . . . value timeliness—or what audiences are interested in watching right now" (9). But studios invest in the supposed timelessness of 1980s television series and feature films. The idea behind remaking is that these properties retain their commercial and cultural value over time and can be easily revived to be sold to both the original generation of viewers and a new one. The remaking formats draw their appeal from the pleasure of recognition, which is guaranteed by marketing and merchandising as well as by textual strategies that do not necessarily disavow earlier texts. The *21 Jump Street* remake acknowledges the (existence and) timeliness of the 1980s film cycle and inserts overt references to the current remaking practice in Hollywood. At the same time, it mocks the notion of timelessness ascribed to many originals of the 1980s by poking fun at the premise, 1980s fashions, and the action and high school scenes of the television series it is based on. The show exposes itself to be a product of its time and not timeless at all. This insight is crucial, since retro-remaking does in fact not turn the original into a timeless classic, but rather into a classic in (a particular) time. Retro-remaking, in other words, creates pop-cultural temporality in the sense that the 1980s become recognizable, through particular codes and iconographies, as a distinct period.

PAST AND PRESENT:
NOSTALGIA AND THE 1980S FILM CYCLE

Reviewers immediately labeled the films discussed in this chapter as 1980s remakes, linking them discursively to a cycle—a cycle that reconstructs not a historical past but a glossy "pastness" for the present (Jameson 1991, 19). This identification sheds light on the fact that memories of the decade, or its "1980s-ness," are themselves manufactured, a product of pop-cultural media representations. It also raises questions about nostalgia, which is commonly understood to be a feeling of loss or a yearning for an idealized past. For Fredric Jameson, nostalgia is symptomatic of a postmodern condition characterized by "the waning of historicity, of our lived possibility of experiencing history in some active way" (21). Nostalgia, he argues, substitutes for "genuine historicity" a "vast collection of images" (18); it is a cultural style that commodifies the past and "empties history of politics, reducing it to a recombination of stereotypes of the past" (Drake 2003, 189). Retro-remaking remembers, reproduces, and sells recognizable pop-cultural bits and pieces of the 1980s in ways that Jameson describes. Yet his critical view neglects the cultural work that nostalgia performs in the present, or as Paul Grainge puts it: "Jameson fails to account for memory and identity being negotiated by the nostalgia mode" (2002, 6).

Nostalgia manifests itself, for instance, in the sentimental attachment to a simpler (childhood) past and its defining cultural touchstones, and this understanding has become a standard feature of the critical discourse that surrounds the 1980s remaking cycle. Thus, Michael Cieply (2012) writes that feature films and television shows from the 1980s "are making a comeback . . . because they mean something to a new generation of filmmakers" and studio executives, while David Gritten (2010) speaks much more critically of their "dismaying obsession with remaking movies from their childhood." In response to his question "Who'd want to be reminded of [the 1980s]?" Gritten states:

> The average Hollywood executive with the power to green-light movies. You know the type. He (it's still usually a he) would be in his mid-thirties. He's ego-driven, socially dysfunctional, badly behaved to subordinates, neurotic and essentially lonely. Oh, and he has little regard for film history.
>
> Why does he want to foist remakes of awful films such as *Conan the Barbarian*, *Tron*, *Police Academy*, and *The Neverending Story* on us? Because he loved these movies as a kid, so they remind him of the last time he felt happy.

Whereas Gritten's harsh comment claims that childhood nostalgia is the driving force behind remaking 1980s properties, this same nostalgia essentially translates into a feeling of apprehension on the part of cinema goers. Guy Adams (2010) describes it in the *Independent* as "that all-too-familiar feeling that accompanies the desecration of a childhood memory: anger, resentment, and a deep, almost primeval sense of sorrow." Adams laments that studios "have decided to use our nostalgia against us": to watch *The A-Team* "is to have a sledgehammer taken to rose-tinted memories," and *The Karate Kid*, "which my generation watched over and over on the family Betamax, has fallen victim to a grimly predictable makeover." Interestingly, similar arguments surface in discussions about possible cameo appearances by original cast members. Ralph Macchio, who played Daniel LaRusso in *The Karate Kid* and two sequels, said in an interview: "I'll forever be attached to that role . . . but I don't think it makes sense to show Daniel as an adult since I think he represents so many people's childhoods. I think seeing him as a grown man could sully that legacy and I just want the film to be what it was" (quoted in Wieselman 2009). His words resonate with the desire of many film critics to preserve and protect the originals and the memories attached to them. Some of these critics label retro-remaking "cultural vandalism" (Gritten 2010) or liken it to "an effort to trammel the memories of an entire generation" (Adams 2010).

Statements like these reveal the extent of personal investment in an idealized pop-cultural past that is still considered to be meaningful in the present. By expressing feelings of nostalgia and generational belonging, these film critics condemn retro-remaking, sometimes in an attempt to save favorites from what they consider to be the most recent excess of cinematic self-cannibalization: "As long as the Reboot Squad keeps its hands off *Back to the Future, ET, Blue Velvet, Brazil,* and *Ferris Bueller's Day Off,* I won't mind too much," writes Gritten (2010), for example.

These largely negative views, however, are not always shared by general audiences, which enjoy the updated versions. "Popular culture loves repetition," Frank Kelleter has observed (2012, 33). And for him, remaking in particular "has a stabilizing function, as each new variation reinforces the entire system of cultural self-generation and furthers the culture's belief in its own existence and continuity" (38). From this perspective, retro-remaking is not (only) "a mark of cultural solipsism or creative bankruptcy, but a way of acknowledging that the past exists through textual traces in cultural and ideological mediation with the present" (Grainge 2002, 55).

Films of the 1980s cycle, then, rely on commercial and textual strategies "that operate as catalysts for recollection, and stand in for a historical 'feeling'" (Drake 2003, 189). More precisely, they evoke a sense of "pastness" derived from the mediated memories of the 1980s in feature films and television series that have generally retained their cultural currency in the present. Retro-remaking constructs a "1980s-ness" based on what Alison Landsberg has termed "prosthetic memories"—memories that "are not 'authentic' or natural, but rather . . . produced by an *experience* of mass mediated representations" (2003, 149, emphasis in the original). At the same time, the re-made properties offer something new, a variation in narrative, style, setting, and cast that clearly locates them in the present (as timely contributions to the film cycle). Feelings of generational belonging among the audience are re-created and reinforced in relation to the dialectics between repetition and innovation. For the generation that consumed the originals in the 1980s, the remaking cycle is repackaging (mediated) memories of its past, endowing them with new cultural capital and a sense of nostalgia for the entire decade. For the new generation (which might be familiar with the originals through pop-cultural references, television reruns, or DVDs), the films provide access to representations of the 1980s past and produce new (mediated) memories linked to their own experiences in the present.

The 1980s moment in contemporary Hollywood cinema has not yet passed. Retro-remaking continues to be a profitable business practice that will add still more film remakes, sequels, prequels, and TV-to-cinema adaptations to the 1980s film cycle in the years to come. When exactly the cycle will end is impossible to predict. According to Klein, "A film cycle can only court the audience for so long. . . . Audiences may fall in love with cycles quickly, but if those same audiences lose interest in a particular cycle, they may become annoyed or frustrated if it continues to be produced for too long" (2011, 14). It is probably safe to say that, irrespective of the 1980s cycle, retro-remaking is here to stay.

NOTES

1. Films in different stages of development include *Gremlins, Police Academy, The Neverending Story, Private Benjamin, Overboard, WarGames, Videodrome, Endless Love, Romancing the Stone, Pet Sematary, Scarface, Highlander, Ghostbusters III, The Goonies 2,* and *Top Gun II* (Allen 2010; Chivers 2010; Graser 2010; Gritten 2010; Meslow 2013).

2. They include action, martial arts, and urban police films; science fiction, horror, and fantasy films; musicals, dance films, and romantic comedies.

3. Frank Kelleter and I are investigating this broader concept of remaking in the subproject "Retrospective Serialization: Remaking as a Method of Cinematic Self-Historicizing," which is part of the research unit Popular Seriality: Aesthetics and Practice, funded by the German Research Foundation (DFG), http://www.popularseriality.de; see also Kelleter and Loock, forthcoming.

4. For discussions of remaking practices in different historical stages of American cinema, see Forrest 2002; Forrest and Koos 2002b; Jess-Cooke 2009, 15–51; Oltmann 2008, 55–77; and Proctor 2012.

5. For example, *The Flintstones* (1960–1966), *The Addams Family* (1964–1966), *Mission: Impossible* (1966–1973), or *Charlie's Angels* (1976–1981).

6. *Conan* cost $90 million and pulled in only $48.8 million worldwide; *The Thing* cost $38 million and made $27.4 million. The other films fared a little better: *Arthur* (budget: $40 million; gross: $45.7 million), *Fright Night* (budget: $30 million; gross: $41 million), and *Footloose* (budget: $24 million; gross: $62.7 million); all figures are from Box Office Mojo.

7. Merchandise tie-ins in the 1980s included action figures, comic books, novelizations of episodes, and records with the *A-Team* theme and music from the series.

8. The opening airplane sequence of *Charlie's Angels* (2000, McG [Joseph McGinty Nichol]) is a case in point, as Verevis has shown (2006, 51).

9. Holly Robinson has a brief cameo appearance as officer Judy Hoffs, and old

footage from the series showing officer Harry Truman Ioki (Dustin Nguyen) is flickering on a television screen during the shootout finale.

WORKS CITED

Adams, Guy. 2010. "Hollywood Ate My Childhood: Why Film Remakes Are Desecrating Our Most Precious Memories." *Independent*, 22 July.

Allen, Nick. 2010. "Hollywood Goes Back to the Future with '80s Remakes." *Telegraph*, 19 April.

Chivers, Tom. 2010. "1980s Movie Remakes: 10 of the Most Ridiculous." *Telegraph*, 8 May.

Cieply, Michael. 2012. "In Hollywood, an '80s Moment." *New York Times*, 29 March.

Densetsu, Shin. 2009. "Jazzwares [sic] Announces *The A Team* Movie Toy Line." Toyark.com, "News," 17 December.

Drake, Philip. 2003. "'Mortgaged to Music': New Retro Movies in 1990s Hollywood Cinema." In Grainge 2003, 183–201.

Ebert, Roger. 2010. Review of *Tron: Legacy*. RogerEbert.com, 15 December.

———. 2011. Review of *Footloose*. RogerEbert.com, 12 October.

Elsaesser, Thomas. 1998a. "Cinema Futures: Convergence, Divergence, Difference." In Elsaesser and Hoffmann 1998, 9–26.

———. 1998b. "Fantasy Island: Dream Logic as Production Logic." In Elsaesser and Hoffmann 1998, 143–158.

Elsaesser, Thomas, and Kay Hoffmann, eds. 1998. *Cinema Futures: Cain, Abel, or Cable?* Amsterdam: Amsterdam University Press.

Forrest, Jennifer. 2002. "The 'Personal' Touch: The Original, the Remake, and the Dupe in Early Cinema." In Forrest and Koos 2002, 89–126.

Forrest, Jennifer, and Leonard R. Koos, eds. 2002a. *Dead Ringers: The Remake in Theory and Practice*. Albany: State University of New York Press.

———. 2002b. "Reviewing Remakes: An Introduction." In Forrest and Koos 2002, 1–36.

Goss, William. 2011. "Review: Footloose Follows Well in the Original's Footsteps." Film.com, 14 October.

Grainge, Paul. 2002. *Monochrome Memories: Nostalgia and Style in Retro America*. Westport, CT: Praeger.

———, ed. 2003. *Memory and Popular Film*. Manchester, UK: Manchester University Press.

Graser, Marc. 2010. "Hollywood Heads Back to the '80s." *Variety*, 16 April.

Grierson, Tim. 2011. "Apparently, People Don't Want '80s Remakes—They Just Want Movies That Remind Them of the '80s." Yahoo! Movies, 17 October.

Gritten, David. 2010. "Leave the '80s in the Past, Hollywood." *Telegraph*, 23 April.

Hakashima, Ryan. 2011. "Hollywood and Big Budget Movies: Is the Love Affair Over?" *Huffington Post*, 17 September.

Horn, John. 2010. "'Karate Kid' Update Breaks Down Some Chinese Walls." *L.A. Times*, 30 May.

IDW (IDW Publishing). 2010. "IDW Partners with Twentieth Century Fox Licensing & Merchandising to Release New Comic Book Series Based on *The A-Team*." IDW Publishing, 22 February.

Jameson, Fredric. 1991. *Postmodernism; or, The Cultural Logic of Late Capitalism*. Durham, NC: Duke University Press.

Jess-Cooke, Carolyn. 2009. *Film Sequels: Theory and Practice from Hollywood to Bollywood*. Edinburgh: Edinburgh University Press.

———. 2010. "Sequelizing Spectatorship and Building Up the Kingdom: The Case of *Pirates of the Caribbean*, Or, How a Theme-Park Attraction Spawned a Multibillion-Dollar Film Franchise." In *Second Takes: Critical Approaches to the Film Sequel*, ed. Carolyn Jess-Cooke and Constantine Verevis, 205–223. Albany: State University of New York Press.

Kelleter, Frank. 2012. "'Toto, I Think We're in Oz Again' (and Again and Again): Remakes and Popular Seriality." In Loock and Verevis 2012, 19–44.

Kelleter, Frank, and Kathleen Loock. Forthcoming. "Hollywood Remaking as Second-Order Serialization." In *Media of Serial Narrative*, ed. Frank Kelleter. Columbus: Ohio State University Press.

Kit, Borys. 2011. "Warner Bros. Readying 'Clash of the Titans 3' (Exclusive)." *Hollywood Reporter*, 2 November.

Klein, Amanda Ann. 2011. *American Film Cycles: Reframing Genres, Screening Social Problems, and Defining Subcultures*. Austin: University of Texas Press.

Landsberg, Alison. 2002. "Prosthetic Memory: The Ethics and Politics of Memory in an Age of Mass Culture." In Grainge 2003, 144–161.

Leitch, Thomas. 2002. "Twice-Told Tales: Disavowal and the Rhetoric of the Remake." In Forrest and Koos 2002, 37–62.

Loock, Kathleen. 2012. "The Return of the Pod People: Remaking Cultural Anxieties in *Invasion of the Body Snatchers*." In Loock and Verevis 2012a, 122–144.

Loock, Kathleen, and Constantine Verevis, eds. 2012a. *Film Remakes, Adaptations, and Fan Productions: Remake/Remodel*. Basingstoke, UK: Palgrave Macmillan.

———. 2012b. Introduction. In Loock and Verevis 2012, 1–15.

Meslow, Scott. 2013. "13 Utterly Unnecessary 1980s Movie Remakes That Are Actually in Development." *The Week*, 12 April.

The Movie Report. 2010. Review of *The A-Team*. 18 June.

Oltmann, Katrin. 2008. *Remake/Premake: Hollywoods romantische Komödien und ihre Gender-Diskurse, 1930–1960*. Bielefeld, Germany: transcript.

Plumb, Ali. 2011. "Bradley Cooper: There'll Be No A-Team 2." *Empire*, 10 March.

Proctor, William. 2012. "Regeneration and Rebirth: Anatomy of the Franchise Reboot." *Scope* 22 (February).

Reynolds, Simon. 2011. *Retromania: Pop Culture's Addiction to Its Own Past*. London: Faber and Faber.

Short, Daniel. 2010. "Marketing Campaign for *Tron Legacy* Exciting Fans." Examiner.com, 27 February.

Sofge, Erik. 2010. "The Not-So-Karate Kid." *Slate*, 11 June.

Time. 2010. "2010: The Year of the '80s Remakes." www.time.com/time/photogallery/0,29307,1977221,00.html.

Trowbridge, Robin. 2010. "Catapult Back to 1982 at Flynn's Arcade at ElecTRONica." *Disney Parks Blog*, 7 October.

Verevis, Constantine. 2006. *Film Remakes*. Edinburgh: Edinburgh University Press.

Wickman, Kase. 2012. "Confirmed: Garrett Hedlund Will Star in 'Tron 3.'" Next-Movie.com, 13 December.

Wieselman, Jarrett. 2009. "Ralph Macchio: I Won't Cameo in 'The Karate Kid' Remake!" *New York Post*, 13 July.

Zeitchik, Steven. 2011. "'Footloose': The '80's Are Dead, Long Live the '80's." *L.A. Times*, 17 October.

CHAPTER 17

I CAN'T LEAD THIS VACATION ANYMORE: MUMBLECORE'S AMERICAN MAN

AMY BORDEN

IN ITS CRITICAL AND POPULAR USE, the name "mumblecore" achieves a sort of self-fulfilling indecipherability that may be traced back to its notably nonmythic origin story. Interviewed by Indiewire in 2005 at the South by Southwest Film Festival, the director Andrew Bujalski recycled the name from the sound mixer Eric Masunaga, who coined the term to describe a group of ultra-low-budget features he had worked on that were playing at the festival.[1] The films most often labeled mumblecore by critics and scholars are conversation-driven, minimalist productions reflective of a generation whose preferred inarticulateness marks a rising affective cultural currency that asks its characters and its audience to understand what they mean and not what they say.

The core group of mumblecore films are those written or directed by Andrew Bujalski, Mark and Jay Duplass, Aaron Katz, Frank V. Ross, Kentucker Aubrey, Joe Swanberg, and Greta Gerwig, although the label has been applied also to films made by Lynne Shelton, Kelly Reichardt, and Noah Baumbach. Both the *New York Times* writer Dennis Lim's oft-cited 2007 mainstream introduction to the cycle and the filmography that appeared alongside Aymar Jean Christian's 2011 *Cinema Journal* essay are emblematic of how critics and scholars classify as mumblecore such varied films as *Funny Ha-Ha* (2002, Andrew Bujalski), *Wendy and Lucy* (2008, Kelly Reichardt), *Baghead* (2008, Mark and Jay Duplass), *Greenberg* (2010, Noah Baumbach), and *Tiny Furniture* (2011, Lena Dunham). Reading this list might leave one with the head-scratching sense that the movement could broadly include any film made from 2002 to 2011 that exhibits the traits of either the art cinema genre described by David Bordwell (1979) or by Michael Newman's "indie-film culture," particularly its use of characters that "are to be read as emblems of their social identities" in a "character-focused realism" (2011, 245–246).[2]

The mutability of the term in popular and scholarly writing is part of what makes it difficult to provide a definitive taxonomy. My goal, instead, is to highlight how the careful dissection of American masculinity typified in *Uncle Kent* (2011, Joe Swanberg), *Hannah Takes the Stairs* (2007, Joe Swanberg), and *The Puffy Chair* (2005, Mark and Jay Duplass) marks the critical response that mumblecore has received and sets it apart from other cycles and sensibilities of indie-film culture, such as smart cinema. By engaging with questions of masculinity, I address how and where to locate mumblecore within indie cinema in order to understand it as a cycle and to ask how mumblecore, like the indie-film culture of which it is part, "demands that our notions of community be redefined, reconfigured, and in some cases radically reconceived" (Newman 2011, 34).

Mumblecore offers a blueprint for understanding a version of contemporary American masculinity as a critical and cultural category particular to the tail end of Generation X and the millennial generation, both of whose educated classes have come of age in the midst of Western movements for queer, trans, gay, lesbian, and women's rights. One result of these movements and the academic study of masculinity, according to Bryce Traister, is "that the masculine gender's presumed invisibility as epistemological foundation is . . . rendered visible as [a] foundation, and a 'constructed' one at that" (2000, 281). This visibility is actualized in the mumblecore cycle's depiction of masculinity through the proliferation of recording devices used in these films, the tendency of characters to perform in various ways, and the emphasis on a do-it-yourself (DIY) craft culture both in the films and in their production histories.

My interest in mumblecore's masculinity does not suggest that the cycle is unconcerned with women or that female characters are not critically featured in its films. For instance, *Beeswax* (2009, Andrew Bujalski) features the sisters Tilly and Maggie Hatcher in lead roles that do not revolve around men even as the film's subplot engages with the roles men inhabit. Rather, the predominantly male-auteur-driven nature of mumblecore masks how these filmmakers have internalized masculinity as both a prescribed norm and a category to be understood within a community that values introspection as the primary mode of self- and group communication. We can see this internalization and introspection at just about the halfway point of *Un-*

cle Kent when the title character (Kent Osborne) walks out of an LA grocery store, carrying four plastic bags filled with alcohol, beer, and snacks. He walks in front of his two companions: Kate (Jennifer Prediger), an environmental writer in her early thirties whom he met on Chatroulette and has come to visit for the weekend, the first time the two have met in person, and Josephine (Josephine Decker), a twenty-something librarian whose Craigslist classified Kent and Kate have answered.[3] In her ad, Josephine seeks a lesbian-curious woman who is game for "friendship and fun." Commenting on the fact that Kent is carrying all their purchases, Josephine turns her head slightly toward Jennifer, who leans against her as they walk, emphasizing their obvious attraction, and says, "He's such a man; he's taking care of us."

To catch this line, Swanberg eschews his tendency to frame in close-up. Instead, he shoots adjacent to Kate and Josephine to frame Kent in a midshot in the grocery store's doorway, catching the two women slightly out of focus in the foreground as they follow him. In this framing, Kent is the leader of the group—he walks in front of the women, allowing his body to activate the automatic doors as he carries their groceries, but his leadership position is rote rather than asserted; he is part of the threesome but distinct from it. Kent's slight glance backward as he leaves the frame shows that he heard the comment and the swallowed laughs it evoked from both women, and that he feels it as a mark of exclusion. He is there to be commented on, and he knows it. He is *such* a man: hilarious.

Kent hopes his night will include a threesome—there is the suggestion of amateur porn in Swanberg's setup—but he is dismissed, feels a bit heartsick, and reverts to documenting the evening's conversation and soft-core petting on his video camera, a self-documentation he constantly engages in throughout the film. With *Uncle Kent*, we see how the preponderance of women in these films and their privileged cinematic and narrative positions situate the male characters as responsive to actions and events rather than as driving the plot or story.

WHY ISN'T MUMBLECORE JUST SMART?

The title of this section isn't a dig; rather, I mean to distinguish mumblecore from the independent cinema sensibility that Jeffrey Sconce diagnoses as smart cinema: "an American school of filmmaking that survives (and at times thrives) at the symbolic and material intersection of 'Hollywood,' the 'indie' scene and the vestiges of what cinephiles used to call 'art' films" (2002, 351). Unlike previous modes of art cinema, smart cinema—epitomized by the films of Wes Anderson, Noah Baumbach, Todd Solondz, and Hal Hartley—relies on a return to classical narrative form with character-driven stories that hinge on the white middle-class family "as a crucible of miscommunication and emotional dysfunction" (358).

Both smart cinema and mumblecore focus on white educated-class relationships, although mumblecore films focus their attention on postcollege twenty-somethings who are often in their first, noncareer jobs. Newman explains, "Smart film is a more specific category than the indie film, one that has little currency outside of academic discourse" because as a tone, it is less concerned with institutions (2011, 13). The nihilism and irony at the core of smart cinema's sensibility "bifurcate one's audience into those who 'get it' and those who do not." This differentiation is intentional: "The entire point of ironic address is to ally oneself with sympathetic peers and to distance oneself from the vast 'other' audience, however defined, which is often the target of the speaker's or artist's derision" (Sconce 2002, 352). Unlike smart cinema, mumblecore has no trace of irony. It is decidedly unironic. In fact, it is so earnest we can almost read mumblecore as the anti–smart cinema. They are perhaps the most earnest set of films ever made, which is in part why they are often attacked for their myopic worldview. Amy Taubin finds "reason enough to reinstate the draft" in Joe Swanberg's assessment that he has nothing much to say about the Iraq War; his films are about his friends and his life in his neighborhood (2007, 47).

The significant differences between smart cinema and mumblecore are overlooked if smart cinema is recognized only as an academic category. Such a classification contributes to a perception in the mainstream press that mumblecore and smart cinema tendencies are interchangeable features of independent film or that the two forms may simply be classified as independent film in their common examination of white middle-class life. This is why *Greenberg* gets classified as "mainstream mumblecore," yet except for Greta Gerwig's costarring role, its depiction of the anxious misanthrope Roger Greenberg (Ben Stiller) has very little in common with character portrayals in the mumblecore cycle.[4] Baumbach's film has much more in common with smart cinema's blank affect, suspicion of the middle-class family, and depiction of the veiled hostility and jealousy embedded in consumer culture than it does with mumblecore's earnest observation of heterosexual relationships and neighborhood life.

Confusion about mumblecore's tendencies helpfully places its style in relief. Surveying the aforementioned movies grouped under the mumblecore label allows for the emergence of narrative and stylistic features that help pinpoint key aspects of the cycle's style. In what follows, I focus on two such aspects to highlight how narrative conventions and their corresponding articulations within the mise-en-scène stress how public and private spaces are gendered in mumblecore. This is reflected in the cycle's minimally dressed sets, home work sites, and the ubiquitous presence of the machines of digital life—computers and cell phones, for example—which support the portability of work for the educated class, thereby blurring the boundaries between traditionally gendered spaces. Mumblecore documents an erasure of the distinctions between traditionally understood public work spaces as masculine and private, and home spaces as feminine. A renewed flexibility in these sites supports the construction of contemporary masculinities that the cycle undertakes.

During the nineteenth century, the concept of the American self-made man—a neologism from 1832—shifted from its seventeenth-century meaning of an independent man in control of his own property, liberty, and life to the concept of the breadwinner, a term coined between 1810 and 1820. The concept of the male breadwinner affirmed the values of nineteenth-century emerging markets and denoted the responsible family man of a rising middle class in which men were no longer bound to their land or to the republican values of New England communities (Kimmel 2011, 14, 15, 17). This development revises the conception of self-sufficient American manhood from the frontier and the community to the marketplace, where survival depends on a restless striving for middle-class status "in the midst of abundance" (Tocqueville, quoted in Kimmel 2011, 18). No longer did manhood rest on "craft traditions, guild memberships, or participation in the virtuous republic of the New England small town" (17). Instead, manhood derived its identity from marketplace successes: "The central characteristic of being self-made was that the proving ground was the public sphere, specifically the workplace. And the workplace was a man's world (and a native-born white man's world at that). If manhood could be proved, it had to be proved in the eyes of other men" (19).

One way to distinguish mumblecore from other indie-film cy-

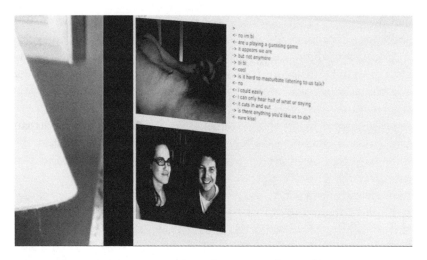

FIGURE 17.1. In *Uncle Kent*, Kent and Jennifer use Kent's home office to visit Chatroulette.

cles is that mumblecore may be recognized via its characters' not yet established work lives or by their work as professional performers. In either case, public spaces—like work spaces—function like home spaces, and vice versa. Tracing the entwined representation of the public sphere and masculinity, Susan Jeffords argues that in 1980s and 1990s American cinema, the workplace is a central male-dominated site in which manhood is proved in the eyes of other men (1993, 200). Taking Jeffords' observation into the twenty-first century, depictions of work and home spaces in mumblecore complicate the distinction between the two spaces and correspondingly allow a disruption of traditional definitions of American masculinity as created in the public sphere. It does this both in its depictions of men and women working in office spaces and in its depiction of home spaces as work spaces. For example, the retail vintage shop owned by Amanda (Anne Dodge) and Jeannie (Tilly Hatcher) in *Beeswax* is the site of personal crises often unrelated to its function as a work space; the nondescript office space in *Hannah Takes the Stairs* is the site of emotional encounters not unlike those that might occur in a living room; and Kent is a cartoonist who works from a home office in which he also views pornography and accesses Chatroulette.

Correspondingly, home spaces are work sites for many of the performers who rehearse or write music at home, as we see in both *Mu-*

tual Appreciation and *Alexander the Last* (2009, Joe Swanberg). In both films, Justin Rice's character rehearses at home with his band, and in the latter his wife, Alex (Jess Weixler), rehearses her off-off-Broadway production at home with her male costar. These dispersals of work spaces into home spaces and vice versa cloud the divide between the home space as private and feminine and the workplace as a site of public masculine identity formation.[5] The decentralization of work spaces and the desire to turn a work space into a home space, as in the use of the break room as the site of emotional and personal discussions and hot cider in *Beeswax*, destabilizes both the site and the ability to assert one's self-made identity.

Mumblecore's indistinct public and private spaces create a world where one's proving ground is no longer apparent, and where community members must enact their own processes of identity formation and gender relations. The sociologists Máirtín Mac an Ghaill and Chris Haywood point to late modernity's shifting gender relations as "an effect of western societies experiencing a surge of individuation," adding "The effects of the freeing of individuals from the normative demands of established social categories is that late modernity subjects (individuals) are impelled to forge their own identity" (2007, 28). The mumblecore cycle dramatizes this experience via its depiction of media reflexivity and its emphasis on performance as a mode of being. Artistic self-creation is mapped onto professional life to such an extent that mumblecore characters normalize self-reflexivity as a mediated process required by their roles as performers. This dynamic is emphasized in the obligatory party scene that nearly every mumblecore film stages. In *Funny Ha-Ha*, Bujalski's intermittent midshots and close-ups create separate spaces where each of the partygoers performs his or her part before the camera cuts to a new "player." The group party scenes are shot and staged to isolate a character as she rehearses her most recent problems with finding both a job and a boyfriend or girlfriend.

The presence of an audience and a performance is not consigned to party scenes or actual staged performances; those two components pervade the actual and mediated interactions that fill the mumblecore universe. The extensive use of cell phones contributes to this aesthetic, since they provide on-screen space for near soliloquies, thus emphasizing the staged nature of the film along the lines of Todd Berliner's reading of John Cassavetes's realism as enforced theatricality.[6] This device is used in *Beeswax* when Jeannie calls her ex (Alex Karpovsky) for advice about her business partnership with Amanda, and in *Nights and Weekends* (2008, Greta Gerwig and Joe Swanberg) as Mattie (Gerwig) and James (Swanberg) maintain their long-distance relationship. This aesthetic invites viewers to confront their own status as eavesdroppers and voyeurs. Thus, mumblecore uses the communication devices of contemporary life to emphasize performance as a central component of identity formation by normalizing a deconstruction of the unified self.

The DIY ethos of mumblecore productions reflects the increasing emphasis on individuals that Mac an Ghaill and Haywood write about and that runs through mumblecore's diegesis. In each case, the emphasis on individuality should be considered from within group and community dynamics, but even within those dynamics, there is on-screen space that emphasizes the relative importance of self-identity formation versus a collective identity that could be articulated by a movement manifesto, as seen in past collective film movements such as neorealism, Dogme 95, and the New American Cinema Group. Mumblecore's DIY aesthetic is an ethos that has no need of a manifesto, lest the group identity supersede the individual.

Maria San Filippo considers how mumblecore is mobilized and motivated "less by concerted effort or collective ideology than by increased access both industrial and political" (2011, 4). This approach is reminiscent of the New American Cinema Group's comparable engagement with the economic limits of independent production, distribution, and exhibition. The group's September 1962 manifesto is notable for articulating the hurdles that both avant-garde and independent narrative filmmakers found when trying to distribute and exhibit their films, and for arguing for an alternative distribution and exhibition network. Mumblecore draws from those of the New American Cinema Group who voiced a desire to join "together to make films" because of their "common beliefs, common knowledge, common anger and impatience" with the conditions of production, distribution, and exhibition of the time (Film-Makers' Cooperative 1962).[7] Alternatively, mumblecore filmmakers, who are predominantly young members of Generation X or millennials, embrace branding their films under the mumblecore label as a means of entering the marketplace.[8] They perform in an era when people are increasingly comfortable with establishing communities and practices by borrowing from market-driven and alternative economies. Considering mumblecore in this context shifts critical emphasis from its talkie aesthetic to the way that its diegetic structures and locations resonate with the material conditions of its productions. Instead of issuing a manifesto or founding a filmmakers' co-op, they distribute online, via curated DVD producers, and are supported by video-on-demand (VOD) release platforms at IFC.com.[9]

Admittedly, there is something very mumblecore about a commercial grouping that creates a product with little to no conscious direction on the part of its key players. I cannot help imagining mumblecore's origin story playing out like the scene from *Hannah Takes the Stairs* when Paul (Andrew Bujalski) builds a story around his announcement to his coworkers Matt (Kent Osborne) and Hannah (Greta Gerwig) that his blog has been noticed by a New York agent and that he has received an e-mail suggesting that maybe—"two or um three or five or six or seven steps ahead"—possibly, it could be published as a book. His demure announcement, framed in an off-center close-up of Paul in the midground of a two-shot, with Hannah in the foreground, is meant to impress Hannah, whose reaction dominates the shot as she turns to the offscreen Matt and enthusiastically echoes Paul's news. He has transcended the blogosphere for the tangibility of print culture, achieving something unnamed yet clearly meaningful while also mumbling that achievement away. It is in that desire to be noticed and to fall away from attention—to occupy a land defined by intuitive affectation and uncertainty—that mumblecore's sensibility finds its intellectual home.

"I CAN'T LEAD THIS VACATION ANYMORE"

As we have seen, the mumblecore label is applied to such a diverse group of independent films because, in part, its practitioners don't subscribe to recognizable movement practices. Another reason is the discomfort it produces through its self-reflexive construction of contemporary forms of American masculinity found in the white intellectual class represented in these films. Dismissal of white heterosexual masculinity is embedded in the critical responses to mumblecore. Writing in the *New York Times*, Nathan Lee suggests that *LOL* (2006, Joe Swanberg) is "a movie about the way we live— or rather about the way white, urban, heterosexual circuit boys are failing to live" (2006). Tim Grierson (2012) describes mumblecore as "the epitome of Hipster White People Problems." With the exception of films by Bujalski and Aaron Katz, mumblecore gets a lukewarm re-

ception from the critics Amy Taubin and J. Hoberman (2007). Swanberg takes the most heat, particularly from Taubin, who finds him
to be "the DIY Judd Apatow," which, she assures her readers, is in no
way a compliment (2007, 46).

Mumblecore's ability to articulate hipster problems, as Grierson
suggests, should be read alongside the cultural history of masculinity that Michael Kimmel and others have written about over the past
thirty years. The craft culture that directs both mumblecore's DIY
aesthetics and its production, distribution, and exhibition conditions
also speaks to the individual self-invention that the films display
and depict. DIY or craft culture does not distinguish between work
space and home space. In their fusion of private and public spaces
as sites of individual and gender invention, mumblecore films push
back against the workplace as a man's world. Instead, mumblecore's
men (and women) rely on and participate in small-scale communities
that resurrect "craft traditions" and participation in a self-made "republic" of like-minded, educated millennials (2011, 17). If you have
ever wondered why muttonchops, homemade jam, and natural clean-
ers populate hipster enclaves like Brooklyn and Portland, look no further than early nineteenth-century America, before market-based industrial capitalism became the overwhelming norm.

The cultural suspicion of men unsure of their own privilege and
unable to articulate their desires dogs mumblecore. Considering *Uncle Kent* alongside Katz's *Dance Party, USA*, which Taubin puts in
her "pantheon of coming-of-age movies" (2007, 47), highlights how
the struggle for self-knowledge is acceptable when you are an adolescent boy—one who has sexually assaulted a passed-out young
woman, as in Katz's film—but not when you are an adult involved
in complex sexual and emotional relationships. The coming-of-age
genre's overt performance of self-reflexivity protects Katz's film from
Taubin's critique of Swanberg's characters as clueless narcissists (46).

One can certainly read Kent in *Uncle Kent* as a narcissist: he
spends the entire movie filming himself and his guests; however,
mumblecore's near-requisite media reflexivity and depiction of romantic or quasi-romantic relationships asks us to consider how performance and vulnerability go hand in hand. Following Judith Butler's arguments for an understanding of gender as a denaturalized
process achieved by "performativity" and "a heterosexual cultural
matrix," Mac an Ghaill and Haywood explain the popular and critical receptivity to the idea that "decentered female and male gay sub-
jectivities provide concrete evidence that femininity and masculinity

FIGURE 17.2. Kent's renaturalized masculinity embraces his vulnerability.

is . . . an active process of achievement, performance, and enactment" (2007, 240).[10] Yet, decentered male heterosexual identities come under fire when engaged in a similar process. Their vulnerability can be seen only as adolescent unless deliberately stylized as a self-reflexive space.

Swanberg manages to create vulnerability in *Uncle Kent* by juxtaposing Kent's constant filming of his life with a series of still and moving images more than midway through the film. These images pull the viewer out of the film's story into a bucolic landscape where Kent is made vulnerable by his apparent aloneness, except for the unassigned view of the camera. He is captured with flowers in his hair, smiling and posed for the camera in a long shot that is held long enough for the viewer to see his near-naked middle-aged tattooed body. This scene displays Kent's vulnerability outside his hybrid home space and work space. It renaturalizes his complex masculinity in a site more akin to a Thomas Eakins painting than to Chatroulette. In doing so, *Uncle Kent* adds nature as yet another space to mumblecore's work spaces and home spaces. Here Kent may experience a desocialized naturalization of masculinity in a process of reseeing himself. In these images, he gives up his role as visual autobiographer and is freed of the self-aware roles of chronicler and performer. Surrendering these positions suspends his active, nearly tortured performance of masculinity as measured against and alongside Kate and Josephine.

Indeed, the men of mumblecore are in a constant state of anxiety about their place in their communities and their status as men.

Are they jokes for the women they hope to bed? Are men and women so similar culturally and socially in the educated class depicted in the majority of these films that any sexual or gender difference can be asserted only in the most fumbling and awkward ways? Are they trusted ex-boyfriends who are there to offer counsel when business discussions go wrong, as in *Beeswax*? Or are they supposed to be incarnations of an idealized American *Father Knows Best* (1954–1960) version of masculinity, as in *The Puffy Chair*?

In her reading of 1990s cinematic masculinity, Jeffords suggests that the problem "men confront in the narrative is that they did their jobs too well, at the expense of their relationships with their families"; as a result, "nineties films are telling audiences that these men were actually being self-destructive" (1993, 200). These self-destructive tendencies are taken up in *The Puffy Chair*. The film consciously engages with the norms of heterosexual masculinity in order to disrupt a traditionally privileged form of American masculinity—more so than the films previously discussed. The film's two male leads play as deliberate echoes of each other. Josh (Mark Duplass) performs the clear archetype of straight American breadwinner and would-be family patriarch; he leads the road trip that Emily (Kate Aselton) and his younger brother, Rhett (Rhett Wilkins), have invited themselves to join. The trip is inspired by Josh's purchase of an oversize used maroon recliner he believes to be a replica of one that his father owned during his childhood.

The chair is a garish emblem of Josh's inability to assert control and direction in his life. Recently dismissed as the keyboardist and singer in his band, he is hustling as a concert promoter while desperately trying to maintain an air of normalcy in his obviously strained relationship with Emily. As a gift for his father, the chair functions as a reminder of the oversize role that fathers play in sons' lives—a reading accentuated by the end of the film when Josh, finally alone and drinking a beer with his father on the family home's back porch, asks him how he knew he wanted to marry, which the film positions as the most significant commitment of heterosexual masculinity.[11]

The characterizations of masculinity presented by Josh and Rhett are accentuated by Josh's assertions of his will against that of his younger brother. Josh's role as the symbolic father is emphasized by the fact that Josh, and only Josh, ever drives the van during the trip. He determines when and where to stop, he pays for all accommodations, and he actually chastises his younger brother with the

FIGURE 17.3. In *The Puffy Chair*, Josh marries his younger brother, Rhett, and Amber in a late-night ceremony witnessed by his long-term girlfriend, Emily.

line "You're a child, you have no money, and you don't know how to take care of yourself." Rhett provides a counterpoint to Josh's nearly hyperbolic performance of a self-styled conservative father figure. Compared to Josh's frequent angry outbursts and efforts to manipulate the world for his own gain—he forces his passengers to engage in an outrageous set of deceptions in order to save ten dollars on the occupancy rate at a roadside motel—we first meet Rhett when he is crouched low in some bushes to film a gecko.[12] He is taken with the beauty of the animal and its habitat. Against Josh's archetypal alpha male, Rhett is cast as a soft-spoken romantic; he is a contemporary hippie. After Rhett figuratively marries a girl he has just met, "because it's just right, man," he is framed with flowers in his hair and beard, like Kent in *Uncle Kent*. Josh acts as the officiant at the wedding, using the opportunity to voice his own insecurities and desires for marriage. In asserting himself in this role, he adopts yet another performance of male privilege: the traditional role of men as representatives of a Christian god. While the use of flowers in *Uncle Kent* works with Swanberg's long-shot framing and Osborne's near-naked appearance to convey Kent's vulnerability, here it reads as an affirmation of multiple articulations of masculinity occupying the same social and cultural spaces.

Josh's use of aggression achieves short-term goals, such as having the purchased chair reupholstered when it is found to be in far worse condition than its eBay advertisement suggested. Yet Rhett usurps

Josh's control over the road trip by burning the chair in a motel parking lot, believing that it contains negative energy that is poisoning the group's interrelationships. Ultimately, the film depicts Josh's coming to consciousness that contemporary identity and gender roles are self-constructed and not entirely adopted from past models. By the end of the trip, Josh learns that being the alpha male is frustrating and exhausting. Furthermore, it is a role that he chose unconsciously for himself.

In the penultimate moment of the film, Josh, framed in a close-up, defeated by the setbacks he has suffered throughout the road trip, says to Emily, "I can't do it anymore." "Do what?" she asks. "I can't lead this vacation anymore," Josh replies. Using an eyeline match to cut from Josh to Emily, the camera frames her reply in close-up: "No one asked you to lead anything, Josh." Emily's role in this exchange is vital. She provides the guidance and control that Josh seeks. It is Emily who gently suggests that Josh took on his role, and it is Emily who ultimately ends things with Josh, answering affirmatively his question whether they should break up. As soon as Josh yields control of the narrative—on the final leg of his road trip, no less—his role shifts alongside Emily's as she becomes the plot's catalyst. The scene ends and the next begins with a close-up of a napping Josh in the passenger seat, his brother driving the van. *The Puffy Chair* is as much about Josh's journey to relinquish control as it is about enacting a visible process of denaturalized straight masculinity.

AMANDA KLEIN SUGGESTS THAT film cycles should be understood to enact a pragmatics of cultural values (2011, 8). The principal players of the mumblecore movement reject their similarity—Bujalski finds it silly to group their films together—yet the critical attention that mumblecore has garnered suggests that it taps into a sensibility that popularly and critically coalesced around the label.[13] It may be that this cycle is not rooted in initial gross financial success, but instead enacts the processes of a brand-driven economy while simultaneously opting to demarcate that drive from other forms of market capitalism in its depiction of work spaces, home spaces, and identity formation. Following this idea, it may be worthwhile to ask whether mumblecore's DIY aesthetic and ethos, along with its representation of nondiscrete identities, may be considered openings into Christine Gledhill's diagnosis that "sexual identities have become increasingly available as commercial style-choices" (2012, 2).

Constance Penley and Sharon Willis end their introduction to *Male Trouble* with the suggestion that feminists must move to the "riskier politics of possibilities—for femininity and masculinity, for women and men" (1993, xix). While perhaps not realizing the riskiest of possibilities, mumblecore masculinity performs its skepticism toward a singular heterosexual masculinity as an implicitly known ideal. The impetus to actualize the processes of a deconstructed American masculinity—mumblecore masculinity—stages an uncomfortable and often unsuccessful process of self-actualization.

NOTES

1. *The Puffy Chair* (2005, Jay and Mark Duplass) won the festival's Audience Award that year. Joe Swanberg made his feature debut with *Kissing on the Mouth*, and Bujalski's *Mutual Appreciation* played in competition.

2. Newman (2011) describes indie-film culture "as a shared way of thinking about films" that formally vary from mainstream Hollywood (245), and that share three tendencies: "character-focused realism, formal play, and oppositionality" (15).

3. Chatroulette is an international online chat site that lets users quickly cycle through other users' live feeds. A user may stop to chat with whoever appears on the screen and just as quickly move on to another user's feed.

4. See Pahle 2010, White 2010, and *Economist* 2010.

5. An interesting forerunner to some of the tendencies that I link to mumblecore may well be *thirtysomething* (1987–1991); see Torres 1993.

6. "In capturing the artistic quality of real life, Cassavetes films exploit the resonances between the systems of representation within both drama and reality" (Berliner 1999, 9).

7. "I think that there are a bunch of us coming up now who have many of the same influences, and the same anti-influences, i.e. some of the crummier aspects of the indie scene that we'd all like to bury" (Bujalski 2005).

8. Taubin (2007, 45) makes the point that many of these titles are helped theatrically by mumblecore's brand. The initial theatrical run of *Hannah Takes the Stairs*, in August 2007, was part of the IFC-programmed series "The New Talkies: Generation DIY."

9. The filmmakers, writers, and actors of mumblecore collaborate on one another's productions, in part because of the limited economic potential of their films, which, in turn is driven partly by their limited budgets, their small-scale, curated theatrical runs, and the self- and curator-issued DVD and web-based distribution networks in which they participate. Andrew Grant, a blogger and critical champion of the cycle, distributes a number of mumblecore titles on DVD through his Benten Films—tagline: "DVDs curated by critics."

10. See Butler (1990) and Butler (1993, 139–141).

11. Notably, Mark and Jay Duplass's parents play Josh and Rhett's parents.

12. Both Josh and Rhett are either professional performers or amateur cre-

ators. The film begins with Josh framed in a close-up while using a chicken leg as a microphone to lip-synch for Emily. This shot sets up the importance of performance for Josh now that he has lost his previous musical outlet. The scene continues, culminating in a massive argument between Josh and Emily when he takes a call during dinner. The call interrupts their domestic space and highlights how Josh has no work space; his work space is his cell phone.

13. Bujalski acknowledges the artificiality of the mumblecore moniker: "It makes perfect sense for bloggers to sift through the films and pluck out commonalities," he said. "But the reductive concept that we're somehow the same—that bugs me" (quoted in Lim 2007).

WORKS CITED

Berliner, Todd. 1999. "Hollywood Movie Dialogue and the 'Real Realism' of John Cassavetes." *Film Quarterly* 52, no. 3 (Spring): 2–16.

Bordwell, David. 1979. "The Art Cinema as a Mode of Film Practice." *Film Criticism* 4, no. 1 (Fall): 56–64.

Bujalski, Andrew. 2005. "The Mumblecore Movement? Andrew Bujalski on His *Funny Ha-Ha*." Interview by Michael Koresky. Indiewire, 22 August.

Butler, Judith. 1990. *Gender Trouble*. New York: Routledge.

———. 1993. *Bodies That Matter: On the Discursive Limits of Sex*. New York: Routledge.

Christian, Aymar Jean. 2011. "Joe Swanberg, Intimacy, and the Digital Aesthetic." *Cinema Journal* 50, no. 4: 117–135.

Economist. 2010. "Mumblecore Meets the Mainstream." 22 April.

Film-Makers' Cooperative. 1962. "The First Statement of the New American Cinema Group." September 30. http://film-makerscoop.com/about/history.

Gledhill, Christine. 2012. *Gender Meets Genre in Postwar Cinema*. Chicago: University of Illinois Press.

Grierson, Tim. 2012. "Say Goodbye to Mumblecore: How the Duplass Brothers Rise above the Ramble." Deadspin.com, 14 March.

Hoberman, J. 2007. "It's Mumblecore! Films by, for, and about Twenty-Somethings Are Having a Moment. IM Someone about It." *Village Voice*, 14 August.

Jeffords, Susan. 1993. "The Big Switch: Hollywood Masculinity in the Nineties." In *Film Theory Goes to the Movies*, ed. Jim Collins, Hilary Radner, and Ava Preacher Collins, 196–208. New York: Routledge.

Kimmel, Michael. 2011. *Manhood in America: A Cultural History*. New York: Oxford University Press.

Klein, Amanda. 2011. *American Film Cycles: Reframing Genres, Screening Social Problems, and Defining Subcultures*. Austin: University of Texas Press.

Lee, Nathan. 2006. "Logging On for Love, Tuning Out the Realities." *New York Times*, 23 August.

Lehman, Peter, ed. 2001. *Masculinity: Bodies, Movies, Culture*. New York: Routledge.

Lim, Dennis. 2007. "A Generation Finds Its Mumble." *New York Times*, 19 August.

Mac an Ghaill, Máirtín, and Chris Haywood. 2007. *Gender, Culture, and So-*

ciety: Contemporary Femininities and Masculinities. New York: Palgrave Macmillan.

Newman, Michael. 2011. *Indie: American Film Culture.* New York: Columbia University Press.

Pahle, Rebecca. 2010. "Mumblecore Goes Mainstream." *MovieMaker,* 28 March.

Penley, Constance, and Sharon Willis, eds. 1993. *Male Trouble.* Minneapolis: University of Minnesota Press.

San Filippo, Maria. 2011. "A Cinema of Recession: Micro-Budgeting, Micro-Drama, and the Mumblecore Movement." *Cineaction* 85.

Sconce, Jeffrey. 2002. "Irony, Nihilism, and the New American Smart Film." *Screen* 43, no. 4 (Winter): 349–369.

Taubin, Amy. 2007. "All Talk?" *Film Comment,* November–December, 45–48.

Torres, Shasha. 1993. "Melodrama, Masculinity, and the Family: *thirtysomething* as Therapy." In *Male Trouble,* ed. Constance Penley and Sharon Willis, 283–302. Minneapolis: University of Minnesota Press.

Traister, Bryce. 2000. "Academic Viagra: The Rise of American Masculinity Studies." *American Quarterly* 52, no. 2 (June): 274–304.

White, Armond. 2010. "My *Greenberg* Problem—And Yours." *New York Press,* 17 March.

CHAPTER 18

SERIALIZED KILLERS: PREBOOTING HORROR IN *BATES MOTEL* AND *HANNIBAL*

ANDREW SCAHILL

IN 2013, TWO HORROR FILMS held in high esteem by fans and critics alike—Alfred Hitchcock's *Psycho* (1960) and Jonathan Demme's
The Silence of the Lambs (1991)—were adapted for television. The
programs, named *Bates Motel* and *Hannibal*,[1] contain a few notable
similarities: both frequently repeat character types and situations
from the films in order to reward spectators familiar with the original texts. Further, each program is billed as a prequel to its "original"
text, and yet both abandon chronological continuity, setting their
stories in a contemporary narrative setting.

Though perhaps popularized in the lexicon by George Lucas's *Star
Wars* prequel trilogy (1999–2005), the prequel has existed as a mode
of filmmaking since at least the 1970s. A text such as *The Godfather
Part II* (Francis Ford Coppola, 1974), for instance, contains features of
both the prequel and sequel, weaving together past and present narratives. The *Planet of the Apes* series (1968–1973) adopted a prequel
format in the last three of the five films in order to expand the narrative universe established by the first two films. But the term "prequel" seems to exist as a defined Hollywood category and has been
a means of marketing and promotion since at least as early as Richard Lester's *Butch and Sundance: The Early Days* (1979). For audiences, the prequel offers the pleasure of familiar characters and settings while further exploring the narrative world of the existing text
and possibly deepening the audience's connection with central characters. Like a feature-length flashback, the prequel extends the story
world backward to an earlier period in the characters' lives, providing further character development, perhaps during a formative stage.
As an industrial mode, the prequel provides the financial safety of a
tested story line with a built-in audience.

This mode includes television adaptations also, including programs such as *Muppet Babies* (1984–1991), *Star Trek: Enterprise* (2001–2005), *The Young Indiana Jones Chronicles* (1992–1996), *Young Hercules* (1998–1999), *X-Men Evolution* (2000–2003), *The Sarah Connor Chronicles* (2008–2009), *Smallville* (2001–2011), *Caprica* (2010–2011), and recently the *Sex & the City* prequel *The Carrie Diaries* (2013–), which explores the high school adventures of the familiar adult protagonist. Nor does this trend show any sign of halting: in 2014, *Better Call Saul* and *Gotham* were created to explore the events leading up to AMC's *Breaking Bad* and the *Batman* franchise.

What sets *Bates Motel* and *Hannibal* apart from traditional prequels is that both programs eschew continuity and choose to update the story's setting rather than place it within the time period of its original text. Further, the programs seem to demonstrate no necessary allegiance to the original text—both are willing to retroactively rewrite or reimagine elements of the original and create new and unexpected plot twists. This approach is similar to that of *Smallville*, which functioned as a prequel to the *Superman* franchise, but also set its narrative in modern time and introduced characters and conflicts that effectively rewrote the "known" narrative of the comic books and films. As a ten-year series, *Smallville* effectively rebooted the franchise through the generic form of teen melodrama.

Rebooting has become a popular way to promote films and other media forms that revisit familiar narratives with an altered origin story, narrative approach, or artistic aesthetic. Whereas a remake is normally made as an act of reverence toward the original (Martin Scorsese's *Cape Fear* [1991] as a remake of J. Lee Thompson's 1962 *Cape Fear*), a reboot is often made in contrast to the original, most famously in the recent *Dark Knight* franchise reboot, which distanced itself from both the television series and the Tim Burton films. The word "rebooting" suggests that these franchises have died—as if repeated sequels had depleted the original text of vitality. The reboot seeks to make a familiar narrative legible as "modern" within a more contemporary cinematic style. Often, this means "rescuing" texts from being read as ironic or camp with an infusion of realism and violence, as is the case with *Dark Knight* (Batman), *Man of Steel* (Superman), even *Miami Vice*.

Within the horror genre, audiences have seen upward of a dozen modern remakes of horror films from the 1970s and early 1980s, including *It's Alive* (Larry Cohen, 1974), *Friday the 13th* (Sean S. Cunningham, 1980), *The Hills Have Eyes* (Wes Craven, 1977), *Night of the Demons* (Kevin Tenney, 1988), *The Last House on the Left* (Wes Craven, 1972), *Black Christmas* (Bob Clark, 1974), *Halloween* (John Carpenter, 1978), *Piranha* (Joe Dante, 1978), *When a Stranger Calls* (Fred Walton, 1979), *My Bloody Valentine* (George Mihalka, 1981), *The House on Sorority Row* (Mark Rosman, 1983), *Amityville Horror* (Stuart Rosenberg, 1979), *Prom Night* (Paul Lynch, 1980), *The Wicker Man* (Robin Hardy, 1973), *Dawn of the Dead* (George A. Romero, 1978), *Invasion of the Body Snatchers* (Philip Kaufman, 1978 [also a remake]), *A Nightmare on Elm Street* (Wes Craven, 1984), *The Fog* (John Carpenter, 1980), and *The Omen* (Richard Donner, 1976), to name a few. Forthcoming remakes include *Children of the Corn* (Fritz Kiersch, 1984), *The Eyes of Laura Mars* (Irvin Kershner, 1978), and *Hellraiser* (Clive Barker, 1987). Four of these have become rebooted franchises themselves. If, as Linda Hutcheon notes, sequels are about "never wanting the story to end," and remakes are about "wanting to retell the same story over and over in different ways" (2006, 9), then we may say that the reboot is tantamount to a desire to make stories relevant again, to rescue the story from the distancing effects of time.[2]

Using *Bates Motel* and *Hannibal* as case studies, this chapter examines how these television cycles function as both prequels and reboots, and considers them as an altogether different mode—an origin remake, or a "preboot." Despite their similarities, however, *Bates Motel* and *Hannibal* offer different strategies for using the serial form of television and delivering on the promise of familiarity and revision. One series crafts the preboot as an alternative perspective that rewrites the audience's understanding of the original, and one sees the preboot as a first draft of the cinematic texts, which confirms the original as complete and coherent. *Bates Motel* engages in an inverted repetition, in which familiar events are replayed with roles reversed as a means of rewriting or deconstructing assumptions about the original text. *Hannibal* engages in an incomplete repetition, in which character types or events mimic familiar moments, but in a way that lacks the "trueness" of the original.

NARRATIVE COMPLEXITY

In addition to their horror film source material and the series' updating of their stories to a modern era, both programs share a similar high-concept aesthetic that vacillates between objective reality and subjective states of madness (possibly a response to the popularity of *American Horror Story*'s frenzied art-horror aesthetic). Indeed, both *Bates Motel* and *Hannibal* employ a notable art-cinema aesthetic—recalling David Bordwell's reference to films that abandon cause-and-effect relationships, favor an episodic plot construction, and eschew narrative closure (1979, 56–62). The series regularly structure their plots through a dream logic rather than linear, objective narrative. Spectators are often forced to engage with tableaus of beautiful weirdness with little recourse to causality or explanation, and both series use the continued breakdown between the subjective (dreams, madness, drugs) and objective points of view. Most importantly, however, each series relies on the audience's prior knowledge of the original film, offering the promise of taboo breaking (incest, cannibalism) as a tantalizing mode of suspense.

There are, however, notable differences: whereas *Bates Motel* centers on Norman Bates and his mother, Norma, purchasing the motel, *Hannibal* is presented through the stories of both Hannibal Lecter and the criminal profiler Will Graham. *Bates Motel* is more narrowly focalized, to borrow Gérard Genette's term from *Narrative Discourse* (1972) for the perspective through which a narrative is presented. Rarely in *Bates Motel* is the audience given a point of view that is not the Bateses', whereas *Hannibal* provides a variety of characters' perspectives on narrative events. *Bates Motel* relies greatly on seriality—that is, on foregrounding relationships over events and allowing for a perpetual lack of narrative closure. In generic classification, it exists somewhere between family melodrama and domestic thriller. Though *Hannibal* has serial qualities, its employment of the police procedural (resembling most closely the *X-Files*'s "monster-of-the-week" model) brings about more frequent narrative closure (cases are solved, killers are brought to justice). This may be owing to the programs' authorships: Roy Lee, the producer of *Bates Motel*, comes from Hollywood cinema, and *Hannibal*'s Bryan Fuller is a veteran of television production.

As a producer, Lee is best known for his American translations of foreign horror and thriller cinema: *The Ring* (2002, Gore Verbinski), *The Grudge* (2004, Takashi Shimizu), *Dark Water* (2005, Walter Salles), *The Eye* (2008, David Moreau), *The Departed* (2006, Martin Scorsese), *Quarantine* (2008, John Erick Dowdle), *The Uninvited* (2009, Charles and Thomas Guard), and *Oldboy* (2013, Spike Lee).[3] Indeed, we may think of Lee as a type of horror-remake auteur, since his future projects (Stephen King's *IT* and Tobe Hooper's *Poltergeist*) place *Bates Motel* in a larger trajectory of making past or foreign horror texts "accessible" to contemporary American audiences. *Hannibal*'s producer, Bryan Fuller, is a television veteran with a penchant for varied, genre-busting television series, including *Dead like Me* (2003–2004), *Wonderfalls* (2004), *Pushing Daisies* (2007–2009), and *Heroes* (2006–2010). Finally, there are format differences: *Bates Motel* is broadcast on the cable channel A&E, whose lineup tends to focus on "true crime" reality shows and blue-collar masculinity. *Bates Motel* is part of the network's foray into "quality television," following the model of successes such as AMC's *Mad Men*. Alternately, *Hannibal* is a product of network television, broadcast on NBC. Despite this, the show is surprisingly violent for FCC-regulated network television, leading some affiliates to censor the series or for the network to pull particularly provocative episodes from broadcast (Bibel 2013).

Despite generic and exhibition differences, both programs use the original films as the constant subtext against and through which the scrics derive meaning. Viewers of both programs are therefore invited to consider the complex interrelationship between the original film text and its television preboot. Useful here is Jason Mittell's notion of an "operational aesthetic"—a mode of pleasurable engagement concerned with the formal construction of a program. Within the operational aesthetic, Mittell says, we are "both actively engaged in the story and successfully surprised through storytelling manipulations—we want to enjoy the machine's results while also marveling at how it works" (2006, 38). Since the long story of both programs has already been written, the operational aesthetic of *Bates Motel* and *Hannibal* is to marvel at the sophisticated play of references, the modes of reflection, and the interaction between known narrative ("now") and newly constructed narrative ("then").

Mittell notes the increasing shift in American television programming toward "narrative complexity," which includes, among other elements, a mix of closed and open narrative forms. He follows a number of scholars who have noted a similar shift in televisual narrative. In "Television and the Neo-Baroque," Angela Ndalianis distinguishes between classical and neo-baroque narrative, claiming that "television series since the 1950s have increasingly favoured an open narrative form [neo-baroque] that . . . weaves into and between multiple story formations that traverse episode and story time" (2007,

84). Kristen Thomas sees this as part of an overall shift in storytelling modes in which the seriality of television provided a template for other mediums. As she says, "The notion of firm and permanent closure to any given narrative has loosened across media. Series television, with its broad possibilities for spinning out narratives indefinitely, has been a major impetus in these tendencies" (2003, 105).

Complex narrative uses the operational aesthetic and tends to move away from episodic closure in favor of a hybrid of contained and open plotlines—season-long or multiseason plot arcs rather than enclosed, per-episode stories (*Seinfeld*, *Buffy the Vampire Slayer*, *Law & Order: SVU*). Ndalianis echoes this notion, claiming that in contemporary television, "the series (which consists of a succession of self-contained narrative episodes that progress in a sequence) and the serial (which comprises a series of episodes whose narrative resists closure and continue into the next episode[s] within the sequence) have increasingly collapsed into one another [making it] difficult to tell one form from another" (2007, 84).

Mittell states that the long narrative of complex television tends to derive from plot developments rather the melodramatic conventions of soap opera. Put another way, complex television narratively seeks to balance "the competing demands and pleasures of episodic and serial forms" (2006, 35). Mittell notes a number of reasons why complex television has become an increasingly dominant mode in televisual storytelling, including technological transformations, such as the VCR and the DVR, that let consumers record, rewind, and rewatch select episodes or scenes, allowing for repeat viewership and close reading practices. In addition, the recording of television programs on DVDs, with their huge storage capacity, allows for "binge viewership," in which spectators can screen episodes back-to-back rather than being tied to a weekly viewing schedule. Finally, contemporary television often uses online media as sites of narrative extension, places where audiences can explore a story world or the backstory of a minor character, often rendering the televisual experience incomplete without it (*Heroes*, *Lost*, *The Office*).

For these reasons, modern television increasingly engages its viewers in a challenging and varied manner, requiring a mode of active viewership often absent from critical accounts of the televisual. It is also a "living narrative" in that it may be altered and transformed from season to season based on audience feedback and fan interaction. As Mittell notes, modern television spectatorship "demands an active and attentive process of comprehension to decode both the complex stories and modes of storytelling offered by contemporary television" (2006, 32).

All these modes of complex televisual address are relevant to a discussion of *Bates Motel* and *Hannibal*. Both series employ intertextuality and repetition, but in different ways and for different aims. Both ask the viewer to marvel at the operational aesthetic of the shows, which may join the television series to the original, remake the original in a new, modern setting, or completely rewrite the narrative of the cycle altogether.

RETHINKING REPETITION

Neither *Bates Motel* nor *Hannibal* is a sequel, though they share many semiotic features of this mode of narrative reiteration, and are mobilized by the sequel's enabling interest in repetition, difference, continuation, and retroactivity (Jess-Cooke and Verevis 2010, 4). Like a sequel, the prequel or preboot must read as a continuation of the original text even if it takes place chronologically earlier. Whereas a sequel may provide the pleasure of recognition by echoing a familiar narrative event (Jason Vorhees stalks another set of teens at Crystal Lake), repetition in prequels takes on the form of premonitions or causes of later events (Jason discovers his hockey mask for the first time). The programs repeat familiar iconography, situations, and characters—either in actual "younger" form or in new characters that evoke known characters or settings. As Paul Sutton notes in "The 'Afterwardsness' of the Sequel," the sequel is designed "to provoke the spectator into recollection and retranslation while at the same time providing pleasurable repetition" (2010, 148–149). Part of the draw of these programs for fans is surely the pleasure of recognition, or "getting" the reference: Norman discovering taxidermy for the first time, or visiting the plastic cell that will become Hannibal Lecter's eventual home.

The narrative premonitions are, in a way, sequels to their original films (they come, to most spectators, after the original texts upon which they are based), but they are complicated by their narrative "beforeness." Indeed, *Bates Motel* and *Hannibal* are more properly deemed prequels because they explore the becoming of their central monsters. This interest in becoming follows a greater trend within rebooted horror film franchises, which seem to take a noted interest in the monster's origins—both *Friday the 13th* (2009, Markus Nispel) and *Halloween* (2007, Rob Zombie) revisit their character's childhoods as a means of eliciting an almost-but-not-quite sympathy for the homicidal maniacs at their center. Rob Zombie's remake of *Halloween* expands the famous child's-POV opening to a forty-minute origin narrative that details the abuse leading to the killer's dissociative disorder. *Friday the 13th* takes the death of Jason's mother in the original film as the site of childhood trauma that will create the grown killer. In a nod to Lila Crane's exploration of the Bates home in *Psycho*, one set of unwitting victims stumbles across Jason's cabin with his tiny boyhood bed, seemingly held in stasis from the moment of his childhood trauma.

Since the prequel discloses events that occurred before the original, it is perhaps most useful to think of this device as an extended or even feature-length flashback— it manipulates our understanding of known events by providing alternative contexts or motivations for those actions. Sutton argues that the prequel "is structured by the logic of 'afterwardsness,' that it possesses a peculiar dual temporality that enables it to both precede and follow the film or films to which it is a prequel" (2010, 141–142). The slasher film often relies on seemingly unmotivated murders to shock and confuse its audience. For spectators familiar with the original film, a prequel offers a peculiar pleasure—the pleasure of understanding what led to what seemed like unmotivated murder and monstrosity. Slasher prequels complete the semiotic circle by providing motivation to their killers, often humanizing them in the process. Jason in *Friday the 13th* becomes a sort of mentally unstable isolationist, attacking teenagers who dare to venture onto his land—more Ted Kaczynski than Frankenstein. In *Halloween*, Michael Myers emerges as a bullied man-child with explosive fits of rage, transformed from a lumbering golem into a steroidal juvenile delinquent.

Most pertinent for considering *Bates Motel* and *Hannibal* is how the preboot structure of the programs relies on audience knowledge of what these stories will become—and how this elicits a very particular type of audience pleasure. It may well be that the programs will contradict the familiar narrative of the original films—as is the case with J. J. Abrams's *Star Trek*. But since audience expectation is that the original and preboot narratives will "meet" in the future, the narratives take on a decidedly Oedipal tone: for all the stories' machinations, the characters' fates have already been written. This is wholly appropriate for both programs and their original texts, since intensely Oedipal struggles animate both *Psycho* and *The Silence of the Lambs*. The repetitions in *Bates Motel* and *Hannibal*, however, are quite different from those in a sequel that takes place chronologically after the original. Since these repetitions come chronologically "before" *Psycho* and *The Silence of the Lambs*, they gain a kind of originary status. In providing what I call incomplete or inverted repetitions, these programs employ the seriality of television and the inevitability of the programs' "known" conclusions—but for different aims: *Bates Motel* deconstructs the original text, and *Hannibal* reaffirms it.

BATES MOTEL: REPETITION AS INVERSION

Bates Motel is a prequel to *Psycho* set in contemporary America. The show begins with Norma Bates (Vera Farmiga) and her son Norman (Freddie Highmore) beginning life anew in a small Oregon community after the accidental death of Norma's husband. They purchase what will become the Bates Motel, are joined by Norman's estranged brother, Dylan (Max Thieriot), and slowly discover that the town is full of secrecy and violence. Season 1 reveals that it was Norman who killed his adopted father, and that the Bateses' frequent moves are the result of Norman's violent dissociative disorder. In the season cliffhanger, we are led to believe that Norman has murdered his schoolteacher, Mrs. Watson (Keegan Connor Tracy) after being sexually aroused by her.

Bates Motel's creative team is dominated by industry veterans from *Friday Night Lights* and *Lost*, series that were likewise deeply focused on character development and deploying the long-form narrative of television. In art design and visual style, *Bates Motel* recalls a David Lynchian aesthetic. Like Lynch's own renowned long-form TV series *Twin Peaks*, *Bates Motel* is set in a bucolic community in the northwestern United States—in this case, White Pine Bay, which offers artisanal cheeses and organic pig farming while hiding a seedy underworld of drug trafficking and the human sex trade. The show's advertising campaign teases viewers with unfamiliar, uncontextualized images (a body on fire, a dismembered hand, a field of marijuana, a woman chained to a hotel sink) and with the promise of "known" future transgressions, namely, incest. In the show's teaser trailer, Norman's tagline from *Psycho*, "A boy's best friend is his mother,"

FIGURE 18.1. Norma and Norman Bates are temporally out of place in the modern world of *Bates Motel*.

accompanies a shot of Norman and his mother alone on a hotel bed as abrasive industrial music plays. The raw, scratchy music suggests the tearing apart that will happen in the program—revealing the criminal world of the town as the libidinal undertones of the mother-son dynamic become clear. Perhaps more appropriately, it represents the tearing apart of *Psycho*'s narrative—by providing an alternative perspective on the history of the Bateses, it inverts the victim-aggressor roles of the original and crafts a tragic, Oedipal trajectory.

One of the most dynamic features of *Bates Motel* is its status as both a prequel to *Psycho* and a "modern reimagining" of the story. But instead of bringing Norman and his mother into the contemporary world, it uses their chronological stasis to specifically code them as removed from modernity. The design of their previous home, their dress, their early-seventies automobile, and Norman's preference for decades-old music and movies are all temporally dislocated from the contemporary setting of the program. Indeed, we may think of *Bates Motel* as an "elsewhen" narrative (Tudor 1989, 12) that seems to coexist in multiple time periods simultaneously, as do *Twin Peaks*, *Bride of Frankenstein*, *Edward Scissorhands*, or *Napoleon Dynamite*. *Twin Peaks*, of course, employed a similar postmodern temporal pastiche and is perhaps *Bates Motel*'s nearest aesthetic and narrative cousin.

In "elsewhen" texts, chronology functions symbolically rather than realistically. Images of the present, like the cell phones used by the young girls at Norman's school and the drunken rave they attend, seem linked to disconnectedness, numbness, and voyeurism. At the rave, the episode lingers on Norman's subjective point of view as he silently surveys the contemporary yet foreign teenage culture, finally stating, "There's a lot to look at." Indeed, the sex-trafficking ring and drug trade that forms the underbelly of the small town is shown to be symptomatic of modernity, and antithetical to the Bateses' anachronistic sensibilities. Though Norma may represent the danger of oppressive maternal affection, the show presents the alternative—giving in to modernity and forward movement—as the more dangerous option for Norman.

Generically, *Bates Motel* offers an interesting blend of bildungsroman and family melodrama. The story belongs largely to Norman, who is at first an awkward, sheltered young man controlled by an overprotective mother. The show strengthens our identification with Norman through a number of narrative features. First and foremost, the show is almost exclusively presented through the point of view of Norman and Norma—we know only what they know, and they serve as our point of entry into this strange town and its inhabitants. The program develops an antagonistic relationship between the Bateses and the town of White Pine Bay: Norma is raped by the former owner of the motel (leading Norman to murder the rapist in order to protect his mother), the police force is corrupt, and the community hides a long history of criminality, kidnapping, and torture.

Though the series constructs Norman as a sympathetic man-child, much as *Psycho* uses victimization to foster our identification with him, *Bates Motel* does not position Norma as an antagonist. In the context created by *Psycho* (what we believe about the Bateses before watching *Bates Motel*), our ire is directed at the destructive mother love of Norma—through the 1960 film, we "know" her to be the puritanical superego of Norman's psychosis. But the series reveals and rewrites her rather as Norman's protection against himself, a prophylactic presence whose eventual absence will surely result in Norman's descent into madness. Though we "know" Norman (and Norma?) will be killers and sociopaths in the future, Norman draws our identification because of both his relative innocence within a depraved community and his ignorance of his psychotic condition. As Norma explains to Dylan, "All I know is that he's innocent of it [the murder

FIGURE 18.2. Inverted repetition: In *Bates Motel*, Norma is responsible for cleaning up the murder scene caused by Norman.

of his father]. He doesn't know he needs to be protected." This formulation of Norman as victim and Norma as protector sutures the spectator to son and mother, constructing them both as largely innocent victims—simultaneously a repetition and reversal of their "known" personas from *Psycho*.

Through what I call inverted reflections, the program offers hints of future narrative events, but structures the episodes of Hitchcock's film as inverted reiterations of what occurs in *Bates Motel*. Discussing his fascination with mirrors in a mise-en-scène, Douglas Sirk (1977) once remarked that reflections are deceptive in that they show us our opposite. Similarly, *Bates Motel* is a program of opposite reflections or inversions in which characters' roles are swapped and narrative events are replayed with their identifications reversed. In its inverted reflections, *Bates Motel* relies on audience foreknowledge of the original film for an added layer of pleasurable recognition. Scenes replay (or "preplay") to reward engaged spectatorship: Norman and Norma flee the law like Marion Crane in their vintage car, Norma is terrorized by a psychotic tenant in the hotel, the pair dump a body in the hotel shower, and Norman takes a Milton Arbogast–style turn as a detective in search of a missing person.

One of the cleverest inversions in the series involves the murder of Norman's father. The series opens with Norman discovering his father's body, suspiciously dead after falling off a ladder. *Bates Motel* immediately directs suspicion at Norma, who emerges unceremoniously from the bathroom and provides unconvincing sorrow at the sight of her husband's body. This suspicion continues until the flashback revelation in episode six that Norman, in order to protect his mother from abuse, killed his father in a fit of catatonic rage. Norma's discovery and disposal of the body "preplays" the famous scene from *Psycho* in which Norman must clean up the hotel room after "mother" murders Marion Crane. *Bates Motel* employs the same free-floating camera technique seen in *Psycho* as this time Norma, not Norman, discovers the body and cleans up after the crime. The program realistically renders Norma's disgust at the blood (*Psycho*'s Norman would yell, "Mother, what have you done? The blood!"). But like *Psycho*, it also registers her calculated, step-by-step cleanup. Like Norman, she drags the body out of the crime scene and hides it while Norman awakes from his catatonic state. In this—functionally, a flashback within a flashback—the program disintegrates the image of Norma as dominant mother, which was constructed by the original film and seemingly propagated by the beginning of the series.

Through preplaying and inverting, *Bates Motel* produces strong identificatory effects by casting Norman and Norma as the victims of events already familiar to us. In doing so, it effectively unravels much of what is known to us from the 1960 film. There is certainly an operational aesthetic of pleasure here—joy at the play of references and plot machinations made possible by this alternative perspective. Norman can be seen as the victim of his environment rather than his mother's domination; further tying us to him, he seems to perpetuate violence learned from the corrupt world around him. Finally, this operational aesthetic further mobilizes the ironic tragedy of the show's long narrative: Norman will terrorize Marion and Lila Crane in the very same way that he and his mother were once victimized. The tension of this Oedipal narrative is that the victim will become the aggressor—once of age in his bildungsroman, he will redirect his victimization outward.

Whereas *Bates Motel* uses seriality to narrate a tragic loss of self-control, *Hannibal* is about the acquisition of control. *Bates Motel* is about things falling apart, but *Hannibal* is about things coming together. *Hannibal*—a show all about appetite—makes its audience salivate for Lecter's acts of absolute mastery.

HANNIBAL: REPETITION AS INCOMPLETION

NBC's prime-time police procedural *Hannibal* follows a Quantico professor named Will Graham (Hugh Dancy), who consults on serial murder investigations conducted by the FBI, which is led by Jack Crawford (Laurence Fishburne). The forensic psychologist Hannibal Lecter (Mads Mikkelsen) initially serves as Graham's therapist, but is eventually brought on to help with investigations. Behind the scenes, Lecter goads his patients into committing homicides while at the same time perpetrating a string of unsolved serial murders. *Hannibal* is notable for its large and active fan community (whose members dub themselves "Fannibals"), which creates a level of discourse usually reserved for the "Big Three" television fan communities (those for *Supernatural*, *Doctor Who*, and *Sherlock*), despite only being on air for a few months (Hall 2013).

Too much time is spent discussing Graham's rare skills of perception *Hannibal* is heavily populated with investigators— therapists, reporters, and police agents. The program's signature shot is a subjective point-of-view sequence that occurs in nearly every episode to illustrate Graham "entering" the mind of the killer to explain his or her motives. Recalling the "crimeporn" aesthetic of the *CSI* programs, each sequence uses a swinging pendulum of light to transition into a subjective point of view, and the sound track contains only the sound of a heartbeat, static, and the whoosh of the pendulum. The scene then rewinds through Graham's eyes, rendering an aesthetically gorgeous sequence of blood splatter droplets and mutilated bodies returning to cohesion. Then Graham, as the killer, navigates the crime scene in complete mastery and narrates the scene in real time, often repeating the phrase "This is by design." In each sequence, the pendulum of light causes Graham to psychologically replay the trauma and articulate it through speech.

Much time is spent discussing Graham's rare skills of perception and his Holmesian ability to make logical leaps unavailable to others. It is suggested that Graham exists somewhere on the far end of the autism spectrum, though later it is revealed that he suffers from a rare condition called anti-NMDA receptor encephalitis, which produces symptoms of psychosis. Still, this *Rainman*-esque construction of autism is fairly common within the procedural genre, from the benign (*Psych*, *Numb3rs*) to more flagrant Asperger's-as-superpower treatments (*Perception*, *Touch*). More troubling, and perhaps following HBO's *Dexter*, is the program's conceit that Graham's supposed autism places his on a spectrum of sociopathology, psychologically linking him to the sadists and serial killers that he pursues. Indeed, the representation of exceptional, or even "magical," autistic characters has followed the increasing prominence of autism diagnoses culturally. One of the show's dramatic tensions, then, is that every act of "knowing" the killer places Graham closer and closer to "becoming" the killer—incorporation threatens transformation. Graham is continually haunted by a nightmare of Lecter as wendigo, the Algonquian myth of a man who is turned into a beast after consuming human flesh. This dream dually links Graham and Lecter, since it alludes to the transformative power of his investigations (becoming animal) and aligns his acts of consumption with Lecter's literal cannibalism.

Hannibal obsesses over the notion of a world "by design." The series takes the pleasure of the operational aesthetic further than *Bates Motel*: Lecter emerges as an orchestrating presence within the text, directing the machinations of the plot with complete control, placing the program in proximity to another genre-busting police procedural, *Dexter*. Since the audience is privy to both Graham's uninformed point of view and Lecter's grand schema, much of the pleasure of the program results from Lecter's ability to dominate the narrative and remain undiscovered. It is no accident, then, that in addition to being a therapist, Lecter is consistently referred to as an architect. His drawings are found repeatedly in the mise-en-scène, a constant reminder that Lecter constructs and manipulates the space around him. Indeed, it is fitting that an architect's trade involves drafting—*Hannibal* is a series all about first drafts. By repeating incomplete or sufficient versions of "known" later events, *Hannibal* creates the impression of a first attempt, and in doing so elevates the film to the level of final draft.

Hannibal continues a number of the central motifs found in *The Silence of the Lambs*, notably, the notion of therapy as murder. Therapy, in the diegetic space of *Hannibal*, is tantamount to psychological dismemberment, and is frequently used to parallel the instances of physical mutilation within each episode. Through the therapeutic, memories can be implanted, morality disbanded, free will subverted, and identities annihilated. Indeed, of the program's many therapist figures, none approach therapy as curative. In *Hannibal*, murder is only one way in which victims may be dissected.

The greatest of therapist-butchers is of course Hannibal Lecter, whose name alone evokes his loquacious (*lector* means "reader" in Latin) power over others. As in the original films, Lecter's interiority remains remarkably opaque; his motivations are less important than his machinations. Much like Norman in *Bates Motel* (though to a lesser degree), Lecter is also temporally dislocated: his dandyish style of dress and speech mark him as an anachronistic presence within the contemporary world of *Hannibal*. Lecter is, at turns, a puppet master, a grand experimenter, a modern Moriarty, a Svengali, Lucifer, and Dr. Frankenstein.[4] In the appropriately titled "The Demon Therapist and Other Dangers," David Sundelson describes Lecter as "an updated 'behavioral science' Dracula—elegant, voracious, and unkillable—and also a ferocious Houdini who escapes inescapable fetters to wreak havoc" (1993, 14). *Hannibal* is about control as consumption: to be the master is to swallow your prey whole and keep it in your belly. The incomplete repetitions, then, serve as a type of aperitif mode—they whet the appetite for the full version to come.

The program proceeds with a number of character repetitions that reward spectators familiar with the original film. One of the series-long narrative arcs involves a copycat killer who mimics Lecter's serial crimes, but without his artistry or architectural vision—an incomplete mimesis. A number of moments allow for the pleasure of recognition (in the literal sense, "to know again") with *Hannibal*, as is common with the enabling structure of the prequel, remake, or reboot. In *Bates Motel*, inverted reflection reinscribes Norman and Norma as victims of the same type of violent acts that they would later commit. Uniquely, *Hannibal* uses reflection to reinscribe the authenticity of the original. Like *Bates Motel*, the show preplays events from its originating film. For example, the psychopathic Dr. Abel Gideon (Eddie Izzard) functions as kind of first-draft Hannibal Lecter. The casting of Izzard, best known as a cross-dressing stand-up comedian, contrasts sharply with the gravitas of the film performance by Anthony Hopkins. Indeed, Izzard's delivery overall makes his scenes read as comedic. In *Hannibal*, Gideon fakes a heart attack at the hospital for the criminally insane where he is institutionalized and attacks a young nurse (in *The Silence of the Lambs*, Lecter, in the same hospital, commits the same kind of attack during a checkup), and FBI psychologists visit him in a plastic-walled cell, seeking information. And yet both of these instances of reiteration read as incomplete: Gideon is an opportunistic copycat killer (Lecter is sometimes opportunistic, but never imitative), and the FBI

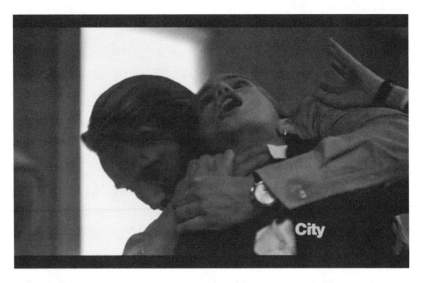

FIGURE 18.3. Incomplete repetition: Agent Miriam Lass in *Hannibal* functions as a first-draft Clarice Starling, but lacks her intuition and grit.

psychologists in the television program lack the insight and daring of the films' Clarice Starling. Gillian Anderson's turn as the psychologist Dr. Du Marier—Lecter's therapist—is a fascinating employment of star image: her character Dana Scully in *X-Files* was directly modeled on Jodie Foster as Starling in *The Silence of the Lambs*. Through Anderson, Clarice Starling reappears in type.

Perhaps the most interesting moment of incomplete reflection is the narrative of a young, ambitious female agent, Miriam Lass (Anna Chlumsky), who is plucked out of the CIA program to pursue an intuitive lead. The series directly preplays the narrative of *The Silence of the Lambs* as Lass tracks her leads to Lecter, and like her second-draft persona, Clarice Starling, engages him in word craft and psychological sparring. But she fails where Starling succeeds, and is overtaken by Lecter. A "lass," she is a girl and not yet the woman who is to come. Narrated in a black-and-white flashback, Lass's demise is shown when she stumbles upon Lecter's drawings that refer to a particular murder—one of the few characters to see the architect at work, an act of discovery for which she pays the price. A flashback within a flashback (the preboot), the sequence functions as a de facto past version of Clarice Starling, placing Starling within a trajectory from failed copy to authentic original.

THE CYNICAL VIEW MIGHT BE to see these programs as conservative or creatively bankrupt reiterations of existing properties. But *Bates Motel* and *Hannibal* offer a much more complex spectatorial experience than such accounts would suggest. As preboots, they make use of multiple modes of repetition, rewriting, and narrative extension; they are thus unique cultural products worthy of academic study. Additionally, their play with chronology and temporality, audience memory, and creative reinterpretation demand audience engagement with a complex constellation of meaning. Despite their similarities, *Bates Motel* and *Hannibal* demonstrate how the serial form of television can deliver on the promise of pleasurable repetition in divergent ways. Whereas *Bates Motel* crafts the preboot as an alternative perspective that rewrites the original, *Hannibal* uses the preboot as a first draft to confirm the original as complete and coherent. Continued study of the preboot offers an opportunity to examine how narrative extension and reiteration may make new and dynamic demands upon audience memory, recognition, and identification.

NOTES

1. *The Silence of the Lambs* is the second in a series by author Thomas Harris, but because of its popularity, I consider it the "original" text when discussing *Hannibal* as a reboot. The first book, *Red Dragon*, was filmed as *Manhunter* in 1986 with Will Graham as a central character. The success of *The Silence of the Lambs* caused the studio to remake *Red Dragon* in 2002 as a prequel. The narrative of *Hannibal* predates that of *Red Dragon*—Bryan Fuller has said in interviews that he plans a seven-season run; the first three seasons will be original material, the fourth will span *Red Dragon*, the fifth *The Silence of the Lambs*, the sixth *Hannibal*, and the seventh will be an original conclusion to the series.

2. The reboot has had a more long-standing relationship in other genres, particularly the superhero film, which has produced several iterations of central characters—Superman, Batman, Spider-Man—without troubling its core constituency of spectators. Comic book fans are used to "retconning," or retroactive continuity, a process that resets a narrative past within the diegetic world of graphic novels. Comic book readers are also more accustomed to conceiving of a story world as an expansive universe that can be altered, reset, or reauthored to meet the desires of writers or a shifting readership. Further, comic book readers are willing to accept simultaneously running and often contradictory accounts of major characters (*Sensational Spider-Man*, *Astonishing Spider-Man*, *Amazing Spider-Man*, *Ultimate Spider-Man*) and their exploits.

3. Original texts, in order: *Ringu* (1998, Hideo Nakata), *Ju-On: The Grudge* (2002, Takashi Shimizu), *Dark Water* (2002, Hideo Nakata), *The Eye* (2002, Oxide and Danny Pang), *Infernal Affairs* (2002, Wai-keung Lau), *REC* (2007, Juame Ballagero), and *Oldboy* (2003, Chan-wook Park).

4. Mikkelsen has said that he is playing Lecter as, in effect, Satan: "He's not a classic psychopath or a classic serial killer. I believe that he's as close to Satan as can be—the fallen angel. He sees the beauty in death. And every day is a new day, full of opportunities" (Associated Press 2013).

WORKS CITED

Associated Press. 2013. "A Tasty Turn by Mads Mikkelsen as NBC's 'Hannibal.'" 2 April.
Bibel, Sara. 2013. "NBC Pulls Episode of 'Hannibal' about Children Who Murder Other Children." TV by the Numbers, 19 April.
Bordwell, David. 1979. "The Art Cinema as a Mode of Film Practice." *Film Criticism* 4, no. 1 (Fall): 56–74.
Genette, Gérard. 1972. *Narrative Discourse: An Essay in Method.* Translated by Jane E. Lewin. Ithaca, NY: Cornell University Press.
Hall, Ellie. 2013. "Meet the 'Hannibal' Fannibals, TV's Newest and Most Intense Fandom." BuzzFeed, 31 May.
Hutcheon, Linda. 2006. *A Theory of Adaptation.* London: Routledge.
Jess-Cooke, Carolyn, and Constantine Verevis. 2010. Introduction to *Second Takes: Critical Approaches to the Film Sequel,* ed. Carolyn Jess-Cooke and Constantine Verevis, 1–10. Albany: State University of New York Press.
Mittell, Jason. 2006. "Narrative Complexity and Contemporary Narrative Television." *Velvet Light Trap* 58 (Fall): 29–40.
Ndalianis, Angela. 2007. "Television and the Neo-Baroque." In *The Contemporary Television Series,* ed. Michael Hammond and Lucy Mazdon, 83–101. Edinburgh: Edinburgh University Press.
Sirk, Douglas. 1977. "Two Weeks in Another Town: Interview with Douglas Sirk." Interview by Jane Stern and Michael Stern. *Bright Lights Film Journal* 6. http://brightlightsfilm.com/48/sirkinterview.php#.UlcIl2TWxcQ.
Sundelson, David. 1993. "The Demon Therapist and Other Dangers: Jonathan Demme's *Silence of the Lambs.*" *Journal of Popular Film and Television* 21, no. 1: 12–18.
Sutton, Paul. 2010. "Prequel: the 'Afterwardsness' of the Sequel." In *Second Takes: Critical Approaches to the Film Sequel,* ed. Carolyn Jess-Cooke and Constantine Verevis, 139–152. Albany: State University of New York Press.
Thompson, Kristen. 2003. *Storytelling in Film and Television.* Cambridge, Mass.: Harvard University Press.
Tudor, Andrew. 1989. *Monsters and Mad Scientists: A Cultural History of the Horror Movie.* Oxford: Basil Blackwell.

CONTRIBUTORS

Elizabeth Birmingham is a professor of English and associate dean of the College of Arts, Humanities and Social Sciences at North Dakota State University. Her doctorate from Iowa State University is in rhetoric and professional communication with a thirty-hour specialization in architectural history, theory, and criticism. Her recent published research is on gender in anime and manga, including the topics of incest tropes in *shōjo* manga, the antimodernist rhetoric of steampunk anime, feminist ecocriticism, and the films of Hayao Miyazaki. Her media-related research has been published in edited collections such as *Clockwork Rhetoric: The Language and Style of Steampunk, Finding McLuhan: The Mind, the Man, the Message,* and *Manga and Philosophy,* as well as in journals such as the *Journal of Popular Film and Television,* the *NWSA Journal, Feminist Media Studies,* and *Intensities: Journal of Cult Media.* She and her husband live in Fargo, where they are raising five children.

Amy Borden is an assistant professor of film at Portland State University, where she specializes in silent film history and classical film theory. She is currently writing a book-length study about the theorization of motion pictures in Gilded Age American magazines. She has presented papers on the involvement of periodical publishing personnel in film marketing during the first decade of the twentieth century. Her interest in film cycles and silent cinema are combined in her most recent work, in which she considers how the vaudeville prop of the sausage machine was featured in a group of films during the silent era. She has presented papers at conferences of Domitor and the Society for Cinema and Media Studies, and her work has appeared in the journal *Jump Cut* and the anthology *Beyond the Screen: Institutions, Networks, and Publics of Early Cinema.*

Chelsey Crawford is currently a PhD candidate in screen studies at Oklahoma State University where she teaches courses in Media Studies, Composition, and Literature. She is writing a dissertation entitled "The Permeable Self: Quotation and the Moving Image," which highlights her broad interests in theorizing the ways in which various forms of moving image production—film, television, and relevant forms of new media—come to participate in the writing of media history itself. She recently served as an assistant editor of the online journal *World Picture* and her essay "The Permeable Self: A Theory of Cinematic Quotation" is forthcoming in *Film-Philosophy.*

Steven Doles received his PhD from Syracuse University in 2014. His research focuses on the social problem genre, making a case for the contribution of such films to public debate and deliberation. He is currently an instructor in the English Department at Syracuse, where he has recently taught courses on the social-problem film and on noir.

Vincent M. Gaine is an independent researcher based in Norwich, England. His research focuses on the intersection of film and philosophy, authorship and genre, in contemporary Hollywood cinema, with particular interest in auteurs, including Michael Mann, James Cameron, and Christopher Nolan. He has published a monograph, *Existentialism and Social Engagement in the Films of Michael Mann* (2011), articles in *Cinema Journal* and the *Journal of Technology, Theology, and Religion*, and book chapters on postfeminism, the superhero genre, transnational cinema, and race in historical film. He is a regular contributor to the *Directory of World Cinema*, on both Hollywood and American independent cinema, and to the *Journal of American Studies in Turkey*. He publishes film reviews and commentary on the blogs *Thinking Film* and *Vincent's View*, and on the website Critical Movie Critics.

Amanda Ann Klein is associate professor of film studies at East Carolina University. She is the author of *American Film Cycles: Reframing Genres, Screening Social Problems, and Defining Subcultures* (2011). Her work on film and television has been published in the journals *Quarterly Review of Film and Video, Jump Cut, Flow, Antenna, Avidly*, and in numerous edited anthologies. She is currently working on a manuscript about MTV reality programming and youth identities. She blogs about film, television, online media, and higher-education issues at *Judgmental Observer*.

Sarah Kornfield is an assistant professor of communication at Hope College in Holland, Michigan. She specializes in the feminist rhetorical analysis of television entertainment and public culture. Primarily concerned with the construction, portrayal, and mobilization of gender norms, her research focuses on how public discourse is televised and how televisual narratives invite viewers to make sense of cultural debates. Her research has been published in journals such as *Women's Studies in Communication, Critical Studies in Media Communication*, and *Communication, Culture, and Critique*.

Kathleen Loock is a postdoctoral research associate at the John F. Kennedy Institute for North American Studies, Freie Universität Berlin, and a member of the research unit Popular Seriality: Aesthetics and Practice. She is currently working on a book that examines the cultural history of Hollywood remaking, from the transition to sound and its so-called talker remakes to the remakes, sequels, and prequels of the franchise era. She received her PhD in American studies from the University of Göttingen; her dissertation, on the commemorative constructions and deconstructions of Christopher Columbus in the nineteenth- and twentieth-century United States, was published as *Kolumbus in den USA: Vom Nationalhelden zur ethnischen Identifikationsfigur* (2014). Her other publications include the coedited collections *Of Body Snatchers and Cyberpunks: Student Essays on American Science Fiction Film* (2011) and *Film Remakes, Adaptations, and Fan Productions: Remake/Remodel* (2012). She has edited a special issue on serial narratives for the journal *Literatur in Wissenschaft und Unterricht* (2014), and is currently preparing a coedited special issue on film seriality for *Film Journal* (2017).

R. Barton Palmer is Calhoun Lemon Professor of Literature and director of film studies at Clemson University. He is the author or editor of nearly forty books on literary and cinematic subjects, as well as the general editor of another thirty. His most recent edited collections include (with Murray Pomerance) *George Cukor: Hollywood Master* and (with William Epstein) *Invented Lives, Imagined Communities: The Biopic and American National Identity*. His latest monograph is *Shot on Location: The Real in Postwar Hollywood Film*.

Claire Perkins is a lecturer in film and screen studies in the School of Media, Film and Journalism at Monash University, Melbourne, where she researches in the areas of American independent cinema, contemporary "quality" television, feminist media and cultural studies, and film and television performance and stardom. She is the author of *American Smart Cinema* (2012) and coeditor of *US Independent Filmmaking after 1989: Possible Films* (2015), *B is for Bad Cinema: Aesthetics, Politics, and Cultural Value* (2014), and *Film Trilogies: New Critical Approaches* (2012). Her writing has appeared in the journals *Camera Obscura, Critical Studies in Television, Velvet Light Trap, Celebrity Studies*, and *Studies in Documentary Film*.

Murray Pomerance is professor in the Department of Sociology at Ryerson University, Toronto. He is the author of *Alfred Hitchcock's America* (2013), *The Eyes Have It: Cinema and the Reality Effect* (2013), *Tomorrow* (2012), *The Horse Who Drank the Sky: Film Experience Beyond Narrative and Theory* (2008), *Edith Valmaine* (2010), *Michelangelo Red Antonioni Blue: Eight Reflections on Cinema* (2011), *Savage Time* (2005), *Johnny Depp Starts Here* (2005), *An Eye for Hitchcock* (2004), and *Magia d'Amore* (1999). He has edited numerous volumes, including *The Last Laugh: Strange Humors of Cinema* (2013) and *Cinema and Modernity* (2006).

Robert Rushing is associate professor of Italian and comparative literature at the University of Illinois, Urbana-Champaign, where he also holds affiliate appointments in the Department of Media and Cinema Studies and the Unit for Criticism and Interpretive Theory. He is the author of *Resisting Arrest: Detective Fiction and Popular Culture* (2007) and coeditor of *Mad Men, Mad World: Sex, Politics, Style, and the 1960s* (2013). He recently finished a monograph on peplum cinema and biopolitics (1914–2014), and has published widely on Italian cinema (the peplum, the spaghetti Western, neorealism, Antonioni) and literature, generally in a comparative context.

Andrew Scahill is an assistant professor in the English Department at Salisbury University in Maryland. His research focuses on issues of genre and historical reception, specifically queer spectatorship. His book *The Revolting Child in Horror Cinema: Youth Rebellion and Queer Spectatorship* (2015) argues that the monstrous child stands in for the queer child by taking on its various incarnations. He has additionally published work on intertextuality, television, adaptation studies, censorship, stardom and celebrity, disability and eugenics, queer spectatorship, Cold War culture, children's media, Japanese cinema, and contemporary horror. He is currently at work on a monograph entitled *Washington, DC: The Movie*, which examines the nation's capitol as a cinematic locale and highly potent symbol.

Noah Tsika is assistant professor of media studies at Queens College, City University of New York. He is the author of *"Gods and Monsters": A Queer Film Classic* (2009) and *Nollywood Stars: Media and Migration in West Africa and the Diaspora* (2015). His articles have appeared in the *African Studies Review, Black Camera, Cineaste,* and *Velvet Light Trap,* among other journals. He has contributed essays to numerous edited collections, including *The Brokeback Book* (2011) and *Film Criticism in the Digital Age* (2015). His book *Pink 2.0: Encoding Queer Cinema on the Internet* is forthcoming from Indiana University Press.

Constantine Verevis is associate professor in film and screen studies at Monash University, Melbourne. His work moves between a number of disciplines spanning both film theory and cultural studies, and takes a special interest in media seriality. He is author of *Film Remakes* (2006) and coauthor of *Australian Film Theory and Criticism, Vol. I: Critical Positions* (2013). His coedited volumes include *Second Takes: Critical Approaches to the Film Sequel* (2010), *After Taste: Cultural Value and the Moving Image* (2011), *Film Trilogies: New Critical Approaches* (2012), *Film Remakes, Adaptations, and Fan Productions: Remake/Remodel* (2012), *B Is for Bad Cinema: Aesthetics, Politics, and Cultural Value* (2014) and *US Independent Film after 1989: Possible Films* (2015). His current projects include coedited works on transnational film remakes and transnational television remakes.

Kathleen Williams is a lecturer in journalism, media, and communications at the University of Tasmania, Australia. She completed her doctoral thesis at the University of New South Wales on recut film trailers, anticipation, and nostalgia. Her research is broadly concerned with charting how media technologies are co-opted from their intended uses and how film and television media histories inform the present. Her work has been published in *Transformative Works and Cultures, M/C Journal,* and collections on fandom and Australian media.

Faye Woods is a lecturer in film and television at the University of Reading. Her research interests include popular music in film and television, youth representations, and television industries. Her work has appeared in the journals *Television and New Media, Critical Studies in Television,* and the *Journal of British Cinema and Television,* as well as in the edited collections *Television Aesthetics and Style* (2013) and *Shane Meadows: Critical Essays* (2013). She is currently writing a monograph on British youth television.